Introduction to Criminal Justice

ASPEN COLLEGE SERIES

Introduction to Criminal Justice

THE ESSENTIALS

L. THOMAS WINFREE JR.
Arizona State University

G. LARRY MAYS
New Mexico State University

LEANNE FIFTAL ALARID
University of Texas at El Paso

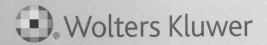 Wolters Kluwer

Copyright © 2015 CCH Incorporated.

Published by Wolters Kluwer in New York.

Wolters Kluwer serves customers worldwide with CCH, Aspen Publishers, and Kluwer Law International products. (www.wolterskluwerlb.com)

No part of this publication may be reproduced or transmitted in any form or by any means, electronic or mechanical, including photocopy, recording, or utilized by any information storage or retrieval system, without written permission from the publisher. For information about permissions or to request permissions online, visit us at www.wolterskluwerlb.com, or a written request may be faxed to our permissions department at 212-771-0803.

To contact Customer Service, e-mail customer.service@wolterskluwer.com, call 1-800-234-1660, fax 1-800-901-9075, or mail correspondence to:

Wolters Kluwer
Attn: Order Department
PO Box 990
Frederick, MD 21705

Printed in the United States of America.

1 2 3 4 5 6 7 8 9 0

ISBN 978-1-4548-3568-4

Library of Congress Cataloging-in-Publication Data

Winfree, Latham T. (Latham Thomas), 1946- author.
    Introduction to criminal justice : the essentials / L. Thomas Winfree Jr., Arizona State University; G. Larry Mays, New Mexico State University; Leanne Fiftal Alarid, University of Texas at El Paso.
        pages cm. — (Aspen College Series)
    Includes bibliographical references and index.
    ISBN 978-1-4548-3568-4 (alk. paper)
    1. Criminal justice, Administration of—United States. 2. Criminal law—United States. 3. Law enforcement—United States. 4. Probation—United States. 5. Community-based corrections—Law and legislation—United States. I. Mays, G. Larry, author. II. Alarid, Leanne Fiftal, 1967- author. III. Title.
    KF9223.W59 2015
    364.973—dc23

                                                                                          2014039430

SUSTAINABLE FORESTRY INITIATIVE

Certified Chain of Custody
At Least 20% Certified Forest Content
www.sfiprogram.org
SFI-01042

SFI label applies to the text stock

About Wolters Kluwer Law & Business

Wolters Kluwer Law & Business is a leading global provider of intelligent information and digital solutions for legal and business professionals in key specialty areas, and respected educational resources for professors and law students. Wolters Kluwer Law & Business connects legal and business professionals as well as those in the education market with timely, specialized authoritative content and information-enabled solutions to support success through productivity, accuracy and mobility.

Serving customers worldwide, Wolters Kluwer Law & Business products include those under the Aspen Publishers, CCH, Kluwer Law International, Loislaw, ftwilliam.com and MediRegs family of products.

CCH products have been a trusted resource since 1913, and are highly regarded resources for legal, securities, antitrust and trade regulation, government contracting, banking, pension, payroll, employment and labor, and healthcare reimbursement and compliance professionals.

Aspen Publishers products provide essential information to attorneys, business professionals and law students. Written by preeminent authorities, the product line offers analytical and practical information in a range of specialty practice areas from securities law and intellectual property to mergers and acquisitions and pension/ benefits. Aspen's trusted legal education resources provide professors and students with high-quality, up-to-date and effective resources for successful instruction and study in all areas of the law.

Kluwer Law International products provide the global business community with reliable international legal information in English. Legal practitioners, corporate counsel and business executives around the world rely on Kluwer Law journals, loose-leafs, books, and electronic products for comprehensive information in many areas of international legal practice.

Loislaw is a comprehensive online legal research product providing legal content to law firm practitioners of various specializations. Loislaw provides attorneys with the ability to quickly and efficiently find the necessary legal information they need, when and where they need it, by facilitating access to primary law as well as state-specific law, records, forms and treatises.

ftwilliam.com offers employee benefits professionals the highest quality plan documents (retirement, welfare and non-qualified) and government forms (5500/PBGC, 1099 and IRS) software at highly competitive prices.

MediRegs products provide integrated health care compliance content and software solutions for professionals in healthcare, higher education and life sciences, including professionals in accounting, law and consulting.

Wolters Kluwer Law & Business, a division of Wolters Kluwer, is headquartered in New York. Wolters Kluwer is a market-leading global information services company focused on professionals.

In memory of Alice Norton Jeffery, my favorite mother-in-law, my only mother-in-law, my last mother

—L. Thomas Winfree Jr.

To Mina, Robert, and Knox and Lucy, Oliver, Cooper, and Maggie from their crazy grandpa

—G. Larry Mays

To all the UTEP students along the border, who inspire others with a dose of daily gratitude

—Leanne Fiftal Alarid

SUMMARY OF CONTENTS

CONTENTS

PART II
Responding to Crime and Criminals

CHAPTER 4
An Introduction to Policing

CHAPTER 5
U.S. Law Enforcement Agencies

CHAPTER 6

Issues in Law Enforcement

PART IV

Punishment and Community Reentry   243

CHAPTER 10

Probation and Community Corrections   245

FOREWORD

There are a lot of textbooks that introduce students to the field of criminal justice. These books have much in common. They review the legal foundation of the criminal justice system; discuss police, courts, and corrections; and perhaps offer a view of community corrections. Many of these books treat the criminal justice system as if it were a factory processing cases from one function to another. These books are generally not very engaging; they are chock-full of facts but miss most of what is really interesting about the system.

Tom Winfree, Larry Mays and, Leanne Alarid have written a different kind of book. Their book is committed to presenting the *essentials* of criminal justice. It is not an encyclopedia or a book that presents the criminal justice system from a particular political or social perspective. It focuses on the essential elements of criminal justice by presenting the stages, processes, and challenges of the American criminal justice system. Certainly all the key actors and steps in the criminal justice process are covered here. But the book is unique because it includes an "issues" chapter for each segment of the criminal justice system, and these chapters apply the principles of the system to real-life decisions and challenges. Most important, Winfree, Mays, and Alarid use these chapters to dispel the many myths about criminal justice that are perpetrated by the media, especially television and movies. These myths are important to understand, as they can present impediments to people who want to work with or in the criminal justice system.

There has been an unfortunate trend in introductory criminal justice over the past decade or so. Many of the textbooks have moved away from presenting a broad look at the legal foundation of the criminal justice system. Such an approach ignores the key features of how the legal system constrains the way criminal justice operates. The rule of law limits the behavior of citizens as well as the government officials who work in the criminal justice system. No understanding of criminal justice processes is complete without a grasp of the legal foundations of the system. An important strength of this book is the detailed exposition in Chapter 3 of criminal law and the legal environment. In many ways, this is the most integral chapter to the book, as it provides the foundation that links all the chapters together.

Another unique feature of the book is its orientation toward students who want to work in the criminal justice system. Too often students don't receive adequate preparation for a career in criminal justice because of the failure of texts, courses, and instructors to teach the basics of the system and how it works. There are no such worries with this book. One of its great strengths is its focus on preparing students for what to expect when they get into the field. I am convinced that students who complete an internship in the criminal justice field will get more from their internship for having read this book. All too often students enter an internship without knowing enough about the criminal justice system to get much out of their experience. All students who have read this book will find themselves ahead of other students and in a position to better understand what is happening and why.

The authors are able to accomplish all this because they combine many key qualities that produce a great book. The first and most important of these ingredients is their experience. In the preface they indicate that they have more than 100 years of teaching experience combined. This is a remarkable base of experience from which to lead students through the criminal justice system. These authors (especially Mays and Winfree) have been around a long time, have seen a lot of changes, and in many ways have been a part of those changes. Such changes include the advent of community-oriented policing, which has altered law enforcement forever; the growth of community corrections; and significant modifications in the courts and the legal system. A long perspective on change is an important component of the book. Alarid has worked closely with prisons throughout her career, and that experience gives the chapters on prison and community corrections a strong sense of reality. But perhaps the most critical quality in the background of all three authors is their involvement in research. Mays, Winfree, and Alarid present much of the research about the criminal justice system that allows us to better understand what it is, how it works, and why it works the way it does. Their experience allows the authors to translate research (some of it their own) to practice in this book.

This is also an approachable book for students. It is clearly written with a transparent organizational scheme. When readers finish the book, they will understand how the parts of the criminal justice system are tied together and interdependent. The writing is engaging and provides numerous examples that students can use to better understand the general principles illustrated in each chapter. The book includes an excellent concluding chapter, "The Future of Criminal Justice: Making Sense of It All." This is perhaps the most engaging chapter of the book, and it also performs an important function by connecting the various issues covered in other chapters. This is a nice feature typically missing from textbooks. Especially thoughtful is the focus on global issues, and the strengths of this section of the chapter reflect Winfree's vast international scholarly experiences.

This is a solid introductory textbook for criminal justice courses. Students and instructors alike will find that it covers the essentials in a way that is engaging and thorough. Let these three master teachers and scholars take you through the maze of the criminal justice system and explain it in ways that prepare you to be a better citizen and perhaps to better enjoy and function in a career in criminal justice.

Scott H. Decker, Ph.D.
Foundation Professor
School of Criminology and Criminal Justice
Arizona State University

PREFACE AND ACKNOWLEDGMENTS

Over the course of our combined 100-plus years of undergraduate teaching, we have reviewed and used many different introductory textbooks for criminal justice. Indeed, two of us, Larry Mays and Tom Winfree, began our undergraduate studies during the 1960s and 1970s, when there were few colleges or universities that even offered coursework in this subject. By the mid- to late 1970s, as Larry and Tom began teaching in criminal justice departments, introductory textbooks were very new and more resembled sociology of criminal justice textbooks than ones dedicated to the emerging discipline of criminal justice. For her part, Leanne Fiftal Alarid is a product of the second generation of introductory criminal justice textbooks, published in the 1980s. Leanne, like her two coauthors, has contributed to the discipline of criminal justice, through both research and textbook authorship. In short, we began this effort with a wealth of experience and knowledge about the discipline of criminal justice, in both its contemporary form and its historical context.

Several years ago, we began a discussion about what we thought was missing at the introductory level. We have taken our experiences as students and teachers to heart and crafted what we believe is a textbook that is student-centric and informative without being encyclopedic. We relate the origins and development of criminal justice as an academic area of study and its potential as a workplace, since an entry-level position within the criminal justice system is often an eventual career choice for those beginning such a course of study. We do not sugarcoat the work world of criminal justice, revealing it instead as it is described and understood through the best scholarly evidence available. As authors, we are a mix of former practitioners and current academics who believe that whether the readers of this textbook seek careers as scholars or practitioners or simply wish to be better-informed citizens of the community, it is best to make decisions that are based on carefully reasoned arguments and highly verified evidence. This perspective guided us in the preparation of this textbook.

Our textbook is a departure from many other introductory textbooks currently available. First, this is an *essentials* book. As you hold the book or view it electronically, you know that this subtitle does not literally translate as "shorter" or "the basics." Rather, the material we included in this textbook is what we believe is necessary to achieve the following goals.

- First, the text provides the casual readers with sufficient information and understanding of how the nation's criminal justice system functions so that they might be better-informed citizens.
- Second, and along the same line, for students of this subject who intend to further their studies, this text establishes a foundation for the essential tools required to advance their interest in criminal justice. These tools include general critical thinking skills, an analytical and evidence-based approach to the subject matter, and a generalist perspective that can be expanded on by advanced studies in criminal justice.
- Third, for those who intend to pursue a career in criminal justice, this book gives unvarnished, balanced, and current insights into how the system should function and how it does function. This information should allow the preservice individual or the current CJS employee seeking advancement through academics to approach his or her respective goals in a better-informed manner.

How do we achieve these goals? The answer to this question is straightforward. We employ four specific teaching devices. First, we emphasize the historical development of all the component parts of the nation's system of criminal justice, including its evolution as an area of academic study. As George Santayana famously stated, "Those who cannot remember the past are condemned to repeat it" (1905: 284). As you will learn in this text, many criminal justice pundits and even so-called experts have shown that there is much truth in Santayana's aphorism. As importantly, and as observed by William Shakespeare in his play *The Tempest*, "What's past is prologue." For those studying criminal justice, this quotation means that we need to understand the past, since history influences and sets the context for the present. The past is often the path to the future. The truth of this statement will also become clear as, for example, we look at such things as the militarization of policing agencies throughout history and societal tinkering with various punishments intended to reduce crime. A historical perspective is essential if one is to understand more fully where we are now in terms of the administration of justice and where we are headed.

Second, throughout the text we encourage the reader to develop a cross-national or comparative orientation. Whether studying criminal justice in a historical context, as with the development of policing in England and Wales or the evolution of Roman laws, or in its contemporary variant, as with examples of how other nations approach the same crime and justice issues that confront the United States, we strongly encourage students to look beyond this nation's borders. Crime is increasingly a global issue, respecting neither international borders nor geographic barriers. When looking at crimes with the global reach of human trafficking or artwork stolen by the Nazis during World War II that later surfaces in a national gallery, having a comparative criminal justice perspective informs our responses to a wide range of criminal activities. Indeed, the final chapter of this book explores a series of such concerns, all through a comparative lens.

Third, we present this material in a consumable, student-friendly fashion. We provide many definitions, as evidenced by the extensive glossary. We relate the information in as nontechnical a fashion as possible but build on the readers' early knowledge throughout the text, so that by the final chapter, they are able to apply the lessons of the previous thirteen chapters in the exploration of this final set of national and international challenges.

The fourth teaching device we employ—one related to issue of student consumption—is the inclusion of a series of review questions at the end of each chapter. These are more than make-work assignments. In most cases, the answer to the question does not lie in the regurgitation of a series of facts found within the text. In some cases, readers may need to look more broadly for supporting evidence or provide their own analysis. We are strong proponents of the exercise and development of critical thinking skills, and these questions should help to hone those of readers on the whetstone of criminal justice.

A brief review of the text's content may prove useful at this juncture, if only to give readers a sense of what lies ahead.

Chapter 1 ("Criminal Justice: An Overview").

This chapter provides a definitional framework for the remaining chapters. A key part of this chapter is simply defining justice and criminal justice. While these terms may seem intuitively straightforward, Chapter 1 reveals that this is far from the case as it explores their more subtle and complex natures. The chapter ends with an overview of the meaning of the criminal justice system in contemporary society.

Chapter 2 ("Defining and Reporting Crime").

Crime is more prevalent today than ever before, right? In fact, the rate of crime is lower today than in previous decades, even if the volume of crime is, in some cases, higher. Readers who think that this answer is a case of weasel wording should read Chapter 2 very carefully. What they will learn is that there are many ways to measure and report crime. Knowing how much crime there is and the trends in its occurrence is central to understanding how a society responds to it.

Chapter 3 ("Criminal Law and the Legal Environment").   It is often said that we are a nation of laws, and this chapter provides an overview of criminal law and the broader legal environment within which criminal law is created, interpreted, and enforced. To understand fully the criminal justice processes in the United States, readers must have at least a basic appreciation for key concepts embodied in criminal law.

Chapter 4 ("An Introduction to Policing").   For many students of criminal justice, this chapter signals the beginning of the core of the course. It is here that they will begin to appreciate the true impact of history on the evolution and development of a central piece of the criminal justice system. In addition, this chapter introduces them to contemporary policing, including its goals and objectives, structure and organization, and activities.

Chapter 5 ("U.S. Law Enforcement Agencies").   Few textbooks contain the breadth of coverage on law enforcement that we provide. From local and state agencies to the range of federal responses to crime and justice, this chapter reveals a great deal about the agencies and the people who populate them, serving their communities and the nation.

Chapter 6 ("Issues in Law Enforcement").   If a textbook claims to cover all the issues related to a single element of the criminal justice system, that claim is probably false. In this chapter, we reveal essential information about the following topical areas in law enforcement: professionalism, corruption, use of force, and police-judiciary interactions. There are certainly other issues confronting law enforcement agencies today, as instructors may indicate during the course of covering this content area. Indeed, Chapter 14 discusses at least one more, police militarization. Chapter 6 is intended to give readers an understanding of several of the key problem areas that confront police in the 21st century.

Chapter 7 ("Local, State, and Federal Courts").   Many people have only a passing familiarity with this nation's courts. Usually that knowledge comes through appearing for a traffic ticket or after receiving a summons to serve on a jury. This chapter provides a review of the different kinds of courts found at all three levels of government in the United States. In addition to giving basic definitions, it also explains the functions of different types of courts at all levels.

Chapter 8 ("Trials and Trial Procedures").   Much of what the average person knows about court processes comes from television and movie depictions of various aspects of trials. Some of this information is accurate, and some is inaccurate (to provide greater drama). This chapter follows criminal cases through the various stages that occur when cases go to trial. However, one important point is worth emphasizing again and again: Somewhere between 80 and 90 percent of all of the criminal cases filed in this country are resolved with something other than a trial, most through a process of negotiated settlement known generally as plea bargaining.

Chapter 9 ("Issues in the Judiciary").   As with the other "issues" chapters, there is no end to the possible questions and controversies that could be covered here. We have chosen to focus on how attorneys are provided for the majority of criminal defendants who cannot afford to hire their own; how judges are selected in the United States and their qualifications; and how we discipline judges who misconduct themselves in their personal and professional lives. Although other issues are included, three in particular are likely to spark interest and classroom discussion: the use of scientific evidence in court (such as DNA testing), wrongful convictions and the impact they have on the perception of justice, and the lingering controversies surrounding the death penalty. We expect this chapter (along with the other issues chapters) to draw students and instructors into serious discussions.

Chapter 10 ("Probation and Community Corrections").   Since the vast majority of sentenced offenders serve their correctional sentence on probation in the community, we thought it important to introduce the most common ways that individuals serve correctional sentences while living at home. We address how restitution, fines, and community service are used to financially compensate victims and help the community. We also discuss technological advances in electronic monitoring of offenders, including the ramifications that technology has for the increased chance of registering probation violations and how this has contributed to net widening and jail crowding.

Chapter 11 ("Institutional Corrections").   This chapter reviews the historical background of punishment and penitentiaries to address the full context behind how penitentiaries began and how incarceration rates in the United States became so high. Students will understand how the United States is different from other Westernized countries in response to crime. This chapter covers the different types of correctional institutions, including jails, prisons, youth detention centers, and private facilities, all of which have the primary goal of depriving offenders of their liberty and various freedoms as part of their sentences.

Chapter 12 ("Living and Working in Prison").   Students of criminal justice have always been interested in what prison might be like; often they believe that prisoners have an easy life. This chapter challenges that argument and gives students a glimpse into life behind bars. They will read what doing time is like, why prisons can be violent and unsafe places, why decent prison conditions are important, and how women's prisons are different. The goal of this chapter is to enlighten the student on the importance of having a safe environment for the correctional staff members who make up the foundation of the prison environment.

Chapter 13 ("Issues in Corrections").   The corrections system currently faces a multitude of challenges. This chapter examines five of the most important issues of our time that include why racial/ethnic disparities exist in corrections, why a disproportionate number of persons with mental illnesses are in jails and prisons, and what happens when prisoners leave early to reenter the community. We highlight the effectiveness of correctional treatment and of imprisonment itself in deterring crime.

Chapter 14 ("The Future of Criminal Justice: Making Sense of It All"). This chapter is ambitious. As in other chapters in which central concerns of the criminal justice system components are discussed, we selected topics that experts tell us will be areas of concern for years if not decades: global crime, models or theories of justice, policing, judicial decision making, corrections, and juvenile justice. We examine the topical issues and how they are informed by cross-national or comparative criminal justice studies. Our intent in this chapter is to leave readers with a greater appreciation for what they will confront as criminal justice consumers, scholars, and practitioners.

All textbook authors owe debts. No book is simply the work of those writing it. This book is no exception. First, we thank the tens of thousands of students who have sat through our lectures. They inspired us to write a textbook that would hold readers' attention and inform them. Second, we thank the external reviewers of this text, including Joe M. Brown, Fayetteville State University; Jennifer Christman, Ball State University; Craig Curtis, Bradley University; Brian Donnelly, Rutgers University–New Brunswick; Eric A. Gentes, Rivier University; Patrick Ibe, Albany State University; Joseph Schafer, Southern Illinois University; Rick Seniff, Indiana University–South Bend; James Sobel, Buffalo State University; Cindy Stewart, College of Saint Joseph; and Lecinda Yevchak, Pennsylvania State University.

Third, four students, past and present, helped us at several stages of the process. Kimberly Kaiser (Arizona State University) and Randy Snyder (Arizona State University and Pima County Sheriff's Office) read all or some of the chapters. Our thanks go to Elizabeth Gandarilla and Areli Guajardo, both students at the University of Texas at El Paso, for helping with the PowerPoint presentations. Finally, Eileen Winfree read, commented on, and asked for clarification of information contained in each chapter. However, any mistakes of fact or other errors are ours alone.

Is this a perfect introductory textbook? Probably not. Nevertheless, it is one that we wish we had had access to as students and professors earlier in our careers. It takes the student on an informed journey across several thousand years of societal responses to crimes and criminals. We ground this journey in the most relevant and recent insights we have on these issues. It is our hope that this text serves to stimulate students' appetite for insights into criminal justice and that they seek even more definitive answers for the questions that we pose—and ones that occur to them as well. Enjoy *Introduction to Criminal Justice: The Essentials*, and enjoy the search that is about to begin. We are still on that journey. Perhaps we will meet at some juncture.

Fundamentals of Criminal Justice

Criminal Justice: An Overview

LEARNING OBJECTIVES

At the conclusion of this chapter, you should be able to:

- Understand the origin and evolution of key terms associated with crime and justice.
- Define the key terms associated with the contemporary administration of criminal justice.
- Understand and correctly employ all the terms linked to criminal justice, such as administration, process, system, and the like.
- Describe the component parts of the criminal justice system and their interrelationships.

INTRODUCTION

For all of recorded history—and perhaps even before—stories of crime and justice have fascinated people. The "why" behind this fascination could fill several books. Tales of wrongdoings and wrongdoers are the foundation of humanity's nightmares and daydreams alike. Humans seem to fear both the acts and the actors. Nonetheless, they are drawn to them, if only to know why the latter engage in the former. Acts of rule breaking often form the lessons against which human conduct is measured, as in, "Don't do that, or you will suffer a horrible fate." They have become part of our folklore and culture. For example, nearly all the world's religions include references to violations of rules—laws, really—handed down by a supreme being or, in some cases, supreme beings, along with the punishments for their violation. Often, parables or stories lay out the rule, examples of their violation, and the punishments the rule violator will likely suffer. Cain killed Abel, becoming, in the Jewish, Christian, and Islamic traditions, the first murderer. Interestingly, God did not kill Cain for his wrongful acts, which included not only a murder but also lying about it. Instead, God cursed Cain and marked him and his descendants with a visible stigma to signify His displeasure at Cain's sins. The world's largest religions—Christianity, Judaism, Islam, Hinduism, and Buddhism—and many others share a concern with both justice and injustice.

Religion is not our only source of information about crimes and criminals. Balladeers, poets, and assorted tellers of tales have endowed nearly every culture with stories of crimes and punishments. Generations of writers have given us tales of crime and justice, whether as morality plays intended to teach both sacred and secular lessons to the masses or as pure entertainment; in most cases, right prevails over wrong, and justice triumphs over injustice. In ancient Greece, for example, Sophocles gave us Oedipus Rex, who kills Laius, his father, and marries Jocasta, his mother. Oedipus learns these facts only after he kills them both, and then he blinds himself and is driven into exile by the community. The medieval poet and philosopher Dante Alighieri's *Divine Comedy*, written in the early 14th century, came to define the fates that await wrongdoers of all sorts, but especially what happens within the nine circles of hell, reserved for those who transgress against the most serious of society's rules. Many of Shakespeare's late 16th- and early 17th-century historical and tragic plays involved deceit, crimes on an epic scale, and eventually justice.

This cultural obsession with crime and justice—the criminals, their victims, and the fates of both—continues today, in both fictional and "real life" crime dramas, whether the medium is a book, television drama, or motion picture. Shows like *CSI: Crime Scene Investigation* and *NCIS* have become worldwide phenomena and virtual franchises

(CBS Corporation 2010); they influence how the public sees the operation of the criminal justice system, often relaying incorrect information, especially about the processing of forensic evidence and its availability at all crime scenes (Lovgren 2004). There is even something called the *"CSI effect,"* which critics of such shows charge causes juries to expect DNA forensics and other scientific evidence, without which they are less inclined to believe the charges against criminal defendants, although scholars disagree as to the veracity of this claim (Lawson 2009; Schweitzer and Saks 2007; Shelton 2008).[1] Even social media, general news media, and the quickly disappearing print media are not exempt from the time-honored dictum: If it bleeds, it leads. Crime stories—and the Bible—are among the best-selling books on the market today. Real-life and fictional accounts of crime, no matter how they are presented to the public, account for a large portion of the news and entertainment businesses across the globe.

Clearly, society cannot get enough information, factual or otherwise, about crime and justice, whether that society existed 2,500 years ago or today. Does the same level of interest exist for *real* criminal justice? Is it as interesting as the fictional accounts or those represented and packaged as real but that often include more than a little "literary license"? Does reality get in the way of what we think we know about the administration of justice in contemporary society? When does reality cross the line into fictional accounts?

With these historical and contemporary contexts in mind, we have three main goals for this textbook. First, we frame the questions and answers surrounding crime, criminals, and justice in the terminology of the academic disciplines of criminal justice and criminology. We discuss more about this framework later in this chapter. The information contained in this text may challenge some of your existing beliefs about crime and justice. Second, we employ a systemic model for viewing the criminal justice process that is based on the best current scholarship and research on the various topics captured by this term, including law, police, courts, and corrections. Third, as we seek to achieve closure with the first two elements, we hope to increase your interest in criminal justice, whether this is your only class on the subject or the beginning of a career-long (or lifelong) search for insights into crime and justice. A good place to begin this quest is to define justice.

DEFINING CRIMINAL JUSTICE

Justice is, quite simply, an abstraction, something that by itself is hard to understand or describe to another person, even if we think we know what justice is. Justice actually has many meanings, and even with

"CSI **effect":**
the idea that juries and other decision makers in criminal justice case processing have come to expect either supporting or exculpatory scientific evidence, including DNA testing, in nearly every criminal case

shared definitions, people can look at the same events and outcomes and come to different conclusions about whether justice was served. Taken by itself, then, the term "justice" exists apart from concrete realities, specific examples or instances, or other ideas that ground it to the world in which we live. For example, the *Oxford Dictionary* (2014) defines **justice** as "the quality of being fair and reasonable." Clearly, we need a bit more information if we are to use this term in any meaningful way. In this regard, consider the four forms of justice described in Box 1.1. Each form defines a rarely achieved ideal state, leaving the door open to forms of injustice, a situation without fairness. Each form is important to our overall understanding of the term justice. All of these terms share the same noun; however, the modifiers differ, and for the present task—defining criminal justice—we must begin with a common understanding of legal justice, crime, and criminal.

Justice:
fairness or reasonableness in the way people are treated or decisions are made

Legal Justice

Box 1.1 reviews several definitions of justice. The modifiers are meaningful, designating the kind of justice sought. As we move to define criminal justice, the focus of this text, we should remember these other forms of justice. Indeed, several of them, including retributive and restorative justice, enjoy some prominence in any discussion of criminal justice. What is generally missing from them is an important legal element. Codified law is not essential for the enactment of distributive, contributive, or restorative justice, and, to a lesser extent, it is not even necessary for retributive justice.[2] **Legal justice**, an essential part of criminal justice, refers to fairness as specifically defined by law. It may involve other forms of justice, including the types we have described. At its core, criminal justice is about fairness based in the laws of the land. What, then, is a crime, and who is the criminal?

Legal justice:
the fairness being sought, which is specifically defined by law

Crime, Criminals, and Criminal Justice

Laws—as written codes—are a topic explored in detail in Chapter 3. It is sufficient to say at this point that laws define the forms of appropriate or inappropriate behavior for those who come under the authority of those laws, sometimes called **jurisdiction**. In most cases, political geography defines jurisdiction as a physical area under the control of those persons mandating, creating, and enforcing the laws. Those persons could be sovereigns, legislatures, or city councils. Criminal law is a unique form of law—one that protects the entire community and individuals within it from harm and injury or, when such acts occur, seeks redress from those responsible in the form of punishment (retributive justice). Criminal law must specify the undesired acts, the methods by which the legal system can lawfully demonstrate that they occurred,

Jurisdiction:
the right of a recognized legal entity to govern or otherwise exert control over a specific geographic area

Box 1.1 Four Forms of Justice

Distributive justice refers to a form of economic justice, whereby all members of a society fairly share the accrued benefits, services, rewards, and resources. Of course, there may be disagreement as to what is fair, which can lead to conflict between individuals and groups in a given society. If people feel shortchanged in the distribution of resources and that they disproportionately carry its burdens, they will often act out against those who seem to be in control. Social justice is a form of distributive justice. Interestingly, distributive justice is at the root of communism and is part of Islam, Judaism, Christianity, and other of the world's great religions.

At the polar extreme from distributive justice, but rarely considered, is **contributive justice**, which looks not at what people can expect from society, but rather what society can expect from them. John F. Kennedy's famous inaugural speech on January 20, 1961, embodied this difference: "[A]sk not what your country can do for you—ask what you can do for your country." According to this form of justice, we, as individuals, have an obligation to contribute to the collective well-being of society to the best of our abilities. Such ideals are rarely met, and what often happens is something akin to neither contributive nor distributive injustice.

Retributive justice is associated with retribution, or punishment for the sake of punishment, with no other goals in mind. It is backward looking, in that an act committed in the past receives a deserved punishment in the present for no other reason than punishing the actor is the correct response. This is not the same as vengeance since the object of scorn is not a specific individual or group, but rather a behavior defined as illegal by a government agency acting in the name of the people. To be truly retributive in form, the punishment must also be proportionate, equal to the offending act itself.

Retributive justice essentially is not individual revenge but rather a form of highly stylized, procedurally correct societal revenge, captured by the phrase "Let the punishment fit the crime." Standing in opposition to this perspective is **restorative justice**. Retributive justice sees crimes as wrongdoings committed against the state or nation; restorative justice refocuses society's energies back on the victim of crime but includes both the perpetrator and the larger community. Restorative justice sees rule violations as rips in the social fabric—ones that, if not addressed, threaten to tear the community apart. Repairing social harm is the catchphrase of restorative justice. The harm that is the object of repair is between the offenders and victims and between both of these groups and the general society. These processes occur at the micro level, as in victim-offender mediation programs that seek to restore the balance in a local community, or at the macro level, as in truth-and-reconciliation commissions that seek to overcome such horrific events as genocide, also called "ethnic cleansing," and other war crimes.

This description presents four forms of justice, yet no single one truly defines criminal justice. Instead, they form the philosophical bedrock from which many in society draw their reactions to criminals and their views of the justice system, and as such, they are essential to a complete understanding of criminal justice.

Distributive justice: a form of economic justice, whereby the benefits, services, rewards, and resources accrued by the society are shared fairly with all members

Contributive justice: a form of justice that essentially focuses on what the individual can bring to the group or society

Retributive justice: associated with retribution, or punishment for the sake of punishment alone, with no other more lofty goals in mind

Restorative justice: an approach to justice that takes into account the needs of the victim, the offender, and the larger community; provides a means of individual and community healing for all three in the aftermath of a criminal event

SOURCES: Murphy 1992; Sayer 2009; Weitekamp 1993.

at what point a specific person or persons engaged in such acts, and the punishments or sanctions for the acts' commission.

"Breaking" a law—not strictly adhering to the formal written conduct norm embodied in that law—is to commit a crime. A police officer may suspect this is the case but cannot state definitively that something is a crime; at best, he or she may have probable cause that a crime has been committed and that the identified suspect did the deed. A prosecutor decides to proceed against the suspected offender and brings the allegations of wrongdoing before an impartial tribunal for a preliminary or grand jury hearing. A judicial officer (or grand jury) may weigh this evidence and decide that there is sufficient basis in fact to believe a crime has been committed and that a trial is the next step. At trial, a person (a judge in a bench trial) or a group of citizens (jurors in a jury trial) considers the questions and facts in the matter: Has a crime been committed, and does the evidence prove beyond a reasonable doubt that the accused person is guilty of the crime? (We discuss this further in Chapter 8.)

For its part, "criminal" is also a unique word with several important meanings. In the sense that the word is used in criminal justice, "criminal" does not refer to the person who engages in crime, which you might think is the case.[3] Instead, "criminal," as used in the term "criminal justice," is an adjective that simply means of or relating to the violation of law or crimes. Thus, **criminal justice** refers to the entire sociolegal process whereby fairness is sought in matters involving laws that define what is a crime, as well as what happens to those found to be engaged in such activities (see Pound 1930). Interestingly, as we next explore, the merger of the noun "system" to criminal justice as a way of referring to the entire process of criminal justice administration is relatively new, its origins spread over roughly 100 years of the nation's crime history.

Criminal justice:
the entire sociolegal process whereby fairness is sought in matters involving laws that define what is and is not a crime, as well as what happens to those found to be engaged in such activities

Criminal Justice: The Search for Identity

From our vantage point in the second decade of the 21st century, we could easily conclude that the term "criminal justice system" has been in use since the first formal responses to crime through a primitive judiciary. Perhaps a medieval king's appointment of local judges to rule on matters of law and carry out the king's justice far from the royal court created such a system. Alternatively, you might think that it is a product of the 19th or certainly the 20th century, when formal policing and an expanding system of prisons brought the final pieces to the administration of justice. Actually, there is some truth in each of these statements, as later chapters make clear. After all, we can hardly appreciate our current system of justice unless we know what preceded it, why those changes took place, and what these "lessons" suggest about the future.

Had you been a student of crime and justice prior to the end of the 19th century, it is likely that you would have sought answers in the field of medicine. You also might have looked into the emerging academic and practical discipline of psychology. Of course, there existed several strange "sciences" such as physiognomy and phrenology, where facial features or the shape of the head revealed a person's criminal proclivities. By the third decade of the 20th century, law schools and sociology departments around the world began to view **criminology**—defined as the scientific study of crime, criminals, and society's response to both—as an appropriate area of academic study. Law schools in particular saw criminal law as a natural part of their curriculum. Nowhere, however, was anyone studying or even talking about something called the criminal justice system. Crime and delinquency were receiving a great deal of attention on the local level, as cities and states attempted to respond to adult criminals and delinquent youths, but these efforts were not systematically organized into something that we would recognize today as the criminal justice system.

Criminology:
the scientific study of crime, criminals, and society's response to both

In the 1930s, academic programs emphasized the more practical aspects of "crime work." Law enforcement academic programs emerged first at the University of California at Berkeley in the 1920s, followed by programs at San Jose State University (1930), Indiana University (1935), Michigan State University (1935), and Washington State University (1943); however, such programs were slow to take hold in the halls of academia. Moreover, researchers at these institutions studying crime tended to address local rather than national crime problems.

In the years preceding World War II, citywide crime commissions and some congressional committees investigated corruption and organized crime, as well as other emerging crime trends. In 1919, for example, the Chicago Crime Commission, an independent "watchdog" group of local business leaders, began tracking and reporting on organized crime, street gangs, and related crime activities. This group is famous for creating the first "public enemy" list in 1930, with Al Capone as "Public Enemy Number 1" (Sifakis 2005).[4] The FBI subsequently adopted the public enemy list in its first major coordinated anticrime effort in 1933 (Burrough 2004), eventually morphing in the 1950s to the "10 Most Wanted" list. For its part, Congress held hearings regarding organized crime, perhaps the most famous of which Senator Estes Kefauver chaired from 1950 to 1951.[5] However, despite the work of these crime commissions and congressional hearings, coordination of crime-fighting activities or information gathering was not a national priority through the 1950s, regardless of public admissions that interstate and organized crime were beyond the control of the FBI (Friedman 2005).

Finding the Criminal Justice System: The Contributions of the Turbulent 1960s

Changes began to occur in the 1960s, just as the nation wrestled with several divisive social and political issues, including an increasingly unpopular foreign war (the Vietnam conflict) and a social movement (civil rights) that was galvanizing the nation's attention to the plight of African Americans 100 years after emancipation. In July 1965, President Lyndon B. Johnson, expanding the social agenda of John F. Kennedy and responding to concerns about increasingly violent civil unrest throughout the nation, established the President's Commission on Law Enforcement and Administration of Justice through an executive order. This commission's goals included fighting crime and reducing occurrences of injustice. As the group's chair, Attorney General Nicholas Katzenbach, wrote, establishing the commission recognized "the urgency of the Nation's crime problems and the depth of ignorance about it" (President's Commission on Law Enforcement and Administration of Justice 1967a).

The final report, titled *The Challenge of Crime in a Free Society*, was the work of 19 commissioners, 63 staff members, 175 consultants, and hundreds of advisors. It made more than 200 recommendations, many of which subsequently became common practices, significantly changing the administration of justice and the federal government's involvement in the overall process.[6] Indeed, this report became the catalyst behind the **Omnibus Crime Control and Safe Streets Act of 1968**, an act of Congress that, once signed into law, helped to change the role of the federal government in helping to shape and direct local, state, and federal crime-fighting efforts. The federal government no longer played the role of sideline observer, particularly in matters that influenced the nature and extent of justice administered at the state and local levels. In the past, entities such as the Federal Bureau of Investigation (FBI) only rarely became involved in nonfederal cases, functioning largely in a support role for the creation of the now famous Uniform Crime Report (UCR), a topic to which we return later in this text.

In the years following the commission's report, new federal bureaucracies coordinated the distribution of crime-fighting funds and provided direct assistance to state and local governments. The crime information vacuum that, outside the UCR, had existed since the nation's founding began to fill with the output of other federal agencies whose job it was to collect, analyze, and disseminate detailed information about crime and criminals. The specifics of these changes are the content of subsequent chapters. It is sufficient to note here that we can mark the history of contemporary criminal justice as beginning in 1965 and, in particular, as reflected in Box 1.2, the rapid growth of criminal justice as an academic discipline.

Omnibus Crime Control and Safe Streets Act (1968): a sweeping anticrime act of Congress that created a number of federal bureaucracies, including LEAA; suspended interstate trade in handguns; and provided direct funds to deal with urban riot control and organized crime

Box 1.2 The Forces Behind the Growth of Academic Criminal Justice

While we acknowledge that the term "criminal justice" is itself a relatively new one, criminal justice as an academic discipline shares an equally recent origin, although as previously noted, some programs have existed since before World War II. What changed in the 1960s were the monetary incentives linked to the **Law Enforcement Assistance Administration (LEAA)**, created by the Omnibus Crime Control and Safe Streets Act of 1968. The **Law Enforcement Education Program (LEEP)** was also part of this congressional act. Congress intended for LEEP to provide college-educated police and correctional officers, who would usher in a new era of enlightened and informed criminal justice. As the U.S. General Accounting Office noted in 1980 upon the demise of LEAA,

> Since 1969, the Law Enforcement Education Program (LEEP) made over $278 million in loans and grants without adequate management controls. The program was originally established by Congress in 1968 [for] the purpose of assisting those working in law enforcement or planning to work in law enforcement to obtain a higher education. . . . The grants and loans are canceled without repayment if the recipient works for a publicly supported law enforcement or criminal justice agency for a specified period. Otherwise, the recipient must repay the grant or loan with interest. (1980: i)

In the wake of this report and owing to political pressures exerted in 1982 by Ronald Reagan's more fiscally conservative administration, the federal government abolished LEAA (and LEEP). Its successor agencies, the Office of Justice Assistance, Research, and Statistics (1982-1984) and the Office of Justice Programs (1984-present) have been less concerned with education and far more concerned with evaluating criminal justice policies and practices.

The combined legacy of LEAA and LEEP, however, is indisputable. In 1960, there were only 40 associate and 15 baccalaureate and graduate programs in criminal-justice-related areas across the nation. A decade later, there were more than 1,000 such programs, nearly all of which received funds from LEEP. The current state of criminal justice academic development—there are well over 1,500 associate, baccalaureate, master's, and doctoral degree programs—owes much to this initial infusion of federal funds into the academic arena.

Law Enforcement Assistance Administration (LEAA): a part of the federal government from 1969 to 1982 that administered funding to state and local law enforcement agencies

Law Enforcement Education Program (LEEP): a part of LEAA intended to provide free or nearly free college and university education for police and correctional officers

SOURCES: U.S. General Accounting Office 1980; Office of Justice Programs 1996; Senna 1974; Southerland 2002.

Figure 1.1   Sequence of events in the criminal justice system

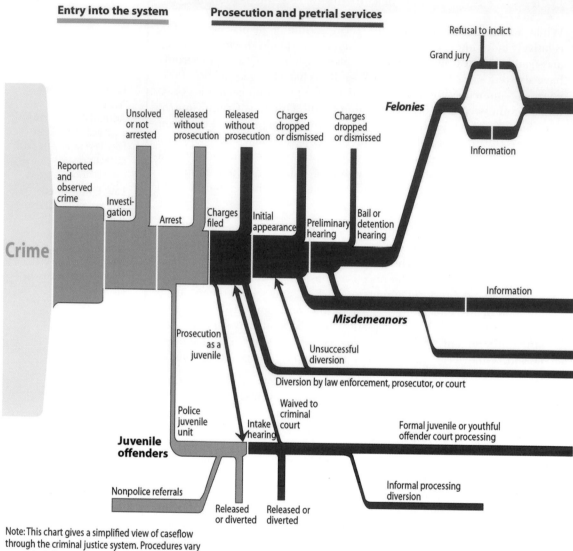

Note: This chart gives a simplified view of caseflow through the criminal justice system. Procedures vary among jurisdictions. The weights of the lines are not intended to show actual size of caseloads.

Outside of these developments, perhaps the most important contribution of the commission and its final report was an important linguistic change. As mentioned previously, we define criminal justice as the entire sociolegal process whereby fairness is sought in matters involving laws that define what is a crime, as well as what happens to those found to have engaged in such activities. The commission report provided the first succinct definition of the **criminal justice system**

Criminal justice system: an apparatus society uses to enforce the standards of conduct necessary to protect individuals and the community

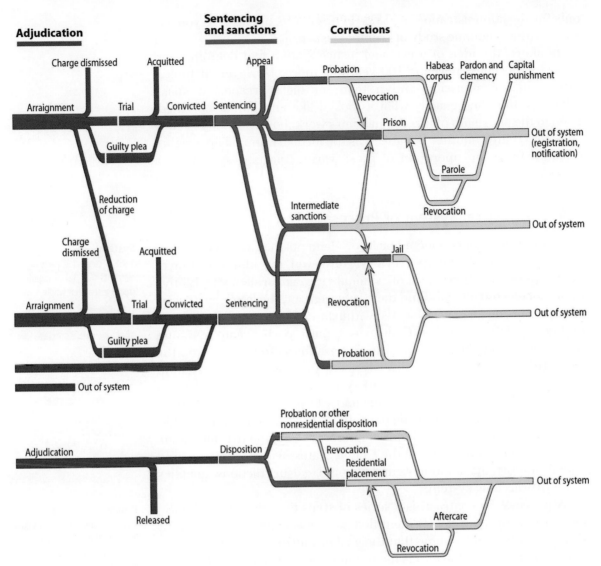

Adjudication

Sentencing and sanctions

Corrections

Charge dismissed   Acquitted   Appeal   Probation   Habeas corpus   Pardon and clemency   Capital punishment

Arraignment   Trial   Convicted   Sentencing   Revocation   Prison

Guilty plea

Out of system (registration, notification)

Reduction of charge

Parole

Charge dismissed   Acquitted   Intermediate sanctions   Revocation   Out of system

Arraignment   Trial   Convicted   Sentencing   Jail

Guilty plea   Revocation   Out of system

Probation

Out of system

Adjudication   Disposition   Probation or other nonresidential disposition   Revocation   Residential placement   Out of system

Released   Aftercare   Revocation

SOURCE: Adapted from President's Commission on Law Enforcement and Administration of Justice 1967a: 8-9.

as "an apparatus society uses to enforce the standards of conduct necessary to protect individuals and the community" (President's Commission on Law Enforcement and Administration of Justice 1967a: 7). The report also included the first diagrammatical representation of that apparatus, reproduced in Figure 1.1, calling it "A General View of the Criminal Justice System." Today, roughly 50 years after the report's declaration, this idea is accepted as a given. At the time, however, it represented a quantum leap forward in thinking about criminal justice. This figure stands as an organizing framework not only for the administration of justice in this nation but also, as you will see, for the academic study of criminal justice.

In short, the idea of a criminal justice *system* had been in operation for decades, perhaps 100 years or more. However, it took a presidential commission—and a team of highly respected social scientists—to define exactly what it looked like and how it operated. Even in the aftermath of this commission's work, however, the resulting "model" created another debate. Was the form of criminal justice that resulted from the operation of these various parts a system or a process?

Criminal Justice: System or Process?

A **system** is a set of connected parts or elements that, taken together, create a complex whole. As previously observed, the administration of justice requires the creation of criminal laws, generally by legislative bodies of elected officials, and their enforcement, the latter by a series of key actors and agencies located within law enforcement, the courts, and correctional agencies. Collectively, these parts create a system dedicated to sanctioning or punishing those found to have broken the laws. However, as we have already seen, there is not one system of justice, but rather several levels of systems operating in the United States. Each has a relatively unique and well-established jurisdiction, although there may be some dispute about this characterization, a dispute to which we return in later chapters. Clearly, the overall administration of criminal justice in the United States, with its separate and equally important components and various legal jurisdictions, qualifies as an overarching system.

A **process**, by contrast, is a series of steps or actions taken in the furtherance of some clearly identified goal or outcome. In the current situation, you could assume that the goal or outcome sought is justice, but then you would have to refer to the various definitions of justice, which can cause some confusion. Let us assume for the moment that in this context we define justice as fairness in the application of law to situations wherein a person is accused of a crime. The process, then, includes a review of the level of fairness reflected in the laws themselves and the lawful actions of the subparts of the criminal justice system at their respective jurisdictional levels. Confounding even this relatively straightforward definition is another set of questions: What is the role of the victim and the larger society in this process? What is justice for them?

The good news is that someone has dealt with this puzzle and provided an answer. In 1968, Herbert Packer authored a work titled

System:
a set of connected parts or elements that, taken together, create a complex whole

Process:
a series of steps or actions taken in the furtherance of some clearly identified goal or outcome

The Limits of the Criminal Sanction, which changed how people characterized the criminal justice process. The thrust of this work is that there are two ways or models to view criminal justice and the sanctioning process associated with it. On the one hand, the **due process model (DPM)** endorses certain principles found in the first ten amendments to the U.S. Constitution. As expressed by the due process clause of the Fourteenth Amendment and as interpreted in many decisions of the U.S. Supreme Court, due process translates into a familiar phrase and means that which is "fundamentally fair." The criminal justice process, according to this view, should consist of a series of hurdles or barriers that the state, in its efforts to prove guilt, must overcome. **"Obstacle course" justice** protects the rights of the accused, who is presumed innocent until proven guilty. To punish the accused and remain true to the notions endorsed in due process, the state bears the burden to demonstrate legal guilt. This finding must be based on evidence presented at court in a procedurally correct fashion in accordance with the full range of legal protections afforded the accused. In this context, **legal guilt** becomes what the prosecutor can "prove" in court. At the end of the day, the search for justice becomes a formal fact-finding activity predicated on slow and deliberate actions, all directed by Blackstone's edict: "It is better to let ten guilty persons escape, than one innocent suffer" ((1771) 1979: 4:358). The goal of the DPM is, after all, fairness.

On the other hand, Packer suggested that in the United States there exists another perspective on justice: the **crime control model (CCM)**. According to this model, criminal justice protects the peace and security of the community. At trial, there remains little doubt that the accused is guilty, which constitutes a presumption of guilt rather than a presumption of innocence, as found in the DPM. The overall criminal justice system should be concerned with the volume of cases processed and should adopt a perspective on achieving justice that is efficient in operation, a regimen often referred to as **"assembly line" justice**. The facts in the case, no matter how they came into the prosecution's possession, should be sufficient to determine guilt, as true justice is based on **factual guilt** (versus the DPM's legal guilt). After all, the overriding goal of the CCM is crime suppression.

Figure 1.1, with its linkages between the central components of criminal justice, reinforces the systemic view, just as Packer's distinctions between the due process and crime control models of justice (see Table 1.1) support the notion of justice as a process. Hence, criminal justice is both a system and a process, and we treat it as such throughout this text.

Due process model (DPM):
a way of viewing the administration of justice in which the goal is fairness; includes the ideas of presumed innocence, legal guilt, and "obstacle course" justice

"Obstacle course" justice:
the method by which the due process model ensures the protection of the rights of the accused, creating hurdles or barriers for the state to overcome as it demonstrates legal guilt

Legal guilt:
the due process model idea that only factual evidence obtained and presented in a procedurally correct fashion may be used in a court of law to substantiate a criminal charge

Crime control model (CCM):
a way of viewing the administration of justice in which the goal is crime suppression; includes the ideas of presumed guilt, factual guilt, and "assembly line" justice

"Assembly line" justice:
the method by which the crime control model enables crime suppression, ensuring the swift and expeditious movement of a defendant through the justice system to punishment predicated on factual guilt

Factual guilt:
the CCM idea that only all evidence, no matter how obtained, may be used to establish a defendant's guilt in or out of a court of law

Table 1.1	Comparing and Contrasting the Crime Control and Due Process Models of Justice	
SOCIOLEGAL ELEMENTS	**CRIME CONTROL MODEL**	**DUE PROCESS MODEL**
View on justice processing	Protects the peace and security of the community	Threatens the liberty of the individual
Principal legal assumption	Presumes the guilt of the accused	Presumes the innocence of the accused
Goal of justice	Crime suppression	Fairness
Endorsed type of justice processing	Quantity justice (i.e., high-volume processing)	Quality justice (i.e., careful, thoughtful decisions)
Method of achieving justice	Efficiency of operation (i.e., "assembly line" justice)	Thoroughness of decision making (i.e., "obstacle course" justice)
Requirement for criminal sanction	Factual guilt	Legal guilt

SOURCE: Packer 1968.

AND JUSTICE FOR ALL

Justice has been a central part of the nation's fabric almost since its founding. Perhaps nowhere is that summarized better than in the national pledge, which stated in 1923, "I pledge allegiance to the flag of the United States of America, and to the Republic for which it stands, one Nation indivisible, with liberty and justice for all." In 1954, Congress added the phrase "under God" between "Nation" and "indivisible." Whatever changes occurred over the years, the phrase "justice for all" captures one of its enduring elements—one included in the pledge of allegiance since first proposed in 1892.[7] In fact, the best place to seek a more complete understanding of this phrase and its significance for criminal justice in the United States is in the U.S. Constitution.

Constitutional Guidance

The U.S. Constitution is the basis of much of what we consider criminal justice in the United States today. For example, Article III of the Constitution provides the broad outlines of the court system at the national level. Furthermore, elements of the **Bill of Rights** (the first ten amendments to the Constitution) have proven essential to administering justice in this country. Consider the various ways that just four amendments affect the administration of justice, as summarized in Box 1.3.

Branches of Government

The federal government, along with state and local governments, is tripartite, which means there is a distribution of power over three parts, or branches: legislative, executive, and judicial. In most cases, we say that the legislative branch enacts the laws and provides funding for the various justice agencies. The executive branch must enforce the laws; police and correctional agencies are located in this branch of government. Finally, the judicial branch is responsible for interpreting the laws. As we see at several points in this book, laws often contain broad and potentially vague terms, and this practice requires the courts to interpret what the statutes really mean. Ultimately, the courts must decide if actions of the legislative and executive branches are consistent with constitutional requirements. We call this process **judicial review**.

Levels of Government

In addition to the three branches of government, governmental agencies also exist at the federal, state, and local (city, county, etc.) levels in the United States. Each of the three branches of government exists at the national or federal level. For example, we have the U.S. Congress (legislative); the president of the United States, the president's cabinet, and other supporting agencies (executive); and the U.S. Supreme Court and other lesser federal courts (judicial). In addition, states and local governments have similar structures. In simplest terms, this means that the entity that we call criminal justice is not one system but many independent and interrelated systems that exist in a vast matrix of justice agencies.

Jurisdictions and Justice

A new question emerges when we have the vast array of justice agencies that we have described: How do we know who is responsible for what? The simple answer rests with the word we introduced earlier in this chapter: jurisdiction. Within criminal justice, the various legal jurisdictions inform us about which agency at which level of government has the responsibility for processing a case. Sheppard says that jurisdiction is "[t]he power of a government, court, or official over a given matter, person, or place. . . . It is also the power conferred by the relevant constitution and statutes upon a court or an

Bill of Rights: collective name for the first ten amendments to the U.S. Constitution, passed largely in response to Anti-Federalists who were concerned about the expanding power of a strong central government

Judicial review: the idea that the courts must decide if actions of the legislative and executive branches are consistent with constitutional requirements

Box 1.3   The Bill of Rights and Criminal Justice Administration

Four amendments to the U.S. Constitution play particularly important roles in guiding the criminal justice system in accordance with the framers' wishes. First, the **Fourth Amendment** has two provisions that will be important during our journey into criminal justice. First, this amendment says that "[t]he right of the people to be secure in their persons, houses, papers, and effects against unreasonable searches and seizure, shall not be violated." This means that when the police carry out a search and seizure, this action must be "reasonable" within the meaning established by law and legal custom.

Second, the amendment contains a so-called **warrant clause**. This clause says, "No Warrants shall issue, but upon probable cause, supported by Oath or affirmation, and particularly describing the place to be searched, and the persons or things to be seized." Therefore, search warrants and arrest warrants must be based on the notion of probable cause (not merely the suspicion of one or more criminal justice actors) in order for a warrant to be issued and the search or arrest to be reasonable. We consider many of the elements associated with this amendment in some of the following chapters.

The **Fifth Amendment** to the Constitution is also central to criminal justice. This amendment requires a grand jury indictment for serious crimes, although this provision still only technically applies to federal cases. The Fifth Amendment also protects against double jeopardy (being tried twice for the same crime) and against criminal defendants being compelled to testify against themselves (self-incrimination). Finally, this amendment guarantees that no person shall be "deprived of life, liberty, or property, without due process of law." While the notion of "due process" troubles many students of criminal justice, in simplest terms it means that the government must ensure that all legal proceedings involving a suspect or an accused person adhere to the appropriate rules and policies.

In some ways, the **Sixth Amendment** is the **"trial amendment."** It contains a variety of provisions related to the administration of justice, including the rights to a jury trial, speedy trial, and public trial; the right to know the charges; the right to confront accusatory witnesses; and the right to assistance of counsel. These provisions originally applied only to federal cases in the context of criminal trials, but some (like the assistance of counsel) have worked their way into other "critical stages" of the criminal justice process, including interrogations and lineups.

Finally, the **Eighth Amendment** contains two provisions often raised in the course of criminal prosecutions. It prohibits the levying of excessive bail (whatever the word "excessive" might mean) and the imposition of cruel and unusual punishment. Death penalty cases often include mention of the cruel and unusual punishment clause, especially in recent years with new (and untested) protocols finding their way into the lethal injection method of execution.

Fourth Amendment:
the legal protections governing search warrants and arrest warrants; they must be based on the notion of probable cause in order for a warrant to be issued and the search or arrest to be reasonable

Warrant clause:
the part of the Fourth Amendment stating that no warrants "shall issue, but upon probable cause, supported by Oath or affirmation, and particularly describing the place to be searched, and the persons or things to be seized"

Fifth Amendment:
constitutional amendment that requires a grand jury indictment for serious crimes (although this provision still only technically applies to federal cases); protects against double jeopardy and against criminal defendants being compelled to testify against themselves; and guarantees that no person shall be deprived of life, liberty, or property without due process of law

Sixth Amendment:
a variety of provisions related to the administration of justice, including the rights to a jury trial, speedy trial, and public trial; the right to be informed of the charges; the right to confront accusatory witnesses; and the right to be assisted by counsel; also called the trial amendment

Eighth Amendment:
constitutional amendment that prohibits the levying of excessive bail and the imposition of cruel and unusual punishment

officer lawfully to assert authority over a person or a subject matter or a place" (2012: 1449). Therefore, in any criminal case, we must always ask who has jurisdiction over this matter.

Juvenile Justice

The question of jurisdiction has more than a geopolitical context to it. Age may also be crucial. Therefore, it is important to note at the beginning of our discussion of criminal justice that in the United States we have a parallel **juvenile justice system** operating alongside what we have called the criminal justice system, the former being responsible for processing youngsters, generally defined as persons under a statutorily defined age, who have violated the law. This has not always been the case. In fact, early in our nation's history (and in many other nations as well), children and adults were treated much the same by the criminal law. As we will see later, all of that changed in 1899 when the state of Illinois created the first juvenile court, a model subsequently followed by governments at all levels.

Juvenile justice system: a part of the overall justice system that is responsible for processing those youngsters, generally viewed as legal minors, who have violated the law

THE CRIMINAL JUSTICE SYSTEM

We often say that the criminal justice system in the United States is composed of three types of agencies: police, courts, and corrections. As previously mentioned, however, the legislative branch of government also plays a critical role in the administration of justice.

Laws and Legislatures

The legislative branch, especially at the national and state levels, performs two very important functions in relation to criminal justice. First, legislatures define what constitutes a criminal act and what is necessary to prove in a court of law that a suspect has committed that act. Second, legislatures provide the funding necessary to staff and operate criminal justice agencies. Funding is essential for us to have the police departments, courts, and correctional agencies necessary to have any semblance of justice in this country.

Agents of Law Enforcement: Policing in the United States

Describing the law enforcement apparatus in the United States is a daunting task. At the federal level, there are hundreds of different law enforcement agencies, each with its own unique set of tasks. At the state level, there are 49 state police agencies (known by a variety of different names), along with specialized law enforcement departments and bureaus that are assigned duties relating to game and fish enforcement, law enforcement in state parks (rangers), gaming (legalized gambling) enforcement, and even some exotic duties such as cattle-brand enforcement. However, in terms of personnel and expenditures, the bulk of law enforcement in the United States occurs at the local level. Even here, we have an array of agencies, such as police departments for cities, towns, and townships, along with more than 3,000 county sheriff's departments. As of the last census, the nation's nearly 18,000 law enforcement agencies employed 765,237 sworn personnel enforcing the laws at all levels of government in the United States (U.S. Census Bureau 2012).

Judicial Responses to Crime and Criminals

Again, as we have previously mentioned, courts exist at all three levels of government. In the federal system, we have the U.S. Supreme Court. In addition, there are 12 regional U.S. Courts of Appeals and a Court of Appeals for the Federal Circuit. The basic federal trial court is the federal district court, and there are 94 federal court districts covering the United States and its territories (Administrative Office of the U.S. Courts, n.d.).

At the state level, each state has a court of last resort—often, though not always, called the state supreme court. Many states also have intermediate appellate courts, frequently called the courts of appeals. At the trial court level, there is a variety of configurations, with states often having multiple general trial jurisdiction courts as well as courts of limited or inferior jurisdiction (see, especially, Rottman and Strickland 2006). In some ways, each of the courts at all levels of government has its own unique jurisdiction, but in some cases, there is overlapping or concurrent jurisdictions between courts at different levels of government and even between courts at the same level.

Punishing the Offender: Contemporary Corrections

After the courts process the criminal cases and convictions result, correctional agencies take control of the convicted offenders. Once again, these agencies exist at the federal, state, and local levels, and they process offenders in a number of different settings. In broadest terms, we can divide corrections into institutional and community-based domains. Institutional corrections include secure places of confinement, such as federal and state prisons. They also consist of various local detention facilities, such as jails, workhouses or penal farms, and juvenile detention centers. By contrast, community-based corrections involve probation, parole, halfway houses, residential treatment centers, day reporting centers, and a number of similar treatment programs.

These distinctions become clear later in this text. Suffice it to say at this point that corrections is big business—today, 6,977,700 adult offenders are under some form of correctional supervision (Glaze and Parks 2012).

SUMMARY

Simply defining the subject matter of this textbook is no easy task. Criminal justice refers to the entire sociolegal process whereby fairness is sought in matters involving laws that define what is a crime, as well as what happens to those found to be engaged in such activities. Our views of this system owe much to legislative and policy developments that took place in the 1960s but continue to evolve well into the 21st century.

The quest to provide justice in the United States looks to the U.S. Constitution for guidance. All branches and levels of government must actively engage in this pursuit for fairness and justice to acquire more than symbolic meaning. Jurisdictions also emerge in this chapter as a critical topic, as in answering the question: Who has jurisdiction in this matter? Finally, while juveniles, particularly those defined as legal minors (i.e., under a specific age), have their own justice system, no review of the U.S. system of criminal justice is complete without considering what the overarching system does to and for children.

In conclusion, his chapter provides a review of the subject matter—the systemic approach to criminal justice—that is the heart of the rest of this textbook. From laws and legislatures to contemporary corrections, each plays central and decisive roles in how the U.S. criminal justice system operates.

REVIEW QUESTIONS

1. Define each of the following and explain their significance for the term "criminal justice": justice, legal justice, and criminal.

2. Complete the following sentence, and explain how you arrived at your conclusion: "The mass media, but particularly television programming in the form of law-enforcement-related shows, has influenced how I see the administration of justice in the following ways: . . ."

3. Define each of the following forms of justice, indicating which one is most important to you and why: distributive justice, contributive justice, retributive justice, and restorative justice.

4. What is the most important part of the evolution of the term "criminal justice" as popularly used in the United States today? Explain your answer.

5. Why are the findings of the President's Commission on Law Enforcement and Administration of Justice important in the second decade of the 21st century?

6. What does "justice" mean to you? Is it attainable in the area of criminal justice? Why or why not?

7. Is the phrase "and justice for all" as relevant today as it was in 1893, when it was first proposed? Explain your answer.

8. Do you have a favorite part of the criminal justice system? What is it and why? (Note: Keep a copy of this answer, and review it at the end of the class.)

KEY TERMS

"assembly line" justice
Bill of Rights
contributive justice
crime control model (CCM)
criminal justice
criminal justice system
criminology
"*CSI* effect"
distributive justice
due process model (DPM)
Eighth Amendment
factual guilt
Fifth Amendment
Fourth Amendment
judicial review
jurisdiction
justice

juvenile justice system
Law Enforcement Assistance Administration (LEAA)
Law Enforcement Education Program (LEEP)
legal guilt
legal justice
"obstacle course" justice
Omnibus Crime Control and Safe Streets Act (1968)
procedural criminal law
process
restorative justice
retributive justice
Sixth Amendment
substantive criminal law
system
trial amendment
warrant clause

NOTES

1. A second form of the "*CSI* effect" has been the proliferation of forensic science academic programs in the United States and around the world (Stephens 2006-2007). Currently, the supply of CSI techs far exceeds the reasonable expectation of employment (Lovgren 2004).

2. While it is true that various legal tracts, ranging from the Law of Moses to the Code of Hammurabi, are closely tied to retributive justice, as in the phrase "an eye for an eye," it is just as likely that retribution as a form of community revenge preceded inclusion of this form of justice in codified law. In short, retribution and retributive justice do not need state mechanisms to function, which are essential for legal justice, a necessary precursor for criminal justice.

3. Thus, criminal justice does not mean justice for criminals.

4. The Chicago Crime Commission continues its work in the 21st century, focusing largely but not exclusively on local corruption and street gangs.

5. In 1953, Kefauver was involved in another set of congressional hearings called the Subcommittee on Juvenile Delinquency. One target was comic books, which were viewed as a source of violent imagery unsuitable for young minds (Wertham 1954). What would Kefauver make of today's "graphic novels"?

6. One might assume that such commissions evaluating and assessing the nation's criminal justice system are a regular occurrence. In fact, there has not been another one in the past 50 years. Calls for new national crime and justice studies occur on a regular basis, the most recent being made by Philadelphia police commissioner Charles Ramsey at the 2013 meeting of the International Association of Chiefs of Police, a group dedicated to improving law enforcement around the globe ("Ramsey Renews" 2013).

7. The irony and conflict between "justice for all" and "under God" have been noted in many legal challenges to the Pledge of Allegiance.

Defining and Reporting Crime

LEARNING OBJECTIVES

At the conclusion of this chapter, you should be able to:

- Distinguish between the different types of sociological and legal definitions used to describe crime.

- Describe the origin and evolution of the *Uniform Crime Report* (UCR) and its significance for measuring crime in the nation.

- Distinguish between different types or classes of crimes, including how the UCR counts and classifies them.

- Understand the future of official crime statistics in the United States, including the application of the National Incident-Based Reporting System.

- Define victimization surveys and distinguish them from crime reports.

- Distinguish between different types of crimes, including how the National Crime Victimization Survey (NCVS) counts and classifies them.

- Understand the future of victimization surveys in the United States, including changes to the NCVS.

23

INTRODUCTION

The year is 1965. A man rapes a woman who is a member of his household. Two police officers respond to a call for service made by a next-door neighbor who heard a woman screaming and begging for help. Arriving at the scene of the disturbance and evaluating the situation, the officers can do nothing. The reason: This was a sexual act between a husband and a wife, covered by law under the **marital rape exception**. Only beginning in the late 1970s could a husband be charged with and convicted of raping his wife and then only in a limited number of states (Finkelhor and Yllo 1985). Not until 1993 would all 50 states and the District of Columbia uniformly criminalize nonconsensual sex in marriage, or **spousal rape** (Mahoney and Williams 1998).[1] The reasons behind these changes are complex and related to social movements during the 1960s and early 1970s, such as the growth of feminism and women's liberation, changing social values and norms, and greater knowledge about the nature and extent of marital rape generated by criminal justice scholars. Judges also began to question the marital rape exception. As New York Court of Appeals judge Sol Wachtler famously observed as late as 1984, "[A] marriage license should not be viewed as a license for a husband to forcibly rape his wife with impunity. A married woman has the same right to control her own body as does an unmarried woman" (*People v. Liberta* (1984)).

As this example suggests, the intertwined processes of defining, categorizing, and measuring crimes owe much to both the scholarly and practical worlds of criminal justice. These two groups do not always communicate well with each other, but each must use the work of the other. Legislators make laws, sometimes informed by academics and practitioners and sometimes in direct contradiction to the best advice of both (Walker 2011). The police formally and informally, consciously and perhaps even unconsciously, utilize academic criminal justice insights into crime and criminals in their work to reduce crime and catch criminals. U.S. Supreme Court and other appellate court decisions often reference the work of psychologists, sociologists, criminologists, and criminal justice scholars, if only in the footnotes. The work of those defining and measuring crime also influences judicial sentencing practices. Correctional systems have long understood the value of the insights provided by criminal justice scholarship, even when politicians seem to ignore those insights. For their part, criminal justice scholars, academics, and researchers work to understand and explain the crime-related statistics generated by the nation's systems of law enforcement, courts, and corrections.

To gain a better understanding of the operation of the contemporary criminal justice system, we must first look at these intertwined processes, starting with how we define crime.

Marital rape exception: the archaic and currently unlawful idea that a husband may rape his wife, even using force, as this is an act permissible under the bonds of marriage

Spousal rape: the crime committed when a husband engages in nonconsensual sex with his wife; in theory, could involve the reverse case as well or same-sex rape in marriage

DEFINING CRIME

In Chapter 1, we define criminal justice, both as an organized response to crime and as an academic discipline. We employ the term "crime" in Chapter 1, defining it only as a violation of criminal law. Is that enough information for you? Probably not. Hence, we review two approaches to defining "crime"—one based in sociology and the other based in law. In the end, both are important. However, the latter drives the criminal justice system and quite literally circumscribes its subject matter.

Sociological Definitions

Sociologists allow communities to create their own definitions of the social phenomena that affect them. From this perspective, then, there is no single universally accepted definition of crime. One definition is instructive: A crime "is any behavior contrary to the group's moral code for which there are formalized group sanctions whether or not they are law" (Theodorson and Theodorson 1969: 86). Fully understanding the links between crimes and moral codes requires a bit more detail.

First, there are many types of norms, but the point of divergence is the nature of a society's reactions to violations of its norms. A **norm** is a shared rule or expectation regarding acceptable and unacceptable behavior and what happens when someone fails to conform to the standard. Social norms give us guidelines for behavior and allow for predictability in social relations. Consider William Graham Sumner's (1906) classical distinction between folkways and mores. A **folkway** is an informal norm based on traditional ways of acting in social relationships. As a behavioral standard, folkways rank rather low, controlling relatively unimportant conduct. For example, if one blows his or her nose in public and fails to use an appropriate disposal method for the product of this action, those around that person may say something about the inappropriateness of the act or make an unkind remark about the actor. In short, the sanction is mild, usually only viewed with social disapproval or perhaps disgust. If, however, the act violates a **mos**, then the social reaction is likely to be extreme, perhaps resulting in the death of the violator. Why? The **mores**, the plural form of mos, are normative acts that strike at the heart of a group's moral standards: Conformity is not optional, and violations of any given mos will generally receive a severe sanction. The actions defined by such mores or moral codes are viewed as so important to the society's existence that their violation simply cannot be tolerated, hence the extreme reaction.

Second, sociologically a crime is distinguishable from a deviant act. Both involve normative violations, but societal reactions to deviance generally lack formalized group sanctions. That is, there is no institutionalized structure—agencies or agents—to effect the punishments on

Norms:
rules or expectations shared by at least two people regarding behavior that is considered acceptable and unacceptable and, moreover, what happens when someone fails to conform to these standards

Folkway:
an informal norm based on traditional ways of acting in social relationships

Mos (mores):
a moral code of significant importance to the group

the guilty or even to decide guilt. Rather, the group responds as a collective entity, or individuals take it on themselves to act informally for the group, as a form of **vigilantism**. As communities grew larger and formal agencies emerged, some but not all social deviance morphed into crime. In some cases, later generations of lawgivers changed the rules. What was once deviance became criminal, what was criminal became deviance, and what was once classified as either deviant or criminal became normative. For example, consider the case of sodomy, which in the United States is no longer illegal (*Lawrence v. Texas* (2003)). However, some groups ostracize people for it or morally condemn it, especially when it involves persons of the same sex. In other parts of the world, such as Sudan, Somalia, Iran, Saudi Arabia, Brunei, and Yemen, sodomy is a capital crime (Altstein and Simon 2003; Shalakany 2006).

> **Vigilantism:**
> a form of behavior whereby an individual or group of individuals claims to act on behalf of the community in catching and punishing norm violators

What is critical to remember about deviant behavior is its group context. Even when the larger society that creates the laws views a behavior as normative, a smaller group within that society—a subculture—could see the act in very different terms. Concisely, all crime is deviant, but not all deviant behaviors are crimes.

In sum, sociologists recognize a range of crime definitions, from behavior that is socially dangerous to behavior that violates a criminal law. Nevertheless, even this latter definition is unhelpful if what we are trying to do is answer the question: How much crime is there? The search for an answer to that question takes us into a more legalistic and less sociological realm. The sociology of crime informs this search, specifically the significance and meaning of the unlawful act for the community.

Legal Definitions

Chapter 3 includes a detailed discussion of the legal elements of a crime. For our purposes here, it is sufficient to say the following about the legal definition: **Crime** is the violation of an existing statutory (written) *criminal* law for which there is a process to determine the guilt in an acceptable fashion and the trial court has pronounced a sentence (sanction) on a now-convicted offender.

> **Crime:**
> any behavior contrary to the group's moral code for which there are formalized group sanctions, whether or not they are law (sociological); an act or failure to act proven in a court of law to be in violation of a criminal code and punished by a lawful authority (legal)

The existing criminal laws must specify exactly the prohibited behavior. There can be no question or equivocation about the act itself. Hence, clear and concise definitions of the behavioral elements of the act in question are essential. For example, see Box 2.1 for the elements of the crimes of first- and second-degree murder as a form of homicide under federal law.[2] A given jurisdiction's criminal code formalizes these definitions. Variability across jurisdictions—say, within a nation such as the United States—concerning a specific crime can be troubling for those trying to count and measure those crimes, a monumental task to which we next turn.

> ## Box 2.1   Federal Definition of Homicide
>
> Title 18—Crimes and Criminal Procedure
>
> Part I—Crimes
>
> Chapter 51—Homicide
>
> §1111. Murder
>
> (a) Murder is the unlawful killing of a human being with malice aforethought. Every murder perpetrated by poison, lying in wait, or any other kind of willful, deliberate, malicious, and premeditated killing; or committed in the perpetration of, or attempt to perpetrate, any arson, escape, murder, kidnapping, treason, espionage, sabotage, aggravated sexual abuse or sexual abuse, child abuse, burglary, or robbery; or perpetrated as part of a pattern or practice of assault or torture against a child or children; or perpetrated from a premeditated design unlawfully and maliciously to effect the death of any human being other than him who is killed, is murder in the first degree.
>
> Any other murder is murder in the second degree.
>
> (b) Within the special maritime and territorial jurisdiction of the United States,
>
> - Whoever is guilty of murder in the first degree shall be punished by death or by imprisonment for life;
> - Whoever is guilty of murder in the second degree shall be imprisoned for any term of years or for life.
>
> (c) For purposes of this section—
>
> (1) the term "assault" has the same meaning as given that term in section 113;
>
> (2) the term "child" means a person who has not attained the age of 18 years and is—
>
> (A) under the perpetrator's care or control; or
>
> (B) at least six years younger than the perpetrator;
>
> (3) the term "child abuse" means intentionally or knowingly causing death or serious bodily injury to a child;
>
> (4) the term "pattern or practice of assault or torture" means assault or torture engaged in on at least two occasions;
>
> (5) the term "serious bodily injury" has the meaning set forth in section 1365; and
>
> (6) the term "torture" means conduct, whether or not committed under the color of law, that otherwise satisfies the definition set forth in section 2340(1).

SOURCE: 18 U.S.C. §1111.

UNIFORM CRIME REPORT PROGRAM

In the United States, we have several different ways of classifying crimes. We can find one of the most generally accepted in the annual report compiled by the Federal Bureau of Investigation (FBI), officially called *Crime in the United States* or, more commonly, the **Uniform Crime Report** (UCR). Any given year's UCR contains information related to 28 types of offenses. State and local law enforcement agencies send the relevant information monthly, and the FBI compiles and publishes the data annually. The Uniform Crime Report Program (UCR Program) essentially divides the offenses into two groups, Part I offenses and Part II offenses, the former viewed as more problematic to society than the latter. To reach this point in its

Uniform Crime Report **(UCR):**
a summary of crime in the United States as gleaned from the nation's local-, county-, and state-level law enforcement agencies

development, however, the UCR Program had to pass through a number of historical stages.

Development of the Uniform Crime Report Program

In 1870, the U.S. Congress authorized the attorney general to begin collecting information on the incidence of crime in the nation. As it turned out, this task was easier to mandate than put into practice. In 1927, the International Association of Chiefs of Police (IACP), a professional organization about whom you will learn more in this text, reached an agreement in principle with the FBI to establish an advisory board that would work with the FBI to collect the kind of information about crime authorized by Congress 60 years before. In 1930, Congress further authorized the FBI to take over the role of national clearinghouse for crime statistics, a voluntary effort on the part of local police departments. It took another 36 years before the National Sheriffs' Association (NSA) established its own advisory board and encouraged its members to participate, also on a voluntary basis. The advisory groups for both organizations continue to participate in the UCR Program. The Association of State UCR Programs, along with the IACP and NSA, works to promote participation and interest in the UCR Program (Federal Bureau of Investigation 2004). As evidence of their efforts, law enforcement agencies participating in the UCR Program represented 97.8 percent of the total U.S. population in 2011 (Federal Bureau of Investigation 2012).

The content of the UCR Program remained largely unchanged for decades. In 1952, cooperating police agencies started to provide information on arrestees' age, sex, and race. In 1958, the FBI established the Crime Index, a summary measure of all crime intended to give an overall picture of crime in the nation, but suspended it in 2004 because such summary measures do not provide an accurate representation of crime. In 1960, 30 years after the program's initiation, the UCR provided the first report of crime in all 50 states and gave statistics for the first time on the number of law enforcement officers killed in the line of duty. The 1962 UCR included the **Supplementary Homicide Report**, which was the first representation of the age, sex, and race of murder victims; the weapon used; and the circumstances surrounding the offense. The 1982 UCR Program permanently added arson to the Part I offenses. Following the **Hate Crimes Statistics Act of 1990**, the UCR Program began to collect bias motivation data or hate crimes, expanding it in 1994 to include mental and physical biases (Federal Bureau of Investigation 2004).

Finally, it is worth noting that the UCR Program has evolved over the years into a document that its creators would little recognize. Besides the changes noted above, there are at least three additional

Supplementary Homicide Report:
a part of the *Uniform Crime Report* after 1962 that provides the age, sex, and race of murder victims; the weapon used; and the circumstances surrounding the offense.

Hate Crimes Statistics Act of 1990:
law passed by Congress requiring the U.S. attorney general to record and report on hate crimes or hate-motivated crimes

unique reports. First, beginning in 1937, law enforcement agencies began reporting the number of police officers killed in the line of duty. These data received special attention in detailed analyses during the 1970s; in 2011, the FBI analytically separated such deaths into accidental and intentional. Second, the FBI began to encourage law enforcement agencies to report any theft of cargo, using a form that is free of the UCR Program's **hierarchy rule**. That is, given the offense ranking system, the UCR includes only the most serious crimes (UCR-1 versus UCR-4). For example, if a rape (UCR-2) occurs with a robbery (UCR-3), the police count only the rape. In 2008, the FBI received authorization to begin collecting human trafficking data, an effort that formally began in 2013.

Currently, the UCR Part I offenses fit into two categories: crimes against persons and crimes against property. The FBI reports information on both crimes known to the police and crimes resolved by an arrest for the eight Part I offenses; it reports only arrest information for the remaining 20 crimes, called Part II offenses. Our primary focus is on Part I offenses. We return to Part II offenses later in this chapter, as well as reviewing other crimes and crime categories used in criminal law.

The UCR Program provides expanded analyses for Part I offenses, which generally include such things as two-year trends, where the crimes occurred or the specific type of offense involved, whether a weapon was involved, and the clearance rates. The latter rates summarize two types of activities. First is **clearance by arrest**, the meaning of which is straightforward. The second is **clearance by exceptional means**, which includes known offenders who have died, nonextraditable suspects, or suspects against whom a key witness or victim is unwilling to testify. In the interest of simplicity, we limit our analyses to the definition, numbers, and per capita rates of Part I offenses between 1960 and 2012.

Part I Offenses: Crimes Against Persons (1960-2012)

Crimes against persons require a personal victim to be present when they are committed. The UCR Part I crimes against persons category covers four offenses: murder and nonnegligent manslaughter (UCR-1), forcible rape (UCR-2), robbery (UCR-3), and aggravated assault (UCR-4). For example, Table 2.1 shows the *number* of crimes against persons reported in the UCR for the years 1960-2012 (with five-year intervals). Figure 2.1 reveals the *per capita rate* for a given type of crime across these same years. We must examine both the table and figure, as they reveal very different information about the same events. For example, there has been a recent downward trend in the number of Part I violent crimes. The per capita rate trend is generally

Hate crime:
a criminal act in which the perpetrator intentionally selects the victim because of the actual or perceived race, gender, religion, sexual orientation, ethnicity, or disability of the victim

Hierarchy rule:
a technique used in the UCR Program whereby only the highest-ranked-category crime in any criminal event is reported in the annual report

Clearance by arrest:
classifying a crime as cleared by arrest

Clearance by exceptional means:
classifying a crime as cleared by means other than arrest

Crimes against persons:
a category of crime whereby the victim of the crime is an actual person or persons

Table 2.1	**UCR Part I, Crimes Against Persons: Annual Counts (1960-2012)**			
YEAR	MURDER/ NONNEGLIGENT MANSLAUGHTER	FORCIBLE RAPE	ROBBERY	AGGRAVATED ASSAULT
1960	9,110	17,190	107,840	154,320
1965	9,960	23,410	138,690	215,330
1970	16,000	37,990	349,860	334,970
1975	20,510	56,090	470,500	492,620
1980	23,040	82,990	565,840	672,650
1985	18,976	87,671	497,874	723,246
1990	23,438	102,555	639,271	1,054,863
1995	21,606	97,470	580,509	1,099,207
2000	15,586	90,178	408,016	911,706
2005	17,740	94,347	417,438	862,220
2010	14,722	85,593	369,089	781,844
2012	14,827	84,376	354,522	760,739

SOURCE: Federal Bureau of Investigation, n.d.b.

similar. The per capita rate is a normalized statistic since it is a rate per 100,000 persons living in the United States. This standardization means that, while the numbers in Table 2.1 could rise or fall just because of changes in U.S. population, the per capita rate found in Figure 2.1 is adjusted for the inevitable increases in the nation's population over time. We begin this discussion of serious crimes in America with a review of murder and nonnegligent manslaughter, also known as UCR-1.

The combined UCR Program category of **murder and nonnegligent manslaughter** actually covers several different offense types. For example, some states follow the pattern established by Pennsylvania in 1794 and have different categories of first-degree murder and second-degree murder (American Law Institute 1985: 117). These states often distinguish degrees of manslaughter, such as voluntary manslaughter and involuntary manslaughter. However, at the most basic level, murder and nonnegligent manslaughter involve "the willful (nonnegligent) killing of one human being by another" without excuse or justification (Federal Bureau of Investigation 2010b).

Table 2.1 shows the number of murders for the period 1960 to 2012 in five-year intervals to 2010. As this table shows, the number of such crimes had more than doubled by 1975, where it stayed, with some up and down fluctuations, until 1995. In that year, it began a downward spiral, a pattern that repeats in Figure 2.1. Murder rates peaked in 1980 at 10.2 per 100,000 population (actual rate), starting to drop

Murder and nonnegligent manslaughter: the willful (nonnegligent) killing of one human being by another

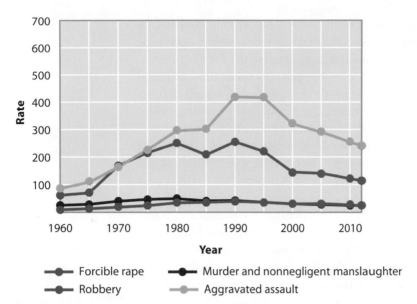

Figure 2.1
UCR Part I offenses, crimes against persons: annual per capita rates (100,000 population), 1960-2012.

NOTE: The murder and nonnegligent manslaughter rates are multiplied by five for comparison purposes.
SOURCE: Federal Bureau of Investigation, n.d.b.

throughout the 1980s, rising again to above 9 in the 1990s, and then dropping off as the century ended and the new millennium began. Indeed, the murder and nonnegligent manslaughter rates in 2012 were the lowest this nation has seen since the mid-1960s.

Among the UCR Part I personal crimes, **forcible rape** is unique for at least four reasons, beyond those noted in this chapter's introduction. First, the UCR traditionally employed a common law definition in which forcible rape "is the carnal knowledge of a female forcibly and against her will." Under such a definition, forcible rape could occur against only female victims. However, in December 2011, the director of the FBI authorized the following definition of **rape**: "penetration, no matter how slight, of the vagina or anus with any body part or object, or oral penetration by a sex organ of another person, without the consent of the victim" (U.S. Department of Justice 2012). This definition allows for the offender and victim to be of either gender. However, it is important to note that the FBI continues to use the historical definition in its statistical reporting of "forcible rape" in the Summary Reporting System of the UCR. In this transition period there is the potential for some confusion about the crime of rape: "forcible" has been removed from the definition, but the UCR summaries may include rapes that reflect both the traditional definition and the new definition of the crime. Second, because of the restrictiveness of the common law definition, in the past 30-plus years a number of states have changed their laws from rape to "criminal sexual penetration" (or a similar designation), also allowing for the collection of offense data when the offenders and

Forcible rape:
by the traditional UCR definition, the carnal knowledge of a female forcibly and against her will, including attempts or assaults to commit rape by force or threat of force; however, statutory rape (without force) and other sex offenses are excluded

Rape:
by the new UCR definition, penetration, no matter how slight, of the vagina or anus with any body part or object, or oral penetration by a sex organ of another person without the consent of the victim

victims are of either gender. Third, based on victim surveys, a technique we examine later in this chapter, it has become apparent that forcible rape is among the most underreported of the Part I offenses. Fourth, law enforcement agencies over the past 20 years have become sensitized to the unique status of rape victims, with many jurisdictions sending a specialized team to interview the victim and providing "rape collection kits" that maintain the all-important chain of evidence.

Criminologists suspect that for these reasons and not changes in their prevalence, rape statistics have fluctuated over the past 40 years (Felson and Paré 2005; Jensen and Karpos 1993; Rennison 2002; Tjaden and Thoennes 2006). For example, reporting of this crime to police increased in the 1970s, particularly in situations involving nonstranger rapes; by the 1990s, differences between reporting for stranger and nonstranger rapes were insignificant (Baumer, Felson, and Messner 2006). Nonetheless, forcible rape numbers and rates are considered among the least trustworthy statistics reported by the FBI in the UCR.

As reflected in Table 2.1, the number of reported forcible rapes more than tripled between 1960 and 1975, nearly doubling again between 1975 and 1990. The volume of forcible rapes peaked in 1992 (109,062). It is important to observe that the number of rapes reported in 1992 was more than six times higher than the 1960 figure. By 2012, the number of reported forcible rapes dropped to a 20-year low, but there were still four times as many reported as in 1960. In terms of per capita rates, they also reached their peak rate in 1992 (42.8). While the per capita rates for forcible rape dropped off to numbers not seen since the 1970s, in 2012 they remained at three times the 1960 rate.

Robbery is the final personal crime included among the UCR Part I offenses. Robbery is a crime that some people confuse with burglary. Victims may say that someone robbed their house or car. However, robbery is a crime against the person; therefore, a victim must be physically present at the crime's commission. This means that a carjacking is a robbery, but having your car broken into and something stolen is not. The FBI defines robbery as "the taking or attempting to take anything of value from the care, custody, or control of a person or persons by force or threat of force or violence and/or putting the victim in fear" (Federal Bureau of Investigation 2010c).

As revealed in Table 2.1, between 1960 and 1980, the number of reported robberies increased fivefold. The peak for robberies between 1960 and 2012 occurred in 1993, around the same time that rapes and murders/nonnegligent manslaughters peaked. In addition, robberies also began to drop in the mid- to late 1990s, achieving levels by 2012 not seen since 1970. The per capita rates for burglary began at 60 and started to increase dramatically in the mid-1960s, peaking first

Robbery:
the taking or attempting to take anything of value from the care, custody, or control of a person or persons by force or threat of force or violence and/or by putting the victim in fear

in 1981 and then dropping off slightly, only to peak again a decade later. Since 1991, the burglary rate has dropped substantially to levels reported in the 1960s. To reiterate, robbery, as with the other three forms of violent offending included in the Part I offenses, generally increased both in volume and per capita rates throughout the 1960s, 1970s, and 1980s. A downward spiral began in the early 1990s, although the downward trend was not as dramatic as, for example, the rate for murder and nonnegligent manslaughter.

As with robbery, the average person sometimes confuses the different forms of assault. A simple assault occurs when a person perceives a physical threat that puts that person in fear for his or her life or safety. Often, simple assaults are misdemeanors and are not counted in the UCR Part I offenses (they are included in the UCR Part II offenses). By contrast, **aggravated assaults** are felonies and are defined as "an unlawful attack by one person upon another person for the purpose of inflicting severe or aggravated bodily injury." Additionally, "this type of assault is usually accompanied by the use of a weapon or by other means likely to produce death or great bodily harm" (Federal Bureau of Investigation 2011a). For an incident to progress from a simple assault into an aggravated assault, some additional condition or circumstance must be present. Several factors can account for this transformation, such as assault and battery, assault with a deadly weapon, assault with intent to commit rape, and assault with intent to commit bodily harm. Therefore, once the act goes from simply a threat that causes fear to striking a person or significant physical harm, an aggravated assault has occurred.

Aggravated assault: an unlawful attack by one person on another for the purpose of inflicting severe or aggravated bodily injury

Aggravated assaults were by far the most commonly committed crime against persons included in the 1960 UCR. The number reported was roughly 50 percent higher than for robbery, its nearest "competitor" offense. By the time the number of aggravated assaults peaked, in 1993, they were nearly twice the number reported for robberies (1,135,607 versus 659,870). There were also more than seven times as many aggravated assaults reported in that year as in 1960, the greatest proportional increase for any Part I offense. Their incidence also began to decline shortly thereafter despite their continued relatively high volume. By 2012, there were still more than three-quarters of a million reported aggravated assaults, a number that was on par with the volume reported in 1985 and five times that reported in 1960. As for the population adjusted rates, there were 242 aggravated assaults reported per 100,000 people in 2012. That figure represented a 45 percent reduction from the 1993 high (442) but was still three times the rate reported in 1960. As the line for aggravated assaults reported in Figure 2.1 suggests, there was a decline, but it was not as deep as the declines reported for robbery or murder/nonnegligent manslaughter.

Part I Offenses: Crimes Against Property (1960-2012)

The UCR records four property crimes among the eight Part I offenses, including burglary (UCR-5), larceny-theft (UCR-6), motor vehicle theft (UCR-7), and arson (UCR-8). As a rule, the FBI's expanded analysis for these offense types is greater than that for the Part I personal crimes. For example, larceny-thefts may include such information as the type of theft (e.g., from a motor vehicle or coin-operated machine, or a purse snatching) or, for a burglary, the location (e.g., residence or nonresidence) and time of day (e.g., night, day, or unknown). Again, such information, while interesting, is not part of the current analysis.

As mentioned previously, burglary is a crime sometimes confused with larceny-theft or robbery. However, the UCR Program definition of **burglary** is "the unlawful entry of a structure to commit a felony or theft. . . . [T]he use of force need not have occurred" (Federal Bureau of Investigation 2010a). Thefts, as previously noted, can occur in a residence or business, at night or in the daytime; for law enforcement purposes, such distinctions are important for criminologists who try to explain such events. In contrast to larceny-theft or robbery, burglary must involve entry into a building or vehicle, either by force or by other means, and it does not involve direct personal contact with a victim.

Burglary:
the unlawful entry of a structure to commit a felony or theft; to classify an offense as a burglary, the use of force to gain entry need not have occurred

As seen in Table 2.2, in 1960 burglaries were the second most frequently occurring type of crime, exceeded only by larceny-thefts.

Table 2.2   **UCR Part I Offenses, Crimes Against Property: Annual Counts (1960-2012)**

YEAR	BURGLARY	LARCENY-THEFT	MOTOR VEHICLE THEFT
1960	912,100	1,855,400	328,200
1965	1,282,500	2,572,600	496,900
1970	2,205,000	4,225,800	928,400
1975	3,265,300	5,977,700	1,009,600
1980	3,795,200	7,136,900	1,131,700
1985	3,073,348	6,926,380	1,102,862
1990	3,073,909	7,945,670	1,635,907
1995	2,593,784	7,997,710	1,472,441
2000	2,050,992	6,971,590	1,160,002
2005	2,116,531	7,092,267	1,228,391
2010	2,168,459	6,204,601	739,565
2012	2,103,787	6,150,598	721,053

SOURCE: Federal Bureau of Investigation, n.d.b.

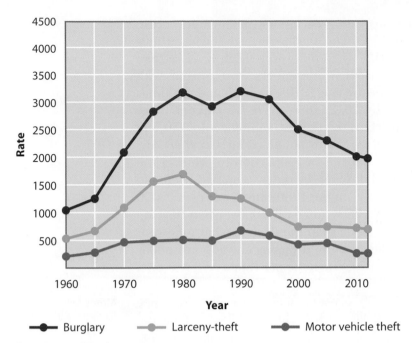

Figure 2.2
UCR Part I offenses,
crimes against prop-
erty: annual per capita
rates (100,000 popu-
lation), 1960-2012

SOURCE: Federal Bureau of Investigation, n.d.b.

By the early 1970s, the number of burglaries had increased threefold, peaking in the late 1980s, several years before the peaks noted for UCR Part I personal offenses. Burglaries remained high, more than 3 million a year, through the early 1990s, and then, about the time that the other offenses began to decline, so did burglaries. However, although they declined by the late 1990s to levels not seen since the early 1970s, their numbers did not dramatically decrease even into the current century. As we have seen previously, gross numbers tell only part of the story, and if the acts stabilized and the population increased, then we would expect that the rates would decline, which they did as well. For example, between 1960 and 1975, the rates reported in Figure 2.2 tripled (509 to 1532). The per capita burglary rates actually peaked in 1980 (1,684) and began a gradual decline throughout the 1990s. By 2012, the burglary rate stood at a level unseen since 1965.

The most common Part I offense by far is **larceny-theft**. The FBI defines larceny-theft as "[t]he unlawful taking, carrying, leading, or riding away of property from the possession or constructive possession of another" (Federal Bureau of Investigation 2009). It is different from burglary in that it does not involve a breaking into a structure and it is different from robbery in that it does not involve the taking of property directly from a person.

The claim that larceny-theft is a common offense is substantiated by the numbers reported in Table 2.2. In 1960, there were more larceny-thefts than all of the other UCR Part I offenses combined (1,855,400

Larceny-theft:
the unlawful taking, carrying, leading, or riding away of property from the possession or constructive possession of another

versus 1,528,700). It took a decade to reach the 4 million mark, cresting at just below 8 million in 1995. The decline through the late 1990s was slow. Indeed, even by 2012, when there were slightly more than 6.1 million larceny-thefts reported, the numbers were on par with those found in UCR volumes for the late 1970s, more than three times than that reported in 1960. By 2012, there were 50 percent more larceny-thefts than all other Part I offenses combined (6,150,598 versus 4,039,304). Thus, in terms of raw numbers, larceny-thefts declined over the past 20 years but not in proportion to other crime categories. This observation is borne out by the per capita rates found in Figure 2.2. The increases between the 1960 rate of just over 1,000 and the twin peaks of the early 1980s and early 1990s, when the rate reached above 3,000, were steeper than the declines that followed. Moreover, the declines were less severe, dropping down to just under 2,000, a rate first achieved in 1970, when the per capita rate was on a very steep upward climb.

Motor vehicle thefts (MVT) present a complex picture, since thefts of personal motor vehicles such as automobiles and pickup trucks are included. Additionally, thefts of recreational vehicles, buses, motorcycles, snowmobiles, and other vehicles also fit within this category. The offense of taking and abandoning a vehicle for temporary transportation is not included here. In many states, this crime is labeled "joyriding" or something similar. As reflected in Table 2.2, MVT outnumbered all of the Part I offenses against persons but were less than half as frequent as burglary and about one-sixth as frequent as larceny thefts. Their numbers increased, taking until 1968 to double, and then doubled *again* by 1986. MVT peaked in 1991, a figure that was five times the number reported in 1960. Only forcible rapes and aggravated assaults exceeded this proportionate increase in the number of offenses reported to the police over these 50-plus years. The rates for MVT generally leveled off near their peak level until the mid-1990s, when, like most other crime rates, they began to fall. They did not drop much below the rates reported in 1970.

Arson became a Part I offense in 1979. **Arson** is defined as "any willful or malicious burning or attempting to burn, with or without intent to defraud, a dwelling house, public building, motor vehicle or aircraft, personal property of another, etc." (Federal Bureau of Investigation 2011b). Local law enforcement agencies have been slow to embrace this criminal act in their reporting, partly because in many jurisdictions, specially trained members of the local fire department or arson investigators within local law enforcement investigate arsons. Whatever its cause, the FBI is very cautious about reporting on

Motor vehicle thefts:
the theft or attempted theft of a motor vehicle, defined as a self-propelled vehicle that runs on land surfaces and not on rails

Arson:
any willful or malicious burning or attempting to burn, with or without intent to defraud, a dwelling house, public building, motor vehicle or aircraft, personal property of another, etc.

arson given the different classification and reporting systems used by the various jurisdictions. There is a great deal of fluctuation in the number of months that a given policing agency may include in reporting these events—the FBI (2011b) describes this phenomenon as "unevenness of reporting"—varying from 1 month of arson statistics to a full 12 months in agency reports. For these reasons, there is no trend analysis available for arson.

UCR Part II Offenses: Other Crimes

UCR Part II offenses are those with an impact on society that is judged to be less serious than UCR Part I offenses, but they are nonetheless important to count. For this reason, the UCR Program collects only arrest data for Part II offenses, consisting of 20 criminal activities, which can be grouped into four offense clusters. First are crimes against public morals, including prostitution and commercialized vice (UCR-16), sex offenses (except forcible rape and prostitution and commercialized vice) (UCR-17), drug abuse violations (UCR-18), and gambling (UCR-19). Another group involves financial crimes, including forgery and counterfeiting (UCR-10), fraud (UCR-11), embezzlement (UCR-12), and stolen property—buying, receiving, and possessing (UCR-13). A third group consists of crimes against public order and the administration of justice, including the following offenses: simple assault (UCR-9); vandalism (UCR-14); weapons—carrying, possessing, etc. (UCR-15); driving under the influence (UCR-21); liquor law (offenses) (UCR-22); drunkenness (UCR-23); disorderly conduct (UCR-24); and vagrancy (UCR 25). Three more have to do with the family or children, mainly juveniles, including offenses against the family and children (UCR-20), and curfew and loitering law violations (juveniles) (UCR-28).[3] The final two offenses are nondescript and include all other offenses (except traffic offenses) (UCR-26) and suspicion (UCR-27), the latter referring to an arrest for no specific offense, where the person was released without formal charges.

Future of the UCR Program

Criminologists and others interested in the true meaning of the UCR have long questioned the utility of this approach. Moreover, those who would like to study specific forms of crime find the information they contain to be useful only in giving the big picture. In 1985, a Uniform Crime Report Program advisory group released the *Blueprint for the Future of the Uniform Crime Reporting Program*, calling for a redesign of the program. Following a series of meetings and confer-ences, the FBI began managing the **National Incident-Based Reporting System (NIBRS)** in 1989. This new program looked at criminal incidents, collecting 57 different pieces of data about 46 specific crimes known as Group A offenses, including but not limited to information about the offense, victim, property, offender and arrestee, all linked together into a criminal incident information file; NIBRS records arrests only for a second category of crime, Group B offenses. By 2011, 15 states submit-ted all crime information for both UCR and NIBRS programs via the NIBRS mechanism; altogether, 32 states are NIBRS compliant.

NIBRS, like the UCR Program before it, will take decades to achieve a proportionality of reporting that parallels that of the senior crime statistics reporting method. In the interim, the standard method will provide a robust picture of crime in the nation, at least in terms of crimes that come to the attention of the police. Eventually, NIBRS may replace the UCR Program entirely, although not for several decades.

Both official crime-reporting systems have faults. Statistics they provide on criminal homicides, or murder and nonnegligent homi-cides, are reasonably reliable because the bodies nearly always show up. The same is true of motor vehicle theft, because most insurance companies require a police report prior to paying on a loss. Never-theless, for the remaining categories, there are legitimate concerns about underreporting, especially for the sex-related offenses such as rape. In short, there is a **dark figure of crime**, those criminal acts about which the police are ignorant and that do not appear in either program. It is unlikely, however, that, outside of full compliance with NIBRS, we will see a change in what we have reported here as the traditional UCR Program and its annual report, *Crime in the United States*. Even if NIBRS becomes the norm, it remains a representation of crimes known to the police, and as such is a measure of the effi-ciency of those organizations in collecting and disseminating crime information.

As the brief overview in Box 2.2 suggests, there are other ways to think about crime. The FBI has shown some flexibility, adding cargo theft and hate crimes to its inventory of recorded crimes, although neither is a Part I or Part II offense. In an effort to breach one of these problems, the question of unreported crime and the dark figure of crime, the U.S. Department of Justice began employing victimiza-tion surveys in the 1970s, a topic to which we next turn.

National Incident-Based Reporting System (NIBRS): crime statistics collection method that looks at every crime as an incident with several possible parts and possibly multiple participants, with the information coming voluntarily from local law enforcement agencies

Dark figure of crime: used by sociologists and crim-inologists to refer to unreported or unrecorded crimes

Box 2.2 Alternative Crime Categorization Schemes

Besides the UCR Program's crime categories, politicians, criminologists, and others in the public find it useful to categorize crime into ever more discrete groupings. For example, **public welfare crimes** would be "the manufacture or sale of impure food or drugs to the public, antipollution environmental laws, as well as traffic and motor-vehicle regulations" (Dressler 2009: 147). There is also a group of activities classified as **crimes against public decency and morality**, including offenses such as prostitution and gambling, which are Part II offenses. Interestingly, the FBI's NIBRS program includes a third category of crime, after crimes against persons and **crimes against property**, called **crimes against society**. Crimes against society represent society's prohibitions and include such specific crimes as gambling (see crimes against public decency and morality), weapons violations, prostitution, child pornography, and drug abuse offenses.

In the wake of the attacks of September 11, 2001, another category of crimes has gained notoriety: **crimes against the state** or offenses related to the administration of justice. Crimes against the state include treason and terrorism. Treason is "[w]aging war against one's country or aiding at war against it" (Sheppard 2012: 2843). Terrorism is "an act of violence or harm against a civilian population, members of the public, infrastructure, places, or vehicles that is intended to sow fear within the population or to intimidate a government or retaliate against a government, people, or state for past actions" (Sheppard 2012: 2784). Administration of justice offenses also involve crimes that generally receive little attention until a well-publicized trial; these include the crimes of perjury, bribery, misconduct by public officials, and obstruction of justice.

Finally, there are specific categories of offenses, including **organized crime**, **corporate crime**, and **occupational crime** (or white-collar crime), that, while important to criminologists and crime fighters alike, have few national benchmarks, as they are not subjected to the same level of legal responses or data collection as, for example, UCR Part I offenses. Most states do not have separate organized crime statutes and treat these offenses as personal or property crimes. By contrast, federal prosecutors have at their disposal the **Racketeer Influenced and Corrupt Organizations (RICO) statutes** that they can use against different types of organized criminal activities. Furthermore, crimes committed by corporations and occupational crimes such as embezzlement, both referred to as white-collar crimes, often are prosecuted under traditional criminal statutes and not necessarily as unique forms of crime.

SOURCES: Dressler 2009; Sheppard 2012.

Public welfare crime: a criminal activity related to an act that normally would be lawful, but owing to certain qualities of the activity, it becomes a crime by placing portions of the public at risk for some loss, including health- and welfare-related problems

Crimes against public decency and morality: public order offenses, generally considered as classic examples of *mala prohibita* crimes or victimless crimes; the "victims" are often willing participants and can include public indecency, prostitution, and public intoxication

Crimes against property: a category of crime whereby the victim of the crime is property owned by an individual or individuals; the UCR Program includes burglary, larceny-theft, motor vehicle theft, and arson

Crimes against society: like many *mala prohibita* crimes, these represent society's prohibitions and include such specific crimes as gambling, weapons violations, prostitution, child pornography, and drug abuse offenses

Crimes against the state: crimes that threaten to disrupt the operation of the government; include treason and terrorism

Organized crime: any group with a formalized structure whose primary objective is to obtain money through illegal activities

Corporate crime: an offense committed either by a corporation or individuals acting on behalf of a corporation or other business entity

Occupational crime: an unlawful act committed by a person through an opportunity created in the course of a legal job or vocation

Racketeer Influenced and Corrupt Organization (RICO) statutes: laws passed first by the federal government and then by states to control organized crime

VICTIMIZATION SURVEYS

For decades, groups critical of official crime statistics warned about the previously mentioned dark figure of crime. Underreporting of crime to the police can occur for any number of reasons, including the culpability of some victims who are also engaged in crime at some levels and the embarrassment and social stigma associated with certain crimes, particularly sex-based crimes such as rape. Some men, for example, are unlikely to report a rape under almost any circumstances unless the injuries associated with the attack are so self-explanatory as to be undeniable. In the minds of some critics, the official crime statistics are simply bureaucratic products, measuring only the effectiveness of the criminal justice system at receiving information about crime, processing that data, and sharing it. They suggested a more direct approach to measuring crime. One answer was the victimization survey.

Development of Victimization Surveys

The modern victimization survey dates to 1966, when three successively larger crime surveys examined victimizations: the first in the high-crime areas of Washington, D.C.; the second in all of the District of Columbia, Boston, and Chicago; and the third nationwide, in a pilot study intended to reveal whether it was feasible to examine this topic on a national basis (Abadinsky and Winfree 1992: 60-61). Based on the pioneering work of the National Opinion Research Center and the President's Commission on Law Enforcement and Administration of Justice (see Chapter 1), the nation saw the first federally sponsored national crime survey in 1972. These first surveys included several parts, most of which were dropped by the mid-1970s. The only part to continue virtually unchanged for 20-plus years was the National Crime Survey (NCS). Given modifications to the NCS from 1992 to 1993, when it became the National Crime Victimization Survey (NCVS), it is impossible to compare the results of surveys conducted prior to 1993 with those after that year; hence, the analyses that follow focus on the 1993 NCVS forward to the most recent survey.

Unlike the UCR and NIBRS programs, which attempt to gather statistics on all crimes known to the police and arrest statistics for certain crimes, the NCVS is based on a sample. It would be impossible to survey every victim in the nation. Hence, the NCVS employs a sophisticated method of data collection called a multistage cluster sample. All of the details and intricacies of the sample method are beyond the scope of this text. The information obtained from the NCVS represents a reasonably representative estimate for the nation as a whole.

Personal Victimization Crimes (1993-2012)

The 1993 restart of the NCVS signaled a new era in the national crime surveys. This was roughly the same time that the annual UCR began showing a generally downward trend in the crime rate. These two sets of crime data cannot be compared; nonetheless, it is interesting to note that the annual victimization surveys showed an even earlier downward trend than did the UCR. The annual crime count estimates (Table 2.3) for personal offenses declined beginning in 1994, dropping to decade lows by the end of the 1990s, rising slightly in the early 2000s, and then dropping off again. By the early 2010s they were lower than had been observed 20 years earlier, a fact reinforced by the per capita rates in Figure 2.3. The per capita rates for all personal

Table 2.3	NCVS Personal Crime Victimizations: Annual Count Estimates (1993-2012)			
YEAR	RAPE/SEXUAL ASSAULT	ROBBERY	AGGRAVATED ASSAULT	PERSONAL THEFT/ LARCENY
1993	898,239	1,752,667	3,481,055	481,384
1994	674,291	1,675,840	3,412,978	502,966
1995	563,249	1,350,577	2,894,387	414,140
1996	437,198	1,425,448	2,877,246	382,772
1997	553,523	1,188,879	2,895,381	369,860
1998	391,101	970,713	2,318,424	295,622
1999	591,460	1,019,159	1,961,820	238,381
2000	366,747	866,123	1,564,737	273,958
2001	476,578	667,736	1,383,667	188,368
2002	349,805	624,391	1,332,518	155,397
2003	325,311	708,376	1,362,267	208,909
2004	255,769	616,419	1,418,657	224,066
2005	207,760	769,148	1,281,491	229,459
2006	463,598	932,397	1,753,819	173,224
2007	248,277	775,522	1,218,923	224,765
2008	349,691	679,789	969,216	171,179
2009	305,574	635,073	1,028,273	133,210
2010	268,574	568,519	857,751	138,341
2011	244,188	557,258	1,053,391	165,770
2012	346,830	741,756	996,106	153,583

SOURCE: Data compiled from Bureau of Justice Statistics NCVS Victimization Analysis Tool (http://www.bjs.gov/index.cfm?ty=nvat).

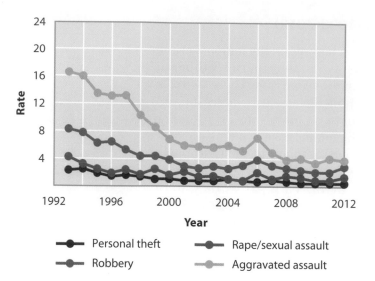

Figure 2.3
NCVS personal victimizations: annual per capita crime rate estimates (1,000 population), 1993-2012

SOURCE: Data compiled from Bureau of Justice Statistics NCVS Victimization Analysis Tool (http://www.bjs.gov/index.cfm?ty=nvat).

crime victimizations dropped steeply throughout the late 1990s and generally stabilized or continued to drop through the first decade-plus of the 21st century. The year 2006 stands as a bit of an oddity in this regard, as the rates for three of the four personal crimes spiked in that year. When it comes to crime statistics, yearly comparisons can be misleading. It is best to take the long view, examining the movement of offense frequencies and rates over multiple years.

Household Victimization Crimes (1993-2012)

Just as with the UCR Program, the NCVS reveals that there are far more household or property victimizations than personal ones (see Table 2.4). In 1993, the overall figure stood at more than 35 million; 20 years later, in keeping with the entire trend data described so far, this annual statistic experienced a decline to 19.6 million, a reduction of nearly 45 percent in the annual count. This drop is interesting because in the early 2010s, the volume of such crimes actually began to climb again from across-the-board lows in 2010. As with personal crimes, which also experienced fluctuations at the beginning of the 2010, these particular statistics bear watching to see if a new trend is emerging. In this regard, the per capita rates (see Figure 2.4) are also instructive, as they have remained reasonably flat since all three dropped at the end of the 20th century. The theft rates have shown far more volatility than the other two, fluctuating up or down every couple of years since 2000; it is currently experiencing a sharp increase. Again, it is too early to determine if a pattern is emerging, given such volatility in both rates and the raw estimates of offenses.

Table 2.4   NCVS Household Crime Victimizations: Annual Count Estimates (1993-2012)

YEAR	HOUSEHOLD BURGLARY	MOTOR VEHICLE THEFT	THEFT
1993	6,378,721	1,921,179	26,793,987
1994	6,328,669	1,924,020	26,058,898
1995	5,524,203	1,739.088	24,758,298
1996	5,425,992	1,419,576	22,864,784
1997	5,036,240	1,460,748	21,274,435
1998	4,517,565	1,216,505	19,241,136
1999	4,111,440	1,068,125	17,388,065
2000	3,718,406	949,580	15,965,944
2001	3,404,382	1,034,419	15,034,396
2002	3,251,812	1,018,688	14,283,819
2003	3,648,671	1,032,471	15,111,310
2004	3,598,571	1,068,480	14,727,728
2005	3,584,847	1,003,150	14,085,360
2006	3,875,155	1,019,761	15,019,296
2007	3,572,218	988,090	13,956,126
2008	3,470,183	795,158	13,012,317
2009	3,411,298	735,765	12,075,913
2010	3,176,181	606,991	11,628,437
2011	3,613,838	628,220	12,821,090
2012	3,764,539	633,742	15,224,695

SOURCE: Data compiled from Bureau of Justice Statistics NCVS Victimization Analysis Tool (http://www.bjs.gov/index.cfm?ty=nvat).

Future of the NCVS Program

A few years ago, the Bureau of Justice Statistics (BJS) began to consider a major redesign of the survey to meet challenges to its viability and ability to meet the long-established goal of providing insights into the dark figure of crime. This project is presently ongoing. Two additional BJS-sponsored projects are also underway that are intended to identify, develop, and test the "best methods for collecting self-report data on rape and sexual assault" (Bureau of Justice Statistics 2014). As with NIBRS, which focuses on crimes known to the police, the goal is to provide the best possible information about criminal victimizations. However, it is doubtful that these changes will result in major alterations to the NCVS before the end of the next decade.

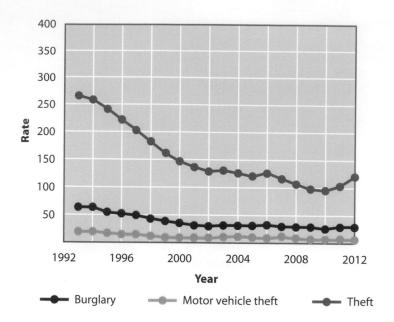

Figure 2.4
NCVS household crime victimizations: annual per capita crime rate estimates (1,000 population), 1993-2012

SOURCE: Data compiled from Bureau of Justice Statistics NCVS Victimization Analysis Tool (http://www.bjs.gov/index.cfm?ty=nvat).

SUMMARY

Even a quick reading of this chapter reveals several key facts. First, no matter which ones you rely on, our crime statistics are estimates and are unable to provide a complete picture of the nature and extent of the true amount of crime. Each system has its unique strengths and weaknesses. At present, there is no superior method, so we have what we have in the way of crime statistics.

Second, irrespective of whether you look at the annual *Uniform Crime Report* or the NCVS reports, crime has gone down since the 1990s. Twenty years of crime victimization surveys that date from 1973 to 1992 also tell us that the falloff in crime volume and rates predates even the past 20 years of UCR statistics about a crime decline (Bastian 1994). Thus, while there are annual fluctuations—ones that may or may not portend future trends—the nation's crime in the early 1990s was more violent and at higher rates than is the case today.

Finally, nothing in criminal justice is static, including its crime statistics. The latter changes in terms of what they tell us about crime and the methods we use to collect, categorize, and report it. What does not change, however, is our need to possess the best possible insights into the nature and extent of crime. This remains a constant, as it informs the rest of the criminal justice system, its policies, and practices.

REVIEW QUESTIONS

1. As we learned in the opening section of this chapter, the criminalization of some behaviors, such as spousal rape, took quite some time. Human trafficking is a crime that has only recently come to the public's attention. A federal statute (18 U.S.C. §§1581-1592) defines the crime. Look up this statute. What is the year of the statute? What is human trafficking? What is the law on human trafficking in your state? What are the penalties in both jurisdictions? (Hint: Try a web search for "human trafficking law in [state]" or some variant of it.)

2. Box 2.1 contains the federal code definition of homicide. Look up the statute for homicide in your state. Does it differ from the federal statute? How does your state's statute differ from the federal code?

3. Attack or defend the following statement: "Sociological definitions of crime are of little use to a person interested in crime statistics, information gathered that is based on acts defined by law."

4. Summarize the UCR personal crime trends between 1960 and 2012. What do they reveal about general trends in personal crime? What do they say about the trends for specific personal crimes?

5. Summarize the UCR property crime trends between 1960 and 2012. What do they reveal about general trends in property crime? What do they say about the trends for specific property crimes?

6. Summarize the NCVS personal victimizations between 1993 and 2012. What do they reveal about general trends in personal victimizations? What do they say about the trends for specific personal victimizations?

7. Summarize the NCVS household victimizations between 1993 and 2012. What do they reveal about the general trends in household victimizations? What do they say about the trends for specific household victimizations?

8. When it comes to crime in the United States, which of the two types of statistics do you trust more—the *Uniform Crime Report* or the reports generated from the National Crime Victimization Survey? Explain your answer.

KEY TERMS

aggravated assault
arson
burglary
clearance by arrest
clearance by exceptional means
corporate crime
crime
crimes against persons
crimes against property
crimes against public morality
crimes against society
crimes against the state
dark figure of crime
folkway
forcible rape
hate crimes
Hate Crimes Statistics Act of 1990

hierarchy rule
larceny-theft
marital rape exception
mos (mores)
motor vehicle thefts murder and nonnegligent manslaughter
National Incident-Based Reporting System (NIBRS)
norms
occupational crime
organized crime
public welfare crime
Racketeer Influenced and Corrupt Organization (RICO) statutes
robbery
spousal rape
supplementary homicide report
Uniform Crime Report
vigilantism

NOTES

1. There are three approaches in law to marital rape today. The neutral approach removes the exception and makes all cases of rape essentially the same. The proactive approach specifically indicates that marriage is not a defense in cases of rape. Finally, the separation approach creates a new crime category to distinguish this type of rape from "normal" rape, with the former often accorded a much more lenient judicial response at sentencing (LaMance 2013).

2. Homicide is the one crime for which there is a high degree of national and international definitional consensus, although particulars can vary from state to state and nation to nation.

3. Until 2010, the annual *Uniform Crime Report* reported on runaways (persons under age 18), or UCR-29.

Criminal Law and the Legal Environment

LEARNING OBJECTIVES

At the conclusion of this chapter, you should be able to:

- Explain the differences between civil law and criminal law.
- Distinguish procedural law from substantive law.
- List and define the various sources of law in the United States.
- Define crimes based on the level of seriousness.
- Explain the various elements associated with crimes.
- Provide examples of inchoate crimes.

INTRODUCTION

As we explain in Chapter 1, the criminal justice system is generally characterized by its three primary components: police, courts, and corrections. However, legislatures play a major role in criminal justice operations in the United States. For instance, legislatures provide funding for criminal justice operations, and a key legislative function is passing substantive and procedural criminal laws. In this chapter, we examine the historical development of criminal law, the differences between criminal law and civil law, the sources of law in the United States, the different degrees of crime seriousness, the elements of criminal offenses, incomplete (or inchoate) offenses, the defenses that are used in some criminal trials, and the ways we can classify crimes based on the nature of the offense and the objective of the criminal activity.

THE HISTORY OF LAW

You could say that human social communities have always had laws, although the nature of these laws may have been different from the laws we have today. This section considers three historical periods in the development of law. These periods are classified as the prehistorical era, early historical era, and modern era, each associated with, in order, the following legal systems: primitive, transitional, and modern (Vago 2009).

Prehistorical Era

Even the most primitive societies that have existed have had what we would call laws. Such societies were organized around clans, tribes, or kinship. Most of these groups' laws would be considered **customary law**. This means the laws come from norms, mores, and folkways that evolve over many generations. The result is these laws become so much a part of the society that no one remembers when or how they originated. Typically, they are handed down from those in positions of authority and exist in unwritten form. Children are taught very early on what is expected of them and how to behave in ways that are acceptable and unacceptable.

Customary law:
unwritten laws that develop in tribal or primitive societies; based on group norms, mores, and folkways

Law enforcement in primitive societies is informal but effective. All members of the group become enforcers, and norm violations can bring swift and sometimes severe sanctions. Judges within primitive societies are the tribal chiefs or ruling elders, who judge controversies and dispense the appropriate sanctions (Vago 2009: 43). The penalties in such societies resemble what is called **restitution** in contemporary justice systems. Stolen property may call for repayment that is equal to or greater than the value of that which was taken, and apologies before the entire group may be required. Primitive societies seldom imposed the death penalty on group members, and this meant that banishment often was the most severe sanction that was imposed.

Restitution:
a means of paying back a crime victim for losses or damages suffered

German economist Max Weber (1954) called primitive legal systems "khadi justice." These are systems marked by procedures that are informal, particularized, and nonrational (that is, there are no written rules or procedures). Nonrational justice systems "rely on ethical or mystical considerations such as magic or faith in the supernatural. . . . [They are] based on religious precepts and [are] so lacking in procedural rules as to seem almost completely arbitrary" (Vago 2009: 52). Today, in Islamic societies, khadis (or qadis) apply **sharia law** based on the teaching of the Quran and the example of the Prophet Mohammed. This type of law deals not only with what could be characterized as secular issues but also with moral and religious issues.

Sharia law:
religious law in Islamic countries that covers all aspects of human interaction, both secular and moral

Such legal systems work, depending on the context in which they are applied. In societies based around tribes or kinship, this approach to law creation, enforcement, and adjudication is effective. When societies become more complex and pluralistic, other legal mechanisms become necessary and emerge.

Early Historical Period

It is difficult to pinpoint the exact development of law during this time period. The Egyptians, Babylonians, Hebrews, and other groups in that part of the world had written legal codes 3,000 or 4,000 years ago. The Greeks and Romans also developed systems of laws that would influence modern Europe and the United States (Calvi and Coleman 2008: 19-23). Modern translations of some of these early documents sound very much like the laws we have today (see, for example, Box 3.1, which contains excerpts from the Code of Hammurabi). Some of the punishments that it prescribed were monetary in nature, and others involved corporal punishments such as floggings.

The transitional legal systems that developed in the early historical period are important for several reasons. For example, they developed written codes, and the roles of different actors in the legal system started to emerge (Vago 2009). Transitional legal societies distinguished between those who enacted the laws (what today we would call legislative bodies), those responsible for enforcing laws, as well as those who advocated for or judged between the disputing parties. In both Greece and Rome, the role of lawyer (an orator or skilled public speaker) began to appear (Vago 2009).

Box 3.1   Excerpts from the Code of Hammurabi

- If a man has borne false witness in a trial, or has not established the statement that he has made, if that case be a capital trial, that man shall be put to death.
- If a man has stolen goods from a temple, or house, he shall be put to death; and he that has received the stolen property from him shall be put to death.
- If a man has stolen a child, he shall be put to death.
- If a man has broken into a house, he shall be killed before the breach and buried there.
- If a man has committed highway robbery and has been caught, that man shall be put to death.

- If a man's wife be caught lying with another, they shall be strangled and cast into the water.
- If a man has divorced his wife, who has not borne him children, he shall pay over to her as much money as was given for her bride-price and the marriage-portion which she brought from her father's house, and so shall divorce her.
- If a son has struck his father, his hands shall be cut off.
- If a man has knocked out the eye of a patrician, his eye shall be knocked out.
- If a builder has built a house for a man, and has not made his work sound, and the house he built has fallen, and caused the death of its owner, that builder shall be put to death.

SOURCE: "Code of Hammurabi," n.d.

All of these societies influenced the development of laws in both Europe and the United States, and that influence continues today. During the early historical period, another influence on legal systems began to emerge: **canon law** (church law). After the fall of the Roman Empire, the influence of the Roman Catholic Church was significant from Constantinople (modern Istanbul, Turkey) to the land that is now Great Britain. The Church exerted its influence over the remains of the Roman Empire, and church law often became the law of the land. As a result, some behaviors that were defined as criminal (for example, adultery and suicide) were against the law because the Church defined them as crimes against morality.

Canon law:
religious or church law

Modern Era

The modern era in the development of law actually goes back several centuries. The origins of this period can be traced to the Renaissance (1300s to 1600s) and the Age of Enlightenment (1700s). During this time, the notion of **natural law**, which had developed under Greek and Roman philosophers, began to move into a place of prominence. Behind the concept of natural law was the notion that there is a higher source of law (the Divine) than that of either earthly governments or the Church. Natural law is so fundamental and immutable that it does not change over time. This perspective holds that natural law governs the universe and the lives of all people, whatever country in which they live (Walsh and Hemmens 2008: 5-6).

Natural law:
the notion that law is unchangeable; its source is divine authority

In contrast to natural law is the concept of positive law. **Positive law** (or **legal positivism**) is the perspective that law is valid not because it was given by divine authority but as a result of the human processes through which it was established (Currier and Eimermann 2009: 22). Stephen Michael Sheppard says that "legal positivism rejects the idea that law is recognized or created by morality or justice, contending instead that while law may reflect morality or an idea of justice, what makes it law is the action of the creation of laws according to the rules for their creation" (2012: 1471).

Positive law (legal positivism): the notion that law is not derived from divine authority but that it results from the interactions and processes that occur within a society

COMPARING CIVIL LAW AND CRIMINAL LAW

The term **civil law** has to be used cautiously because this phrase has two meanings. To begin with, civil law (sometimes called code law) is distinct from common law. James Calvi and Susan Coleman (2008: 23-24) note that civil or code law is the world's dominant legal system. They explain, "In civil law countries, the law is extensively codified, and decisions are based on the code as designated by the legislature rather than on binding judicial precedent" (24). In legal terms, a **precedent** is a decision by a court or other body in a particular case that may serve as the basis for resolving other legal disputes in similar cases in the future (see Sheppard 2012: 2121). France, Italy, and Spain, along with most other continental European countries, have civil law traditions where all infractions are carefully defined in the criminal code, and there is no tradition of judge-made law.

Civil law: in contrast to criminal law, legal disputes involving private parties; may involve civil wrongs or torts

Precedent: a decision by a judge or other body that decides an issue in one case and may serve as the basis for resolving similar cases in the future (see also *legal precedence*)

There is a second way that the term civil law is used. In countries like the United States, Canada, England, and Wales, as well as many former British colonies and protectorates that have a common law tradition, civil law is distinct from criminal law in that the former deals with disputes between private parties—such as torts, breaches of contract, divorces, and personal injury claims—and the latter deals with offenses against society, called crimes. This means that in criminal cases, the government serves as the party bringing the action on behalf of the people. We explain this further in the following sections.

Examining the Differences

It is important to note that civil law and criminal law have different goals. For instance, civil law attempts to make the plaintiff "whole," or to return the person to his or her original position prior to the wrong or breach occurring. By contrast, one of the key objectives in criminal law is to provide some type of punishment for convicted offenders (we address this issue further in the chapters on corrections).

One way to understand the differences between civil law and criminal law is through the use of some illustrations. For example, cases that involve personal injuries resulting from traffic accidents, along with divorces and breaches of contract, are addressed by civil law. That stands in contrast to offenses that deal with burglaries, homicides, and motor vehicle theft, which are crimes.

While these illustrations are straightforward, it is important to remember that many times civil suits arise out of criminal incidents. For example, a traffic accident resulting in injury might have criminal charges filed against the driver for driving while intoxicated (DWI) as well as a civil case based on injuries resulting from negligent behavior. This means that while we often view civil law issues and criminal law issues as separate and distinct, the two can be linked when a crime is committed against another person or someone's property.

Features of Civil Law

A key point to remember is that civil cases typically involve disputes between private parties. As previously mentioned, examples include breaches of contract, divorces, and personal injury claims. These are situations that occur regularly between individuals and within groups. At times, these cases are settled informally, but often they end up in court. An individual or group of people bring the issue, and the government provides a place (courtroom), a group to decide (a jury), and a person (judge) to facilitate a dispute resolution.

In some states (for example, Tennessee and Texas), there are courts that handle only civil cases and courts for criminal cases. Most states, by contrast, have unified judicial systems where the same courts can hear both civil cases and criminal cases (Rottman and Strickland 2006). Whatever the structural arrangement of the courts, the state legislature—and sometimes the courts themselves—will create civil procedures to govern the processes related to these disputes.

A second difference between civil cases and criminal cases involves the labels given to the parties in a case. In civil cases, the party who initiates a suit is called the **plaintiff**. The party against whom the suit is brought is called the **defendant**. In the next section, we see that these labels are similar to but slightly different from those in criminal cases.

A third distinction between civil and criminal law has to do with jury size. Most states require 12-member juries in felony criminal trials, although some lower trial courts may permit juries of fewer than 12 in misdemeanor cases. In contrast, some states and the federal courts use 6-member juries in many civil trials.

Probably the clearest difference between civil procedures and criminal procedures has to do with the nature of jury verdicts and

Plaintiff:
in civil law, the person who brings suit against another (the defendant)

Defendant:
in civil law, the person against whom a suit is brought; in criminal law, the person charged with committing a crime

what is called the **weight of evidence**. In civil cases, juries decide cases on the **preponderance of the evidence**. This simply means that the verdict should go in favor of the party that presents enough evidence to convince the jury slightly more than the other side. Some people would say that the winning party must tip the decision-making scales just over 50 percent, but judges and lawyers resist such efforts to provide a precise quantification of the jury's decision-making process. The key point here is that civil cases require only a small difference between the disputing parties to win a case.

However, it is important to note that in civil law, both parties may be at fault. In a case involving an accident between two automobiles, for example, the jury could find that one party ran a traffic light and the other party was speeding, and the actions of both contributed to the accident. This is called contributory negligence (Calvi and Coleman 2008: 255-256). In cases such as this, the jury could find that the plaintiff was speeding and the defendant ran the traffic light. This means the jury must decide to what extent each party was to blame. In this example, the defendant might be 60 percent at fault, while the plaintiff was 40 percent at fault. Therefore, the plaintiff's award of damages will be reduced by 40 percent (the amount the plaintiff contributed to causing the accident).

The fourth difference between civil law and criminal law concerns the appointment of attorneys. In civil law, unlike criminal law, there is no constitutional guarantee of an attorney when a person cannot afford one. However, many lawyers are willing to take civil cases on a **contingency fee** basis. This is illustrated by advertisements for lawyers that say "no recovery, no attorneys' fees." Attorneys evaluate the merits of the case and the likelihood of recovering their fees as a percentage of their clients' monetary awards. It is also worth noting that in civil cases, a judge could order the losing party to pay the attorneys' costs on the winning side; this is above and beyond any monetary or property settlement reached as to the tort damages that initiated the suit.

The final difference is that in civil cases, there is no possibility of incarceration. This means that defendants in civil cases cannot be locked up if they lose their case. In most civil suits, plaintiffs seek monetary damages, but they also might seek **equitable relief**. This could include requesting an injunction to halt some action or to put things back the way they were originally before the dispute arose.

Features of Criminal Law

As mentioned previously, some states operate separate civil and criminal courts. The trend since the 1960s has been to have unified court systems in which there are no specialized courts. However, even in unified systems, judges may specialize in hearing only civil

Weight of evidence: the amount of proof necessary to secure a conviction (in criminal law) or a judgment (in civil law)

Preponderance of the evidence: in civil law, the standard of proof that must tip the evidentiary scales in favor of one side or the other

Contingency fee: the practice by attorneys of accepting civil cases based on the likelihood of winning and receiving a certain percentage of the award

Equitable relief: in civil law, the legal remedy that intends to put all parties back to their original status before some act or injury took place

cases, criminal cases, family law cases, and so on. In states with separate civil and criminal courts, judges typically handle only one type of case.

In civil cases, the party bringing a suit is called the plaintiff. By contrast, in **criminal law**, the government initiates a case, and the attorney responsible for presenting the case is called the **prosecutor**. Prosecuting attorneys present criminal charges on behalf of a state's citizens or, in federal cases, for the U.S. government. In both civil and criminal cases, the person against whom the case is brought is called the defendant.

Criminal defendants can choose to have a **bench trial** before a judge with no jury. Nevertheless, most cases that go to trial have juries. In most states, either the constitution or statutes require criminal court juries to be composed of 12 members. The U.S. Supreme Court has permitted criminal trial juries with as few as 6 jurors—in cases such as *Williams v. Florida* (1970)—but 12 is the most common number nationwide in felony cases.

In comparing the rules of civil procedure with those of criminal procedure, two issues are particularly important. First, on the issue of the weight of evidence in criminal cases, juries are instructed that they must find the defendant guilty based on the standard of **beyond a reasonable doubt** (American Law Institute 1985: 16). Once again, it is difficult to say precisely what this means. However, the U.S. Supreme Court, in the case of *Victor v. Nebraska* (1994), said, "The beyond a reasonable doubt standard is a requirement of due process, but the Constitution neither prohibits trial courts from defining reasonable doubt nor requires them to do so as a matter of course." In most cases, judges tell jurors that the evidence presented should clearly point to the defendant's guilt, and if there is a reasonable doubt as to the defendant's guilt, they should vote to acquit. Box 3.2 provides a brief overview of the idea of reasonable doubt.

Second, in criminal cases, the **burden of proof** or the burden of persuasion rests with the prosecutor (Dressler 2009). This means that it is the state's responsibility to prove the defendant guilty, not the defendant's responsibility to prove innocence. Given the resources the state has in prosecuting cases, this requirement helps somewhat to level the playing field for the defendant.

Unlike civil cases, criminal defendants are entitled to the appointment of an attorney since they may be sentenced to incarceration or death. The Sixth Amendment to the U.S. Constitution—applied to the states through a series of U.S. Supreme Court decisions—provides for the **right to counsel**. This right even extends to first-level appeals but not beyond (see, for example, *Douglas v. California* (1963) and *Ross v. Moffitt* (1974)). Both state and federal governments use several methods to provide lawyers for the large number of criminal defendants who

Criminal law:
laws that define wrongful acts in which the prosecutor acts on behalf of the citizens of the state; often called penal law in that it provides for various punishments for those convicted of violations

Prosecutor:
the attorney representing the state (government); initiates criminal charges against the accused (defendant)

Bench trial:
any trial before a judge without a jury

Beyond a reasonable doubt:
the standard of proof in criminal cases necessary to establish guilt

Burden of proof:
the notion in criminal law that the prosecutor (state) bears the responsibility for proving to the jury the defendant's guilt

Right to counsel:
based on the Sixth Amendment of the U.S. Constitution, the protection that accused criminal defendants have to be represented by an attorney at all critical stages of the legal proceedings

---

Box 3.2   Reasonable Doubt

One of the ideas with which juries often struggle is the idea of guilt "beyond a reasonable doubt." Judges give juries instructions on this notion, but it still may seem difficult to grasp. Reasonable doubt does not mean that jurors cannot have some doubts relative to the defendant's guilt. Essentially, reasonable doubt means that there is no other logical explanation concerning the defendant's guilt or for the defendant's actions based on the level of proof presented by the state. Mixed in with this notion is that of the "reasonable person." What the courts are asking jurors to do is to decide what a reasonable person (really, each member of the jury) would conclude from the evidence the state has presented. There is no real way to quantify the notion of reasonable doubt, and jury instructions often include terms such as "moral certainty" or "abiding doubt" to try to help clarify the deliberation process. In the end, jurors must answer the question "Do you *really* believe this person committed the act (or acts) alleged by the state?"

Box 3.3   Key U.S. Supreme Court Cases on Right to Counsel

- *Powell v. Alabama* (1932): In the famous "Scottsboro Boys" case, the Supreme Court ruled that the convictions had resulted from a number of deficiencies, particularly ineffective (or nonexistent) assistance of counsel. The Court held that when the death penalty was a potential outcome, the state was obligated to provide defendants with adequate legal representation.
- *Gideon v. Wainwright* (1963): This case overruled the decision in *Betts v. Brady* (1942) and provided that states must appoint attorneys for indigent defendants in all felony cases.
- *Argersinger v. Hamlin* (1972): The decision in this case extended the right to counsel to serious misdemeanor cases in which there was the possibility of incarceration for any length of time.
- *In re Gault* (1967): This case involved a juvenile accused of making obscene or annoying phone calls to a neighbor. A number of constitutional rights issues were raised by this case, but chief among them was the right to counsel in delinquency proceedings. The Supreme Court held that just like adults accused of crimes, juveniles also have the right to legal representation in delinquency proceedings in which they might be incarcerated.

---

cannot afford to hire an attorney. We discuss this right more fully in Chapter 8 when we deal with criminal trials, but Box 3.3 includes a brief synopsis of some of the major U.S. Supreme Court cases that have addressed this issue.

A final area that distinguishes criminal law involves the variety of sanctions facing defendants. These include fines, forfeitures, and other economic penalties. Courts can also impose probation and other community-based sanctions and, potentially, jail or prison time, or even death. The possibility of incarceration is a major way that civil cases and criminal cases can be distinguished.

COMPARING SUBSTANTIVE LAW AND PROCEDURAL LAW

Now that we have presented some of the differences between civil law and criminal law, we need to distinguish substantive law from procedural law (see Calvi and Coleman 2008: 8-9). Keep in mind that most of what we label substantive law and procedural law today is enacted by legislatures. However, some courts also have rule-making authority over their own procedures.

In terms of criminal law, **substantive law** defines those acts that are crimes. Therefore, substantive law defines what is illegal and what the penalties are for various offenses. As an illustration, for a crime such as first-degree murder, the law typically specifies that there has been an unlawful killing of another human being, that it occurred with malice aforethought (or what often is called premeditation), and that one or more aggravating circumstances must exist. In terms of constitutional law, the prohibition against bills of attainder is an example of substantive law.

Substantive law:
the type of law that defines the nature of criminal offenses

Procedural law, by contrast, defines the means for processing a criminal case and includes constitutional protections for individuals involved in the criminal justice process. This includes protections provided for in the Bill of Rights such as the appointment of attorneys for indigent defendants, the ways juries must be selected, protections against self-incrimination, and questions about the admissibility of evidence. Some observers have called procedural law the "rules of the game," since it defines how cases are handled from arrest through trial and appeal. In effect, procedural law provides the rules by which the government must abide to secure a conviction that is fundamentally fair.

Procedural law:
the "rules of the game"; the processes by which the substantive (statutory) law is to be applied

SOURCES OF LAW

There are primarily five sources of law in the United States today: common law, statutory law, constitutional law, case law, and administrative or regulatory law (Calvi and Coleman 2008: 11-15). This section briefly examines each of these.

Common Law

The fundamental basis for law in the United States is **common law**. We inherited the English common law tradition from Great Britain, and several elements characterize common law. These elements differentiate the common law system from the civil or codified laws of continental European countries.

First, the common law emerged during a period, around the time of the Norman Conquest (1066) and the Domesday Book (1086), when

Common law:
unwritten, judge-made law developed through the application of precedence in deciding similar cases in similar ways over a period of time

there were virtually no written laws, and "[a] rule of law become 'common' not in the sense of being ordinary, but in the sense of being common to all parts of England" (Calvi and Coleman 2008: 14). This type of law is based on the norms of a particular community, and while it is unwritten, a certain consistency develops through the regular and routine application of legal principles. Today we call this concept a **legal precedent**, and it is embodied in the term "stare decisis," meaning "let the decision stand." Thus, as judges decide cases over a long period of time, they apply the same types of rulings to similar cases.

Legal precedent: an established legal standard that exists as a result of a series of cases being decided the same way over some period of time (see also "precedent")

Second, common law is often said to be "judge-made law," as opposed to written or "black letter" law. This means that unlike case law (discussed later in the chapter), which is based on interpreting constitutional provisions or statutes, common law is decided "in the absence of any positive law" (Calvi and Coleman 2008: 14). Since it is not enacted by legislatures, judges "make" law simply by deciding the cases brought before them. Over time, the citizens of a community come to recognize what the legal principles are based on the cases that have been decided previously.

Third, the common law both reflects and shapes community values. Thus, changes in common law principles come about slowly over time.

As previously mentioned, the United States and its territories and protectorates, along with many other former British colonies and parts of the Commonwealth, share a common law tradition with contemporary England and Wales. In most instances, states and the federal government have replaced the common law with written statutes.

Constitutional Law

In the United States, **constitutional law** is the second most influential source of law, following the common law. While this may seem like one source of law, in reality it is 51 sources since each of the 50 states has its own constitution, and the laws of each state must be consistent with its state constitution as well as the U.S. Constitution.

Constitutional law: interpretations of state and federal constitutions by appellate courts; may be called case law

The various state and federal appellate courts are the ultimate arbiters of constitutional law in the United States. These courts review cases that are appealed to them and decide whether executive and legislative actions are consistent with the appropriate constitution. Appellate court decisions illustrate case law, which is discussed later in the chapter.

Legislative or Statutory Law

Criminal law in the United States today is almost exclusively written, or "black letter" law. Legislatures at the local, state, and federal levels enact laws all the time. These written laws, **statutory law**, typically are compiled in volumes that are available in most libraries. Statutory law is especially important today for two reasons. First, it is crucial to understanding the **legality principle**, which says that people have the right to know what is illegal so they will know in advance if they are breaking the law (see Fletcher 1998: 207). Second, in contemporary society, there are so many offenses at all levels of government that laws must be written so that citizens and those who work in the criminal justice system know what is illegal at a particular time.

Statutory law today is pervasive; every state has its own criminal code, and there is also a federal criminal code. This means that by searching a university or law school library or online, one can locate the criminal offenses that are contained in each jurisdiction's criminal code.

Statutory law: statutes (laws) that are passed by legislative bodies and codified (compiled in volumes) to spell out the various elements associated with different crimes

Legality principle: the concept that citizens have the right to know what conduct is illegal and that the law should establish such behavior specifically enough to minimize discretion by law enforcement authorities

Case Law

Students are often taught that the legislative branch makes the law (statutes), the executive branch enforces the law, and the judicial branch interprets the law. In reality, all three branches of government "make" law. For instance, in the process known as **judicial review**, appellate courts often examine a statute enacted by legislative bodies to determine if it is constitutional. Courts also review the actions of the executive branch. As one example, the U.S. Supreme Court was recently asked to determine whether a search by a trained police dog from the front porch of a dwelling constituted a search within the meaning of the Fourth Amendment. In a five-to-four decision, the Court held that the use of the dog prior to a warrant being issued was an unconstitutional search (*Florida v. Jardines* (2013)).

Whenever state or federal appellate courts decide cases, the decisions are published in what are called "reporters." These volumes are available in many libraries and allow lawyers, judges, and other interested people to read what the courts actually said in a particular case. These court opinions provide the basis for case law, and, like common law, they rely on precedence.

Judicial review: the courts' ability to review the acts of executive agencies and legislative bodies to determine the constitutionality of their actions; originally asserted in the case of *Marbury v. Madison* (1803)

Administrative or Regulatory Law

A final source of law, and one that is unfamiliar to many, is **administrative law**. Administrative law can originate from a number of sources in the executive branch of government, but primarily it comes from the federal regulatory agencies. These agencies include such bodies as the Federal Aviation Administration (FAA), the Federal Communications Commission (FCC), the Food and Drug Administration (FDA),

Administrative law: the type of law developed by regulatory agencies, especially those of the federal government

the Environmental Protection Agency (EPA), the Interstate Commerce Commission (ICC), and the Securities Exchange Commission (SEC). It is important to recognize that these agencies have a great deal to do with law. In fact, the Occupational Safety and Health Administration (OSHA) has a major impact on business operations in the United States, and this agency has the authority to impose fines (a criminal sanction) for safety violations.

Administrative agencies are always creating regulations, and these essentially are laws. Federal agencies publish proposed regulations in a document called the *Federal Register*, and after an appropriate period of notice and time for comment, these proposed regulations become regulatory law. If someone challenges a regulation or an agency ruling (for example, in a Social Security disability case), most of these agencies have their own in-house administrative law judges or hearing officers that serve as first-line reviewers of legal challenges. Once these laws are adopted, they are published in the *Code of Federal Regulations*.

DISTINGUISHING OFFENSES

There are a number of different ways of classifying laws. This section addresses the differences based on the perceived wrongfulness of the offenses. Traditionally, actions that were considered wrong were labeled according to what might be called the evilness of the acts. In this regard, the law classifies some acts as *mala in se* and others as *mala prohibita*.

Offenses that are considered bad (or evil) in and of themselves are classified as **mala in se**. Even in cases where there is no written prohibition, these are actions that would be considered inappropriate by nearly all of society's members. This means that these prohibitions are supported by a strong social consensus. For instance, in both primitive and modern societies, killing another person in most cases is considered wrong. In tribal groups, nearly all laws would be considered *mala in se*. This is also true of many of the offenses included in our criminal codes.

In contrast with *mala in se* offenses, **mala prohibita** offenses are wrong because they have been legislatively prohibited, and they are prohibited because we consider them to be wrong. In the study of logic, this is called a tautology, or defining something by itself. *Mala prohibita* offenses are not necessarily inherently evil or less serious than *mala in se* offenses; nevertheless, legislatures have passed laws prohibiting these actions. Today there are many examples of *mala prohibita* crimes, such as seatbelt or motorcycle helmet law violations and

Mala in se **offenses:** behaviors that are considered bad in and of themselves; those types of offenses that are inherently bad or evil

Mala prohibita **offenses:** acts that are not inherently bad or evil but that are prohibited as a result of laws prohibiting them vice offenses (drugs, gambling, and prostitution). Some groups within a society might consider these actions evil, while others might not. For example, recent laws intended to criminalize abortion entirely or at certain points reflect this conflict. Some groups, generally based on their views of conception and life, see abortion as *mala in se*, while others see efforts to criminalize it as overreaching law, or a form of *mala prohibita*. Thus, some acts have moved back and forth between *mala prohibita* and *mala in se* (for example, drugs, abortion, and homosexuality), while others continue to be considered *mala in se* (homicide). This means that there may be a lack of social consensus about whether some behaviors should be criminalized.

Statutory definitions provide another way to classify the degrees of crime seriousness. When a law is enacted, legislatures decide how serious each crime is. The three most common statutory categories are felonies, misdemeanors, and petty misdemeanors (or infractions).

Felonies

Felonies are the most serious crimes in any statutory scheme. Two elements distinguish felonies from less serious offenses: the place of possible incarceration and the potential length of incarceration. People convicted of felonies can be sentenced to serve time in federal or state prisons, although a few jurisdictions allow felons to serve time in local facilities. Most states begin felony sentences at one year; however, some states start felony sentences at 18 months or even two years.

States often have different categories of felonies, and some follow the *Model Penal Code* designation of first-, second-, and third-degree felonies (American Law Institute 1985: 85). This means that not all felonies are considered equally serious, and the penalties associated with each category indicate the relative degree of seriousness. The American Law Institute (ALI), a group that now consists of 4,000 influential attorneys, judges, and legal scholars, originally drafted the *Model Penal Code* in 1962. The most recent edition of the *Code* was completed in 1984. Although no state has completely adopted the *Code* as its criminal statutes, it continues to serve as a model for legislative bodies revising criminal codes in many states. The ALI's website says that the ALI is the "leading independent organization in the United States producing scholarly work to clarify, modernize, and otherwise improve the law" (American Law Institute, n.d.).

In states that use the first-degree felony classification, sentences for such offenses often begin at 20 years and extend to life imprisonment or even the death penalty. The *Model Penal Code* provides that sentences for first-degree felonies should carry a "term the minimum of which shall be fixed by the Court at not less than one year or more than

Felonies:
the most serious crimes calling for incarceration of one year or more in prison; felonies may be graded into different categories of seriousness

Model Penal Code:
a series of volumes prepared by the American Law Institute that provides examples of statutory provisions that can be copied and followed by states seeking to revise their criminal codes

ten years, and the maximum of which shall be life imprisonment" (American Law Institute 1985: 91). Second-degree felonies might call for sentences beginning at 10 years and extend to 20 years, and third-degree felony sentences might be no more than one or two years. Again, the *Model Penal Code* says that sentences for second-degree felonies should be "not less than one year not more than three years, and the maximum of which shall be ten years," and third-degree felonies should have sentences of "not less than one year nor more than two years, and the maximum of which shall be five years" (American Law Institute 1985: 91).

Misdemeanors

The place of incarceration for **misdemeanors** normally will be a local facility like a jail, detention center, workhouse, or penal farm. In many cases, city or county governments operate these facilities; county sheriffs manage just over two-thirds of the jails in the United States. Most state criminal codes and the *Model Penal Code* provide that misdemeanor sentences should not exceed one year (American Law Institute 1985: 94).

Misdemeanors: the least serious crimes; often call for fines or incarceration in a local detention facility of less than one year

Petty Misdemeanors

States may divide misdemeanor offenses into different categories of seriousness, and both state and local governments may have what are called **petty misdemeanors** (or violations of local ordinances may be called infractions). Petty misdemeanors generally have fines assessed and may allow for short jail terms. In some instances, both jail terms and fines may be imposed. The *Model Penal Code* says that incarceration for petty misdemeanors should not exceed 30 days (American Law Institute 1985: 94).

Petty misdemeanors: the least serious misdemeanor offenses; often these violations result in only fines or very short periods of incarceration

ELEMENTS OF CRIMES

The beginning of this chapter mentions that the government bears the burden of proof in criminal cases and that prosecutors must prove every element of the crime. The elements of a crime are known collectively by the Latin phrase *corpus delicti* (that is, the "body of the crime"). The *corpus delicti* represents all of the factors that must be proven to establish that a person has committed a crime, as well as which crime has been committed. Typically, three elements must be present—*mens rea*, *actus reus*, and concurrence; for crimes like homicide, a fourth element, result, must be established.

Corpus delicti: Latin phrase meaning the "body of the crime"; these are the elements the state must prove to establish that a crime has occurred

Mens rea

Mens rea involves the "guilty mind" of the person or persons suspected of having committed a crime (Sheppard 2012: 1730-1731). *Mens rea* is associated with criminal intent and deals with the required mental state that accompanies the wrongful act. It is essential to understand three points when it comes to *mens rea*. First, criminal law does not hold people accountable for their thoughts, and as long as no actions have taken place, no crime has occurred.

Second, there are offenses known as **strict liability crimes** that may not require proof of *mens rea*. Common examples of strict liability crimes include speeding, driving on an expired license, or statutory rape. While most offenses require proof of some degree of thought or contemplation, strict liability offenses may not require such proof (see American Law Institute 1985; Bergelson 2011; Carpenter 2003). Depending on the offense charged, the state may have a difficult or easy job when it comes to establishing the existence of *mens rea*.

Third, while the terms sometimes may be confused, *mens rea* is different from motive. *Mens rea* addresses the offender's intent relative to the commission of the crime, whereas motive is the reason the individual did whatever he or she did. For instance, a man might decide to kill his wife to collect her insurance (motive), but for a crime to be established, the state must prove that he acted with premeditation or malice aforethought. Clearly the two terms are related, but they are distinct concepts, and the state does not bear a burden of proof relative to motive. Nevertheless, knowing the motive may help the prosecutor explain the case more clearly to the jury.

Mens rea:
the guilty mind or criminal intent

Strict liability crimes:
the limited number of cases that do not require the state to prove criminal intent; common examples include speeding in a car and statutory rape

Actus reus

In addition to *mens rea*, or the guilty mind, the state must also prove **actus reus**, or that a wrongful act has occurred. For a crime to exist, there must be some affirmative action or "substantial step" toward completion of the offense. However, in some instances, a failure to act (an omission) also may constitute a crime. For instance, many states now have laws that require reporting of suspected child abuse cases. Failure to report constitutes a violation of criminal law. Furthermore, as we discuss in one of the following sections, offenses do not have to be totally completed for a crime to have occurred.

Actus reus:
the wrongful act associated with a crime

Concurrence

A crime exists at the point where the intent and the act come together. Sometimes this is called **concurrence**; at other times it is known as nexus or some similar term (Dressler 2009: 199). At the time of a

Concurrence:
in criminal law, the meeting of the guilty mind (*mens rea*) and the wrongful act (*actus reus*)

criminal trial, the prosecuting attorney must establish to the satisfaction of the jury (beyond a reasonable doubt) that the offender had the intent necessary and acted on that intention in the commission of the crime.

Result

For some crimes, like criminal homicide, the state must prove a fourth element—result. In simplest terms, result is the outcome of a particular action. In homicide cases, the state must prove that a person died as a result of some action taken by the accused individual. This makes homicide a *result* crime and differentiates it from offenses such as burglary that are *conduct* crimes.

INCHOATE OFFENSES

Previously we discussed the element of *actus reus*, or the wrongful act, as part of a crime. However, we should note that not all criminal offenses that are attempted are completed, but this does not mean that no crime has occurred. This section discusses three types of incomplete offenses, or what are known as **inchoate offenses**: conspiracies, solicitations, and attempts.

Before dealing with each of the different categories of inchoate offenses, it is important to consider why criminal law generally allows for punishment when a crime has not been completed. First, with all types of inchoate offenses, some effort has been made to commit a crime. Second, the offenses undertaken were not completed as a result of some factor beyond the control of the individuals contemplating the crimes. Finally, the law considers those people who are willing to commit a crime, but who for some reason are unable to do so, as being as potentially dangerous as the people who actually commit crimes. George Fletcher says that "the question is not whether the *act* is dangerous to a specific potential victim, but whether the *actor* is dangerous to the society as a whole" (1998: 177). Therefore, the law allows the police to make arrests for inchoate offenses before other, more serious crimes are completed.

Inchoate offenses: incomplete criminal acts, including attempts, conspiracies, and solicitations

Conspiracies

The first type of inchoate offense that this section considers is **conspiracy**.

For our purposes, a conspiracy is said to exist when two or more people agree to commit a crime. Sheppard says, "Conspiracy is a crime committed when two or more people plan or work together to do

Conspiracy: the inchoate offense that results when two or more people plan to commit a crime and have a "meeting of the minds" relative to the commission of a crime

anything that is itself a crime. It does not matter whether the crime itself is ever performed or attempted. Nor does it matter if one participant has no intention to commit the crime; as long as the participant plans or works with at least one other person in support of the supposed future criminal act, that participant is conspiring to commit a crime" (2012: 541). An overt act may not be required as long as there is a "meeting of the minds" relative to the commission of the crime.

For example, two mechanics who work in an auto repair shop plan to duplicate the keys of cars that come in for repair. They decide that since they know where the owners live, once the cars have been repaired and returned, they can then steal the cars and sell them to someone else or strip them for parts. Most legal scholars would say that once the two mechanics agree to commit the vehicle thefts, there has been a "meeting of the minds" and they have entered into a conspiracy. However, the state may have to prove that the conspirators went beyond merely talking about stealing the cars to see whether they engaged in a "substantial step" (some type of overt act) toward committing the crime for there to be a valid charge of conspiracy.

Solicitations

A second type of inchoate offense is **solicitation**. Solicitation occurs when one person tries to convince another person to commit a crime on behalf of the one doing the soliciting (Sheppard 2012: 2640). This may involve an offer of some amount of money or other consideration to get the person to commit the crime. For example, James and Margaret have been married ten years when James decides he no longer wants to be married to Margaret. He is not willing to kill her himself, but he is willing to pay someone to kill her, especially since he has taken out a large life insurance policy on her. One night, while he is drinking in a bar, James strikes up a conversation with a casual acquaintance about the possibility have having his wife "done in." The acquaintance says he might be willing to do the job if the amount of money was right. James says he will pay $3,000 up front and another $3,000 after the deed has been accomplished. Even with no other actions being taken, there has been a solicitation to commit murder, and as with the case of conspiracies, both parties may be guilty of multiple crimes.

Solicitation: the inchoate (incomplete) offense where one person encourages another person to commit a crime on behalf of the person doing the encouraging

Attempts

The third category of inchoate offenses includes **attempts**. Attempts occur when someone tries to complete a crime but for some reason is unable to do so. For example, two people are sitting in an automobile

Attempts: crimes that have been undertaken but for some reason beyond the control of the offender were not completed

behind a fast-food restaurant at 11:00 P.M. A store employee calls the police to report a suspicious vehicle in the parking lot after closing time. A patrol car is dispatched to the scene and stops to investigate. The officers order the two suspects to exit the car with their hands in plain sight; they find a loaded handgun on the front seat. In this case, the police intercepted the would-be robbers before they could rob the night manager as he left with the bank deposit. Though a robbery had not yet occurred, the officers typically would charge the suspects with attempted armed robbery. Once again, as with conspiracies, most jurisdictions require that a "substantial step" toward completing the crime must be taken. Again, it can be a crime to engage in certain behaviors even if the contemplated offense is not completed.

DEFENSES

A number of defenses in the field of criminal law can be used to negate one or more essential elements of the crime. This section addresses several of the most common defenses, particularly those that are labeled **affirmative defenses**.

Affirmative defenses: justifications and excuses offered by criminal defendants explaining why their seemingly wrongful acts should not be considered criminal

Burden of Proof

The burden of proof can also be called the burden of persuasion or even the burden of production. It is different from the standard of proof, or what we previously called the weight of the evidence. As we begin this section on defenses, it is important to note once again that under common law tradition, the state bears the burden of proof (or persuasion) in criminal trials. This means that under our adversarial system of justice, the defendant is not obligated to prove anything in court.

For the most part, the burdens of production and persuasion rest on the state. However, as the following section shows, certain criminal defenses, known as affirmative defenses, may require some degree of proof (persuasion) on the part of the defendant.

Affirmative Defenses

There are two major categories of affirmative defenses: **justifications** and **excuses**. Joshua Dressler (2009: 204, 207) says that justification deals with those acts that are "right or, at least, not wrong," and he adds, "The justified actor [is] free of all legal impediments." Self-defense is probably the most common example of a justification defense. In nearly all cases, the law does not condone the killing of another person, but if a person is truly acting in self-defense, the killing is justified and may even be expected.

Justifications: acts (such as self-defense) that otherwise would be wrong but given the circumstances are allowable and even expected

Excuses: affirmative defenses that acknowledge the wrongfulness of the act but assert that there were acceptable reasons for the act

---

Box 3.4   A Case of Self-Defense?

The Florida case involving community watch volunteer George Zimmerman and Trayvon Martin, the teenager he shot, illustrates one of the ways in which self-defense might be used in criminal law. Zimmerman was concerned about the number of crimes, especially burglaries, that had occurred in his neighborhood. On the night he saw Trayvon Martin returning from the store after buying candy, Zimmerman believed the youngster was up to no good and followed him. Although there was a dispute about who confronted whom, there was a scuffle, and Zimmerman pulled a handgun that he was carrying and shot Martin.

The state of Florida eventually filed criminal charges against Zimmerman for the shooting, and much of his defense centered on his perceived fear for his safety. Florida has a law known as "stand your ground," which allows individuals to use force rather than to retreat. While Zimmerman's attorney did not specifically use it as part of the self-defense argument, this law (and those of other states) drew a great deal of attention during the trial. Eventually the jury believed that the state had not proved its homicide case against George Zimmerman beyond a reasonable doubt. This case illustrates the complicating factors that can arise when someone alleges self-defense.

For excuse defenses, by contrast, someone who has committed a wrongful act acknowledges the wrongness but claims that extenuating circumstances resulted in the behavior or make it unreasonable to hold the accused person criminally liable. Therefore, in an excuse defense, the person "tries to show that [he] is not morally culpable for his wrongful conduct" (Dressler 2009: 205).

In the case of self-defense or possibly in situations involving the defense of others, an individual is allowed to use a reasonable amount of force to repel an attack. Three elements must be present to justify such a defense: necessity, proportionality, and reasonable belief. The *necessity* element means that the individual must be facing an immediate threat and has no possible escape route. However, most jurisdictions do not require people in their own homes to retreat before using deadly force, and Florida and some other states now have "stand-your-ground laws" that have eliminated the general rule requiring escape as long as the person is legally entitled to be in the location (see Box 3.4). The *proportionality* requirement stipulates that the amount of force used in self-defense must be roughly equal to the amount of force that has been threatened. Finally, anyone acting in self-defense must *reasonably believe* that an attacker has targeted him or her (Dressler 2009: 223-225). Box 3.4 discusses one of the nation's recent high-profile cases in which self-defense became a key element.

Most affirmative defenses are excuses rather than justifications; we consider both of these categories. First, some of the most common affirmative defenses are duress, entrapment, infancy, insanity, and intoxication. Courts often treat necessity as a justification—like self-defense—and distinguish it from duress.

When a person is compelled to commit a crime by another, **duress** is said to exist. Typically duress involves the threat of bodily harm to the individual or to another person. Sheppard says that duress involves "any improper threat or condition, such as coercion, that limits a person's ability to think or act independently" (2012: 899). Fletcher (1998: 83) adds that the question we should ask ourselves is: Would we have acted in the same way if we were found in similar situation?

Duress:
the affirmative defense alleging that the wrongful act was committed under some form of external compulsion (such as the threat of bodily harm or death for the person or the person's family)

Necessity is a defense that is related to duress, but it is still separate and distinct from it. The primary difference is that duress is externally imposed: It happens as a result of compulsion from another person. In comparison, necessity often occurs as a result of forces of nature rather than human elements. For example, two people get lost while hiking in a backwoods area. They cannot find their vehicle, and they do not have cell phone communications because of the remote location. They come upon a ranger station that is used seasonally but is now locked up. To secure shelter and in the hope of finding additional food, they break into the structure. In most instances we would say that this is breaking and entering, or at least trespassing, and that would be a crime. However, if the hikers are attempting to save their lives by seeking shelter until they could be located and rescued, the law would treat this as necessity. Necessity can be characterized as a "lesser evil" defense and is "a defense of last resort" (see Sheppard 2012: 1815). It is important to note at this point that in homicide cases, neither duress nor necessity can be raised as defenses.

Necessity:
the affirmative defense alleging that a violation occurred as a result of forces of nature; considered a lesser-of-evils defense

Entrapment is a defense that maintains that the idea for a crime originated with someone else—more specifically, the police. The question of entrapment often arises in circumstances where the police conduct undercover or "sting" operations related to drug sales, prostitution, and the fencing of stolen merchandise, among other crimes. If a case goes to trial, jurors are asked to decide whether the defendant was already inclined to commit the crime and the police merely provided the opportunity, in which case entrapment does not exist. By contrast, if the police instigated a crime by someone who was not predisposed to commit the crime, then entrapment does exist. The U.S. Supreme Court has said that the police are free to use informants and undercover agents in investigating crimes (see, for example, *Hoffa v. United States* (1966)), but the Court has also said that the police must not impermissibly initiate the criminal activity. Box 3.5 contains an excerpt from a U.S. Supreme Court case dealing with the issue of entrapment.

Entrapment:
the affirmative action alleging that law enforcement officials conceived the idea for a crime and that the suspect would not normally have committed such an offense

Another possible criminal defense is infancy. Simply defined, **infancy** means that the person who committed an alleged offense was legally too young to have formed criminal intent. States vary in their definitions of the minimum age for juvenile court jurisdiction,

Infancy:
the affirmative defense alleging that the accused was too young to form criminal intent

---

Box 3.5   *United States v. Russell* (1973)

An undercover narcotics agent investigating respondent and his confederates for illicitly manufacturing a drug, offered them an essential ingredient which was difficult to obtain, though legally available. After the agent had observed the process and contributed the ingredient in return for a share of the finished product, respondent was found guilty by a jury which had been given the standard entrapment instruction. The Court of Appeals reversed, concluding that there had been "an intolerable degree of governmental participation in the criminal enterprise."

[The U.S. Supreme Court held that] the entrapment defense, which, as explicated in *Sorrells v. United States* [1932] and *Sherman v. United States* [1958], prohibits law enforcement officers from instigating criminal acts by otherwise innocent persons in order to lure them to commit crimes and punish them, did not bar the conviction of respondent in view of the evidence of respondent's involvement in making the drug before and after the agent's visits, and respondent's concession "that he may have harbored a predisposition to commit the charged offenses." Nor was the agent's infiltration of the drug-making operation of such a nature as to violate fundamental principles of due process.

SOURCE: *United States v. Russell,* 411 U.S. 423 (1973).

---

but many use the common law standard of seven as the age at which criminal intent can be formed (see, for example, Gardner 2009: 246-247).

Perhaps the most controversial of the affirmative defenses is **insanity**. While it is not used often and is even less often successful, when insanity is employed in a case, it takes on great symbolic significance. Dressler (2009: 339) says, "Since the time of Edward III in the fourteenth century when 'madness' became a complete defense to criminal charges, English and American courts and, more recently, legislatures have struggled to define 'insanity.'" It is important to note that insanity is a legal concept and not a medical one. However, it mixes legal notions such as *mens rea* with concepts that originate in psychology and psychiatry.

Insanity:
a legal (not medical) concept; an affirmative defense alleging that as a result of some mental incapacity occurring at the time of the wrongful act, the accused was incapable of forming criminal intent

Over the years, there have been several legal standards for applying the insanity defense. The oldest is the so-called M'Naughton Rule. This rule says that criminal defendants cannot be found guilty if they are mentally impaired in such a way that they cannot distinguish right from wrong. This was followed in some states by the irresistible impulse test, which said that individuals are not criminally liable in those situations where they are unable to control their behavior. Finally, the *Model Penal Code* provides for the defense of insanity in those situations where the accused lacks a substantial capacity to appreciate the criminality of the act or to be able to conform to the requirements of law (American Law Institute 1985: 61; Sheppard 2012: 1327).

Box 3.6   An Attempted Presidential Assassination

On March 30, 1981, outside the Washington Hilton Hotel, John Hinckley Jr. attempted to assassinate President Ronald Reagan. While Hinckley was unsuccessful in his attempt to kill the president, he did succeed in wounding Secret Service agent Tim McCarthy and District of Columbia police officer Thomas Delahanty and very seriously wounded the president's press secretary, James Brady. The president was hit in the side under his arm by a bullet that ricocheted off of his limousine.

Hinckley was brought to trial in 1982 on 13 federal charges and found not guilty by reason of insanity. As a result of the verdict, he was ordered to be confined in St. Elizabeth's Hospital for treatment of his mental disorders (including a fixation on the actress Jody Foster); while he is still considered a patient at St. Elizabeth's, he has been allowed numerous leaves and unsupervised visits with his family. As a result of this verdict, several states moved to restrict the insanity defense, and Idaho, Montana, and Utah (eventually joined by Kansas) eliminated the insanity defense altogether.

The heart of the insanity defense is that at the time the crime was committed, the person accused of the offense was unable to form criminal intent as a result of some mental incapacity. This inability might be the result of a chemical imbalance in the brain, mental illness, a psychological problem, post-traumatic stress disorder, or even a blunt trauma injury to the head. Whatever the underlying reason, the accused person alleges that he or she was incapable of possessing the necessary criminal intent to commit a crime.

In summarizing the insanity defense, it is important to include a few key points. First, insanity is used in less than 1 percent of the criminal cases in the United States. Second, the insanity defense is used principally in homicide cases (and even then infrequently), and it seldom works. Third, to date, four states (Idaho, Kansas, Montana, and Utah) have completely eliminated the insanity defense. Finally, as a result of the attempted assassination of President Ronald Reagan in 1980, 13 states have retained the insanity defense but allow an additional plea or verdict of "guilty, but mentally ill" (Walker 2011: 183-190). Box 3.6 presents one case in which the insanity defense was successfully used.

Intoxication is a defense that would seem to appeal to many people; however, law and practice tightly define this defense, and there are limited circumstances under which it can be used. For instance, *voluntary* intoxication is never a total defense to criminal behavior. If it were, then there would be no such crimes as driving while intoxicated/driving under the influence (DWI/DUI). However, in cases of first-degree murder, defendants might argue that they were so intoxicated that they could not form the specific intent for that crime and that they should instead be convicted of a lesser offense.

Nevertheless, there are some circumstances where a person might experience *involuntary* intoxication, and judges and juries must weigh

Intoxication:
being under the influence of alcohol or drugs; voluntary intoxication is not a defense to crime, and involuntary intoxication may be a defense in very limited circumstances

these situations to determine whether there was a lack of criminal intent. In most cases of involuntary intoxication, someone was given an intoxicating substance without his or her knowledge. Involuntary intoxication also might result from an *unanticipated* reaction to ingesting alcohol or a legal drug. This is known as pathological intoxication, and the *Model Penal Code* says that it means "intoxication grossly excessive in degree, given the amount of the intoxicant, to which the actor does not know he is susceptible" (American Law Institute 1985: 36).

Finally, **alibi** is probably one of the most misunderstood of the affirmative defenses, and as Sheppard notes, "[i]n most jurisdictions, alibi is not an affirmative defense but a rebuttal to the claims of the prosecutor" (2012: 122). In terms of general usage, people often believe that having an alibi simply means having an excuse (such as "my computer crashed," "my grandmother died [again]," or "the dog ate my homework"), but these are not alibis. Alibi is based on the Latin word that means "elsewhere." Essentially, the defendant is attacking the state's ability to prove guilt by saying, "I could not have committed this crime because I was somewhere else." The state must prove beyond a reasonable doubt that the defendant committed the alleged act, and if a jury believes the defendant's alibi defense, then the prosecutor will have a difficult time proving the case.

Alibi:
Latin term for "elsewhere"; the affirmative defense alleging that the accused could not have committed the crime as a result of being somewhere else at the time

SUMMARY

Criminal law in the United States today represents several centuries of development. Most of our legal structure can be traced to the English common law tradition, but we have also been influenced by ancient codes.

Several features distinguish civil law from criminal law, including the procedures defined for each type of court proceeding. The terms used in civil law and criminal law are sometimes different but similar. The major difference in the two types of law is the weight of evidence necessary to secure a verdict. In civil cases, proof is based on the preponderance of the evidence, whereas in criminal cases, guilt must be proven beyond a reasonable doubt.

There are also several sources of law in the United States. These include the common law that we inherited from England, statutory law, constitutional law, and case law. Law also originates from executive orders, treaties, and international law. Federal regulatory agencies provide a major source of law, and administrative law has become a major factor in the American legal system.

Crimes in the United States can be categorized in several ways. Two of the most common classifications distinguish between *mala in se* and *mala prohibita* offenses and between felonies and misdemeanors.

The different elements of crimes become especially significant during trials. Prosecutors must establish *mens rea*, *actus reus*, and the intersection of the two. It is also important to remember that there can be inchoate crimes that represent incomplete offenses.

Finally, the government bears the burden of proof in criminal trials. However, in cases where affirmative defenses are offered, the burden for these defenses can shift to the defense.

REVIEW QUESTIONS

1. How are customary law and modern criminal law different? What makes one system of laws work better in one setting versus another?
2. How and in what ways are civil law and criminal law different? How are they alike?
3. Are there advantages or disadvantages to having 12-member juries? Does it make a difference if the case is a criminal case instead of a civil case?
4. What are the primary sources of law in the United States? Which of these sources of law seem to play a dominant role today?
5. What are the differences between *mala in se* and *mala prohibita* offenses? Does the public consider one of these categories more serious than the other?
6. What are inchoate offenses? What are the most common types, and why are these activities considered criminal?
7. Which of the affirmative defenses would most likely be employed? Which seem to have to best chance of convincing a jury?
8. Why is an alibi different from an affirmative defense (or other affirmative defenses)?

KEY TERMS

actus reus
administrative law
affirmative defenses
alibi
attempts
bench trial
beyond a reasonable doubt
burden of proof
canon law
civil law
common law
concurrence
conspiracy
constitutional law
contingency fee
corpus delicti
criminal law
customary law
defendant
duress
entrapment

equitable relief
excuses
felonies
inchoate offenses
infancy
insanity
intoxication
judicial review
justifications
legality principle
legal precedent
mala in se
mala prohibita
mens rea
misdemeanors
Model Penal Code
murder
natural law necessity
petty misdemeanors
plaintiff
positive law (legal positivism)
precedent
preponderance of the evidence

procedural law
prosecutor
restitution
right to counsel
sharia law

solicitation
strict liability crimes
substantive law
statutory law
weight of evidence

PART II

Responding to Crime and Criminals

An Introduction to Policing

LEARNING OBJECTIVES

At the conclusion of this chapter, you should be able to:

- Appreciate how order was maintained from ancient times to medieval Europe and Britain.

- Describe how policing changed in terms of policies and practices from colonial times to the era of community policing.

- Explain the structure and function of contemporary police work, including its goals and objectives, structure and organization, and activities.

- Understand the legacy of law enforcers in the past as it shapes policing in the present and the future.

INTRODUCTION

Police are sometimes described as a "**thin blue line**," which indicates the relatively small number of law enforcers—blue-uniformed officers—standing between the lawful citizenry and the nation's criminal element.[1] However, some police critics suggest this phrase means that the police are a subculture unto themselves, detached and removed from the public they are sworn to protect and serve. The former idea is far more supportive of the police than the latter, which itself could be viewed as a summary indictment of the profession. The obvious question, then, is who is right?

At about the same time that this term came into popular use, Arthur Niederhoffer (1969) wrote an incisive work on police culture called *Behind the Shield: The Police in Urban Society,* in which he described life "behind the blue curtain" as something unknown and foreign to most of the public. The "**blue curtain**" served to protect the police subculture. It was a blue curtain of secrecy. This sociological and psychological look into the world of policing was not always sympathetic or even supportive of the police; however, it did provide a real-world perspective on what it was like to be a police officer in a large American city at midcentury. Niederhoffer described a subculture that earnestly served the public, but given what officers saw as their primary public-protection activity—crime fighting—this was often a no-holds-barred engagement with the enemy, the criminals. The police came to view the blue curtain of secrecy as a necessary evil. This was not simply a matter of keeping police officers' illegal activities hidden for fear of prosecution. Rather, it was necessary to keep the public ignorant of what the police had to do to keep the citizenry safe and secure. The police believed that the public did not want to know.

These phrases and the ideas they reflect about policing emerged during a problematic time in American history—the turbulent 1960s. This epoch of social change and conflict, viewed by many students of policing as having culminated in the 1968 "police riot" in Chicago (Walker 1968) had an undeniable and lasting impact on policing in America.[2] In the past 50 years, much has transpired in the profession of policing. At the same time, police history and law enforcement's multiple missions continue to influence contemporary policing. In Chapter 6, we return to the question of problems and issues associated with law enforcement activities, many of which flow from the concept of the thin blue line. To understand better contemporary policing, we begin with its history, followed by a review of what police do in the 21st century.

Thin blue line:
generally refers to the police, who are either socially and psychologically distant from the public or stand between the public and anarchy

Blue curtain:
the veil of secrecy separating the police from the citizenry they protect and serve

THE ORIGINS OF POLICING

The history of policing is the history of humankind, but particularly the history of social communities. As is the case with law and justice (see Chapter 1), when we set out to define policing, we have before us a somewhat daunting task. The term has many meanings, but a good starting place is the following: **policing** involves "the actions of a person or group in authority in order to ensure fairness and legality in an area of public life" (*Collins English Dictionary* 2014). Consider what this term means. The agent of control, a person or a group, operates under a formal legal order, giving that person or that group the power to act. It is not too difficult to see that in the time before there were princes, kings, and other local leaders, the people themselves were responsible for such activities, as they essentially policed themselves. Anthropologists who study tribal groups, even those leading a "stone age" existence, tell us that this is the case. In small residential groups of humans, where nearly everyone is related to everyone else by blood or marriage, adhering to the laws is a very informal and personal matter. If the violations were serious, then the sanctions were also very harsh; however, in most cases, elders in the group mediated between the aggrieved party and the alleged offender. This was to change with the emergence of the city-state and various nations and empires in ancient times, where policing established and maintained order.

Policing:
the actions of a person or group in authority to ensure fairness and legality in an area of public life

Order in Ancient Times

The eons-old status quo changed when city-states began to emerge about 10,000 years ago, as kinship and blood became less important in relations between people, and local rulers or sovereigns and their laws defined and maintained justice. For example, in ancient Mesopotamia, under the Code of Hammurabi (1750 B.C.E.) and other rulers of that era, civil servants, including judges, assumed expanded roles in the lives of the citizens of those early communities (Halsall 1998). Soldiers, serving their sovereigns, enforced a wide range of laws, particularly against robbers on the roadways linking the emerging cities of this region. This dual role of soldiers as warriors and law enforcers was to continue for millennia (Keegan 1993). There is also evidence that in ancient Sumerian and Mesopotamian cultures, African slaves policed other slaves and even free citizens in these early city-states (McNiven 2014). Ancient Athens (about 500 B.C.E.) also used publicly owned slaves as police; however, citizens were responsible for investigating crimes, while the slaves arrested and detained the suspects, pending trials by magistrates or local judges (Hunter 1994).

Critically for the current topic, however, is the observation that among the 51 main ancient civilizations, the creation of a separate and formal policing organization was the exception and not the rule (Banton 2014). Moreover, in many ancient civilizations that had formal policing structures, such as the police prefectures that emerged in China during the 8th century B.C.E. (Finer 2003), there was a cultural preference for mediation over formal governmental involvement (Yao 2001).

Formal Control in Imperial Rome

The Roman Empire (27 B.C.E. to 476 C.E.) provides an exception to the observed historical preference for mediation. Specialized armed forces provided security early in the Roman Empire, but not during the earlier Roman Republic (509 to 27 B.C.E.), as armies were then viewed as threats to republican liberties. Indeed, most "crimes" in the Roman Republic were personal matters between the victims and offenders, including homicide (Gaughan 2010). In the early days of the empire, as the city of Rome became more densely populated, the Emperor Augustus saw the need to exercise increasing control over both the general population and the criminal element (Finer 2003). Augustus formalized law enforcement with the creation of the **quaestores**, who were originally empowered to investigate capital homicide but later became investigators of financial and personal crimes as well (Schmitz 1875).

Quaestores: investigative agents in ancient Rome

More than crime, fire was a central problem in Rome at this time. While we often associate ancient Rome with stone and marble buildings, most of the city was made of wooden structures, which were highly susceptible to fire. An existing bureaucracy, the *triumviri nocturni*, consisted of three magistrates who managed a group of slaves who policed Rome's neighborhoods looking for unsupervised or otherwise dangerous fires. By the end of the Roman Republic, the *vigiles*, a watch organized into seven 100-man cohorts, replaced the largely ineffective *triumviri nocturni*. Each cohort patrolled two Roman administrative areas at night, looking for fires, burglars, thieves, brigands, runaway slaves, and other nighttime criminals (Baillie Reynolds 1926; Lanciani 1898). Eventually, the *vigiles* extended their reach to Roman port cities.

Triumviri nocturni: in ancient Rome, the individuals responsible for organizing and overseeing the slaves, who served as a night watch; translated from the Latin, this term means "the group of three responsible for the night"

Vigiles: public employees in ancient Rome who looked for fires and criminals at night

By the third century, the larger **Praetorian Guard** subsumed the *vigiles*, the former responsible for protecting the emperor and, in times of riot and general civilian unrest, the entire city of Rome. The Praetorian Guard was a highly politicized group, as it actively worked to influence the outcome of imperial successions (Bingham 2013). In addition, the guard spied for the emperor (Bingham 1997). Also

Praetorian Guard: Roman paramilitary group that protected the emperor and the city of Rome; politicized early in its existence; served as an early "secret service," or spy group

by this time, the *vigiles* and their **prefect of the watch** had jurisdiction over daytime petty crimes, as well as firefighting and other nighttime duties. This change brought them into conflict with the **urban cohorts**, a daytime patrol that Augustus founded as a counterbalance to the growing power of the Praetorian Guard. Under the supervision of an **urban prefect**, the urban cohorts dealt with major criminal activities such as roaming gangs and rioting citizens, not only in Rome but also in other urbanized areas of the Empire (Le Bohec 2000). These two groups, the civilianized *vigiles* and the paramilitary urban cohorts, often clashed with one another (Grant 1978).

Policing Medieval Europe

The fall of the Roman Empire in the west caused many changes in how laws were enforced and interpreted. In much of Europe, Roman law remained in force or at least played a major role in day-to-day activities through its influence on the Roman Catholic Church's canon law. Tribal law also reestablished itself throughout much of Europe, with local chiefs and princes assuming greater responsibility for maintaining order as the Roman influence diminished. In this power vacuum, several different models of law enforcement emerged. As various European rulers consolidated power, new laws and systems of social control emerged, representing a second stage in medieval policing. For instance, in the Frankish region of Europe, part of modern Germany and France, the Merovingian kings of the 5th to 8th centuries created the **Salic Code**, which was to form the basic civil law system found throughout much of modern Western Europe. This code, while based on local tribal norms and rules, owed much to Roman law. Local **counts (*comites*)** ruled over a geographic area known as a county and were subservient to the Merovingian kings. They maintained order and protected the roadways between cities and towns through the deployment of their men-at-arms. The counts oversaw local civil governments and resolved disputes. As the Merovingians gave way to the Carolingians in the mid-8th century, there were few changes in the daily administration of justice.

In review, medieval ruling powers and legal systems changed, but responsibility for maintaining local order resided largely in the hands of petty nobility, who had nearly absolute power. These local nobles, many of whom held hereditary positions, addressed issues of law and justice locally through their men-at-arms, who policed civil society generally and in times of war fought as soldiers for the count or the king. This system harkens back to law enforcers in the Ancient world. In fact, semimilitarized organizations policed much of Europe well into the 18th century (Emsley 1984).

Prefect of the watch:
the administrator in charge of the Roman *vigiles* who watched for fires and crimes in ancient Rome

Urban cohorts:
a daytime patrol that Augustus founded as a counterbalance to the growing power of the Praetorian Guard

Urban prefect:
the commander of the urban cohort in ancient Rome

Salic Code:
the basic civil law system found throughout much of modern Western Europe in medieval times; based on local tribal norms and rules, it owed much to Roman law

Counts (*comites*):
a form of medieval political leader under the Frankish kings who was responsible for all elements of civil government

Policing Medieval Britain

For its part, Britain presents a slightly different history of law enforcement. In Anglo-Saxon England, starting around the 7th century until roughly the 11th century, a system of shires or counties emerged, largely as geopolitical and taxation units. A shire was further divided into **hundreds**, groupings of approximately 100 families, itself made up of 10 **tithings**, the latter an even smaller area where 10 families lived. A selected member of each tithing, the **tithingman**, was the group's leader and spokesperson. When a crime was committed, the tithingman was responsible for the **hue and cry**, a call for all able-bodied persons to apprehend the offender. The tithings, hundreds, and shires also constituted the means by which the Anglo-Saxon earls, dukes, and English kings called their people to arms.[3]

At roughly this same time the office of the reeve emerged. Reeves were administrative officials in Anglo-Saxon England who ranked just below the earl. There were reeves of towns, shires, hundreds, and manors, the latter based on the local tithing. Some were appointed while others were elected. The **shire reeve**, however, is of most interest to us. This royal judicial and administrative officer was, even in Anglo-Saxon times, responsible for keeping the king's peace throughout the shire and collecting taxes. The shire reeve is the forerunner of the modern sheriff.

Two other local officials completed the British system, and despite existing in early medieval times, they did not become full-fledged law enforcers until after the Norman Conquest in 1066. First, Edward I (1272-1307), by the **Statute of Winchester** (1285), decreed that each local hundred would have a **constable**, who would serve as parish peacekeepers, while the sheriffs policed the larger counties (Critchley 1978; see also "Statute of Winchester 1285" 2013). Second, by the middle of the 13th century, Britain had developed a **watch and ward system** similar to the Roman *vigiles*. Divided into two shifts, the watchers provided security for London and other urban areas at night, while the warders did the same in the daytime, reporting offenses to the sheriff and eventually the parish constable (*Online Dictionary* 2013; see also Critchley 1978). The watch also announced the passage of the hours, as in "12 o'clock and all is well." These two systems of law enforcement continued for 500 years: sheriffs in the largely rural areas and the parish constables with their watch and ward system in the cities and large towns.

HISTORY OF AMERICAN POLICING

Along with the first colonists to the Americas came laws and the means to enforce them. While a number of European nations maintained colonies in North, Central, and South America, policing in the United

Hundreds:
a sociopolitical unit in Anglo-Saxon Britain based on the geographic area where 100 families resided

Tithings:
an Anglo-Saxon term referring to a group of 10 families; 10 tithings made up a hundred

Tithingman:
an appointed or elected member of a tithing who represented that tithing and was responsible for issuing the hue and cry

Hue and cry:
a call for all able-bodied persons to apprehend the offender

Shire reeve:
an Anglo-Saxon official who represented the king or queen in the county; collected taxes and maintained order; precursor of the modern sheriff

Statute of Winchester:
a decree by Edward I concerning the existing office of constable, which would henceforth be assigned to a local hundred

Constable:
a type of law enforcer dating from medieval England, assigned to a parish or local area in the community

Watch and ward system:
medieval English police protection system whereby watchers looked for fires and criminals at night and warders kept the cities and towns safe in the daytime; also used in colonial America

States owes its greatest debt to the practices brought by the English to North America. Hence, we look primarily at law enforcement practices in the English colonies. For example, almost from the day they landed and established a foothold, colonists selected a sheriff or constable and a magistrate from their midst. Among the first structures they built were a gaol (jail) and stocks, the former intended to hold offenders until trial and the latter intended to execute the authorized sanctions. Local jailers, often under the supervision of the sheriff, charged their detainees fees for the basics of life, food, and clothing.

The British also brought with them the office of marshal, whose law enforcement duties dated from the appointment of London's first city marshal in 1595.[4] The first American night watch system, all community volunteers, was created in Boston in 1631, followed by New York, called New Amsterdam at the time (1658), and Philadelphia (1700) (Bailey 1989; Gaines, Kappeler, and Vaughan 1999). Boston authorized a daytime town watch in 1636; it was to continue in effect for 200 years (Wrobleski and Hess 2000). Town constables in the colonial period were unpaid appointees. They supported themselves with fees collected from local courts for writs and warrants served.

Throughout most of the colonial period, law enforcers, whatever their formal name, were a combination of volunteers and poorly paid public employees. It is interesting to note that after more than 900 years, from the time of the Anglo-Saxons to colonial America, there were few efforts to formalize and professionalize British law enforcement. Policing remained a community responsibility.

The British crown left a lasting legacy in North American law enforcement, even as Britain's political influence decreased and, after the American Revolution, largely but not completely disappeared. The remainder of this section examines three topics related to the evolution of U.S. policing. First, we explore the type of policing services provided in the coastal regions and large cities and in the "hinterland" of the new nation. The second topic is the adaptation of "modern scientific policing" to the United States and the "growing pains" experienced by these agencies. Not the least of these problems was the politicization of the police and the resulting patterns of corruption that existed well into the 20th century, as well as periodic efforts to reform the police. The final topic is the era of modern policing, which generally dates from the mid-1970s and continues to the present. We begin with postrevolutionary policing.

Policing a New Nation

Little about law enforcement agencies and their actions changed in the years following the establishment of the United States. Several entities grew in power. Specifically, town marshals and constables, along with volunteer watch and ward systems, provided security in most urban centers well into the 19th century. Take the case of Boston, which became a city in 1822. Sixteen years later, Boston created a paid police force of six officers under the supervision of the city marshal. The new daytime entity operated independently of the night watch. This emergent force continued to provide nighttime patrols until the creation of a unified police force in 1854. This slow evolution from volunteer night watches to full-time professional police gained traction in the emerging urban centers of the East Coast. Sheriffs continued to serve most of the geographic areas as the chief law enforcement officer of the county.

On the frontier, four entities exercised policing responsibilities. First, the U.S. Army served as a quasi-law enforcement agency, keeping Native American tribal groups on their reservations and protecting civilians from raiding parties of Indian nations with whom the government had no treaties. In 1878 the U.S. Congress passed the **Posse Comitatus Act** (18 U.S.C. §1385). This legislation severely limited the army's power to provide policing services throughout the nation. Initially, the act was a response to federal troops' enforcement of the political conditions of Reconstruction following the Civil War (1861-1865). In the West, it meant that the army could still respond to "Indian problems" but could no longer provide basic law enforcement services in the communities springing up throughout the West. Federal and local law enforcers performed those duties.

Posse Comitatus Act: congressional legislation that limited the use of the U.S. military for essentially policing functions

Second, the **U.S. marshal** was often the only law enforcement presence in much of the West, particularly in the federal territories that had yet to be become states. We return to this federal law enforcement officer in the next chapter. The marshal was an often-overworked member of the U.S. district court system. The jurisdiction of the U.S. marshals, the oldest U.S. law enforcement agency in continuous operation, having been founded in 1789, included federal laws and crimes committed on federal territory. During the post-Civil War era, marshals often assumed the role of mediator between Native Americans and settlers, miners, and the like. They also pursued escaped convicts and wanted persons under federal warrants, an activity that continues to this day. In the pursuit of "desperados," marshals could and often did deputize local citizens and formed posses. Until 1896, U.S. marshals collected fees from the federal courts for their pay and expenses, including the pay of posse members and other expenditures, such as bullets and food, incurred in the apprehension of criminals throughout the West (U.S. Marshals Service, n.d., 2014).

U.S. marshal: an appointed member of a U.S. district court; kept the peace in the court and enforced federal law in the area under the court's jurisdiction, including the apprehension of escape prisoners and warranted offenders

Third, in communities with a sufficient population to support one, there was generally a town sheriff or marshal and, in territories or states that had been divided into counties, a county sheriff. These individuals often competed with one another for graft opportunities and political power. Perhaps the most famous such conflict took place in Tombstone, Arizona, and led to a shootout between the Earps and Clantons. The former allied themselves with Republicans and Union soldiers, while the latter were part of the Democratic and Confederate-leaning "cowboy" faction. A dispute between the town marshal, U.S. marshal, and county sheriff over Tombstone's political and economic control led to the shootout.

Finally, the emerging nation had a long history of **vigilantism**, where local citizens, absent organized or effective law enforcement, took the law into their own hands. There were as many as 500 vigilante movements in the United States from 1767 to 1900 (Klockars 1985). For example, prior to the Revolution, the **regulator movement** in North and South Carolina sought out criminals of all forms, from corrupt British-appointed officials to outlaw gangs (Whittenburg 1977). Even as the new nation moved westward, the practice of taking charge of law enforcement in the absence of other authorities continued from the Appalachians to the Pacific (Brown 1975). Throughout the 19th century, vigilante groups meted out justice as they saw fit, often without due process or judicial actions.

Vigilantism: a situation where local citizens, absent organized or effective law enforcement, took the law into their own hands

Regulator movement: a group of pre-Revolutionary War vigilantes in North and South Carolina who took the law into their own hands

Political Policing and Police Reform

North America in the mid-19th century, but particularly the United States, was heavily influenced by recent revolutionary changes in British law enforcement (see Box 4.1), including the use of uniforms, beats, work specializations, and rank structures. The British continued to influence the administration of justice in the United States nearly 50 years after the American Revolution. Many police scholars view the 1838 creation of a day force to supplement the Boston night watch as the inaugural event in the creation of a modern police force in the United States. In 1851, the two groups became a single unified Boston-wide police force. By that time, New York City had abandoned its two-tiered system and created its own unified police department. Philadelphia unified its police department in 1854, also adopting the London Metropolitan Police model. Indeed, by the start of the American Civil War in 1861, most large U.S. cities had unified police departments.

With the establishment of unified police departments, firearms and uniforms became polarizing issues. It seems a bit odd in the 21st century to think that these elements of policing were actually important in the 19th century, but they were. The London Metropolitan Police did not generally carry firearms; nor did the first wave of officers in unified departments in the United States. This was to change by midcentury. Unofficially, police officers prior to the Civil War often carried

Box 4.1   Sir Robert Peel and the London Metropolitan Police

We often trace modern policing back to Sir Robert Peel. In fact, what happened during Peel's two terms as British Home Secretary represented the conclusion of a long succession of developments, all of which occurred between 1750 and 1830. By the mid-1700s, there was a growing distrust in Britain of a military-style gendarmerie such as was developing in France and Germany. Into the midst of this debate, brothers Henry and John Fielding created the **Bow Street Constables** or the **Runners**, a combination of crime-fighting street officers and detectives. This effort was short-lived, to be followed by Patrick Colquhoun's **Thames Police Office**, a group of constables who patrolled the Thames River docks and, beginning in 1800, were paid from the public purse, whereas the Runners were a privately funded operation. In 1800, Glasgow successfully petitioned the government to allow for the creation of a city police force. Other Scottish cities petitioned London to create similar policing organizations. However, London held out against the rising tide of a professional police force.

A series of events precipitated a change in British sensibilities about police. First, riots over food and military recruiting made people feel vulnerable to the mob, and the mob had recently overthrown the French monarchy. Second, military barracks began to appear around major British cities, including London, which only created more concerns about military control of the civilian government. Third, Parliamentary committees reported on the need for police as an alternative to the military. Fourth, owing to the first three elements, public debate began to turn the tide toward a publicly funded police force. The final element was Sir Robert Peel, who had already organized the Royal Irish Constabulary and, as home secretary, spearheaded the passage of the **Metropolitan Police Improvement Bill of 1829**.

In May 1830, Peel's 2,800-man **London Metropolitan Police**—the Met—was operational. Organized along military ranks and structure, the officers wore civilian-style blue-serge suits, topped by a tall conical hat. Bobbies carried a truncheon and "rattle," the latter being a device loud enough to be heard from up to 800 meters and used to signal for help. In the late 1880s and early 1890s, the rattle gave way to the whistle. As for ranks, while the emblems of rank were similar to the British military, their titles were not, except for the police or detective sergeant.

Called Bobbies by the public, the Met's police had no jurisdiction over the City of London, a one-square mile area in the heart of the London metropolitan district. Hence, a separate City of London force emerged in 1839, when that city disbanded its parish constable system. By the **Rural Constabulary Act of 1839**, local magistrates throughout rural England and Wales had the option to create their own police force, but by 1856, every borough and county was required to form and fund its own police along the same lines as the Met.

SOURCE: Emsley 1984.

Bow Street Constables: a London-based, privately funded policing and investigative agency in the 18th century, operating under the leadership of the Fielding brothers; also known as the Runners

Thames Police Office: an early 19th-century group, placed on the public purse that maintained order on London's Thames River docks

Metropolitan Police Improvement Bill of 1829: English Parliamentary legislation that created the London Metropolitan Police

London Metropolitan Police: a police agency, dating from 1829 and operating today, that is considered the first modern police force

Rural Constabulary Act of 1839: British Parliamentary act that mandated local police organizations throughout Britain along the lines of the London Metropolitan Police

personal weapons with them on duty. By 1900, police officers routinely received service revolvers, often stamped "Police Model" at the factory (Emsley 1984).

Early police officers also resisted wearing uniforms and the badge of office. Officers were not particularly popular with the residents of the cities they policed, especially among newly arrived immigrant groups. New York City police only began appearing in their full uniforms in 1853 (Emsley 1984). Similarly, Boston police began to dress in blue uniforms with white hats in 1859 (Richardson 1974). By the turn of the 20th century, unified police departments, organized along the lines of the London Metropolitan Police but carrying firearms, were commonplace in nearly every U.S. city of any size. A uniformed and armed police force, like other public services, became the hallmark of a modern city or town (Fogelson 1977).

Advances in technology changed policing at the start of the 20th century. Telegraph stations and eventually call boxes with telephones were strategically spaced around police beats in larger cities. These devices allowed backup officers and police "paddy wagons" to be dispatched when and where needed. However, not everything about early 20th-century policing advanced the cause of law enforcement and public safety, especially when it came to public confidence in the police. Policing agencies were heavily dependent on local politicians for funding and, before the advent of civil service protections, their very jobs. Local ward political machines, organized like William "Boss" Tweed's infamous Tammany Hall of New York City, often demanded a payback from prospective officers. Once in uniform, these officers remained under the influence of such political machines, all organized on the same local level as the police themselves (Fogelson 1977; Richardson 1974). An officer ignored the wishes of the local ward politician at his own peril, both for his job and his personal health and welfare. The **spoils system** allowed politicians to appoint individuals to jobs on the public purse based on patronage, political affiliation, and graft. Given the long-standing ties between politicians and formal social control agents, stretching back to the Roman Empire, this development was predictable.

Organized criminals, as distinct from corrupt organized politicians, also had their fingers in police business. The police often provided protection for "racketeers" in the nation's larger cities, like Philadelphia, Chicago, Minneapolis, and New York, in exchange for a piece of the action, usually in the form of cash or an exchange of services (Fogelson 1977; Rubenstein 1973; Steffens 1957). The ties between vice and the police have been observed since Roman times. The big financial incentive for organized crime, however, was Prohibition (1919-1933).

Spoils system:
system that allowed politicians to appoint individuals to jobs on the public purse based on patronage, political affiliation, and graft

The **Volstead Act**, which mandated federally enforced alcohol prohibition throughout the nation, created conditions that were ripe for corruption. The **Wickersham Commission**, also known as the National Commission on Law Observance and Enforcement, reported in 1931 that the Volstead Act was basically unenforceable and the source of much corruption within the law enforcement community. The 21st Amendment, ratified in 1933, repealed the 18th Amendment, but it was too late to reverse the erosion in public trust of police.

By 1930, the political era of policing was drawing to a close (Kelling and Moore 1988). For the first 80-plus years of policing, politicians had been the source of nearly all police authority. Police in that era were torn between responding to the needs of citizens, whose neighborhoods they walked on their beats, and the demands of politicians, who controlled their job security and salaries. As a rule, the local police forces were decentralized down to the local precincts, which tended to parallel political power in the cities, making a bad situation even worse.

From the early1930s to the late 1970s, the reform era of policing brought about many changes, not all of them good for the public or the police (Kelling and Moore 1988). The epoch's chief reformers, including August Vollmer, O.W. Wilson, and J. Edgar Hoover, worked to establish professional police organizations out of the chaos created by the political era of policing. The reformers made officer selection a more rigorous and objective process. They emphasized education and training (see Chapter 1). Police work became, following the precepts of O.W. Wilson's **professional model of policing**, more scientific and more bureaucratic. However, the advent of the radio-dispatched police car and various technological advances and scientific management procedures removed the officer from the beat and regular contact with the public and brought about **depersonalized policing**. Equally troubling in the 1950s was a new wave of policing scandals, particularly those related to the corrupting influence of organized crime. For example, the 1950 **Kefauver Committee** issued a report that served as an indictment of many large city police departments that were, in the committee's estimation, literally on the payroll of organized crime.

Also in 1950, William H. Parker took command of the Los Angeles Police Department (LAPD). Parker was a staunch advocate of higher standards of physical fitness, intelligence, and scholastic aptitude among police recruits, including psychiatric examinations. He believed that urban society was a jungle and all that stood between society and anarchy was the "thin blue line" of a city's police. Importantly, the LAPD policing model, with its high level of professionalism and intractable opposition to restrictions on police methods, became the standard against which police reforms were measured throughout the 1950s (Peak 2012: 30).

Volstead Act:
congressional act that essentially criminalized the manufacture, distribution, transportation, and possession of nonmedicinal alcohol under the provisions of the 18th Amendment to the U.S. Constitution

Wickersham Commission:
commission that reported in 1931 that the Volstead Act was basically unenforceable and the source of much corruption within the law enforcement community; also known as the National Commission on Law Observance and Enforcement

Professional model of policing:
an idea advanced by O.W. Wilson to make the police less prone to corruption

Depersonalized policing:
the idea that removing police officers physically from their beats effectively cut them off and isolated them from the citizenry

Kefauver Committee:
an investigative body in Congress that looked into the ties between organized crime and corrupt police in 1950s America

Even as U.S. police forces became more professional, the social and, often, physical distance between the officers and the people they policed became a problem. Moreover, beginning in the late 1950s and early 1960s, law enforcers began to face a new obstacle: the protest era (see Chapter 1). Police agencies at all levels across the nation had to deal with new challenges, ones for which they were ill equipped to respond. Antiwar and pro-civil rights protesters, along with a growing drug-using counterculture, created new and in many cases insurmountable challenges for most contemporary police departments. The timing could not have been worse, as depersonalized policing was well entrenched. Importantly, however, the protest era also helped to propel law enforcement agencies in the direction of a new policing model, which returned the officers to the communities they served and protected.

Police Services in the Community Policing Era

Throughout the 1960s and into the early 1980s, local commissions, such as that empowered by Mayor Richard Dailey to look at the root causes of the Chicago Police Riot, and national ones, such as the President Lyndon Baines Johnson's Crime Commission, came to a similar conclusion: Police practices were alienating the police from their communities. Moreover, the communities and the police exhibited mutual distrust of each other. Hostility and antagonism defined the relations between police and civilians, but especially urban minority communities.

In response to breakdowns in police authority and respect, several innovative policing programs began to emerge beginning in the 1970s. The problem was that the police were on the defensive, and change was the watchword for police administrators seeking to keep their jobs. **Team policing** is an example of a good idea rushed into practice in cities like Cincinnati and Boston. A study of the New York City Police Department's team policing program found that it was doomed to failure by a lack of proper funding and poor training for involved personnel. In theory, street officers were generalists, working all aspects of all forms of crime in their communities to provide the services that were needed, where and when needed. Detectives became upset that patrol officers were investigating crimes, muddying a turf distinction important to many in law enforcement. Midlevel NYPD police managers also never fully supported the program, and it was judged a failure and abandoned (Walker 1993). An interesting footnote is that team policing remains quite popular and successful in England and Wales, which was where the NYPD initially found the idea for its variant of team policing.

In the 1970s and early 1980s, other jurisdictions returned to Peel's basic strategy, the foot patrol. For example, an experimental field

Team policing: a New York City Police Department program whereby officers were assigned to neighborhoods where they handled all aspects of local crime and disorder

study in Newark, New Jersey, showed that such practices led to higher satisfaction with police services and improvements in other public perceptions of the police; however, it did not result in a crime reduction (Police Foundation 1981). A more recent experiment in Philadelphia found that foot patrols could actually reduce crime (Ratcliffe et al. 2011). Crime rates, however, returned to preexperiment levels within months of cessation of the foot patrols (Sorg et al. 2013). What is not lost on police administrators is that foot patrols are labor intensive, so departments have been slow to (re)embrace them.

At about the same time that team policing grew in popularity, three publications defined a new era into modern policing, one suggested by team policing but that went beyond it in scope and concept. In the first, Herman Goldstein (1979) suggested that rather than a broad-based, shotgun approach to neighborhood crime, police needed to study the problems carefully and construct specific responses to very particular problems. Goldstein, like Albert Reiss (1971) before him, observed that contemporary police work is far more reactive (**reactive policing** refers to actions taken by the police after the crime or in response to it) than proactive (**proactive policing** refers to anticipatory police actions intended to reduce or prevent crime). According to Goldstein, line police, in concert with dedicated police researchers, would target the underlying roots of crime and disorder, working within the community to reduce or eliminate social and physical disorder. This, then, was the essence of **problem-oriented policing (POP)**.

In a second seminal piece titled "Broken Windows: The Police and Neighborhood Safety," George Kelling and James Wilson (1981) noted that social and physical disorder in the nation's inner cities helped to explain the rising crime levels. However, the key to fighting crime was within the neighborhood itself. "Broken windows" were a symptom of a larger community problem: the disconnection of the residents from each other and the larger community, including the police. The police had to work to overcome community malaise and the growing sense of defeatism at the hands of local criminals that led people to ignore the disintegration of their own neighborhood.

Goldstein defined problem-oriented policing as the means of addressing the needs of communities plagued by crime and disorder. Kelling and Wilson provided its theoretical underpinnings. John Eck and William Spelman (1987) described a problem-solving method that evolved into the **SARA model**. "S" is for scanning, which means looking for the clustering of criminal incidents that are interconnected, and the police could approach them using a unified response. "A" refers to analysis, what many view as the heart of the community-policing model. The analyst identifies the crime triangle (which includes the victims or targets), the offender or offenders, and the crime locations and opportunities. "R" is for response. The analysis must articulate the

Reactive policing: actions taken by the police after a crime is committed or in response to it

Proactive policing: anticipatory police actions intended to reduce or prevent crime

Problem-oriented policing (POP): a strategy employed by police agencies to identify, analysis, respond to, and assess specific crime and disorder problems with the goal of creating effective responses to them

SARA model: a method used in problem-oriented policing to provide workable solutions to community-based crime and public-disorder issues

response and provide a viable answer to the identified problem, not just a reaction. Finally, problem-solving policing must include an assessment, the final "A" in SARA. It is not enough to come up with what everyone agrees is a great program and an appropriate response to the problem. Rather, the researchers/collaborators must show the exact nature of the program's impact on the identified problem and that the response was implemented as designed. Only by doing both tasks can replication of the program elsewhere achieve anything like the same results.

By the early 1980s, **community policing** had become the new watchword in law enforcement. This "new" approach to policing was defined as "a philosophy that promotes organizational strategies, which support the systematic use of partnerships and problem solving techniques, to proactively address the immediate conditions that give rise to public safety issues, such as crime, social disorder, and fear of crime" (Scheider 2008). Throughout the 1980s and 1990s, dozens of demonstration projects tested the usefulness of problem-oriented policing, leading some to call it "a new policing" (Glensor, Correia, and Peak 2000). In 1999, Goldstein established the Problem-Oriented Policing (POP) Center, which has since distributed nearly 1 million copies of its guidelines and other supporting materials, much of it in the form of online programming (Center for Problem-Oriented Policing, n.d.). In addition, the Department of Justice established **Community Oriented Policing Services (COPS)** as a standalone office in 1995. COPS has spent $14 billion directly supporting community policing through grants awarded to more than 13,000 state, local, and tribal law enforcement agencies (Community Oriented Policing Services 2013). Agencies used these grants to hire and redeploy approximately 125,000 officers. In addition, COPS has provided a variety of knowledge resource products, including publications, training, technical assistance, conferences, and webcasts (James 2011).

Community policing has its share of critics, including concerns about the validity of its basic theoretical model called "broken windows" (Sampson and Raudenbusch 1999; Thatcher 2004). There may also be an implicit racial bias in the groups and neighborhoods targeted by problem-oriented policing and community-based programs (Sampson and Raudenbusch 1999; Stewart 1998). Furthermore, some midlevel police managers and officers do not view community policing as real police work, a criticism that was also leveled at team policing back in the 1970s (Peak 2000). Still, the body of research on the effects of community policing programs and the level of congressional support suggests that it will continue to guide police policy for the foreseeable future (Maguire and Wells 2009; James 2011). The current community era of policing has demonstrated generally positive results and widespread acceptance by both line police officers and the communities

Community policing: a philosophy that promotes organizational strategies that support the systematic use of partnerships and problem-solving techniques to proactively address the immediate conditions that give rise to public safety issues, such as crime, social disorder, and fear of crime

Community Oriented Policing Services (COPS): an office within the Department of Justice that disseminates information and provides grants for community-oriented policing

they serve. The emergence of community policing also signaled the demise of the professional era of policing that preceded it.

CONTEMPORARY POLICE WORK

A common answer by police officers when asked what they do is "fight crime." In fact, crime-fighting activities account for a small part of what they do, both as individual officers and entire agencies. At a broader level, police officers say that they protect and serve the public. Indeed, this statement, or one like it, is often printed on their police units or the agency's official seal. To gain a better perspective on police work, we begin with the goals and objectives of a 21st-century policing agency and follow that discussion with a brief examination of police agency structures and organizations, which include the work of the police.

Police Goals and Objectives

Given the extensive history of policing, one could ask how has police work changed since the 19th century? How has it changed since the 18th century? How has it changed since the 18th century B.C.E. and the actions of the Mesopotamian law enforcers? These are legitimate questions. A partial answer lies in a series of commonly stated goals associated with the police, including the following (Grant and Terry 2008: 136):

1. The prevention of crime
2. The protection of life
3. The upholding and enforcement of laws
4. The combating of public fear of crime
5. The promotion of community safety
6. The control of motorized and other traffic
7. The encouragement of respect for the law
8. The protection of civil rights and liberties of individuals

Obviously, several of these items would not apply to ancient Mesopotamia or even medieval Europe or Britain. Likewise, the protection of the supreme ruler's personal wealth is missing, which was often the prime directive for ancient and medieval law enforcers. Moreover, the extent to which a given law enforcement agency—and here we are principally talking about **general service law enforcement agencies** (Walker and Katz 2007: 3)—adopts any or all of these goals varies greatly and is generally expressed on each agency's home website or more traditional print media.

The recent history of our nation's policing organizations has taught us that order maintenance largely directed police activities during the

General service law enforcement agencies: agencies that engage in crime prevention, crime investigation and criminal apprehension, order maintenance, and the provision of miscellaneous supportive services

political era, whether it was controlling immigrant populations or striking workers. Police reform efforts set strict law enforcement as the order of the day—the central focus of the police from the 1930s through the 1980s. Given the current emphasis on the community and its engagement with the police, the goals are likely to manifest themselves in different ways, emphasizing community service through a clear mission statement and set of values. Nearly all modern policing agencies have both a mission statement, which describes the reason a particular organization exists, and a list of core values, which defines how they function as law enforcers. Such statements constitute sets of values or beliefs that typically provide guideposts for the employees of that organization, suggesting the benchmarks against which we measure their conduct. For example, consider the mission and values/beliefs statements found in Box 4.2.

Police Structure and Organization

Going back to ancient Mesopotamian and Sumerian cultures and continuing through the days of the Roman Empire, the groups that policed the population often looked like military forces. British and American police forces in the middle of the 19th century adapted this organizational structure to policing. This is still the case today. Specifically, most general services law enforcement agencies today look like paramilitary organizations. There is a bureaucratic hierarchy that generally follows a pyramidal structure. At the top is the **command element**, usually with the rank of chief, commissioner, or sheriff, as well as his or her immediate subordinates, the latter often holding the rank of deputy chief, commissioner, or commander. The duty uniforms usually reflect military rank, ranging from stars to oak clusters. **Middle management** comes next, or those personnel responsible for directly administering or overseeing the operations of the various divisions or units in the agency. In ranks, these individuals include an agency's captains and lieutenants. Next are the **first-line managers**, essentially supervisory staff. In rank, they are typically sergeants. At the bottom are the **line staff**, the sworn officers who populate the operational divisions and units of the agency.

The actual structures employed by the thousands of law enforcement agencies across the nation are many and varied. Historically, agencies followed a centralized policing model, with a rigid chain of command that makes movement of information back up the chain difficult. The removal of bureaucratic levels results in a flattened organizational structure and a decentralization of command and control. Decentralization of command and control is commonly found in those agencies that emphasize community policing.

Command element: the highest-ranking part of an agency, responsible for developing policies and procedures; typically a highly politicized office

Middle management: those personnel in an agency who are responsible for directly administering or overseeing the operations of the various divisions or units in the agency

First-line managers: supervisory staff, usually serving at the rank of sergeant

Line staff: sworn officers who populate the operational divisions and units of the agency

| Box 4.2 | **Police Mission Statements and Core Values** |

Below are the mission statement and core beliefs and values of a large police department. Do they reflect your values?

Chicago Police Department

A. Mission Statement—(A) The Chicago Police Department, as part of and empowered by the community, is committed to protect the lives, property, and rights of all people, to maintain order, and to enforce the law impartially. We will provide quality police service in partnership with other members of the community. To fulfill our mission, we will strive to attain the highest degree of ethical behavior and professional conduct at all times. (B) The Department and all members will act in a unified manner to uphold the Mission Statement. (C) The Department's response to emerging and chronic crime and disorder will be comprehensive and consistent with all aspects of the Mission Statement

B. Core Values—The core values of the Chicago Police Department
  1. Professionalism—We are members of an elite and highly trained profession: law enforcement. We will conduct ourselves in a manner that is consistent with professional standards. These standards include the adherence to our Mission Statement and our Core Values. We hold ourselves and each other accountable for our actions. Professionalism means having a corporate and personal set of standards for performance. We aspire to high ideals: altruism; honor; respect; scholarship; caring, compassion, and communication; leadership; and responsibility.
  2. Obligation—Our obligation is a requirement to take action, be that action either legal or moral. It is a compulsion; we are compelled to act. As police officers, we have the legal obligation to serve and protect the residents of the City of Chicago, and the legal requirement to preserve order and uphold the law. However, our obligation runs deeper than just

legal requirements. For us, there is an obligation to service that is tied directly to personal honor. We act not just because of our legal authority, but because of our personal *duty*.

  3. Leadership—Leadership is influencing people—by providing purpose, direction, and motivation—while operating to accomplish a mission and improve the organization. Each member is expected and encouraged to be a leader. By combining personal knowledge, job skill, and obligation, we are leaders in the community. With a positive attitude and the commitment to our fellow members, we are leaders among our peers in both the Chicago Police Department and the law enforcement profession. We seek out challenging situations and circumstances in order to thrive as leaders: never looking to avoid conflict but instead seeking to resolve it.

  4. Integrity—Integrity, the adherence to moral and ethical principles and the consistency of actions which are value-based, is our standard. We will conduct ourselves in a manner that gains the trust and respect of those whom we serve. We are of strong character, possessing the personal values and mental and emotional attributes that enable us to make ethical decisions and empathize with others. We do what is right not because it brings us personal recognition, but because it is the right thing to do.

  5. Courage—Courage is not the absence of fear, but rather its mastery. We will remain courageous in our actions. We recognize that there are two types of courage: physical courage and moral courage. Physical courage is recognizing danger to oneself or to others, but persisting in our duty regardless. Moral courage is the adherence to principle, integrity, and obligation no matter how convenient it may be to do otherwise. It is putting character ahead of expediency;

of putting what is right ahead of what may be popular. We fulfill our obligation and are leaders because of our courage.

6. Excellence—We recognize that excellence is not an end state, but rather a continuing process. We will continue to seek out innovative ways to work with the members of the community we serve in order to achieve the highest level of quality in our service. We will strive for creative and effective solutions to crime and disorder, and we will work to be the symbol for excellence in the law enforcement profession.

SOURCE: Chicago Police Department, n.d.

Generally, a department has two main elements: **field services**, which provide such activities as police patrol, traffic, community services, and investigations, and **administrative services**, which include recruitment and training, technical services, planning, analysis and research, and records and communications. Again, most 21st-century police agencies provide a great deal of information about their organizational structure on the Internet, which is a good place to begin to learn about your community's agency.

Police Activities

Police work changes with the times, but some elements remain constant. For example, if the community has a gang problem, the agency may have a specialized antigang unit. If there is no large-scale gang problem, then specially designated juvenile officers within the patrol division or by a separate juvenile division may target gang members. Agencies often have a number of different divisions and units, depending on the size and socioeconomic composition of the community served and the agency's specific mission. A **police division** is a group of police personnel who all share a particular police function. For example, the patrol division (sometimes called a patrol bureau) is usually the largest part of any policing agency. A **police unit** is a smaller element within a division or bureau that has a specialized activity to perform. Continuing this example, certain officers within a patrol division may form units that specialize in preventive patrols or traffic patrols. As another example, the department's internal affairs (IA) unit reactively and proactively investigates misconduct by serving officers in the agency. This entity may be part of the investigative division. In other agencies, IA officers work more directly for administrative services or a senior administrator who reports to the chief or sheriff. Small police organizations may not observe the distinctions between divisions and units.

As a rule, specific functions determine the organizational units. In field services, such units would include patrol, traffic, crime prevention, criminal investigations, juvenile services, community services, vice and narcotics, organized crime, intelligence, undercover, and

Field services: services that provide such activities as police patrol, traffic, community services, and investigations; generally sworn police personnel

Administrative services: services that provide for police recruitment and training, technical services, planning, analysis and research, and records and communications; generally but not exclusively nonsworn personnel

Police division: a group of police personnel who all share a common police function

Police unit: a smaller and discrete part of a division that has a specialized activity to perform

special operations. Obviously, large departments have most if not all of these units, and may actually have more, such as a homeland security or antiterrorism units. Smaller agencies may have far fewer units, and general service officers perform multiple functions or rely on other agencies to assist as needed. In administrative services, the following units are common: clerical, finance, personnel, training, records keeping, public information, planning and analysis, intelligence, internal affairs, detention, and prisoner transportation. As with field services, many smaller agencies do not have separate units for all of these tasks; instead, nonsworn or civilian personnel may perform multiple administrative duties.

Finally, we must distinguish between sworn officers and civilian employees. The majority of personnel serving in a policing agency are **sworn officers**, persons certified by the appropriate agency with oversight in such matters, usually organized at the state level. **Nonsworn** or **civilian personnel** have no police powers but perform essential work. Nearly all field services employees are sworn officers, while many who work in administrative services, especially such activities as clerical, financial, records, and planning and analysis, are nonsworn personnel. The civilianization of the nation's policing agencies is a growing trend. Since the 1960s, the percentage of civilian personnel in police departments has tripled (King and Maguire 2000), although there is evidence that considerable variation exists by agency (King 2009). Except for specialized skill areas, such as accounting, budgeting, and personnel, civilians are often less expensive to hire, train, and maintain than sworn officers. Using them allows the civilians to specialize in a narrow support role, while officers directly serve the public.

These are the essential elements and divisions of police work. Police engage in far more activities than we can possibly cover in a part of a single chapter. Specialized units engage in surveillance of repeat violent offenders, seeking to catch them in the act. Directed patrols look for certain types of offenses or offenders and may even focus on "hot spots" or places that have repeated calls for service, often involving the same people. There is far more specialization of tasks and responsibilities than we can possibly cover in an introductory text. We trust that in covering the basics, we have given you a flavor of the range of activities engaged in by today's law enforcement officers.

Sworn officers: police personnel who are certified by a statewide agency and may exercise the full range of police duties, responsibilities, and powers

Civilian employees: nonsworn police personnel

SUMMARY

This chapter covers three main topics. First, we place policing as an activity in its proper social and historical context. From prehistorical times to the emergence of city-states to medieval times, the work of those entrusted with maintaining order and fighting crime changed less than we might think. Paramilitary groups policed ancient Mesopotamian communities but especially the trade routes that were essential to their survival. However, it was in Britain that we see a far more civilianized policing structure emerge—one that colonialists transported to North America.

Second, policing in the United States once again mirrored what had taken place and was evolving in Great Britain. Sheriffs, marshals, and constables kept order in large cities and across the western frontier. At the close of the 19th century, another British export, the London Metropolitan Police, took its own unique Americanized form in U.S. cities, large and small. As the lessons of the past have clearly demonstrated, however, with such immense power as is given to the police, there is the danger that such agencies will be corrupted, which is what happened almost from the creation of the first U.S. police forces to the end of Prohibition and beyond. Reforms did not necessarily bring about a better, more citizen-friendly police. However, in recent years, the police and the community began collaboratively working against urban crime and disorder.

Finally, this chapter provides an overview of police structure, organization, and activities. Police agencies remain paramilitary organizations. They are also bureaucracies in form, structure, and design. Indeed, the size of the geographic area served or its population density can determine the police force's organizational structure. From start to finish, this chapter provides lessons that are rooted in the past yet projected into the future of policing. For example, we are left wondering what practice of the past will be "retuned" to fit a need in the future. This is one of the key lessons found in the study of police history and evolution.

REVIEW QUESTIONS

1. Summarize Roman efforts at policing the empire. Is there something about the Roman Empire that made the role of the police so complicated, especially given the variety of law enforcers present in those days?
2. Medieval policing represented some changes from policing found in Roman times. What were they?
3. What do you make of the fact that in Europe and Britain the concept of the night watch was "reinvented" hundreds of years after it had been abandoned? What does this suggest about other, perhaps more modern police practices?
4. Compare and contrast policing in the political era and the reform era. When do you think the

work of a police officer would have been easier, and why?
5. Community policing and problem-oriented policing are not the same thing. How does each complement the other, and where do they diverge?
6. What is SARA, and what are its ties to problem-oriented policing?
7. The mission statement of the Chicago Police Department is included in Box 4.2. Find a similar statement for a police department in your city or state. Can you detect elements of the different models of policing in each one? How does the statement you found compare and contrast with the Chicago mission statement?
8. Distinguish between police divisions and police units, and explain where those distinctions may not be very useful.

KEY TERMS

administrative services
blue curtain
Bow Street Constables
civilian employees
command element
Community Oriented Policing Services (COPS)
community policing
constable
counts (*comites*)
depersonalized policing
field services
first-line managers
general service law enforcement agencies
hue and cry
hundreds
Kefauver Committee
line staff
London Metropolitan Police
Metropolitan Police Improvement Bill of 1829
middle management
nonsworn personnel
police division
policing
police unit
Posse Comitatus Act
Praetorian Guard
prefect of the watch

proactive policing
problem-oriented policing (POP)
professional model of policing
quaestores
reactive policing
regulatory movement
runners
Rural Constabulary Act of 1839
Salic Code
SARA model
shire reeve
spoils system
Statute of Winchester
sworn officers
team policing
Thames Police Office
thin blue line
tithingman
tithings
triumviri nocturni
urban cohorts
urban prefect
U.S. marshal
vigilantism
vigiles
Volstead Act
watch and ward system
Wickersham Commission

NOTES

1. The "thin blue line" is a phrase popularized in the 1960s, after a documentary film of that same name by William Friedkin (1965). Friedkin is better known for his film *The French Connection* (1971). Chief William Parker of the Los Angeles Police Department generally receives credit for originating the phrase (Peak 2012).

2. A police riot is a violent confrontation between the police and some segment of the public that the police instigate, carry out, and execute. Some see it as a case of the police out of control, while others view it as an act of political oppression (Stark 1972; Walker 1968). To learn more and see period film footage, search the Internet for an answer to the following question: What happened at the 1968 Democratic Convention?

3. Until the Norman invasion, the Anglo-Saxon dukes were the most powerful political figures in Britain. They were descended from the earlier ealdorman, a term eventually replaced by the Danish *eorl* (later earl); the first ealdormen took the title of *duces* (the plural of the original Latin *dux*, meaning "leader").

4. The term "marshal" is of Roman origin, popularized by Charlemagne, a Carolingian king, in the 9th century. The Normans brought the term to the British Isles in 1066. It is similar to "constable" in usage (Bruce 1999).

U.S. Law Enforcement Agencies

LEARNING OBJECTIVES

At the conclusion of this chapter, you should be able to:

- Distinguish between the different forms of general services law enforcement agencies.
- Explain the role of jurisdiction and mission in shaping the structure and form of local versus county versus state police agencies.
- Understand the evolution and development of federal law enforcement.
- Describe the responsibilities of the various federal law enforcement agencies.

INTRODUCTION

Police are the largest, most visible and pervasive part of the U.S. criminal justice system. We see police vehicles on our city streets and interstate highways. In many cities and towns, uniformed officers walk beats or protect buildings. When we fly or take other public transportation such as trains, buses, or subways, they are often in the public spaces or riding along with us. Police protect the nation's infrastructure, ranging from dams to bridges to tunnels. Uniformed and plain-clothes officers protect the president and the president's family, as well as other select politicians. Governors also have special police details protecting them. Even football coaches often have uniformed officers at their side during games.

A natural question to ask is exactly how many police are there in the United States? The answer depends on what is meant by the word "police." The question could be about the number of police forces or agencies. Another determining factor to consider when answering such a question is the jurisdiction of the force or agency. In fact, the number of agencies or police forces is slightly more than 18,000 if the question contains the phrase "all possible jurisdictions," or not quite 75 if the question is limited to federal law enforcement agencies. The question could also refer to the number of sworn officers, or individuals with full arrest powers and authorization to carry firearms. For example, if the question is asked about the number of full-time sworn officers in the Chicago Police Department, the answer would be quite different than if the same question is asked about the Smithsonian Zoological Park Police—the former a local police department and the latter a federal law enforcement agency.[1]

This overview is more suggestive than definitive. Yes, the nation has hundreds of thousands of full-time sworn law enforcement officers operating at the local level, if by local we mean all U.S. villages, towns, cities, and counties. Yes, the nation has far fewer individuals providing police services at the federal level. Moreover, law, custom, and practice define each agency's jurisdiction. Do you now have a better understanding of breadth and depth of contemporary police in the United States? Probably not. At least, not yet. You do have a better sense of policing as a possible vocation, as there are more than a million positions across these agencies, and tens of thousands of them become available every year. To extend our look at local, state, and federal law enforcement, we turn to exactly what the police do for their communities. A good place to start is with general services law enforcement agencies—those organized at the local, county, and state levels.

LOCAL, COUNTY, AND STATE LAW ENFORCEMENT

Nearly every level of government across the nation has some form of **general services law enforcement agencies**, with mission statements that include crime prevention, crime investigation, and criminal apprehension, maintenance of order, and related law enforcement services. In this section, we examine three such organizations or agencies. Jurisdiction and sworn personnel are central to this discussion. The first type of police organization, the local police agency, employs by far the largest number of sworn police personnel. In terms of size, they range from small, employing fewer than 10 sworn officers, to large, with 1,000 or more such officers. A very few are megadepartments, with as many as 30,000-plus officers. The key to understanding the scope of their legal duties is the jurisdiction that provides the funds to pay them. The police provide services to a specific geographically based unit of government or the political entity that funds them. In the case of the local police, that unit is an individual village, town, city, or municipality. The second type of policing organization, the county sheriff, is a descendant of the shire reeve of pre-Norman England. In many counties across the nation, the sheriff, a mostly elected position, is the chief law enforcement official; however, four states—Alaska, Connecticut, Hawaii, and Rhode Island—have no sheriff's offices; instead, the law enforcement duties that usually fall to that office are delegated to other local law enforcement agencies. Finally, nearly all states operate a broad-based policing organization, generally known as the state police, that has wide-ranging law enforcement powers. The exception to this generalization is Hawaii, although even in that state there is the Department of Public Safety, which has some investigative/policing powers.

The number of police agencies and employees is a key question for this chapter. Table 5.1 summarizes the nation's general service police agencies at all important jurisdictional levels.[2] The nation has almost 18,000 such agencies of all types and more than 1.1 million employees, roughly three-fourths being sworn officers. Local police account for seven in ten general service policing agencies and employ slightly more than 50 percent of all total employees but more than 60 percent of all sworn personnel. Sheriff's offices, with the exceptions noted above, are found at the county level and account for about one in six of all general services police agencies. Slightly less than one in three personnel employed by policing agencies in this country work at the county level, but only one in four sworn officers are sheriff's deputies. At the state level, there are 50 state police agencies. However, while the Hawaiian Department of Public Safety is included in this list, the

General services law enforcement agencies: public agencies with mission statements that include crime prevention, crime investigation, criminal apprehension, maintenance of order, and related law enforcement services

Table 5.1	By the Numbers: State, County, and Local Law Enforcement, Full-Time Employees			
		NUMBER OF FULL-TIME EMPLOYEES		
TYPE OF AGENCY	NUMBER OF AGENCIES	TOTAL	SWORN	NONSWORN
All agencies	17,985	1,133,915	726,246	368,669
Local police	12,501	593,013	561,063	131,950
Sheriff's office	3,063	353,461	182,979	170,482
Primary state	50	93,148	60,772	32,376
Special jurisdiction	1,733	90,262	56,968	33,294
Constable/marshal	638	4,031	3,464	567

NOTE: Excludes agencies employing fewer than one full-time officer or the equivalent in part-time officers.
SOURCE: Adapted from Reaves 2011: 2.

department's law enforcement division, which consists of both a narcotics enforcement division and sheriff's division, provides police services across the archipelago, making it a unique state general services police agency. When totaled, state police agencies employ about 8 percent of all full-time law enforcement employees and the same percentage of all sworn personnel.

Table 5.1 reveals the breadth of nonfederal law enforcement agencies across the nation. Two categories merit special mention. Special jurisdiction agencies either serve a unique geographical area or have special enforcement or investigative responsibilities (Reaves 2011: 2). The former would include those sworn officers that protect public hospitals, colleges and universities, and other governmental buildings. Natural resources law enforcement officers—park or forestry rangers—are also in this category. Special investigation agencies working at the state, county, and city level constitute other examples, as do transportation police. Constables and marshals are the heirs to a tradition that began centuries ago in France and England. There are few of them, mostly in Texas (Reaves 2011). The remainder of this section focuses on the three other types of local law enforcement. Later in this chapter, we explore the federal agencies and their jurisdictions and subject matter. Before looking at federal law enforcement, however, we turn to a brief examination of the depth, structure, and responsibilities of local and state law enforcement.

Local Police Agencies

The term "local police agencies" is fairly all encompassing and includes small agencies, such as town marshals and village police. It also includes incorporated municipal areas with up to 50,000 residents. When a geopolitical area's population is above 50,000, we generally refer to it as a metropolitan area, a designation recognized by the U.S. Census Bureau. Large metropolitan areas, such as Chicago, New York City, and Los Angeles, have large police departments, yet they are also local law enforcement agencies.

Table 5.2 presents the nation's local policing agencies' employee statistics by the size of the agency involved. Several patterns are apparent in these numbers. First, there are few large local policing agencies, if by large we mean employing more than 1,000 full-time sworn officers. Second, at the other extreme, more than half (53.2 percent) of all policing agencies in the United States have fewer than 10 officers. Another 35 percent have between 10 and 49 officers. More than 10 percent of all general services departments included in this table have only one full-time sworn police officer. Most policing agencies in the nation are small, given that nearly eight in ten have fewer than 50 officers. Third, the 49 largest local police agencies employ one-third of all officers. In sum, most police departments in the nation are small; however, nearly half of the full-time sworn personnel serve in what are arguably the country's largest police departments (i.e., 250 or more officers).

Organizational issues are also important and are tied to the size of the local police department. For thousands of local policing agencies,

Table 5.2	**By the Numbers: Local Policing Agencies, Full-Time Employees**			
		NUMBER OF FULL-TIME EMPLOYEES		
SIZE OF AGENCY	**NUMBER OF AGENCIES**	**TOTAL**	**SWORN**	**NONSWORN**
All agencies	12,501	593,013	461,063	131,950
1,000 or more officers	49	194,829	150,444	44,385
500-999	43	39,447	29,985	9,462
250-499	101	47,910	36,021	11,889
100-249	445	85,345	64,939	20,406
50-99	815	72,701	56,060	16,641
25-49	1,543	67,743	53,465	14,278
10-24	2,846	55,476	44,520	10,956
5-9	2,493	19,687	16,582	3,105
2-4	2,637	8,405	7,694	711
0-1	1,529	1,470	1,353	117

NOTE: Excludes agencies employing fewer than one full-time officer or the equivalent in part-time officers. Size of agency is based on number of full-time sworn personnel.
SOURCE: Reaves 2011: 4.

particularly those with fewer than 25 officers, the organizational chart would look like a small business: the chief or town marshal at the top and an immediate supervisor and support staff below. The chief administrator often directly supervises the officers under his or her command, who are the definition of general services officers. The chief's office usually has direct oversight of the administrative services division of such a department. There probably are no detectives, as all officers are part of the same operations division. Any criminal investigations might be the work of specially trained patrol officers, or the department would request aid and assistance from the local sheriff's office or state bureau of investigation. In major crimes, the local agencies might seek federal assistance.

Small departments consisting of between 25 to 99 officers require a more complex organizational structure. Figure 5.1 reflects a municipal police force of 75 officers serving a community of fewer than 30,000 residents. Even this department has three divisions, similar to the bureaus discussed in Chapter 4. Support services, typically led by a

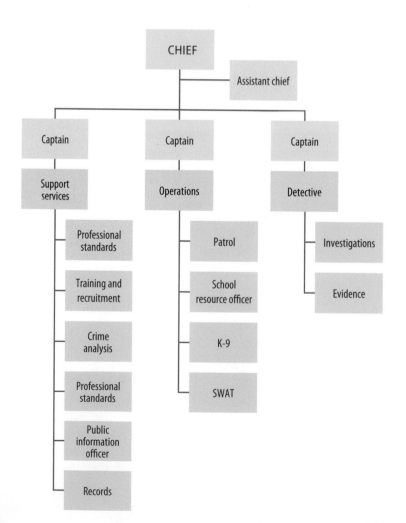

Figure 5.1
Organizational chart for a small police force (fewer than 75 officers)

captain, provide the requisite internal housekeeping units of this size police force. Such subdivisions include the following units: professional standards (internal affairs), which investigates allegations of abuse and misuse of authority against officers; training and recruitment; public information; accreditation; crime analysis; and records. A lieutenant leads each subdivision. Similarly, the operations bureau provides the central services of any police department, patrol, school resource officers, K-9 or dog unit, and special weapons and tactics unit, sometimes called a special response unit. Again, a captain heads this bureau, and a lieutenant supervises each unit. Finally, in this department, a detective bureau investigates all crimes. A captain supervises two units within this bureau: criminal investigations (detective bureau) and evidence, the latter maintaining the chain of integrity of all evidence collected in the investigation of crimes.

A medium-size department employing between 100 and 249 officers generally adds another layer of bureaucracy, as reflected in Figure 5.2. This department of 175 officers serves a community of more than 100,000 inhabitants and has two primary divisions—support services and operations—each supervised by a deputy chief. The **public information office (PIO)** and **professional standards unit (PSU)** work directly under the chief. The operations division divides the city into regional commands, also called police districts. The western and eastern area commands are nearly identical, except that the school resource officers (SROs) are in one command and the prisoner transport responsibilities in the other. Each has a breath ethanol and sobriety testing (BEAST) unit and a traffic-oriented policing squad (TOPS) unit. The special services division includes three units, one of which requires additional explanation. Targeting Neighborhood Threats (TNS) is a community-based program intended to defuse problems early. The neighborhood enforcement teams (NET) work under the traffic section and handle issues related to traffic law violations, making it another community-based program.

The support service division in Figure 5.2 is more complex than for the smaller department (Figure 5.1) and includes an environmental section, a criminal investigations section (CIS), a cross-agency narcotics squad, and general administrative support. This simple chart hides even more organizational complexities. The CIS includes not only the specialized units (e.g., evidence unit, identification unit, victims' assistance unit), but also within its detective division are offense-specific specialized investigators (e.g., crimes against children detectives, crimes against persons detectives, financial crimes detectives, domestic violence detectives).

Larger metropolitan areas present their own unique policing and organizational challenges, largely based on geography and demographics, including the size of the area served and the population

Public information office (PIO): an internal unit that provides information to the media and the general public about programs, projects, and events affecting the community and the police department; community relations unit

Professional standards unit (PSU): an internal unit dedicated to investigating complaints and charges against the police force in question

Figure 5.2   Organizational chart for a medium-size police force (75 to 200 officers)

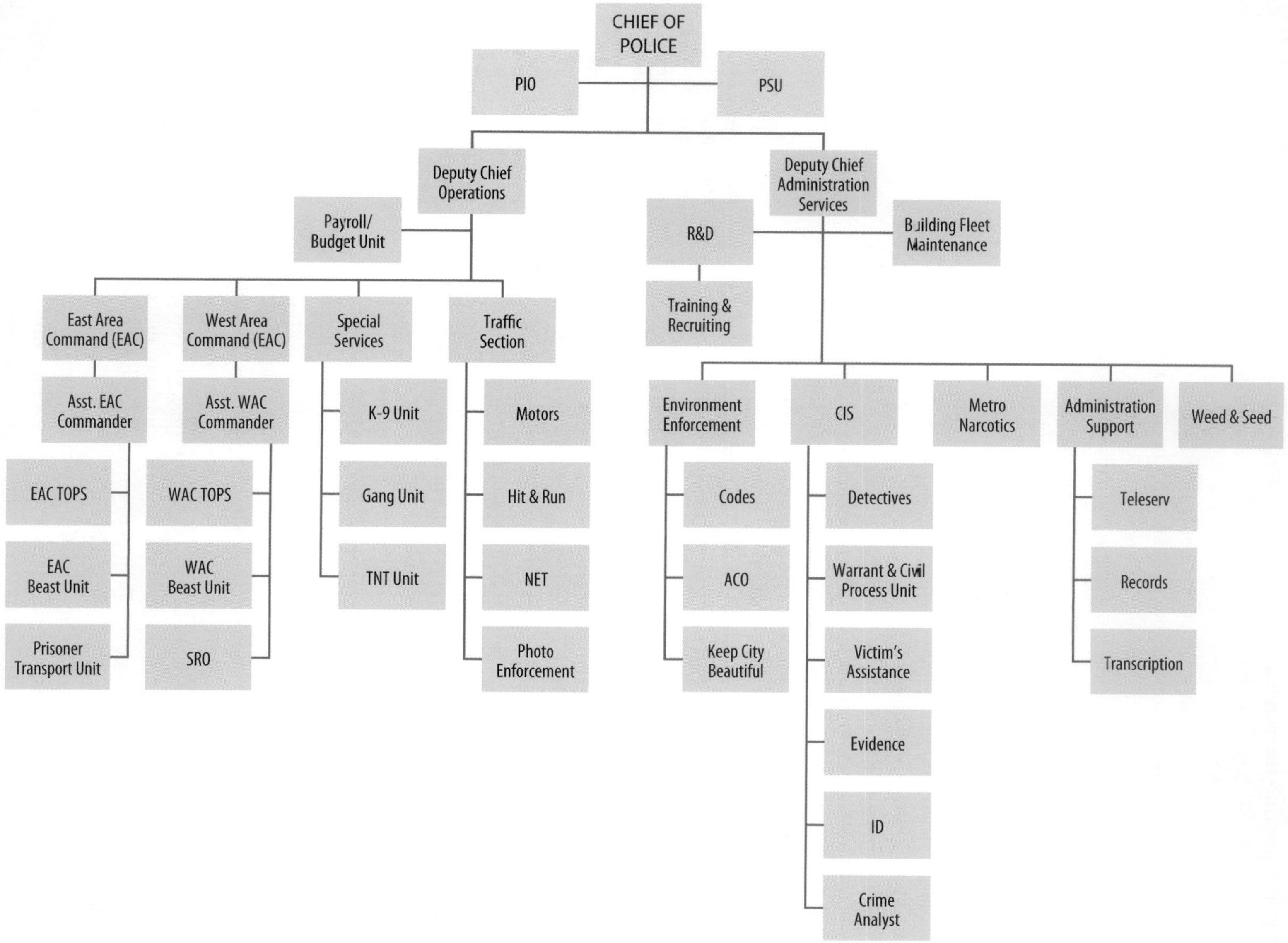

characteristics of the various geographic areas served. Were we to include the organizational chart for a city the size of New York, Chicago, Los Angeles, or Philadelphia—the nation's four largest police departments, where the number of sworn officers range from 36,023 for the NYPD to 6,624 for Philadelphia (Reaves 2011: 14)—we would have to add a half dozen pages of charts. If you are curious, we suggest that you do an Internet search of a large or mega-department near you. These charts have more in common with those for General Motors, Xerox, or any major corporation than the police department portrayed in Figure 5.2.

County-Level Law Enforcement Agencies

The contemporary county sheriff is the modern incarnation of the English shire reeve. The total number of sheriff's offices across the nation represents only 17 percent of all local and state police agencies, while local police departments account for 70 percent. Local police employ 60 percent of all sworn personnel in the nation, and sheriff's offices are next, at 24 percent. It is interesting that sheriff's offices also account for 46 percent of full-time civilian personnel across all policing organizations.

We can make several other important generalizations from Table 5.3. Large (500 or more sworn officers) sheriff's offices, like

Table 5.3	**By the Numbers: County-Level Policing Agencies, Full-Time Employees**			
		NUMBER OF FULL-TIME EMPLOYEES		
SIZE OF AGENCY	NUMBER OF AGENCIES	TOTAL	SWORN	NONSWORN
All agencies	3,063	353,461	182,979	170,482
1,000 or more officers	13	59,981	32,897	27,084
500-999	27	34,348	17,184	17,164
250-499	98	65,704	34,743	29,961
100-249	240	68,265	36,085	32,180
50-99	327	44,772	23,037	21,735
25-49	573	40,988	20,084	20,904
10-24	910	30,121	14,196	15,925
5-9	569	8,485	3,901	4,584
2-4	261	1,615	822	793
0-1	45	182	30	152

NOTE: Excludes agencies employing fewer than one full-time officer or the equivalent in part-time officers.
SOURCE: Reaves 2011: 5.

local police departments, are the exception, accounting for only 1.3 percent of all sheriffs' offices, but they employ more than one in four sheriff's deputies. Nearly 80 percent of all sheriffs' offices employ fewer than 50 full-time sworn officers but account for about one in four of all deputies. Sheriff's offices with between 50 and 499 officers make up 22 percent of all offices; they employ 50 percent of all deputies. Thus, departments at the top and bottom in terms of size employ about the same percentage of deputies (roughly 25 percent each), while the majority of all deputies serve in offices that range between 50 and 499 officers.

Figure 5.3 represents a sheriff's office with just under 250 sworn officers. It serves a county with 389,000 residents. Generally, this chart (and the law enforcement agency it represents) has much in common with the one found in Figure 5.2, but there are some important differences. The sheriff's office has an aviation wing located in its special operations unit, a feature that reflects the county's large size (nearly 5,400 square miles). In other words, this agency serves an area that is larger than most large urban police departments. Second, under a chief deputy for detention, the sheriff's office operates a 1,500-bed capacity jail, a unit that is generally the unique province of the county sheriff's office (see Chapter 11). Third, directly under the supervision of the sheriff is the posse. This is not to be confused with the 19th-century posse of the Old West. Where it exists, the contemporary posse consists of specially trained members of community who aid and assist in the maintenance of law and order in the county. They generally are unarmed and do not have arrest powers, although they may be uniformed personnel and drive sheriff's vehicles. In other jurisdictions, however, "reserve" deputies, who are armed and have limited arrest powers, perform this function. Finally, the sheriff's office represented in Figure 5.3 has a search and rescue unit (see special operations), again owing to the large and rural nature of its jurisdiction.

Individual local law enforcement—whether organized as the village or town marshal, city police, or county sheriff—provides the nation with general police services. In some situations, a consolidated police organization, as described in Box 5.1, serves a regionalized community. As a rule, when we talk about police activities in the nation, we are describing the actions of sworn officers employed by agencies at one of these levels. However, others exist. We turn next to a unique layer of nonfederal, nonlocal policing: the state police.

State-Level Law Enforcement Agencies

Prior to World War I (1914-1918), few states saw the need for a statewide police force. Three exceptions stand out in history; moreover,

Figure 5.3 Organizational chart for a 21st-century sheriff's office

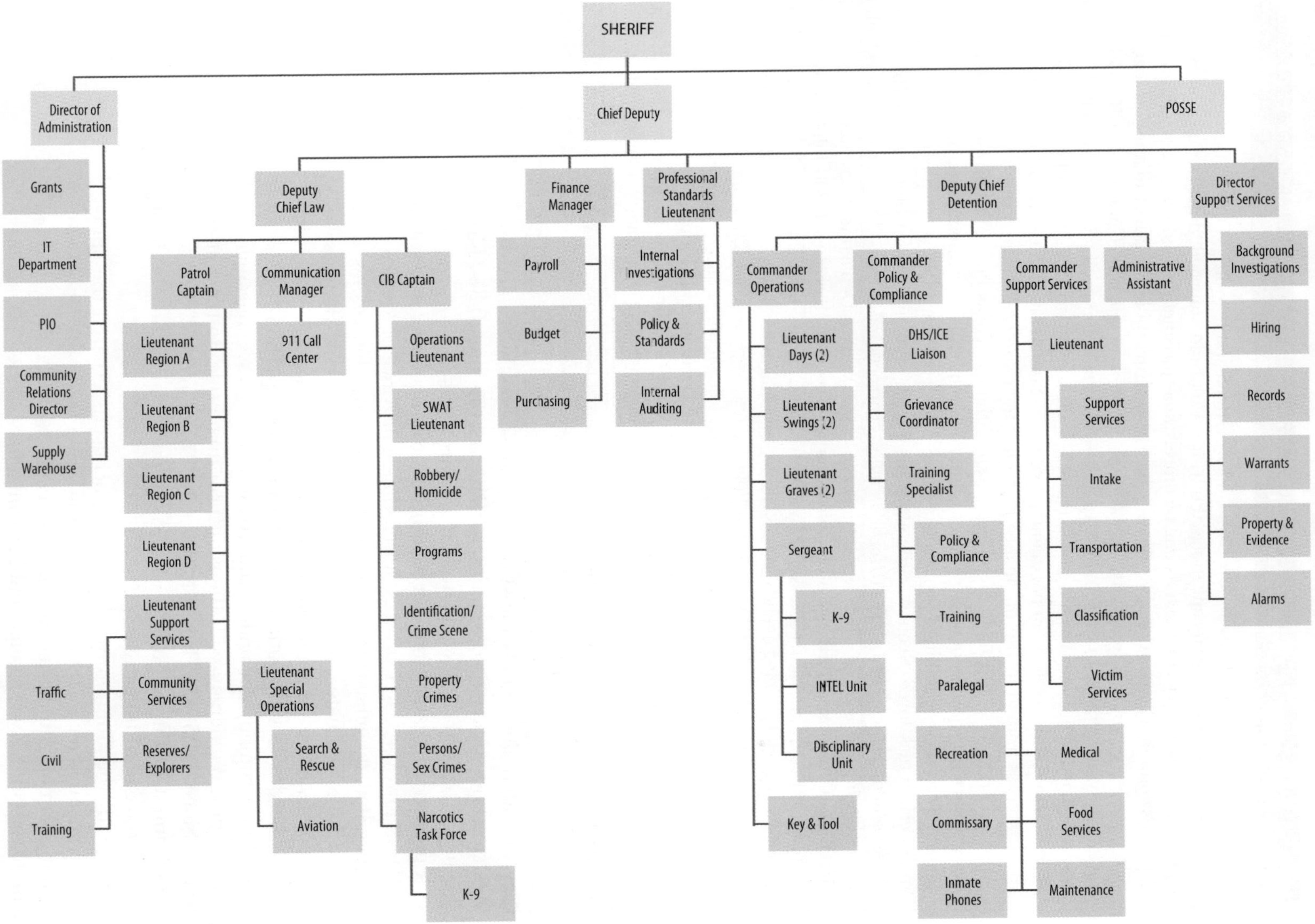

Box 5.1   Consolidated Law Enforcement Agencies

The term "consolidated law enforcement agencies" can mean several different things. First, it can mean shared services, such as one or more agencies combining operational functions, which can include communications networks, SWAT units, or even records. In extremely rare situations, police and fire services have been consolidated into public safety departments, with officers cross-trained in the disciplines of both types of services, as certified officers are essentially police-fire personnel. In Will County, Illinois, 37 agencies combined to provide a single major-crime task force. Second, city-county law enforcement agencies can merge to form a single consolidated police force. Rather than jurisdictional combinations, a third type of consolidation employs a geographical area, essentially creating a new regional policing agency. For example, the Northern York County (PA) Regional Police Department provides police services for two boroughs and six townships. Fourth, local mergers involve separate entities that join to form a new police force, such as when the police

departments in Winter Park and Fraser, Colorado, merged. Finally, an agency serving one jurisdiction could provide, under a formal contract, police services to another legal entity. The Los Angeles County Sheriff's Office has formally contracted with a number of area jurisdictions to provide local police services.

Some consolidated agencies are notable for their size or prominence. For example, in 1973, the Las Vegas Police Department and the Clark County Sheriff combined to form the Las Vegas Metropolitan Police Department, which has 2,700 full-time sworn officers and 750 full-time correctional officers. The Charlotte-Mecklenburg (NC) Police Department, created from a similar merger in 1994, has 1,600 full-time sworn officers. The Indianapolis Metropolitan Police Department has 1,700 full-time sworn officers and represents a 2007 merger of the City of Indianapolis Police Department and the law enforcement division of the Marion County Sheriff's Office; a year later, it moved to the Indianapolis Department of Public Safety.

SOURCES: New Jersey State Association of Chiefs of Police 2007; Stefko and Sittig 2012; Wilson and Grammich 2012; Wilson, Weiss, and Chermak 2014; respective agency websites.

they provided the models for states that subsequently created their own statewide police forces between 1919 and the late 1940s. First, Stephen F. Austin unofficially authorized the Texas Rangers in 1823 as a protection against Indian raiders, Mexican banditos, and cattle rustlers; however, as Texas was at that time a province of Mexico, the Rangers had no official standing. In 1835, during the Texans' war with Mexico to create the Republic of Texas, the Texas Rangers became an official entity of that government and had the task of securing Texas's border to the south. During Reconstruction (1865-1877), the federal government disbanded the Texas Rangers as a paramilitary group, but it reemerged with the return of "home rule" to the state of Texas. Since 1935, the Texas Rangers has been part of the Texas Department of Public Safety, essentially performing the duties of a state bureau of investigation.

Second, the Commonwealth of Massachusetts created the statewide Constabulary in 1865 to control the rising levels of alcohol consumption among immigrant groups, especially the Irish. Once they began to enforce laws against public drunkenness, the Constabulary extended its reach into other areas of Massachusetts, in terms of both legal and physical jurisdictions. The Constabulary disbanded in 1875, largely at the behest of Massachusetts' Irish population, which saw it as an instrument of governmental oppression (Johnson 1981: 158-163). Rural detectives took its place outside of Boston, while the Boston Police patrolled that city. It was not until 1921 that the Commonwealth of Massachusetts joined a relatively small group of states in creating a statewide police force.

Third, in the late 19th and early 20th centuries, the Commonwealth of Pennsylvania experienced a series of events that led to the creation of the nation's first uniformed statewide policing organization (Pennsylvania State Police, n.d.). Similar to what happened in Texas and Massachusetts, the need for a statewide police in Pennsylvania was borne out of the widespread belief that there was a pervasive problem population who disproportionately caused crime throughout the state. In this case, it was not simply immigrants, as was the case in Massachusetts, or marauding Indians, as in Texas, but rather striking workers and their open conflict with iron and coal police. A national investigation blessed by President Theodore Roosevelt, himself a former superintendent of the New York Police Commission, blamed the absence of effective police in the coalfields. Pennsylvania governor Samuel Pennypacker, using the Philippine constabulary as a model, established the Pennsylvania State Police in 1905, which in less than a decade resolved the problems in the coalfields and moved on to policing the entire commonwealth.

In the years following World War I, the idea of state-level police organizations gained traction with state legislatures. A series of inter-related factors shaped this movement (Johnson 1981: 158-163). First, immigrants and unions, two problems of the late 19th and early 20th centuries, were less troublesome in the decades following World War I. Anti-immigration sentiment in Congress resulted in quotas that made immigration difficult; moreover, past immigrant populations began to be assimilated into the nation. Second, the booming pro-business culture of the 1920s slowed the rapid growth of labor unions, and strikes became less of a problem for local and state police. Third, thanks to Prohibition, organized crime became interstate crime as bootleggers transported distilled spirits and beer across national and state boundaries. In the 1920s and early 1930s, many other criminals took advantage of the lack of police coordination, including the likes of Bonnie Parker and Clyde Barrow, John Dillinger, "Machine Gun" Kelly, and Ma Barker and her brood of criminal children. Their combined exploits highlighted the need for not only state-level police organizations but also a strong federal law enforcement presence, the latter focus adopted by J. Edgar Hoover as he sought to expand the power of the Federal Bureau of Investigation. Finally, the growth in private ownership of motorized vehicles meant greater mobility for citizens and criminals alike. Contributing to this trend, Congress passed the first interstate highway act in 1921. The net result was a growing need for statewide law enforcement. The emerging state police organizations assumed a lead role in maintaining order on the interstate and intrastate highways, as well as generally providing safety standards and licensing processes for all vehicles using those byways. Several states expanded the general police powers of their state-level agencies or, as was the case in 34 states, created separate criminal investigation bureaus based on the structure of the Federal Bureau of Investigation (Johnson 1981: 163).

Today state-level law enforcement represents one of the most diversified of all levels of policing. Table 5.1 shows that the states employ 60,772 full-time sworn officers. This simple statistic belies the complexities of state policing. Table 5.4 summarizes the nature and extent of state-level policing across the nation. It includes for each state the specific state-level law enforcement agencies, their major law enforcement-related divisions, and the number of full-time sworn personnel.

There are two types of state-level law enforcement agencies. First, the majority of states operate a full-service police agency, which enforces all state vehicular-related laws, rules, and ordinances, as well as criminal laws. We call the prototypical model of a full-service police agency the state police. Second, the policing agency may be limited to traffic law enforcement, which means that for the most part this agency is responsible for the safety and security of the state and associated interstate highway systems. The dominant model here is the state highway patrol, although a handful of agencies with this designation are actually full-service police agencies. The latter states often operate another agency that is solely investigatory, which means that it has the power to investigate crimes throughout the state and arrest suspects. The most common example is the state bureau of investigation, most often found in the office of the state attorney general or state department of justice (e.g., California, Kansas, Montana, North Carolina, North Dakota, Ohio, South Dakota, Wisconsin, and Wyoming). Less often, the state operates an independent state bureau of investigation (e.g., Florida, Georgia, Nevada, Oklahoma, South Carolina, and Tennessee) or one in the department of public safety (e.g., Colorado and Utah). Typically, full-time sworn peace officers constitute only a small portion of such a bureau's staff.

State-level policing agencies have other responsibilities. Irrespective of their name, all officers have full police powers. In some states, the state police or highway patrol may also provide rural and unincorporated areas with police services under legal agreements or contracts (see also Box 5.1). They may provide security for the state's chief executive—the governor—and patrol the state capitol. Many state

Table 5.4 Structure of State Police Organizations in the United States

STATE	AGENCY (YEAR FOUNDED)	TYPE	MAJOR LAW ENFORCEMENT-RELATED BUREAUS/DIVISIONS/UNITS	SWORN OFFICERS
AL	Department of Public Safety (1939), Highway Patrol (1935); formerly State Law Enforcement Department (1913)	Full service	Highway Patrol; Bureau of Investigation	763
AK	Department of Public Safety (1959); formerly State Troopers (1941)	Full service	Highway Patrol; State Troopers; Investigations	274
AZ	Department of Public Safety (1969), Highway Patrol (1931); formerly Arizona Rangers (1901)	Full service	Highway Patrol; Criminal Investigation Division	1,244
AR	State Police (1937)	Full service	Highway Patrol Division; Criminal Investigation Division	525
CA	Highway Patrol (1924)	Traffic	Field Divisions; Protective Services	7,202
CO	Department of Public Safety (1984), State Patrol (1935)	Traffic	Investigations; Vehicular Crimes; Executive Security; Homeland Security	742
CT	Department of Emergency Services and Public Protection (2011), State Police (1903)	Full service	Office of Field Operations; Bureau of Criminal Investigations	1,227
DE	Department of Safety and Homeland Security (2003), State Police (1923)	Full service	Field Services; Investigations; Homeland Security	658
FL	Department of Highway Safety and Motor Vehicles (1969), Highway Patrol (1939)	Traffic	Patrol Operations; Special Services	1,606
GA	Department of Public Safety, State Patrol (1937)	Traffic	Patrol; SWAT; Criminal Interdiction	1,048
HI	Department of Public Safety, Law Enforcement Division	Full service	Narcotics Enforcement; Sheriff's Division	290
ID	Idaho State Police (2000); formerly Department of Law Enforcement (1919)	Full service	Patrol/Investigations	264

(continued)

Table 5.4 Continued

STATE	AGENCY (YEAR FOUNDED)	TYPE	MAJOR LAW ENFORCEMENT-RELATED BUREAUS/DIVISIONS/ UNITS	SWORN OFFICERS
IL	State Police (1922)	Full service	Operations; Internal Investigations	2,105
IN	State Police (1933); formerly Motor Vehicle Police (1921)	Full service	Operations; Criminal Investigation	1,315
IA	Department of Public Safety (1939)	Full service	State Police; Criminal Investigations; Narcotics Enforcement	669
KS	Highway Patrol (1933)	Full service	Field Operations; Homeland Security; Special Operations; Motor Vehicle Enforcement	525
KY	State Police (1948)	Full service	Operations; Technical Services	882
LA	Department of Public Safety and Corrections (1942), State Police (1922)	Full service	Patrol; Investigations	1,215
ME	State Police (1920)	Full service	Field Troops; Criminal Investigations and Forensics	334
MD	State Police (1921)		Field Operations; Criminal Investigation; Special Operations	1,440
MA	Executive Office of Public Safety and Security, Department of State Police (1992), formerly Constabulary (1865) and State Police (1919)	Full service	Field Services Division; State Police Detective Units	2,310
MI	State Police (1917)	Full service	Crime Prevention, Safety and Police Services; Emergency Management and Homeland Security	1,732
MN	Department of Public Safety, State Patrol (1929)	Full service	Patrol; Special Response Team; Capitol Security Unit	530
MS	Department of Public Safety (1938)	Full service	Highway Patrol; Investigation; Narcotics; Homeland Security	594

STATE	AGENCY (YEAR FOUNDED)	TYPE	MAJOR LAW ENFORCEMENT-RELATED BUREAUS/DIVISIONS/ UNITS	SWORN OFFICERS
MO	Highway Patrol (1931)	Full service	Field Operations; Criminal Investigations; Governor Security	1,028
MT	Department of Justice, Montana Highway Patrol (1935)	Traffic	Field Services; Operations; Executive Protection	218
NE	State Patrol (1937)	Full service	Field Services; Investigative Services	491
NV	Department of Public Safety, Highway Patrol (1981)	Traffic	Traffic Law Enforcement	417
NH	Department of Public Safety, Division of State Police (1937)	Full service	Field Operations; Investigative Services	350
NJ	Department of Law and Public Safety (1948), State Police (1921)	Full service	Investigations; Operations; Homeland Security; Administration	3,053
NM	State Police (1935); formerly Mounted Police (1905)	Full service	Investigations; Uniform; Special Operations	528
NY	State Police (1917)	Full service	Uniformed Force; Specialized Services; Criminal Investigations; Office of Counter Terrorism	4,847
NC	Department of Public Safety (2012), Highway Patrol (1929)	Traffic	Patrol; Inspection; Internal Affairs	1,827
ND	Highway Patrol (1935)	Traffic	Field Operations	139
OH	Department of Public Safety, State Highway Patrol (1937)	Traffic*	Field Operations; Criminal Investigations; Special Operations; Strategic Operations	1,560
OK	Department of Public Safety, Highway Patrol (1937)	Full service	Field Troops; Investigations; Tactical; Executive Security; Capitol Patrol	825
OR	State Police (1931)	Full service	Patrol Services; Field Operations; Criminal Investigation	596

(continued)

Table 5.4   **Continued**

STATE	AGENCY (YEAR FOUNDED)	TYPE	MAJOR LAW ENFORCEMENT-RELATED BUREAUS/DIVISIONS/ UNITS	SWORN OFFICERS
PA	State Police (1905)	Full service	Patrol; Criminal Investigations	4,458
RI	Department of Public Safety, State Police (1923)	Full service	Patrol; Detective	201
SC	Department of Public Safety, Highway Patrol (1930)	Traffic	Field Operations; Specialized Units	967
SD	Department of Public Safety, Highway Patrol (1935)	Traffic	Patrol; Special Services Units	152
TN	Department of Public Safety and Homeland Security, Highway Patrol (1929)	Traffic	Field Operations; Protective Services; Special Investigations; Special Operations	942
TX	Department of Public Safety	Full service	Highway Patrol; Texas Rangers; Criminal Investigations; Intelligence and Counterterrorism	3,529
UT	Public Safety Department (1951), Highway Patrol (1925)	Traffic	Field Sections	475
VT	Department of Public Safety, State Police (1947)	Full service	Field Force; Criminal Investigations	307
VA	State Police (1932)	Full service	Criminal Investigation; Field Operations	1,873
WA	State Patrol (1921)	Full service	Field Operations; Investigative Services	1,132
WV	Department of Public Safety, State Police (1919)	Full service	Field Operations; Special Operations; Criminal Investigations; Executive Protection	667
WI	Transportation Department State Patrol (1939)	Traffic	Field Operations	492
WY	Transportation Department, Highway Patrol (1933)	Traffic	Operations; Field Operations	204

*Investigates crimes committed on state property.

SOURCES: Reaves 2011: 7; Torres 1987. (See respective agency websites for updated information.)

police agencies operate a state-level forensic lab whose services are available for all public policing agencies throughout the state; in some jurisdictions, the state bureau of investigation provides this service. Since September 11, 2001, the state police may house a state-level department of homeland security, although many large cities also operate a division dedicated to this purpose. NYPD's Demographics Unit is an example of this latter type of unit that essentially gathers local intelligence on possible terrorists. The state police may regulate the state gaming industry. They may also provide security on state-run university campuses, including security for coaches of the intercollegiate athletic teams.

There is great variability with respect to size, generally linked to the size of the state. Six state police organizations in the United States have more than 2,000 full-time sworn personnel, including California (7,202), New York (4,847), Pennsylvania (4,458), Texas (3,529), New Jersey (3,053), and Massachusetts (2,310). Combined, these six agencies account for 40 percent of all state police officers in the nation. Importantly among these six, only California Highway Patrol is not a full-service agency.

FEDERAL LAW ENFORCEMENT

For most of U.S. history, there have been few policing organizations at the federal level. Since the founding of the republic, various presidents, members of Congress, and the public at large have expressed concern about the establishment of a national secret police. Such an organization has long been seen as a threat to democratic ideals and basic freedoms. This topic resurfaces whenever Congress proposes a new federal law enforcement agency. Only reluctantly, then, has Congress authorized the creation and fiscal support of such agencies. Congress initially established most of these agencies, including such entities as the Coast Guard, Secret Service, Bureau of Customs, and Bureau of Alcohol and Tobacco, either to protect the nation's monetary system or to generate revenue. Only later did they and others assume general law enforcement missions resembling modern police forces.

Two departments of the federal government have sworn personnel who closely resemble police in the sense used in this chapter: The U.S. Department of Justice and the U.S. Department of Homeland Security. Congress established the former in 1870, and it has assumed a leadership role in the federal law enforcement community, largely owing to the fact that the U.S. attorney general directs it. Congress created the latter agency in 2003 out of a merger and redesignation of existing law enforcement agencies at the federal level, several of which had previously been a part of the U.S. Department of Treasury or the U.S.

Department of Justice. We begin with a look at the current law enforcement agencies and agents operating under the administrative control of the U.S. Department of Justice.

Before we examine each of these departments and their respective law enforcement agencies, two topics merit our attention. First is the question of official designations of the various positions within each agency. The Office of Personnel Management (OPM) classifies most police positions under the 1800 Occupational Series (inspection, investigation, enforcement, and compliance). The most common law-enforcement-related positions are the general agent position (criminal investigator) and the specialized agent (criminal investigator, treasury enforcement agent). Not all federal law enforcement positions possess full police powers. The following discussions are limited to those federal officers with full police powers and responsibilities.

Second is the question of training. Two main federal training agencies exist, outside of specialized training, such as that required generally by the U.S. Coast Guard or for agricultural specialists within the Department of Homeland Security. The Federal Bureau of Investigation and Drug Enforcement Administration train at their own academies located at the Marine Corps Base at Quantico, Virginia. Otherwise, all federal law enforcement personnel train at one of the three domestic Federal Law Enforcement Training Centers (FLETC) operated by DHS, one each in Glynco, Georgia; Artesia, New Mexico; and Charleston, South Carolina. Secret Service agents-in-training begin at FLETC-Glynco and complete their training at the James R. Rowley Training Center in Beltsville, Maryland.

U.S. Department of Justice

The Office of the Attorney General directs the U.S. Department of Justice. The law enforcement functions of the Office of the U.S. Attorney General are under the supervision of the deputy attorney general. Two of these agencies are not relevant for this chapter: The Bureau of Prisons (see Chapter 11) and INTERPOL-Washington (see Chapter 14). This section of the chapter explores the nature and extent of policing services provided by the following agencies: Federal Bureau of Investigation, Drug Enforcement Administration, U.S. Marshals Service, and Bureau of Alcohol, Tobacco, Firearms and Explosives.

Federal Bureau of Investigation

For nearly 40 years after the assassination of President Abraham Lincoln, the U.S. Department of Justice employed private detectives from agencies such as the Pinkertons or temporarily assigned agents from the U.S. Secret Service for its investigations. In 1908, President Theodore Roosevelt directed the U.S. attorney general to develop an investigative unit within the Department of Justice. This agency, known first as the Bureau of Investigation, became the Federal Bureau of Investigation (FBI) in 1935.[3]

It is impossible to discuss the growth and evolution of the FBI without including reference to J. Edgar Hoover, its director from 1924 until his death in 1972. Between assuming control of the FBI and World War II, Hoover oversaw many changes in the agency's mission, from investigating radical political activity, subversion, and espionage to combating interstate transportation of stolen motor vehicles, kidnapping, bank robbery, and interstate fugitives. He established the FBI Laboratory in 1932 and the National Academy in 1935. In the 1960s, Hoover and the FBI turned their attention to the antiwar and civil rights movements, both of which Hoover saw as threats to national security. The legal low point in this type of investigation was **COINTELPRO**, an FBI-sponsored counterintelligence program intended to investigate and disrupt the activities of "anti-American" groups and organizations in the late 1960s and early 1970s (Federal Bureau of Investigation, n.d.a). COINTELPRO often used illegal methods to survey, infiltrate, discredit, and disrupt domestic political organizations viewed as enemies of the administration. Because of several congressional investigations and in the wake of Hoover's death, the FBI instituted reforms to prevent future such abuses of power (Federal Bureau of Investigation, n.d.a).

The modern FBI has a much-expanded mission, especially since September 11, 2001, and the USA PATRIOT Act. The FBI's mission "is to protect and defend the United States against terrorist and foreign intelligence threats, to uphold and enforce the criminal laws of the United States, and to provide leadership and criminal justice services to federal, state, municipal, and international agencies and partners" (Federal Bureau of Investigation, n.d.c). It achieves these goals by focusing on the following types of crimes: terrorism and terrorist attacks, cybercrime and other high-tech crime, organized crime, public corruption, white-collar crime, and significant violent crime. It also provides support services upon request to state and local partners. One of the ways it achieves this latter goal is by providing advanced training for police officers at its FBI Academy in Quantico, Virginia. Another way is through its highly regarded Critical Incident Response Group, home to the FBI's Special Weapons and Tactics (SWAT) team and **Hostage Rescue Team (HRT)**, which together have 1,200 FBI agent-members. HRT is in Quantico, Virginia, and 56 FBI field offices have SWAT teams.

Drug Enforcement Administration

Beginning in 1912, the United States signed an international agreement to curb the flow of certain drugs, particularly heroin. Congress

COINTELPRO:
an "age of protest" FBI operation that implanted agents in alleged criminal groups and brought much discredit to the bureau

Hostage Rescue Team (HRT):
a highly trained and specialized unit within the FBI dedicated full time to counterterrorism and hostage rescue

passed the Harrison Narcotics Act in 1914 and assigned enforcement duties to the Treasury Department's Bureau of Internal Revenue. Drug enforcement duties shifted to Treasury's Prohibition Bureau in 1919, but that move was short-lived as Congress created the Federal Bureau of Narcotics (FBN) in 1930. Five years after the FBN moved to the Justice Department, President Richard Nixon created the Drug Enforcement Administration (DEA) out of the Bureau of Narcotics and Dangerous Drug, itself the heir to the FBN, plus a cluster of other federal agencies that had antidrug law enforcement duties.

The mission of the modern DEA includes enforcement of all U.S. laws and regulations concerning controlled substances. It brings cases to both the U.S. civil and criminal justice systems. It focuses on the growing, manufacture, or distribution of controlled substances that appear in or are destined for illicit traffic in the United States. Like the FBI, the DEA maintains a strong physical presence in the nation's embassies around the world, particularly those nations that figure strongly in the illicit drug trade as either nations of origin or transit nations. The DEA expends much of its investigative and law enforcement efforts in the domestic trade as well, which, given the recent trends toward the legalization of marijuana in particular, has placed the DEA in an awkward position.

U.S. Marshals Service

The oldest member of the federal law enforcement community, the U.S. Marshals Service, traces its origins to the Judiciary Act of 1789. A presidentially appointed U.S. marshal directs the activities of each of the 94 federal court districts. The competitive federal merit system oversees the selection of U.S. deputy marshals. The U.S. Marshals Service achieved agency status within the Justice Department in 1974.

The U.S. Marshals Service has six distinct functions. First, it provides security for the 94 district courts and 11 circuit courts, essentially protecting the entire federal judicial process. The agency employs more than 5,000 **court security officers**. A second mission, **fugitive operations**, was well established in the 18th and 19th centuries. Deputy marshals, working in collaboration with local and state police, as well as INTERPOL and other international policing organizations, locate and arrest dangerous pretrial and postadjudication fugitives. Third, the U.S. Marshals Service plays a central role in the Justice Department's **asset forfeiture program**, which "strips criminals of their ill-gotten gain." Two operational elements are more akin to corrections than policing, those being prisoner operations and prisoner transportation. In the former case, the U.S. Marshals Service must provide for the housing and care of persons accused of federal crimes, undergoing a legal appeal, or awaiting transfer to a Federal Bureau of Prisons facility, while in the latter, marshals are responsible for the

Court security officers:
nonmarshal members of the U.S. Marshals Service who provide physical security for the nation's federal courts and buildings

Fugitive operations:
a U.S. Marshals Service program intended to bring to justice escaped prisoners and others wanted under federal arrest or detainment orders

Asset forfeiture program:
Justice Department program for taking ill-gotten gains from criminals; run by the U.S. Marshals Service

physical transfer of those prisoners from one location to another, by either ground or air. Sixth, the U.S. Marshals Service operates the **Witness Security Program**, also known as the Witness Protection Program or WitSec. Since the beginning of this program, in 1971, the U.S. Marshals have protected more than 18,000 witnesses (U.S. Marshals Service 2014).

Witness Security Program:
a U.S. Marshals Service program that gives at-risk federal witnesses new identities; also called the Witness Protection Program or WitSec

Bureau of Alcohol, Tobacco, Firearms and Explosives

The history of alcohol control is the history of this nation, especially from the late 1780s to Prohibition. Department of Treasury revenue agents, also called revenuers, were responsible for stopping the highly profitable bootlegging and moonshining businesses before, during, and after Prohibition. From 1920 to 1933, these agents were with the Bureau of Prohibition; with the repeal of Prohibition, the agency became the Alcohol Tax Unit. Firearms enforcement laws became part of its mission in 1942, but the name was not changed. In the 1950s, it became the Alcohol and Tobacco Tax Division. In 1968, with passage of the Gun Control Act, the "ATF" designation, for alcohol, tobacco, and firearms, came into popular usage. Explosives were added in 1970 and arson investigations in 1982; however, the commonly used agency name—ATF—was not changed, even if the formal name did. ATF achieved bureau status under the Treasury Department in 1972 and went to the Department of Justice in 2003, when its tax collection duties for alcohol and tobacco became the work of a newly created Alcohol and Tobacco Tax and Trade Bureau, which remained in the Treasury Department.

The mission of ATF includes four jurisdictional areas. First, ATF regulates the firearms industry, enforces federal laws controlling firearms, and provides technical support to other federal, state, and local agencies regarding crimes involving firearms. Second, control of the explosives industry is also the purview of the ATF; moreover, explosives enforcement officers provide expertise in both investigations of events involving energetic materials (i.e., explosives) and bomb disposal. Third, ATF officers investigate arson-related federal crimes, and the ATF's Fire Research Laboratory provides technical support related to both arson and explosive events. Fourth, ATF combats alcohol smuggling and contraband cigarette trafficking. Agents investigate domestic and international criminals across these four areas.

U.S. Department of Justice: The Agents

Table 5.5 provides a summary overview of the four Department of Justice (DOJ) law enforcement agencies. The DOJ employs nearly 23,000 law enforcement officers, more than half of whom work as FBI special agents, police officers, or criminal investigators. While nearly everyone knows about FBI special agents, less well known

Table 5.5   By the Numbers: Department of Justice Law Enforcement Agencies

AGENCY	LAW ENFORCEMENT DIVISIONS/OFFICES	JOB TITLES	FULL-TIME LEOS*
All DOJ Agencies			22,922
Federal Bureau of Investigation	Counterterrorism; Counterintelligence; Criminal Investigations; Cyber; Critical Incident Response Group; International Operations; Office of Law Enforcement Cooperation; Laboratory Division; Training; Weapons of Mass Destruction Directorate	Special Agent; Police Officer; Criminal Investigator	12,760
Drug Enforcement Administration	Operations; Intelligence; EPIC	Special Agent; Criminal Investigator	4,308
U.S. Marshals Service	Court Security Officer Program; Witness Protection Program; Special Operations/ Special Operations Group; Justice Prisoner and Alien Transportation System; Department of Justice Asset Forfeiture Program; Office of Emergency Management	U.S. Marshal; Deputy U.S. Marshal; Criminal Investigator	3,313
Bureau of Alcohol, Tobacco, Firearms and Explosives	Office of Enforcement Programs and Services; Office of Strategic Intelligence and Information; Office of Field Operations	Special Agent; Criminal Investigator	2,541

*A law enforcement officer, or LEO, is defined for the purposes of this report as a person who has arrest powers and is authorized to carry a firearm.
SOURCE: U.S. Government Accountability Office 2006; Reaves 2012a: 2.

are the FBI police officers, who provide security and basic police services in and around key FBI facilities. The Drug Enforcement Administration has only about one-third as many full-time sworn officers serving as either special agents or **diversion investigators**, the latter focusing on specific drug problems, including Internet pharmacies. The U.S. Marshals Service, with 3,313 full-time law enforcement officers

Diversion investigators: DEA investigators who specialize in finding the ways legal drugs are diverted to the illicit drug market

(LEOs), is third in size among DOJ law enforcement agencies. Assigned to the nation's 94 judicial districts and headquartered near Washington, D.C., U.S. marshals, deputy marshals, and criminal investigators operate numerous programs under the aegis of the U.S. Marshals Service. Detention enforcement officers and aviation enforcement officers are primarily responsible for transporting federal prisoners, the latter exclusively by aircraft operated by the **Justice Prisoner and Alien Transportation System (JPATS)**. Finally, ATF has barely 10 percent of DOJ's complement of full-time LEOs. Industry operations investigators perform inspections and investigations related to that part of the ATF's regulatory mission centering on firearms and explosives. Special agents work in all phases of the ATF's various missions.

Justice Prisoner and Alien Transportation System (JPATS):
the air wing of the U.S. Marshals Service that moves prisoners and undocumented aliens around the nation

U.S. Department of Homeland Security

September 11, 2001, is a date we have referenced several times in this text. Congress and President George W. Bush set about reorganizing the nation's federal law enforcement agencies to meet what was widely viewed as a sea-change event and threat: international terrorists striking the homeland. On March 1, 2003, the newly created **Department of Homeland Security (DHS)** absorbed the Immigration and Naturalization Service (INS) and the U.S. Customs Service. It subsequently split the function of these two agencies into two entities: Immigration and Customs Enforcement and Citizenship and Immigration Services. The former is primarily a law enforcement agency; the latter is largely a civil regulatory agency, although its agents conduct some criminal investigations into fraud. The INS's border enforcement functions, including the U.S. Border Patrol and the Animal and Plant Health Inspection Service, merged into a new agency within DHS, U.S. Customs and Border Protection. In a somewhat controversial move, the U.S. Secret Service left the Treasury for DHS. In addition, the Coast Guard, which had been part of either the Defense Department or Transportation Department, became an agency within DHS. The Federal Emergency Management Agency (FEMA) also became a part of DHS. Finally, Congress created the Transportation Security Agency (TSA) in 2001 and made it part of the Department of Transportation. In 2003, TSA, along with its law enforcement division, the Federal Air Marshal Service, became elements within DHS. Currently, DHS includes five law enforcement agencies that are the primary concern of this chapter, beginning with U.S. Customs and Border Protection (CBP).

Department of Homeland Security (DHS):
a cabinet-level department created in the aftermath of the events of September 11, 2001; includes new law enforcement entities and existing ones taken from other federal law enforcement divisions with the goal of protecting the United States and its territories from and responding to terrorist attacks, human-originated accidents, and natural disasters

U.S. Customs and Border Protection

Customs and Border Protection (CBP) in the United States has a long history. The Customs Service dates from 1789. Until the creation of income tax in 1913, revenue from the Customs Service, located in the

Treasury Department, was the nation's primary source of income. The Customs Service dissolved in 2003 with the creation of DHS's CBP. For its part, immigration control had also been part of Treasury's mission since the late 19th century. Early in the 20th century, Congress authorized mounted watchmen to prevent illegal border crossings, and these evolved in 1915 into "mounted inspectors." The Border Patrol formed in 1924 as part of the Department of Labor but became part of the Justice Department before World War II, where it would remain until 2003.

The largest part of DHS, Customs and Border Protection (CBP) regulates and facilitates international trade, largely by collecting import duties and enforcing trade, customs, and immigration regulations. CBP works with other federal agencies, such as the DEA, to stem the flow of illegal drugs and other contraband items, including but not limited to counterfeit and untaxed products. A significant part of CBP's activities involves securing the nation's border through the actions of either the Border Patrol (BP) or the Office of Field Operations (OFO). BP agents serve in static and mobile activities intended to secure the nation's physical borders. In some rural areas, deputized BP agents enforce local and state or territory laws as well as federal laws. CBP officers in the OFO, generally located at or near border-crossing points, have full law enforcement powers, make arrests, conduct searches, bear firearms, and serve warrants and other legal orders.

Other parts of CBP are less well known. For example, CBP agricultural specialists, part of the Animal and Plant Health Inspection Service, target dangerous diseases and infestations and combat agroterrorism. The second less well-known part of CBP is the Office of Air and Marine (OAM), the world's largest civil aviation and maritime law enforcement organization. OAM's mission, in line with the larger mission of CBP, is to protect the American people and the nation's critical infrastructure through the coordinated use of integrated air and marine forces. These forces detect, interdict, and prevent terrorism and unlawful movement of illegal drugs and contraband, along with undocumented persons, toward or across the nation's borders.

U.S. Coast Guard

Founded in 1790 as a "Revenue Marine," the U.S. Coast Guard is unique among the nation's law enforcement agencies and U.S. military forces. In peacetime, it enforces U.S. laws at sea in the world's largest exclusive economic zone (EEZ). In wartime, it is part of the U.S. Department of Defense. Called the U.S. Revenue Cutter Service from the 1860s to 1915, when it was renamed the U.S. Coast Guard (USCG) and made a part of the Treasury Department, where it remained until it was moved to DHS in 2003. U.S. Code authorizes active and reserve commissioned officers, warrant officers, and petty officers to serve as federal customs officers, granting them general federal police authority.

Today the USCG provides security in the nation's ports and waterways. It participates in federal drug and illegal migration interdiction efforts. The USCG is also involved in the nation's war on terrorism, especially given the nation's huge expanse of coastline. In its non-law enforcement capacity, the USCG also engages in search and rescue operations and marine environmental protection and aids navigation. As part of its EEZ policing duties, the Coast Guard prevents illegal fishing, thereby maintaining the integrity of the nation's maritime borders and protecting the health of U.S. fisheries.

U.S. Immigration and Customs Enforcement

Congress created Immigration and Customs Enforcement (ICE) in 2003, merging the investigative and intelligence resources of the U.S. Customs Service, the detention and deportation resources of INS, and the entire Federal Protective Service. In 2009, the Federal Protective Service moved to the National Protection and Programs Directorate. ICE consists of two law enforcement directorates. First, the Enforcement and Removal Operations (ERO) enforces the nation's immigration laws and makes certain that "removed" aliens depart the United States. Second, Homeland Security Investigations (HSI) has broad legal authority across a range of issues that threaten national security, from all forms of illegal trafficking and smuggling (e.g., humans, drugs, arms) to human rights violations to computer crimes to money laundering. HSI special agents also provide executive protection for visiting dignitaries and witness protection and, as needed, augment the U.S. Secret Service.

U.S. Secret Service

Formed in 1865 with the mission of protecting the nation's currency and other monetary instruments, the Secret Service divided into two missions after the assassination of William McKinley in 1901: Investigations and Protective Services. Until the creation of the Bureau of Investigation in 1908, it had served as this nation's only domestic intelligence and counterintelligence agency. The U.S. Secret Service (USSS) moved to the Department of Homeland Security in 2003.

As an investigative agency, the Secret Service safeguards U.S. payment and financial systems, which includes jurisdiction over any crimes that involve financial institution fraud, computer and telecommunications fraud, false identification documents, access device fraud, advance fee fraud, electronic funds transfer, and money laundering. A recent focus combining several of these areas is identity theft and related crimes. Criminal investigations are often international in nature, as counterfeit currency may originate outside the United States, and counterfeit versions of other nations' currency may originate within U.S. borders. In short, the USSS has within its jurisdiction virtually any monetary instrument, physical or electronic, that is vulnerable to a criminal enterprise.

As part of their protective missions, Secret Service agents protect the following individuals: the president, the vice president (or other persons in order of succession), the president elect and the vice president-elect, immediate family members of all protected persons, former presidents and their spouses for their lifetimes (unless a spouse remarries), and minor children of former presidents. This mission can extend to visiting heads of foreign nations and their families, major presidential and vice presidential candidates and their spouses (within 120 days of a general election), other persons at the order of the president, and national special security events (designated as such by the secretary of the Department of Homeland Security).

U.S. Department of Homeland Security: The Agents

Table 5.6 contains the agencies, associated law enforcement divisions and offices, and law-enforcement-related job titles found within DHS.

Table 5.6 By the Numbers: Department of Homeland Security Law Enforcement Agencies			
AGENCY (YEAR FOUNDED/REFORMED)	**LAW ENFORCEMENT DIVISIONS/OFFICES**	**JOB TITLES**	**FULL-TIME LEOS***
All DHS law enforcement agencies			49,835**
U.S. Customs and Border Protection (1789/2003)	Office of Field Operations; Office of Border Patrol; Office of Air and Marine	Criminal Investigator; Border Patrol Agent; Customs and Border Protection Officer; Police Officer	30,080
U.S. Coast Guard (1790/2003)	Districts; Mission Execution Units; Intelligence and Criminal Investigation	Criminal Investigator; Maritime Boarding Law Enforcement Officers	3,972
U.S. Immigration and Customs Enforcement (1789/2003)	Homeland Security Investigations; Intelligence; International Operations; Enforcement and Removal Operations	Criminal Investigator; Special Agent; Police Officer; Deportation Officer; Immigration Enforcement Officer	10,482
U.S. Secret Service (1865/2003)	Special Agents; Uniformed Division	Special Agent; Criminal Investigator	4,964

* A law enforcement officer, or LEO, is defined for the purposes of this report as a person who can do any of the following activities: (1) conduct criminal investigations, (2) execute search warrants, (3) make arrests, or (4) carry firearms.

** Includes 158 Office of Inspector General special agent, criminal investigator/special agent, criminal investigator, and investigator positions.

SOURCES: Berrick and Wilshusen 2008: 18; U.S. Government Accountability Office 2006.

The first relevant point made in this table is that DHS is enormous, including nearly 50,000 full-time LEO positions. Second and related to the first point, three agencies are preeminent when it comes to DHS's law enforcement activities: U.S. Customs and Border Protection (CBP), U.S. Immigration and Customs Enforcement (ICE), and U.S. Secret Service (USSS). Specifically, CBP employs more than 60 percent of the LEO positions in DHS, which includes the Border Patrol. The next-largest LEO component found in DHS is ICE, which has slightly more than one in five of DHS's allotment of LEO positions. USSS, which has suffered a public-relations problem in recent years, is smaller, with fewer than 5,000 full-time sworn officers, most of whom are special agents. A smaller contingent, the uniformed division, protects the White House. The USCG includes the multimission specialist called the boarding law enforcement officer, accounting for nearly 4,000 LEOs.

Four DHS agencies operate relatively small (all fewer than 100 personnel) LEO contingents (not included in Table 5.6), although the exact number is classified in the case of the TSA's Federal Air Marshal Service. The service has both air marshals and criminal investigators. The various FLETCs around the nation employ few criminal investigators or law enforcement specialists who provide safety and security for the facility itself. For its part, FEMA operates a relatively small security branch with fewer than 100 police officers. Finally, Citizenship and Immigration Services employs a small number of special agents and investigative specialists in its Fraud Detection and National Security Directorate.

SUMMARY

At the outset of this chapter, we suggest not only that the topic of the nature and extent of policing in the United States is central to the understanding of our criminal justice system but also that it is a complex topic. At the local level exist tens of thousands of jurisdictions and empowering entities. As we move to the county-level, the picture becomes no less complex; indeed, not only is county-level law enforcement a question of American justice, but it is also a seminal political institution. At the state level, there is also considerable variation, ranging from small highway patrol agencies to large full-service police forces.

Federal policing tends to intrigue criminal justice students, many of whom see themselves as a future "fed." Statistically, the odds favor securing a law enforcement position at the local or even state level over federal employment. More signficantly, however, the federal agencies have far higher selection requirements and training standards than do most local and even state-level policing agencies.

In closing this chapter, we acknowledge that while on some levels this review of local, state, and federal law enforcement is very detailed and complete, much remains for the serious student of law enforcement to discover. The journey begins at the website of the agency of interest. The next chapter provides another element in that journey, as we explore the issues related to contemporary policing.

REVIEW QUESTIONS

1. When looking at the numerical overview of the nation's state and local general services policing agencies, what surprised you most and why?
2. Does your state certify marshals? Where? What are their duties? How many marshals are there in your state? Is this position outdated in the 21st century?
3. Three organizational charts for policing agencies are included in this chapter. Find the organizational chart for a local jurisdictional (i.e., nonfederal, nonstate) police agency near you. Compare and contrast its organization to one of the charts found in this chapter, addressing how they are similar and different.
4. Do you think police consolidation is a good idea? Explain. Be sure to address all forms of police consolidation in your answer.
5. Examine your state's police agency. What is its subject matter jurisdiction? What is its organization? Is it a full-service or traffic patrol agency? If the latter, who provides for criminal investigations at the state level? Does it include a homeland defense component? If not, who addresses these concerns in your state?
6. Respond to the following statement: We need to create a national police with a stronger local presence and great police powers.
7. If you were to apply to a federal agency for employment, which one would it be and why? Which one would you avoid and why?
8. Complete the following sentence, explaining how you arrived at your conclusion: "The one critical lesson I have learned about the structure of law enforcement in this nation is . . ."

KEY TERMS

asset forfeiture program
COINTELPRO
court security officers
Department of Homeland Security (DHS)
diversion investigators
fugitive operations
general services law enforcement agencies
hostage rescue team (HRT)
judicial marshals
Justice Prisoner and Alien Transportation System (JPATS)
professional standards unit (PSU)
public information office (PIO)
Witness Security Program

NOTES

1. In 2008, the Chicago Police Department employed 13,354 full-time sworn officers, while the Smithsonian Zoological Park Police had 26 officers with arrest powers and authorization to carry firearms (Reaves 2011: 4, 2012a: 5).

2. The following discussion of state, county, and local law enforcement derives from Reaves 2011. The data reported in that document are part of a quadrennial report to the nation on full-service policing agencies of this nature. This report includes the findings of the 2008 survey; the 2012 survey results are not yet available.

3. Unless otherwise stated, the information reported for each of the federal departments and agencies within each one came from the respective agency's website.

Issues in Law Enforcement

LEARNING OBJECTIVES

At the conclusion of this chapter, you should be able to:

- Describe the various issues that threaten to limit the effectiveness of the police, largely by eroding public trust and confidence.

- Understand the role played by (and limitations of) the police professionalism movement in curbing problems related to policing contemporary society.

- Distinguish among the forms of police misconduct, including corruption and the misuse of force, that confront the police in the 21st century.

- Explain the impact the judiciary has on police misconduct and police work generally.

INTRODUCTION

Of the three major components of the criminal justice system (police, courts, and corrections) that we examine in this text, the police seem to have the most public visibility and, as a result, perhaps the highest levels of public scrutiny and criticism. In this chapter, we examine a series of issues that have confronted police agencies throughout their history and those that seem to be particularly relevant. Some issues result from deficiencies in policies and practices, and others derive from the fact that we must recruit officers from the communities they serve. Thus, many police flaws are simply reflections of our flaws as a society.

Moreover, those flaws are not distributed equally across the na-tion. Consider Figure 6.1, which provides a standardized measure of

Figure 6.1 National Police Misconduct Statistics and Reporting Project (NPMSRP) 2009 police misconduct rate density map

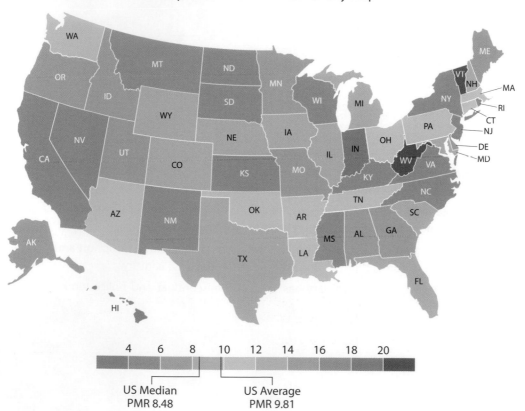

NOTE: PMR is a projected 12-month total of media-based reports of police misconduct, which forms the basis of the per-1,000 officer misconduct rate based on the 2008 UCR statewide sworn law enforcement officer employment rate for that given state.
SOURCE: Adapted from Cato Institute 2010.

the density of state-level **police misconduct**. The types of misconduct summarized in this figure are taken from newspaper and other media accounts of such incidents and include the following: assaults (e.g., physical violence occurring while off duty), brutality (e.g., physical violence occurring while on duty), sexual (e.g., sex-related incidents), theft (e.g., robbery, theft, shoplifting, fraud, extortion, and bribery), shooting (e.g., gun-related incidents both on and off duty, including self-harm), color of law (e.g., incidents that involve the misuse of authority), and perjury (e.g., false testimony, dishonesty during investigations, falsified charging papers, and falsified warrants). If the occurrence of police misconduct was random, then the map would be one color, which is not the case.

On a per capita basis, the five "worst" states—those with the highest officer misconduct densities—are, in descending order, West Virginia, Vermont, Indiana, New Mexico, and Montana. The absolute worst jurisdiction for reported officer misconduct is the District of Columbia. The five states with the lowest per capita rates of misconduct are, in ascending order, Hawaii, New Jersey, Kansas, North Dakota, and Kentucky. While we must consider these rankings carefully, owing to their source, they suggest that officer misconduct is a national problem that also has considerable regional variation. To gain an understanding of what is behind these statistics, we turn to an exploration of police professionalism as a bulwark against misconduct and related concerns.

Police misconduct: any action by a police officer that violates a standard of professional conduct as defined by the employing department

PROFESSIONALISM

One of the most consistent themes to emerge from the national commission reports of the 1960s was the need to professionalize policing at all levels. These reports led to a major expansion of criminal justice education at all levels, from associate degrees to doctoral programs. The idea driving this movement was that a better-educated and better-informed police force was less likely to experience the kinds of problems that existed between the public and the police.

In the intervening years, a debate has emerged in policing circles that centers on whether policing is a profession or a craft (White 2007). On the craft side of the ledger are those practitioners, researchers, and policy makers who view classroom learning as largely irrelevant to officers in the field (Bayley and Bittner 1984). Indeed, Wilson (1968) argues that police work is heavily dependent on what is learned on the job, a generalist work ethic, a lack of deference to authority, and the existence of an oral tradition; it is more craft than profession (see also Crank 1990). On the other side is the argument that police work is a profession owing to its specialized body of knowledge and skills, national and statewide accreditation, orientation toward clients in a service capacity, high levels of discretion, and nonprofit orientation (White 2007; see also Capps 1998; Crank, Payn, and Jackson 1993; Radelet and Carter 1994).

The merger of the strengths of academia and the street—the theoretical and the practical, classroom learning and on-the-job training—may well direct the police professionalism movement well into the 21st century (White 2007). Training provides the new officer with the basic skills required to perform the job, which are refined and honed during the probationary period and through early work experiences. Education, gleaned from both the police academy and higher education, can provide essential critical thinking skills, a broad understanding of society, and the role of the criminal justice system in it, and insights into crime, justice, and human behavior. The document that initiated this debate also reflects this position. As the authors of *Task Force Report: The Police* expressed it, "The trained man has developed skills and attitudes needed to perform a complex task. The educated man has developed capacity to judge the worth, the performance, and the excellence of human action" (President's Commission on Law Enforcement and Administration of Justice 1967b: 127).

Elements of Modern Police Professionalism

A merger of education *and* training, then, would seem to be the bellwether of modern professional policing. The first factor in defining any profession is the adequacy of the training necessary to do the job. For example, consider the professions of medicine and law. Doctors have a great deal of education, but they also undergo years of rigorous on-the-job training in the form of internships and rotations. Lawyers, by contrast, have about the same number of years of formal education, but the on-the-job training can come at the expense of their clients. Box 6.1 includes a description of the police personality, which in the minds of many police experts is an impediment to police professionalism.

Prior to the 1960s, many police departments largely implemented only on-the-job training, supplemented by a field training officer for new police recruits. Today, all 50 states and the District of Columbia have boards, councils, or commissions that oversee the basic training standards for sworn police personnel. These agencies, often called **police officer standards and training (or POST) commissions/councils**, are responsible for the licensure of peace officers, reserve peace officers, basic training instructors, curriculum, and training centers. The principal goal is to ensure that before commissioning officers to enforce the law, they receive adequate training in a wide variety of subjects. States typically also give the POST the authority to revoke a

Police officer standards and training (POST) commissions/councils: statewide entities that standardize and certify officers and their training

Box 6.1   **The Police Personality: Impediment to Professionalism?**

Arthur Niederhoffer, in his seminal work on police (1969), suggested that the difficulties experienced by police in their interactions with the public, and a possible barrier to seeing police work as a profession, is the high incidence of authoritarianism among police. Aggressiveness, assertiveness, and cynicism characterize this personality type. The nature and extent of the **police personality** has been debated for decades, including whether it is the result of selective recruitment to police work (i.e., recruits are attracted to policing because it fits their existing personality traits) or organizational socialization (i.e., the police department shapes the personality of those admitted to the force). What researchers generally agree on is that the extent to which the police exhibit these characteristics may make for compliant officers within the department but can create problems when they encounter the public.

This debate is far from settled, but there is a measure of truth in each position. Even if police officers are more conservative, more cynical, and more assertive, is this necessarily a bad thing? The answer to this question largely depends on the situations in which the officers find themselves. If they are responding to a call for assistance from the distraught parent of a missing child, an assertive and take-charge attitude might be welcome; if they are responding to an armed, barricaded, and aggressive suspect, this attitude could be like pouring gasoline on an open flame.

Police personality: the idea that there is a special type of person who is either attracted to police work or is produced by it; that person tends to be authoritarian and cynical

SOURCES: Anson, Mann, and Sherman 1986; Poole and Regoli 1980; Niederhoffer 1969; Twerksy-Glasner 2005; Wilt and Brannon 1976.

police officer's commission if the officer is found to have violated certain procedures or laws.

Another challenge for local police that emerged out of the reports of the 1960s involved education. The 1967 President's Commission on Law Enforcement and Administration of Justice recommended that police officers have a four-year degree. This requirement is not yet a universal preemployment requirement for police service. Many of the federal law enforcement agencies require at least a bachelor's degree, and some state and local agencies have followed this pattern. The vast majority of state and local agencies continue to require only a high school diploma or a general education development (GED) certificate for employment, although many reward officers who seek college degrees in the form of pay raises or promotions.[1]

A third factor is the degree to which the community recognizes a particular occupation as a profession. The "traditional" professions are law and medicine, with some adding theology or even business occupations to this short list. As a result, even though the police may approach their duties in a professional way, which August Vollmer and others recommended in the 1940s, it has been very difficult for law enforcement to be formally recognized as a profession by governmental entities and the public at large. For example, the U.S. Equal Employment Opportunity Commission (EEOC) classifies police officers as "service workers," its lowest-ranked occupational category (U.S. Equal Employment Opportunity Commission, n.d.). Law enforcers looking outside their own ranks for validation of police work as a profession versus a craft, as suggested in Box 6.2, face an uphill battle.

The Police Unionization Movement

In the minds of many police experts, the police unionization movement threatens to derail police professionalism. What professions, they ask, are unionized? Are doctors members of unions in the United States? Do lawyers have a trade union? Does not the idea of a trade union fly in the face of the basic elements of a profession? The police unionization movement dates to the years immediately following World War I. The

---

Box 6.2 Police as Professionals: You Be the Judge

Arthur Niederhoffer observed that professions have the following characteristics:

1. *High standards of admission:* Not everyone who applies is accepted.
2. *A specialized body of knowledge and theory:* As a rule, the body of knowledge and theory included has some linguistic elements that are unique to it and unknown to the uninitiated; the emphasis on theory, as a prerequisite for a profession, often surprises undergraduate students.
3. *Altruism and dedication to service ideal:* Lawyers and doctors alike often engage in voluntary or licensure-required *pro publico bono* (i.e., for the public good).
4. *A code of ethics:* The training phase exposes pre-professionals to the elements of a code that serves as a proscriptive guide for ethical behavior; practitioners must hold to it as they engage in their profession.
5. *A lengthy period of training for candidates:* The order is typically education first, followed by pre- and in-service training with the training lasting anywhere from several months to several years.
6. *Licensure of members:* Practitioners are eligible to work in the profession only after passing a national, regional, or state licensing examination.
7. *Autonomous control:* Once admitted to the profession, incumbents have freedom to act without the oversight of others, except the code of ethics.
8. *Pride of the members in their profession:* Given the first seven characteristics, it is easy to understand this one.
9. *Publicly recognized status and prestige:* Both the public at large and governmental agencies, such as the U.S. Equal Employment Opportunity Commission, recognize this by their rankings of various occupations, placing certain professions like law and medicine at the top.

Having reviewed the preceding information, what do you think? Is policing a profession? Does this designation matter?

SOURCE: Niederhoffer 1969.

American Federation of Labor, a predecessor to the American Federation of Labor and Congress of Industrial Organizations (AFL-CIO), chartered a number of police unions, including one in Boston. City administrators argued that police had no more right to organize than did the military (Levine 1988). When Boston city officials did not respond positively to union demands for higher wages, the officers responded in what became a bloody police strike. Calvin Coolidge, governor of Massachusetts and later president of the United States, responded by ordering the city to fire the strikers and dissolve the union.

By 1920, the police union movement went into a 20-year hiatus. Instead, the police joined existing benevolent and fraternal organizations, such as the New York Patrolman's Benevolent Association (PBA) and Philadelphia's Fraternal Order of Police (FOP). These organizations brought their members' demands to the attention of local elected officials. The International Association of Chiefs of Police (IACP) praised the efforts of these groups. In general, the PBAs and FOPs were policy neutral, spending most of their time, energies, and money on issues related to their members' health and welfare, advocating for them with local politicians and the voters (Levine 1988).

A second police unionization movement took place at the start of World War II. This time, the American Federation of State, County, and Municipal Employees (AFSCME) led the campaign. It too was rejected by elected and police officials. Once again, opponents offered the military analogy as a reason to reject unions, and, in a series of legal actions (*City of Jackson v. McLeod* (1946), *Perez v. Board of Police Commissioners* (1947), *King v. Priest* (1947)), state and federal appellate courts upheld the officials' right to ban unions. In 1944, the IACP published a pamphlet listing the reasons against unionizing police officers. Reviewing police departments around the nation, the IACP concluded that besides the emerging body of legal decisions, unions were incompatible with police work and the police profession; moreover, cities could not negotiate with unions. Quietly, behind the scenes, the FOPs and PBAs continued to represent officers in the same way they had for nearly 50 years.

As noted several times, the police often found themselves at the center of the maelstrom during the civil rights and antiwar protests, either holding apart opposing sides or participating in the protests themselves, as in the Chicago Police Riot of 1968. Police staged their own protests during the 1960s, engaging in work slowdowns and similar job actions (Ayres 1977). At the same time, police FOPs and PBAs became politicized, adopting an increasingly militant stand toward candidates for office. The political war cry became, "Recognize our needs and demands or we will do more than simply not support you, we will work to defeat you" (Levine 1988: 341). By the early 1970s,

PBAs and FOPs had become de facto police unions, supported by formal grievance resolution procedures for officers and collective bargaining agreements. They were unions in all but name.

In the 21st century, many organizations compete to represent police officers in those states that allow them to form unions or union-like groups. The **Fraternal Order of Police**, a national organization founded in 1915, is a full-fledged trade union and fraternal organization. Its formal relationship with the entity authorizing the police depends on state laws and local ordinances. The **International Union of Police Associations (IUPA)**, an affiliate of the AFL-CIO, dates to 1978 and is an umbrella group for local police organizations. Depending on state law, police officers have access to unions and collective bargaining. One issue remains: the strike.

Special Case: The Police Strike

The ultimate weapon in every union's arsenal—including police unions—is the strike. The police can threaten a work action if their requests for changes to working conditions or increased compensation are not met. They can engage in work slowdowns. They can call in sick, sometimes called the **"blue flu."** Unless they are willing to strike—to walk the picket line and refuse to provide services—the union is little more than a liaison between the officers and their employers.

The police strike that for a century has defined this issue is the 1919 Boston police strike.[2] In September, most of Boston's police force went out on strike. Governor Coolidge ordered the Metropolitan Park Police to replace the strikers, but that solution proved to be an ineffective stopgap. After several days of violence, Coolidge ordered out the National Guard, who employed all possible means to reestablish order, making the city of Boston resemble a modern urban combat zone. Other unionized workers joined the strike. Reason prevailed as matters threatened to spiral out of control. The city fired the striking officers. The city subsequently hired more new officers than worked on the force before the strike—at higher wages and with more benefits.

The 1919 Boston police strike became a touchstone for antiunionists for the next 50 years or more. Police strikes were relatively rare. However, between 1971 and 1981, New York, New York; Baltimore, Maryland; Las Cruces, New Mexico; Cleveland, Ohio; New Orleans, Louisiana; Birmingham, Alabama; San Francisco and Santa Barbara, California; and Milwaukee, Wisconsin experienced police strikes, sometimes punctuated by acts of violence. In most cases, the aftermath was one of distrust between the citizens and the police and among the officers themselves, particularly between those who struck and those who continued working. The lessons of those years seem to have paid dividends, as a police strike, or even the threat of one, is a

Fraternal Order of Police (FOP):
a social organization for police, begun in the late 19th century, that in 1915 morphed into a formal organization—a police union

International Union of Police Associations (IUPA):
an affiliate of the AFL-CIO that represents police across the nation

"Blue flu":
police work slowdowns, generally achieved by officers calling in sick and failing to report for duty

rare event in the United States in the 21st century. If any single event threatens the public's perception of police, reducing the possibility of its consideration as a profession, it is the strike, especially when that strike involves violence (Anderson et al. 1976; Bopp, Chignell, and Maddox 1977; Palmer 2004).

In closing, the following generalizations seem to characterize the current state of police professionalism, but especially the role played by higher education. First, the police see themselves as professionals, even though the public does not always accept this status. The unionization movement—especially the use of work actions, including the blue flu and strikes—and certain elements of the putative police personality threaten how the public sees the police.

Second, federal law enforcement agencies, more than local or even state police, require a college degree for entry-level positions, although there are some exceptions to that generalization. For example, many jobs in Homeland Security's Transportation Security Administration (TSA) and federal security guard positions do not require more than a high school diploma and the absence of felony convictions, which is the employment norm for the majority of the nation's local law enforcement agencies (Hickman and Reeves 2003).

Third, there is little reason to believe that a college education creates a better overall police officer, although there is some evidence that college-educated officers may make more appropriate judgments in their interactions with the public, particularly being less prone to misuse force than non-college-educated officers (Poaline and Terrill 2007; Rydberg and Terrill 2010). Many departments view a college degree positively when considering a candidate for promotion, although a college degree is not sufficient by itself for either employment or promotion (Gau, Terrill, and Poaline 2013).

Finally, many police officers indicate that they selected their current job partly because of an existing system that rewards college education with pay increases or provides college tuition support for officers or both (Reaves 2012b). Thus, the relationship between police professionalism and higher education in the 21st century remains in flux, but the evidence and trends suggest more rather than less education leads to a more professional and less problematic police force.

CORRUPTION

All forms of **police corruption** involve the misuse of authority. However, some misuses of authority do not fit neatly into the category of corruption, especially if the act rises to the level of a crime. For example, police officers may use their positions to get free items (e.g., coffee or meals) or substantial discounts (e.g., on automobile tires

Police corruption: all forms of law enforcement misuse of authority, ranging from the acceptance of gifts and gratuities to officer-involved criminal homicide

or household appliances). Departments may have policies against accepting **gratuities**, but these are typically administrative matters and not criminal acts. Police actions (and inactions) that rise above administrative malfeasance to the level of crimes not only threaten to erode public confidence in the police but also threaten justice itself.

Gratuities:
gifts, whether solicited or unsolicited, to police officers as a result of their official positions

Nature of Corruption

Waves of corruption have threatened a few police departments throughout their histories. One of the most visible reports of corruption in a major police department came about when New York City mayor John Lindsay appointed a commission to investigate alleged police corruption. Known as the **Knapp Commission**, after its chairperson, Whitman Knapp, this body found a variety of corrupt practices inside the New York City Police Department (NYPD). Included in its findings were situations where police officers were involved in outright thefts (Armstrong 2012). Some officers also accepted money not to enforce the laws against vice crimes such as drugs, gambling, and prostitution. The commission found officers on the payroll of organized crime families and others who alerted members of organized crime to the existence of investigations or possible informants. The commission's final report classified corrupt officers into two broad groups. First were the **"meat eaters."** These officers actively sought corrupt opportunities for personal gain. Second were the **"grass eaters,"** officers who were passive in terms of corruption; they did not seek out opportunities for illegal gain, but they were willing to accept a bribe or kickback if offered one (Knapp Commission 1972).

Knapp Commission:
a special investigation team in the 1970s that found widespread corruption in the NYPD, mostly related to protection and graft

"Meat eaters":
the Knapp Commission's designation for police officers who actively sought opportunities for corruption, mostly related to drug trade and violence

"Grass eaters":
the Knapp Commission's designation for police officers who accepted bribes for overlooking crimes, but who did not actively solicit such bribes

Twenty years later, New York City mayor David N. Dinkins appointed Milton Mollen to investigate allegations of continued corruption in the NYPD. The **Mollen Commission** (1994) reported that the most prevalent forms of police corruption involved the illegal drug trade. This finding contrasted with the Knapp Commission, which found that most police corruption centered on police oversight of illegal activities, most commonly bookmaking, or illegal gambling. The Mollen Commission concluded that whereas in the days of the Knapp Commission corruption generally involved crimes of accommodation—police officers giving and taking bribes or buying and selling protection—20 years later, the corruption was far more brutal, involving theft, high levels of abuse of authority, and active police criminality. The Knapp Commission found that grass eaters were the rule and meat eaters the exception; the Mollen Commission found that this pattern had reversed in the intervening 20 years.

Mollen Commission:
a special investigation team in the 1990s that found widespread corruption in the NYPD

The police today engage in a wide array of illegal behaviors. Two conditions must be met for the conduct to be considered police corruption, both of which are suggested in the two NYPD examples and are

Box 6.3   "Jammed Up": The Lessons of the NYPD and Beyond

Officers in fact and fiction describe being **"jammed up."** This term means that for external or internal reasons, the organization for which the officers work has decided to conduct an investigation into the possible corrupt practices of its officers. Robert Kane and Michael White's (2013) study of 20 years of NYPD disciplinary records for 1,500 officers is instructive in this regard. Overall, they report, the NYPD was twice as likely to separate black officers from the force for misconduct as white officers. In recent years, however, this difference decreased to the point that by 1996 the rates of career-ending misconduct for both groups were virtually the same.

The authors suggest that several factors may account for these racial differences. First, given differential hiring practices, black officers, who were in the minority, could have come under heightened scrutiny by investigators, resulting in more misconduct findings. Second, black officers may have been assigned disproportionately to "high-risk" precincts, those with more social disorganization and citizen-police conflict than was the case for officers of other races. Personal characteristics, including a record of prior bad behavior of even minor crimes (e.g., public order arrests), were the second most important risk factor for misconduct.

In terms of protective factors, education exerted a strong inverse link to being removed from the force for misconduct, with an associate's degree being slightly stronger than the bachelor's degree. While it is possible that the same unmeasured force that causes people to get a college degree also keeps them from getting involved in the continuum of compromise, this finding is nonetheless instructive. Age too was important, as younger officers, who are also more likely to be beat cops, were at the highest risk of separation for corruption.

Another important lesson of the Kane and White study is that the absence of bad policing, the focus of this chapter, does not mean the presence of good policing. Good policing involves looking after people and protecting life. The two are independent and separate features of police work. Police organizations need to be vigilant about and responsive to the symptoms of bad policing and separately work on good policing.

"Jammed up":
the idea that the police are being investigated, internally or externally, for possible malfeasance, misfeasance, or nonfeasance

SOURCE: Kane and White 2013.

elemental to the definition offered at the beginning of this section (see also Box 6.3). First, the conduct must involve misuse of some key element of the police role, such as inappropriate use of authority or official position in the community. Second, the conduct must involve the receipt or expected receipt of some material reward or personal gain. In other words, if they were not peace officers, they could not engage in the untoward act, and the act must benefit the officers.

This latter element—material reward or personal gain—may create problems for investigators or civilians alike, as it may cast doubt on whether the officer truly benefited from the misconduct. Consider the case of a detective who suborns perjury on the part of a jailhouse snitch, the latter giving testimony essential to the conviction of an alleged offender. The officer might commit perjury, lying on an affidavit for a search warrant or in testimony at trial, if there is no other way to make a case against a particularly egregious offender. In both cases, the officer was convinced that the person in custody was the perpetrator, but there was no other way to make the case.

Would the fact that the officer commits the act of malfeasance in the pursuit of "justice" change the equation? Even if the answer to this last question is yes, it is still a crime and part of the **continuum of compromise** (Gilmartin and Harris 1998). That is, an officer can move from "honest cop" to "comprised cop," but in most cases, it is not a one-step slide to the bottom. Police officers, overinvested in the job and seeing themselves as cops first, last, and always, can come to view themselves as victims of criminals, an unresponsive criminal justice system, and a disinterested public. Eventually, they see their work world in different terms from other officers. At-risk officers are entitled, owing to their special status as police, rather than accountable as civil servants (entitlement versus accountability). They must be loyal to each other—the thin blue line—rather than exhibit the public integrity that accompanies law enforcement (loyalty versus integrity).

The continuum of compromise also has behavioral elements. At the first stage, officers commit acts of omission, failing to act when they should, allowing certain low-level crimes to occur and low-level criminals to remain free even when apprehended. Administrative acts of commission, such as accepting "benefits" of the workplace, follow this first step. The next line crossed involves criminal acts of commission, which themselves have gradients of seriousness, based on the laws violated and the punishments available. In this way, officers go from bent officers to broken ones.

Continuum of compromise: the notion that the movement from good cop to bent cop to broken cop is one of stages; a slippery slope hypothesis

Combating Corruption

Law enforcement agencies have long had investigators or even entire units devoted to policing the police. In small departments, these investigators work directly for the chief supervisory official's office (e.g., the chief, sheriff, or marshal). In larger departments, these units carry such names as Professional Standards Unit, Internal Investigations Division, or Bureau of Internal Affairs; a commander or other high-ranking officer generally supervises them, having direct access to the chief supervisory official. In still larger departments, the oversight units report to the police commissioner. At the federal level, these activities come under the Office of the Inspector General or Office of Professional Responsibility. As a rule, they also report to the highest-ranking individual in the agency, for example the U.S. attorney general or the secretary of Veterans Affairs.

For internal investigation units to be effective, as has been shown in both NYPD commission reports, they must proactive rather than reactive; they must also receive the full support and endorsement of the agency's central administration, and the rank and file must clearly understand their function and purpose (Mollen Commission 1994; see also Kane and White 2013). They can investigate on their own, respond to officer-initiated concerns, or address public complaints. However, this is not the only mechanism on guard against police corruption and misconduct.

Beginning in the 1930s and 1940s, cities that experienced high levels of police corruption or general police misconduct created **civilian review boards**. Law enforcement agencies were not trusted to police their own. The IACP and other police advocates considered it a bad idea to place investigative authority in the hands of civilians who did not understand police work. This perspective did not prevail, allowing two models to dominate the 21st century (Goldsmith and Lewis 2000). First, the traditional civilian review board examines only internal investigations initiated and completed by the agency. They make recommendations about that investigation to the agency head. Second, an enhanced civilian review board model includes both review and investigatory powers. Such boards' investigations may parallel internal investigations, or in some jurisdictions, the civilian review boards have the sole power to investigate the police. It would be rare for the civilian review board to have the power to issue a final report and discipline those found in violation of departmental rules and regulations or recommend a criminal investigation based on its findings. Generally, those actions are the sole province of the agency's executive.

New York City's Civilian Complaint Review Board (CCRB) is an enhanced model that traces its origins to the 1950s; however, its most recent incarnation is a direct result of the Mollen Commission report. The CCRB is an independent civilian agency with more than 100 investigators. It works closely with the NYPD to gain access to confidential police records concerning officers. In 2013, the CCRB received 5,410 complaints, conducted 2,082 full investigations, and substantiated 14 percent of all complaints (Civilian Complaint Review Board 2014). Most of these complaints involved abuse of authority (corruption), followed by use of force, discourtesy, and offensive language. The NYPD followed the CCRB's recommended action twice as often as it declined to take action; in a minority of cases, either the statute of limitations had expired or the officer had resigned or retired. In most cases, when the NYPD took action—nearly nine in ten findings of involvement—it issued special instructions to the officers or

Civilian review boards: panels of citizens and police experts that either reviewed the findings of internal police reviews or conducted their own investigations, depending on local police and practice

otherwise disciplined them. Officers were four times more likely to plead guilty or be found guilty as they were to be exonerated.

There can be no letup by police agencies and the public at large in the quest to keep police misconduct, including corrupt practices, to a minimum. It is also doubtful that any actions will eliminate corruption in its entirety. For example, localized crime trends can derail even the best of corrective measures, as the growth of the illegal drug trade in New York City overwhelmed the NYPD by the 1990s. Consider that during the 1990s, nearly half of all FBI-led corruption investigations involved drugs (U.S. Government Accountability Office 1998). One area that merits special attention, therefore, is corruption associated with undercover investigations.

Special Case: Undercover Investigations, Law Breaking, and "Going Native"

Certain criminal acts are difficult to police by "normal" methods. The victims, sometimes willing participants, may not be inclined to report the offenses. The public and the police, under normal circumstances, are largely unaware that they were occurring at all. These offenses are often *mala prohibita* vice crimes, such as commercialized sex and prostitution; illegal drug manufacture, distribution, and sales; and, to a lesser extent, political crimes, including influence peddling and extortion. Police departments may call on undercover officers to observe, facilitate, and prevent crimes. They may have to commit a crime to maintain their undercover status or to provide opportunities for others to commit crimes (Loh 2009). When in the furtherance of a legitimate law enforcement function, these acts are not crimes.

It is not surprising, therefore, that undercover investigations have many strong points in their favor (e.g., there may be no other way to investigate the offense in question). At the same time, such investigations create equally strong pressures on investigators, especially surrounding situational ethics and other moral dilemmas (Marx 1982, 1988). Undercover investigators often find themselves on the edge of legality (Loh 2009; Wachtel 1992). Departments tend to give their work a great deal of autonomy, and, importantly, the administrative rules and regulations that are so clear on the beat may become fuzzy deep in the life. The pressures to step over the line in the interest of developing a stronger case may be undeniable for some officers. This is especially true if, as represented by the continuum of compromise, the officers have already committed acts that violate administrative procedures, which is very likely in the case of undercover police work.

"Playing a crook," with the right set of pressures and circumstances, can lead to being a crook. For example, Gary Marx (1982: 177) offers the example of a police operative who was in "deep cover" with the

Hell's Angels for 18 months. Upon return to his "square" existence as a cop, drug use, alcoholism, and family violence changed his life. He resigned from the force, and he received a lengthy prison term after a bank robbery conviction. Others, including fellow police officers, may confuse the "righteous" undercover cop with a **skell**, an informal police term used to describe a member of the criminal lowlife. In the 1970s in the greater New York area, officers shot eight black undercover officers whom they took to be criminals, killing five of them (Marx 1982: 178).[3]

Without a doubt, much good flows from undercover police work. However, associated with it are a large number of potential pitfalls, corruption being one of them.

Skell:
an informal police term to describe an unsavory character with whom the officer comes into contact on the job

USE OF FORCE

Acts of police violence generally occur in the process of confronting criminal suspects, especially during felony arrests. These acts can include striking suspects with hands or fists, kicking them, deploying batons or other striking instruments, and shocking them with conductive energy devices (CEDs), such as the Taser. In extreme instances, officers use handguns, shotguns, or rifles against suspects, often with deadly results. As Community Oriented Policing Services (n.d.) reports, there is no commonly agreed-on definition of police use of force. Nevertheless, we can define **police use of force** as the "amount of effort required by police to compel compliance by an unwilling subject" (International Association of Chiefs of Police 2001).

Police use of force:
amount of effort required by police to compel compliance by an unwilling subject

Use-of-Force Continuum

The so-called **use-of-force continuum** has been at the heart of much police training over the past 40 years. This continuum contains a number of steps or stages that officers can follow to resolve potentially forceful situations. The National Institute of Justice (2012) says that police use of force can be classified into three broad categories: (1) verbal and physical restraint, (2) **less-lethal force** (sometimes called less-than-lethal force), and (3) **lethal force**. The classification of less-lethal force (rather than less-than-lethal force) recognizes that some actions not intended to be lethal—such as the use of conductive energy devices—can still have lethal consequences.

The steps normally associated with the use-of-force continuum are as follows:

1. *Physical presence:* Merely by being at a scene, one or more officers may be able to control a situation before it gets out of hand.

Use-of-force continuum:
a device designed to guide officer decision making in the process of the use of physical and other force in citizen encounters

Less-lethal force:
types of physical, mechanical, or chemical force used by police officers that are not intended to produce great bodily harm or death

Lethal force:
types of force usually as a result of discharging weapons designed to incapacitate or kill

2. *Verbal commands:* By the use of the spoken word, officers may be able to get suspects to comply with their wishes (commands such as "place your hands on the trunk of the car" or "lay on the ground, face down").

3. *Physical restraint:* This can involve holding or striking a suspect with the hands, the application of holds applied to pressure points, or the use of handcuffs.

4. *Less-lethal force:* In this category are use of the baton, pepper spray or other chemical agents, beanbag rounds fired from shotguns, and conductive energy devices.

5. *Lethal force:* Normally, this will result from the use of firearms of some type.

The use-of-force continuum continues to come under criticism even though it has been around for many years. For instance, critics say that this approach assumes that officers must respond to force or resistance with force. In other words, it does not consider other options or alternatives that might deescalate the situation. In examining this topic, the National Institute of Justice (2012) contends, "Police officers should use only the amount of force to control an incident, effect an arrest, or protect themselves or others from harm or death." The Federal Law Enforcement Training Center abandoned the traditional stair-step continuum in 2005, turning instead to a reality-based scenario training regimen that was part of a Fourth Amendment curriculum. Simply stated, each use of force by the police can be judged as reasonable (or justified) or unreasonable (and, thus, excessive). Ultimately, police supervisors, internal affairs investigations, grand juries and/or prosecuting attorneys, and trial juries make the determination of reasonableness or unreasonableness. A few cases are clear-cut one way or the other, but many are complex and murky.

According to Community Oriented Policing Services (n.d.), in 1999 approximately 44 million people in the United States experienced face-to-face contact with police officers. Of this number, roughly one-half of 1 percent experienced officers threatening them or using some type of force against them. We do not know about all situations involving the use of force; however, police appear to use force infrequently. Any use of force, especially in situations where a suspect is injured or killed, can produce public outrage, protests, and litigation. Less likely to receive such a response is the use of less-lethal force, although, as Box 6.4 reveals, there may be other justice-related concerns associated with its use.

Special Case: High-Speed Pursuits

The police car is arguably the officer's most deadly weapon. It may not have the killing range of a firearm. It may lack the visceral impact of a

> ## Box 6.4   **Less-Lethal Force: Unintended Consequences**
>
> Over the past decade, the Taser has become the preferred less-lethal weapon, used by nearly 7,300 police departments. In fact, police worldwide carry nearly three-quarters of a million Tasers. Three questions surround the use of the Taser unit. First, against whom should it be deployed? Second, does it result in fewer injuries when deployed than other "weapons" in the officer's arsenal? Third, what are its physiological effects on those against whom it is deployed? Departments generally develop policies in response to the first question. In answering the second question, researchers find general agreement that receiving a small bolt that discharges a large but brief electrical current has a lower potential for injury than being on the receiving end of a bullet discharged from a handgun or other police weapon.
>
> It is this third question that White and his associates addressed. When one is on the re-ceiving end of a Taser or similar electrically based "stun gun," the "victim" essentially receives an electrical injury (EI). EI victims report physical, cognitive, and emotional problems; importantly, nearly half indicate that their cognitive functioning slows, a claim reinforced by cognitive testing. In their study, Michael White and his associates pretested their subjects—all police cadets—shocked them, and then post-tested them within five minutes and at the 24-hour mark. Cognitive functioning was impaired at the five-minute mark but restored after 24 hours. The findings suggest that police should not question persons subjected to a Taser device until after they have had an opportunity to have their cognitive functioning restored. Given the fact that before this study, 2 million citizens were on the receiving end of a Taser unit, the authors' suggestion is important.

SOURCE: White et al. 2014.

police baton striking a person about the head and shoulders. Nevertheless, as an instrument of blunt force, the police cruiser is no less deadly and has a higher probability of deployment. An officer rushing to the scene of a crime, flashing lights and sirens engaged, could strike and kill an uninvolved civilian, and such accidents do occur periodically. The high-speed pursuit is defined as "an active attempt by a law enforcement officer operating an emergency vehicle to apprehend alleged criminals in a moving motor vehicle, when the driver of the vehicle, in an attempt to avoid apprehension, significantly increases his or her speed or takes other evasive actions" (Alpert and Anderson 1986: 5).

There are several critical facts to consider about high-speed pursuits. First, most of them begin after a traffic violation. Second, each day in the United States, one person dies because of a police pursuit. Most of those who die—upwards of 70 percent—are those being pursued or others in the vehicle, while innocent third parties account for about 30 percent of the deaths; officer deaths are relatively rare, perhaps as little as 1 to 2 percent of the overall deaths (Hutson et al. 2007: 278). These deaths represent about 1 percent of all fatal crashes in the nation. One in 100 high-speed pursuits results in a death (Schultz, Hudak, and Alpert 2010). Third, unless an officer failed to exercise due regard for property and life so that the behavior amounted to "reckless disregard," these deaths, however tragic and regrettable, are generally not litigable (Cooley and Gavery 2006). Fourth, in most cases—perhaps seven in ten—when the officer breaks off pursuit, the pursued driver slows down (Alpert 1997).

There are three possible high-speed pursuit policy options, ranging from least to most restrictive. First, the department could have a policy that allows virtually any pursuit, limited only by the officer's judgment. Second, more restrictive pursuit policies add some or all of the following possible delimiting elements beyond the driver's judgment: weather conditions, road conditions, traffic conditions, and vehicle conditions. Beyond conditional aspects associated with the likelihood of danger (recall reckless disregard), the department may limit pursuit to violent felonies. In the event of a felony-only policy, the department would likely include some driving-condition elements as well. Finally, the department may have a no-pursuit policy. Whatever policy departments adopt, they must train officers in that policy; moreover, the department must periodically update and reinforce driver training, especially in tactics for use in pursuing suspects (Alpert 1997; Becknell, Mays, and Giever 1999). In short, officers must be taught not only *how* to pursue but also *when* to pursue.

Current and projected technologies provide alternatives to pursuits (Hill 2002). First, many late-model cars have a mechanism that allows for tracking of the vehicle by global positioning system (GPS) satellites (e.g., LoJack, OnStar, or other integrated phone systems). Second, immobilizers also can send a signal to the vehicle, essentially shutting down all of its electronics. In these cases, officers must know the vehicle's identity, which would probably be the case only if the pursuing officer observed its license number or if the owner reported the vehicle as stolen to the police. Third, helicopters allow police to follow the suspect vehicle and coordinate a roadblock or intercept at some point along the vehicle's route. Officers at the intercept point set out spiked strips or "stop sticks" that create a controlled loss of air when they make contact with the suspect's tires. Finally, technology is being developed that will allow an officer to deploy a tracking device that attaches to the fleeing vehicle. One system currently available is StarChase, which consists of a small projectile with a GPS transmitter that the pursuing officer launches using compressed air from the front grill of the police unit.

Force is part of the police work world. It is crucial that departments adequately train officers and that officers understand their department's policies and accepted practices. Failure to do so can lead to individual liability if the officer is at fault, or, in some cases, the agency itself is accountable. Police officers rarely enjoy going to court, and they would rather appear as witnesses than as defendants.

POLICE AND THE JUDICIARY

The police have had a long and dynamic relationship with the courts, which dates to the creation of the law enforcer-judge position of magistrate in medieval England. Today, the police interact with the courts in three primary ways. First, officers serve as witnesses in court and often serve as the chief prosecution witness in criminal trials. Second, on appeal, appellate courts may review officers' actions in cases involving interrogations and searches and seizures. Finally, officers may be defendants in civil (or civil rights) cases alleging that their actions violated the rights of criminal defendants or those against whom the officer used force.

The first area is fairly simple and straightforward. Both uniform and plainclothes officers investigate crimes and gather evidence. They interview witnesses and assist in securing crime scenes. As a result, they appear in court on a regular basis to testify in criminal trials. Defense attorneys may question officers vigorously, but most of these situations are relatively uneventful.

Second, appellate courts may examine officers' actions during an investigation. Of particular interest are cases where the police have interrogated individuals suspected of committing crimes. Supreme Court cases such as *Escobedo v. Illinois* (1964) and *Miranda v. Arizona* (1966) restrain when and how the police can conduct **custodial interrogations**. Box 6.5 provides a brief synopsis of these two cases.

The third area in which the police interact with the courts includes situations in which they are defendants as the result of injuries or deaths of suspects. Two Supreme Court cases are particularly significant here: *Tennessee v. Garner* (1985) and *Graham v. Connor* (1989). In *Garner*, a Memphis, Tennessee, police officer shot and killed a teenage boy who was fleeing from a home burglary. Under Tennessee law at the time, and based on English common law, officers could use deadly force to apprehend a fleeing felon. The **fleeing felon rule** did not distinguish between violent and nonviolent felonies, and it generally did not take into account the threat posed to the officers. In issuing its opinion, the Supreme Court ruled that officers were justified in using deadly force only in those cases where the fleeing felon posed a continuing threat to the officers or to others in the civilian population (Fyfe 2004). Again, while this did not eliminate the use of deadly force with fleeing felons, it significantly restricted its use.

In *Graham*, the Supreme Court said that the prevailing standard for police use of force cases (whether it was deadly force or not) was that of *objective reasonableness*. However, rather than using the standard of a reasonable person, which is applied so often in criminal cases, the Court used the measure of a reasonable police officer acting in the same or similar circumstances. As the Court's majority held, "All

Custodial interrogations: any situation in which the police focus on questioning a person suspected of a crime and the individual cannot leave of his or her free will

Fleeing felon rule: the English common law rule that allowed the police to use deadly force to apprehend any felon who was fleeing arrest

Box 6.5   The Supreme Court and Police Custodial Interrogations

The facts in *Escobedo v. Illinois* are straightforward. The police took Escobedo into custody as a suspect in a fatal shooting. Shortly afterward, his attorney arrived at police headquarters and asked to see his client. The officers informed the attorney that he could not see his client until the police were through interrogating him. Throughout the period of questioning, Escobedo also requested to see his attorney. The officers lied and said that Escobedo's attorney did not want to see him.

The Supreme Court majority opinion held that when an investigation moves from a general area of inquiry into a focus on a particular person, the police must give the suspect the opportunity to consult with his attorney and inform the suspect of the right to remain silent. As a result, the Supreme Court overturned Escobedo's conviction and remanded the case back to the Illinois court system.

Perhaps one of the most famous (or infamous, depending on your perspective) Supreme Court cases of all time was *Miranda v. Arizona*. In *Miranda*, the Supreme Court revisited the *Escobedo* case to determine the specific constitutional guidelines that control police custodial interrogations. The Court said that such interrogations involve "questioning initiated by law enforcement officers after a person has been taken into custody or otherwise deprived of his freedom of action in any significant way." The result was the historic *Miranda* warning: "Prior to any questioning, the person must be warned that he has a right to remain silent, that any statements he does make may be used as evidence against him, and that he has the right to the presence of an attorney, either retained or appointed."

Police officers may question criminal suspects or take confessions from them. However, they are required to follow the guidelines that the Supreme Court has defined and refined over the years.

SOURCES: Escobedo v. Illinois (1964); Miranda v. Arizona (1966).

claims that law enforcement officials have used excessive force—deadly or not—in the course of an arrest, investigatory stop, or other 'seizure' of a free citizen are properly analyzed under the Fourth Amendment's 'objective reasonableness' standard, rather than under a substantive due process standard." Such cases restrict the ways in which the police may act or have further defined permissible police actions.

Civil Liability

Officers and agencies may find themselves as litigants in civil proceedings. Given the level of proof required for criminal prosecutions and basic protections against criminal liability generally accorded officers, proceeding against them in a civil action is often the only chance for a "victim" (i.e., the plaintiff) to seek justice. In such cases, the plaintiff alleges that the actions or inactions of the defendant caused a calculable loss, also called a civil wrong or tort. The plaintiff generally seeks either monetary damages or an injunction (i.e., formal court order) for the defendant to cease and desist the harmful behavior that caused the tort or both.

Do not think that officers are immune from civil litigation. In the absence of a clear case of injustice, however, it is rare for a civil court to allow a case to proceed or for a judgment in favor of a plaintiff.

Special Case: 1983 Suits

Reconstruction (1865-1877) was a dark time in U.S. history. Groups like the Ku Klux Klan (KKK) threatened basic freedoms, especially those of recently freed slaves living in the former Confederate states. With passage of the Civil Rights Act of 1871, Congress authorized President Ulysses S. Grant to suspend the Habeas Corpus Act and use federal troops to apprehend members of the KKK (see Chapter 4 for an examination of the Posse Comitatus Act). Grant's prosecution of the KKK was so successful that the group virtually disappeared until the early 20th century. 42 U.S.C. §1983 codified key elements of the act. Still, as Grant's administration gave way to that of Rutherford B. Hayes and Reconstruction formally ended, enforcement of the act ended for nearly 100 years.

The language of 42 U.S.C. §1983 is important:

> Every person who, under color of any statute, ordinance, regulation, custom, or usage of any State or Territory or the District of Columbia, subjects, or causes to be subjected, any citizen of the United States or other person within the jurisdiction thereof to the deprivation of any rights, privileges, or immunities secured by the Constitution and laws, shall be liable to the party injured in an action at law, suit in equity, or other proper proceeding for redress.

For there to be a 1983 civil rights claim, two factors must apply: (1) the conduct litigated was committed by "a person" under color of state law, and (2) the conduct deprived the plaintiff of rights, privileges, or immunities as reflected in the Constitution or the laws of the United States.

When 1983 suits came back to the halls of justice, many involved the rights of prison and jail inmates (see Chapter 12). Suits typically listed the warden as the defendant, the "person acting under color of law." Until 1978, most jurisdictions escaped litigation involving police officers' actions since the Supreme Court long held that municipalities were not persons for the purposes of 1983 suits. In *Monell v. New York City Department of Social Services*, the Court held that the city could not be held accountable for the actions of its non-policy-making employees, including police officers. The doctrine of *respondeat superior*, or **vicarious liability**, protected the city's actions. However, if the municipality itself caused the harm by its policies or authorized practices, then liability could attach to the act and the city sued for damages. To prevail, the plaintiff's attorney must demonstrate a causal link between the policy and the officer's actions that caused the harm.

Vicarious liability: a form of strict liability; when an employee commits a tort as a result of something that the employer had a responsibility to do or not to do, then the liability passes to the employer (*respondeat superior*), who becomes the tortfeasor

In this regard, you should think high-speed pursuit policy or the use of deadly force in subduing a suspect.

The 1983 suit has several unique features. First, the trials are in federal court under the federal rules of procedure, which are standard across the nation. Second, while many states have instituted caps on damages for certain types of legal actions, there is no cap on actual or compensatory damages for 1983 suits; moreover, the losing party pays attorneys' fees, which can be a substantial amount in its own right. Third, the legal barrier required to be crossed—the deliberate indifference standard—was established in *City of Canton v. Harris* (1989). In that case, the Court wrote, "A plaintiff must be able to show that his injury resulted from the officer's violation of his civil rights and that such an injury would not have occurred if the officer had been trained and/or supervised under a program that was not constitutionally deficient" (Grossman 2008).

Litigation is a part of life. Not everyone is sued, but nearly everyone could be sued. Police officers are no exception to this observation. Given a stressful work environment and the split-second decisions that officers often make, harm is a constant possibility. As the review of women in the police work world in Box 6.6 suggests, the courts also played a large role in facilitating women's advancement into police work, but the work is far from over.

SUMMARY

You might ask yourself: Are there no more issues confronting police today? The obvious answer is yes, there are many more. This review necessarily keys on a limited number of issues. The issues reviewed represent a cross-section of concerns that affect individual officers' lives, the lives of citizens, and the relationships between both groups. What you should take away from this chapter is the realization that issues can be timely, influenced by the pressures of contemporary society, such as what happened in this nation during the civil rights era or in the aftermath of September 11, 2001. They can also be timeless, bound up in the job itself, in this case the work of the police, whether they were enforcing laws in ancient Mesopotamia, Rome, Greece, or Europe during the Middle Ages or in the United States during Prohibition.

In terms of the issues described in this chapter, consider the following:

- Elements of police work exhibit high levels of professionalism, especially as one proceeds up the promotion ladder within a department or agency; street-level police work, however, is more craftlike than professional in nature.

Box 6.6   Women and Policing: The Rest of the Story

From its earliest incarnations, policing has been male dominated. Alice Stebbins Wells, the first female police officer in the United States, began work with the Los Angeles Police Department in 1910. Hiring practices were slow to change over the ensuing 100 years, as departments viewed most female police recruits as best suited for juvenile work or as matrons in the female jail but not suitable for patrol work. Matters have improved for female officers. A 2011 Bureau of Justice Statistics report indicates that females accounted for 15 percent of all federal officers. At the local and state levels, the picture is not quite as positive. Slightly more than 5 percent of all state police officers are women, while around 11 percent of both city police officers and county sheriff's deputies are female. Moreover, the smaller the agency, the proportionately fewer women it has employed.

What can account for this underrepresentation of women in policing? That discussion alone could consume an entire chapter. While discrimination is certainly part of the issue, overt discrimination, as in "women need not apply," is unlikely. What does happen is that certain **bona fide occupational qualifications (BFOQ)** make it less likely that women will become police recruits or pass the physical agility portions of training. There may be height requirements, which often eliminate many female candidates. Largely abandoned tensile-strength tests, which consisted of repeatedly pulling a trigger in a fixed time span, commonly eliminated women. Between 2005 and 2011, the rates at which women passed these physical agility tests were 80 percent lower than those of male candidates. In short, women can apply but may not be selected or complete training at the same rates as men.

These tests may violate Title VII of the 1964 Civil Rights Act, as amended in1991; however, this question has not yet been fully litigated. Other gender-specific issues face females once they join the force, including sexual harassment and pregnancy leave. The former is a matter of settled law, although it does exist in the workplace. The Federal Family Medical Leave Act (1993) and the Pregnancy Discrimination Act (1978) cover the latter; however, agencies may not have clear policies on restricted duty for female officers during pregnancy. A survey conducted by the organization Women in Federal Law Enforcement found that 65 percent of the female officers contacted would leave their organization if it did not support them during their pregnancy or in the matter of child care.

Bona fide occupational qualifications (BFOQ): job requirements that the courts have recognized as necessary prerequisites for employment, either upon entry or because of in-service assessment

SOURCES: Brooks 2001; Fields 2012; Langton 2010; Women in Federal Law Enforcement 2011.

- Whether police work is considered a profession, higher education has a role in shaping its present and future.
- Police misconduct is unlikely to disappear entirely; however, we know what can influence its prevalence in police work.
- Distrust and cynicism, along with several other problematic personality traits, are found in high supply within the police

community; a measure of some of them is good, but too much can spell trouble.

Careers in policing can be rewarding on many levels. Many criminal justice students see the ultimate goal as the position of special agent with the FBI, DEA, or Secret Service, perhaps even being a deputy U.S. marshal. Many would be happy with a career in state or local law enforcement. What this chapter suggests is that no matter where you seek employment, you should understand that such work has costs *and* benefits. In addition, if you are not interested in a law enforcement career, remember that many of the issues this chapter describes will reappear in later chapters about the work worlds of other criminal justice employees. Finally, if your interest in law enforcement is more academic than practical, now you understand that while we need police, those who perform law enforcement functions do so at a cost. Moreover, society must be vigilant in its oversight of police, as the costs of having an out-of-control police force can potentially outweigh the benefits they provide.

REVIEW QUESTIONS

1. Locate your state in Figure 6.1, or look it up at the Cato Institute. How does it rank in terms of per capita police misconduct? Do you have any insights or ideas about why it ranks where it does?

2. In Box 6.2, the question appears to be rhetorical. Now answer it. What fact or series of facts most strongly influenced your position on this matter?

3. Should police be unionized? What role does the idea of striking police play in constructing your answer?

4. What kinds of factors are likely to affect corruption by police officers? Do laws, policies, and administrative practices make a difference? Why or why not?

5. It has been said that Supreme Court cases like *Miranda v. Arizona* have "handcuffed" the police. Do you agree with this characterization? Explain.

6. Do some historical detective work. What was the basis for the fleeing felon rule in England (and later in the United States)? Irrespective of what the Supreme Court said in *Tennessee v. Garner*, does it make sense for the police to be able to employ deadly force in all fleeing felon cases? Is it possible that there are circumstances in which the police do not actually know the nature of the felony that may have been committed?

7. Should officers be exempt from civil liability when they are acting in the public good, no matter how much their actions endanger the public? Explain the reasoning for your answer.

8. How can police agencies do more to rectify the gender imbalance? What approaches to police work or the police subculture might have a positive impact?

KEY TERMS

"blue flu"
Bona fide occupational qualifications (BFOQ)

civil review boards
continuum of compromise
custodial interrogations
fleeing felon rule

Fraternal Order of Police (FOP)
"grass eaters"
gratuities
International Union of Police Associations
    (IUPA)
"jammed up"
Knapp Commission
less-lethal force
lethal force
"meat eaters"

Mollen Commission
police corruption
police misconduct
Police Officer Standards and Training (POST)
police personality
police use of force
skell
use-of-force continuum
vicarious liability

NOTES

1. Some academies, including those sponsored through colleges with open enrollment, meet both requirements and transfer the basic training curriculum toward college credits. Some college-linked academies award up to 33 hours of college credit, allowing cadets to complete their associate's degree in short order after receiving POST certification.

2. Much of the following information about the 1919 Boston police strike is taken from Francis 1975.

3. Larry Mays was an undercover narcotics investigator early in his career. Unable to tell his family about the assignment, Mays was subjected to much social approbation until he was able to don his Knoxville Police Department uniform and "clear" his reputation.

PART III

Defining Justice

Local, State, and Federal Courts

LEARNING OBJECTIVES

At the conclusion of this chapter, you should be able to:

- Describe the nature and operations of local courts.
- Explain the differences and similarities between state courts and federal courts.
- Distinguish courts of limited jurisdiction from those of general jurisdiction.
- Describe the structures and functions of various appellate courts.

INTRODUCTION

The court system in the United States is somewhat unique. There are a variety of types of courts, and they are found at three different levels of government: local, state, and federal. It is even accurate to say that there are more than 51 court systems in this country, since, in addition to the federal courts, many states have local or specialized courts along with the state court structure. This chapter provides a brief overview of local, state, and federal courts in the United States. We examine how these courts are organized and the types of cases heard by the various courts. As you will see, there are some parts of the nation where all of the courts are somewhat similar, but there are also elements that differentiate courts from one another.

LOCAL COURTS

When we talk about local courts in the United States, there are really two different types of court entities. First, we have courts that are created by and serve the needs of villages, towns, townships, and cities. These are almost exclusively courts of limited jurisdiction, also known as inferior courts, but even at this level, there can be some exceptions (such as California's municipal courts). Second, there can also be what appear to be "local" courts, but in reality these are the lowest-level state courts that merely operate at the local level. This second type of court is discussed more fully in the section on state courts.

The judges that preside over local courts hear cases involving minor civil disputes (small claims) and misdemeanor criminal cases, hence their designation as courts of limited jurisdiction. These courts may be called city courts or municipal courts, and a great deal of their caseload involves traffic offenses and violations of municipal ordinances.

Local courts handle a variety of minor cases, and they are the courts with which the average person is most likely to have experience. For many people, going to traffic court may be the only court experience they have.

STATE COURTS

State-level courts handle most of the civil and criminal caseload in the United States. These trial courts can have two types of authority or jurisdiction: **limited jurisdiction** or **general trial jurisdiction**. Limited jurisdiction courts are those that can try only a narrow range of cases, such as misdemeanors (including traffic offenses), as well as civil disputes under a specified amount (such as $2,500 or $5,000). In minor

Courts of limited jurisdiction: trial courts limited to small civil disputes and minor criminal cases (petty misdemeanors or misdemeanors)

Courts of general trial jurisdiction: courts authorized to hear a broad range of civil and criminal cases

civil disputes, these courts serve as "small claims" courts. By contrast, general trial jurisdiction courts can hear the full range of criminal cases, including felonies and misdemeanor convictions that may be appealed from limited jurisdiction courts. They also have trial responsibility for major civil suits (those over the range specified for the limited jurisdiction courts).

As trial courts, they are charged with deciding between several different possible outcomes, all in accordance with defining and guiding principles found in state substantive and procedural law. These courts can have a unified structure, hearing both civil and criminal cases, or they can be specialized courts, handling only one or a limited range of cases. State courts can also handle cases at law, equity cases, or both. "Law is the set of rules, written by legislatures, and enforced by society"; by contrast, "[e]quity is a system of justice administered according to standards of fairness (as opposed to standards imposed by specific laws or rules)" (Legal Grind 2011). This means that equity cases are designed to provide fairness when legal remedies might produce "inadequate or unacceptable results" (Altschuler and Sgroi 1996: 424). Today, virtually all states have merged law and equity courts into one system. However, there are states, such as Arkansas, Delaware, Mississippi, and Tennessee, that have retained separate **chancery courts**, or courts of equity (Rottman and Strickland 2006).

Chancery courts: specialized equity courts found in a limited number of states

Financing for state courts may come from the state general fund, they may be locally funded, or in some instances, they may receive funding from both sources. State courts also can have very simple or extremely complex organizational structures. Most state court judges will be licensed attorneys, but in some inferior jurisdiction courts, they are not required to possess a law degree.

All of these features make it difficult to describe in a simple way what state courts in the United States really look like. Therefore, we use the most general descriptions possible. In some cases, we use specific state court systems to illustrate the points being made. To find the organizational structure of your state's courts, search the Internet, combining "courts" and your state's name.

Creation of State Courts

A point that is frequently made in any description of courts in the United States is that we are a nation of many different courts. Nearly all of them function as trial courts; many, including some that are trial courts, also perform appellate functions, meaning that they may review decisions of lower trial courts, although even on this issue there is some variability, as we make clear. Later in the chapter, we also examine the federal government's trial and appellate court system. Moreover, each state has its own unique court system, which also includes a system of appellate courts. The time during which different states entered the Union explains some of the differences in court structures. The legal cultures and traditions of each state also explain some of the differences. A classic example is Louisiana, which differs from the other 49 states and the federal government in that its legal system is based on the French Napoleonic or civil law tradition; however, in all criminal matters, the U.S. common law system is followed, while the Code Napoleon provides guidance for civil matters (Calvi and Coleman 2008; Vago 2009). Immigration patterns, local traditions, and different historical patterns also influence what is often called the **local legal culture** of each state.

Local legal culture: the legal environment that exists in a particular jurisdiction based on the history and traditions of the location

State Trial Courts

State constitutions ultimately define state court jurisdictions and give legislatures the authority to outline the specifics of its court jurisdictions and structure. Therefore, the simplest statement that we can make is that while there are similar patterns in state court structures, each state actually has a unique organizational pattern. Some of these have changed substantially over the years, while others are much the same today as they were a century ago. In this section, we present state court structures in very general terms; however, it is useful to point out specific states that illustrate what we mean by certain court structures.

One of the key differences among states is the number of tiers or levels of courts. For example, South Dakota has a two-tiered court system. By contrast, Minnesota has a three-tiered court system, and Kentucky has a four-tiered system. In Tennessee—along with some other states—there are lower tiers with several different courts. The simplest way to classify state courts, therefore, is to divide them into two categories: **courts of original jurisdiction** and **courts of appellate jurisdiction**.

Courts of original jurisdiction: courts where civil and criminal cases first originate; may be called trial courts

Courts of original jurisdiction are the courts where civil and criminal cases are first heard. These are what we have previously called trial courts. These are the courts that hear evidence and decide winners and losers in civil cases and determine guilt or innocence in criminal cases. Once liability has been determined in civil cases trials judges and juries decide the appropriate remedies, including monetary awards. In criminal cases, should a conviction occur, the trial court is responsible for imposing fines, probation, the appropriate jail or prison sentence, or other sanction on the criminal defendant.

Courts of appellate jurisdiction: courts that review the proceedings of trial courts in instances where errors of law are alleged

In some states, the original jurisdiction courts occupy one level of the state's court structure. By contrast, some states have more than one level of trial courts. As a result, the courts of original jurisdiction can be divided into two further categories: courts of limited jurisdiction and courts of general trial jurisdiction.

Limited Jurisdiction Courts

As we begin this section, we must consider some of the features associated with the courts of limited or inferior jurisdiction. Some observers have suggested that these courts are inferior courts because they allocate an inferior quality of justice. John Robertson (1974), for one, has described lower criminal courts as dispensing "rough justice." However, we should examine some of the features of these courts before concluding that the quality of justice provided by these courts is itself inferior.

First, the courts of limited jurisdiction handle the bulk of both civil and criminal cases in the United States. One way to illustrate this claim is to look at the number of misdemeanor cases disposed of by state courts; however, a significant problem is that there is no centralized source for this information. Nevertheless, the National Center for State Courts conducted a study on misdemeanor cases for the years 1985 to 1998 for 26 states plus the District of Columbia and Puerto Rico. It found that case numbers ranged from 5.3 million in 1985 to 7.3 million in 1998. Projecting from these jurisdictions to the population of the entire United States would give us an estimated annual misdemeanor caseload of 11,604,745 for all states in 1998 (Cohen 2000). Consistent with these numbers, James Wesley Hall, president of the National Association of Criminal Defense Lawyers, testified before Congress about the state of indigent defense in the United States. In his testimony, Hall estimated that 10.5 million misdemeanor cases were processed in 2006, which would be equivalent to 3.5 percent of the nation's population (Hall 2009). Two additional reports by the Bureau of Justice Statistics estimate that nationwide prosecutors closed 7.5 million misdemeanor cases in 2005 (Perry 2006), and that public defenders' offices were assigned 2.3 million misdemeanor cases to defend in 2007 (Farole and Langton 2010).

To help us understand the qualitative differences in the types of cases processed at the various court levels, we resort to what Samuel Walker (2011) terms the **"wedding cake model."** Walker's model describes the types of cases processed by each layer of the wedding cake:

- The top layer is composed of **celebrated cases**. Such cases are notorious because of the nature of the crime, the celebrity status of the person charged with committing the crime, or the celebrity status of the person against whom the crime is committed. These cases often go through the entire judicial process and they garner public attention as a result of the media focus given them. The Florida case involving George Zimmerman and Trayvon Martin discussed in Chapter 3 is an example of a celebrated case. Many of these cases, such as the Zimmerman trial, involve original jurisdiction issues; however,

Wedding cake model:
the four-layer model developed by Samuel Walker to explain the different ways in which the courts process celebrated cases, serious felonies, less serious felonies, and misdemeanors

Celebrated cases:
high-profile or particularly newsworthy cases

the most celebrated among them are those that essentially change (or fail to change) the law: those cases handled by the U.S. Supreme Court.

- The second level includes serious felonies. These cases involve crimes of personal violence, and they may be as serious as the celebrated cases. Nevertheless, they do not attract the notoriety or the media attention of celebrated cases. Many of the serious felony cases go to trial because the defendants face long prison sentences and they have nothing to lose by going to trial. Only a small percentage of the serious felonies involve plea bargaining.

- Level three is composed of less serious felonies. These include auto thefts, burglaries, and grand larcenies. There are also routine drug and other vice offenses here. Plea bargaining increases as we go down the various levels of the wedding cake and offenders at level three try to have charges reduced to misdemeanors, or try to receive probation and sentences that do not involve prison time.

- At the bottom of the wedding cake is the misdemeanor level. We find significantly more cases here than in the other three levels combined. The misdemeanor cases are handled by the limited jurisdiction courts, sometimes called "the people's courts," and they include a wide variety of personal and property offenses (Mansfield 1999).

From what we know about court caseloads, it easy to see that the lower criminal courts are extremely busy. This very heavy workload limits how much time judges and lawyers can spend with each case and indicates something of the increased likelihood of plea bargaining.

Second, most courts of limited jurisdiction are courts of nonrecord. In other words, the trials conducted in these courts do not use court reporters to prepare verbatim transcripts. Most of the time this is not a problem; however, for cases appealed from limited jurisdiction courts to general trial courts, there must be a **trial de novo**, or a completely new trial, since no transcript is available.

Third, in many cases that come before limited jurisdiction courts, neither side is represented by an attorney. The prosecutor's office will send attorneys for only the most serious misdemeanor cases, but for traffic charges and other petty offenses, police officers and victims may serve as their own prosecutors. Defendants also may represent themselves in what are known as **pro se proceedings**. The U.S. Supreme Court has held that in most circumstances defendants have the right to represent themselves (*Faretta v. California* (1975)), but the absence of attorneys places a greater burden on inferior court judges to ensure that proper legal procedures are followed. This situation can create the

Trial de novo:
to try a case anew; cases appealed from limited jurisdiction courts (courts of nonrecord) go to general jurisdiction courts where a whole new trial is conducted

Pro se proceedings:
court proceedings where parties represent themselves without the assistance of an attorney

potential for judicial misconduct since no lawyers are present to scrutinize the ways in which judges conduct themselves—and there is rarely a record to consult for an appeal (Mansfield 1999).

Fourth, many states do not provide for jury trials at the inferior court level, or they do so in limited circumstances. However, if the case is a non-petty offense—one that could result in incarceration for six months or more—the Supreme Court has held that the Sixth Amendment requires the option of a jury trial (*Duncan v. Louisiana* (1968)). In response to this requirement, some states provide for 6-person (instead of 12-person) juries in inferior courts when jury trials are necessary.

Finally, as previously mentioned, some states allow for lay judges (nonlawyer judges) in limited jurisdiction courts. As one example, the state of New Mexico eliminated the office of justice of the peace in 1968, and replaced it with **magistrate judges** (still nonlawyer judges) who serve in the state's limited jurisdiction courts. These judges are required to meet three general qualifications for elected office in the state: (1) they must be a qualified voter, (2) they must reside in the district from which they are elected, and (3) they must possess a high school diploma or GED (*New Mexico Statutes Annotated* §35-2-1).

Magistrate judges: judges that preside over courts of limited jurisdictions in some states; most are popularly elected and they may or may not be required to possess law degrees

Court participants in limited jurisdiction courts with lay judges are at the mercy of the judges' common sense and training that may have been received after election. Organizations like the state **administrative office of courts (AOC)** or the National Judicial Center at the University of Nevada, Reno offer training programs for nonlawyer judges to assist them in effectively discharging their duties.

Administrative office of courts (AOC): state (or federal) agencies created to administer the ongoing business details of the judicial branch of government

State courts of limited jurisdiction have their authority defined by the state constitution, the state legislature, or both. Texas, for instance, continues to employ the old English common law office of **justice of the peace** (Rottman and Strickland 2006). Justices of the peace are elected judicial officials, with some serving full time and some serving part time. As a result of some of the deficiencies of this judicial office—notably the lack of legal training and the practice of paying justices of the peace through a fee system—most states have eliminated or merged it with other courts of limited jurisdiction (Rottman and Strickland 2006). For instance, as some states reorganized their court systems in the 1960s and 1970s, they abolished the justice of the peace, replacing the office with limited jurisdiction courts—such as magistrates' courts—presided over by magistrate judges. These judges still are elected, but they have regular offices and courtrooms and are paid a salary instead of relying on a fee system. Also, states may allow cities and towns to create their own municipal courts, but these courts are not normally part of the state court system. While municipal court are also courts of limited jurisdiction, they differ from justice of the

Justices of the peace: elected judicial officials who serve in a limited number of states; historically they were paid based on the fees they collected and in most instances were not required to be trained in the law

peace or magistrate courts in that their jurisdiction is limited to municipal ordinance violations.

Many limited jurisdiction courts also hear minor civil disputes, making them small claims courts. In typical cases, creditors can file suits with the courts—often without the need for a lawyer—to recover money owed for a consumer credit loan. These civil cases are limited to disputes of a specific dollar amount, such as $2,000 or $5,000, but the state may set the amounts as much as $25,000 or higher (see Mansfield 1999). Creditors who win such cases obtain a "judgment," which in many cases is no more than an official court document that says they won, and they still may not be able to collect the outstanding debt.

In terms of criminal cases, limited jurisdiction courts can hear and dispose of misdemeanor cases, which include traffic offenses, petty misdemeanors like shoplifting, or serious misdemeanors like simple assault or drunk driving. These cases can result in either fines or periods of jail time up to one year in a county jail; the judge can even order both a fine and jail time.

Limited jurisdiction courts also can have the responsibility for the initial legal processing of felony cases. In other words, these courts may issue search or arrest warrants, hold initial appearances (often within 48 hours of arrest), and conduct preliminary (probable cause) hearings. During the initial appearances judges advise defendants of the charges, deal with the issue of bail, and appoint attorneys if defendants are indigent. For preliminary hearings, if the judge finds that there is sufficient probable cause for further action, the case can be bound over to the grand jury or forwarded to a general trial jurisdiction court.

General Trial Courts

General trial jurisdiction courts are authorized to try any state legal claim of wrongdoing, whether civil or criminal in nature. While minor civil disputes and misdemeanors may be heard in limited jurisdiction courts, major civil cases and felony trials are heard in the general trial courts. Sometimes appeals from inferior courts make the general trial courts ultimately responsible for all state cases.

Several factors differentiate general trial courts from the limited jurisdiction courts. As one illustration, trial courts dispose of significantly fewer cases than the limited jurisdiction courts. For example, from 1990 to 2006, the number of felony cases increased by 302,950 from 829,340 to 1,132,290 (Rosenmerkel, Durose, and Farole 2009: 1). This was an increased rate per 100,000 adult population of 11 percent. These numbers are substantial, but it is only about one-tenth of the number of misdemeanor cases heard. Figure 7.1 provides an illustration of the most serious charges filed against felony defendants in the nation's 75 largest counties from 1990 to 2006.

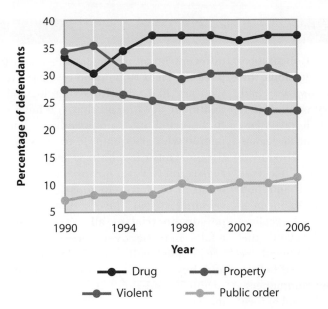

Figure 7.1
Most serious arrest charge of felony defendants in the 75 largest counties, 1990-2006

General trial courts are also **courts of record**. Thus, court reporters are present for all trials and most other proceedings to keep a verbatim transcript. Transcripts become essential when cases are appealed as they become the record on which appeals are based.

The regular presence of attorneys is another distinguishing factor for trial courts. Prosecutors' offices regularly assign a number of assistant prosecutors to trial courts, depending on the size of the jurisdiction. Defense attorneys—either privately retained or court appointed—also represent the criminal defendants charged with felonies (see Farole and Langton 2010). Only occasionally will defendants waive their right to an attorney in these courts.

Juries are also a regular feature of general trial courts. The U.S. Constitution's Sixth Amendment provides the right to a trial by "a jury of one's peers," and the Supreme Court has said that this right applies in all but petty cases (*Duncan v. Louisiana* (1968)). Presumably all felony cases will be tried by a jury. There is always the option to waive the right to a jury trial and proceed with a **bench trial**, which is a trial before a judge with no jury. In some civil cases where understanding complex points of law is crucial, or in criminal cases that may involve a great deal of negative publicity toward the defendant (like child sex abuse cases), bench trials may be preferable. However, in criminal cases, the defendant retains the choice over a jury trial versus a bench trial. Box 7.1 addresses the issue of what it means for defendants to have juries of their peers.

Courts of record:
courts in which a verbatim transcript is kept of the proceedings

Bench trial:
judicial proceedings before a judge without a jury

Box 7.1   A Jury of Your Peers

The Sixth Amendment to the U.S. Constitution provides that "[i]n all criminal prosecutions, the accused shall enjoy the right to a speedy and public trial, by an impartial jury of the State and district wherein the crime shall have been committed." The notion of an impartial jury is often associated with the right to be tried by a jury of one's peers. However, "peers" has two distinct meanings: one sociological and one legal. Sociologically, we use peers to mean a group of people much like oneself. In reality, when juries began to evolve in England, the right to a jury of one's peers meant that members of the nobility had the right to be tried before other members of the nobility, not commoners.

In the United States, the idea of trial before a jury of one's peers has taken on a slightly different meaning. It doesn't mean that you have the right to be tried by 12 (or 6) people who are like you (for example, college students). It does mean that you have the right to be tried by an appropriate number of people who are qualified for jury service. At the most basic level, these are people who are registered to vote, pay property taxes, or are licensed to drive. In most cases (especially criminal cases), jurors don't resemble the person on trial at all. Women and senior adults may be overrepresented, but these are people legally qualified to serve on juries, and they typically take this responsibility very seriously and don't try to get excused from jury duty.

SOURCE: Mays 2012.

There also may be a physical layout difference between courts of general trial jurisdiction and limited jurisdiction courts. In some jurisdictions, both types of courts may share the same courtrooms, although this is somewhat uncommon. In other jurisdictions, the inferior courts dispense justice in small rooms located inside of police stations or county justice centers. Sometimes such courtrooms are located in storefront space, such as a strip mall or disused downtown shopping area. The general trial courts, in contrast, tend to be housed in far more dignified-looking buildings, complete with wood paneling, carpeting, prominently displayed state seals, U.S. and state flags, and other official-looking decorations.

The last factor that is common to general trial courts is the requirement of law-trained judges. Nearly all states require general trial jurisdiction judges to have law degrees. Additionally, many states now require judicial candidates to have been licensed, practicing attorneys for anywhere from five to ten years (Rottman and Strickland 2006).

Specialized State Courts

In closing out this section on state courts, we need to take a brief look at some of the specialized state-level courts. Again, these courts' names and jurisdictions vary from state to state, but we present the categories of specialized courts that are most common.

Juvenile courts represent one of the most common specialized courts. Beginning with the first juvenile court in Cook County, Illinois, in 1899, all states have developed some form of juvenile or children's court (Rottman and Strickland 2006; Snyder and Sickmund 2006). General trial jurisdiction courts handle juvenile cases dealing with delinquency, dependency, and neglect in some states. Other states—such as Georgia and Texas—have separate county-level courts that handle matters concerning individuals under the age of majority; Colorado, which created a juvenile court in Denver in 1899, has some counties that have their own separate juvenile courts and some that do not. The most common age of majority in the United States is 18, so most juvenile courts exercise jurisdiction over youths through age 17.

Family or domestic relations courts represent another category of specialized courts. These courts commonly handle marriage annulments, divorces, paternity suits, custody disputes, and issues of child support. In some states, they also have jurisdiction over delinquency, dependency, and neglect/abuse cases traditionally associated with juvenile courts. For example, Delaware, Hawaii, New York, Rhode Island, South Carolina, and Vermont have these types of specialized courts.

Probate courts are a third common category of specialized courts. These courts are responsible for cases related to wills and inheritances. In some states, they also oversee the legal affairs of orphans, adoptions, mental health issues, and transfers of property. Alabama, Arkansas, Colorado (Denver), Connecticut, Georgia, Indiana, Maine, Maryland (Orphan's Court), Massachusetts, Michigan, New Hampshire, New Mexico, New York (Surrogates' Courts), Rhode Island, South Carolina, Tennessee, Texas, and Vermont have courts that partially or completely are responsible for probate cases.

> **Probate courts:** courts established to deal with issues such as wills, inheritance, and related matters

Beyond these examples, there are states that have created some very specialized courts (see Rottman and Strickland 2006). For example, Arizona, Indiana, New Jersey, Oklahoma, and Oregon have tax courts; Arkansas has police courts; Colorado and Montana have water courts; Louisiana has mayor's courts; Maine has administrative courts; Massachusetts has housing courts and land courts; Montana and Rhode Island have workers' compensation courts; New York and Ohio have courts of claims; and Vermont has environmental courts.

Finally, since the 1980s, there has been the emergence of a group of specialized courts at the state level called **problem-solving courts**. Most of these courts are based on the notion of therapeutic jurisprudence, and their ultimate goal is to solve social problems, not just to adjudicate cases. Examples of problem-solving courts are drug courts (for both adults and juveniles), DWI drug courts, mental health courts, veterans' courts, and domestic violence courts (see Butts and Roman 2004; Mays, Ryan, and Bejarano 1997; Schmitt 2006; Slate 2004). Box 7.2 provides an overview on drug courts, one of the most common of the problem-solving courts.

> **Problem-solving courts:** judicial forums based on the notion of therapeutic jurisprudence; these courts are created to solve social problems rather than merely adjudicating legal cases

---

Box 7.2   Drug Courts

The first drug court was established in Miami, Florida, in 1989, and the concept has since spread nationwide, along with applying it to other social problems. Glenn Schmitt (2006) provides a brief overview of drugs courts and how therapeutic jurisprudence applies to other types of cases:

Traditionally, the courts use legal sanctions, including incarceration, both to punish drug-involved offenders and to deter them from further criminal activity. On the other hand, the treatment community emphasizes therapeutic

relationships to help motivate addicts to reduce their dependence on drugs, change their behavior, and take control of their lives. Drug courts offer an alternative to incarceration, which, by itself, has not been effective in breaking the cycle of drugs and crime. While problem-solving courts such as drug courts have not resolved all of our social problems, they at least offer an alternative to what is often characterized as a revolving door for many people who are processed by the criminal justice system.

SOURCE: Schmitt 2006.

State Appellate Courts

Just like the original jurisdiction courts, states also vary on the numbers of appellate jurisdiction courts they have. Currently, 11 states—Delaware, Maine, Mississippi, Montana, Nevada, New Hampshire, Rhode Island, South Dakota, Vermont, West Virginia, and Wyoming—have only one level of appellate courts. The other 39 states have both a court of intermediate appeals and a court of last resort (Rottman and Strickland 2006).

Intermediate Courts of Appeals

The **intermediate courts of appeal** usually meet in a centralized location such as the state capital; this is the arrangement in most states. For other states, as a result of the state size or court workload, the judges may meet at different locations, or there may be regional divisions of these courts (see Barclay 1998). New York and Texas follow this pattern (see Marvell 1989; Rottman and Strickland 2006). Intermediate appellate courts (often called the courts of appeals) are the first—and normally the last—point of appeal for most state cases.

Intermediate courts of appeal:
those courts that hear appeals from trial courts before they can progress to courts of last resort

Courts of Last Resort

The courts of last resort are known by a number of different names in different state court systems. In many jurisdictions, the state supreme court is the court of last resort for civil and criminal cases. However, in Texas and Oklahoma, the state supreme courts exclusively have jurisdiction over civil matters; the court of last resort for criminal cases in these two states is the court of criminal appeals. New York uses the designation of "supreme court" for the court of general trial jurisdiction (Rottman and Strickland 2006). This makes it difficult to use one label that adequately describes all of the courts of last resort. However, since 48 states use the title of "supreme court" for the court of last resort, that is the label we use.

State supreme courts vary in the number of justices they have: 6 states have nine supreme court justices, 26 have seven, and 18 have five. The judges, or justices as they are often called, are selected in a variety of ways. Some states elect state supreme court justices in partisan or nonpartisan elections. Others appoint justices, and some use a form of merit selection (sometimes called the **Missouri Plan**) to choose judges. Unlike U.S. Supreme Court justices, state supreme court justices normally serve fixed terms—ranging from 6 to 12 years—but there are some exceptions to this. Consider, for example, the following (Rottman and Strickland 2006):

1. In Indiana, justices serve an initial two-year term and then stand for retention election every ten years.
2. In Massachusetts and New Hampshire, justices are appointed by the governor and may serve until age 70.
3. The major exception is Rhode Island, where state supreme court justices have life tenure, like federal judges.

Missouri Plan: merit selection system of choosing judges first established in the state of Missouri in the 1940s; combines some elements of appointment along with retention elections

States also employ a variety of mechanisms for removing judges who prove unfit for service.

As previously noted, every state except Oklahoma and Texas has a single court of last resort with both criminal and civil jurisdiction. Civil appeals constitute most of the appellate workload for these courts. This is also true in federal courts, where in 2011, out of 45,864 appeals pending in the federal courts of appeals, 12,066 were criminal appeals; the remainder were civil cases (see Administrative Office of the U.S. Courts 2012b: 60).

Most state supreme court justices carry out their duties with little fanfare or publicity. In fact, the average citizen would have a hard time naming any of their state supreme court justices. Over the past two decades, some state supreme courts have come under scrutiny whenever they are asked to review a death penalty case. Such reviews might bring unfavorable publicity to state supreme court justices; in Tennessee, there was a successful effort by a citizens' group to defeat Justice Penny White in her retention election to the state supreme court over what were perceived as lenient decisions in death penalty cases (Reid 1999; see also Brown 1998). Cases like this may not occur often, and when they do, they may not be successful. However, the White case and that of state supreme court justice Rose Bird in California illustrate that some groups may give state appellate court judges more publicity than they normally receive. Box 7.3 discusses the issue of death penalty appeals that must be addressed by the majority of state supreme courts.

Box 7.3   The Exception That Proves the Rule: Appealing a Death Sentence

Even though their numbers are small, one type of state supreme court case is particularly important. After the U.S. Supreme Court's ruling in *Furman v. Georgia* (1972), which struck down the death penalty, many states rewrote their capital punishment laws. Now every state except South Carolina that has the death penalty includes a provision allowing for automatic appeals from the trial court to the state court of last resort (see *Gregg v. Georgia* (1976)). These appeals do not have to be filed by the person convicted of the crime and bypass the state intermediate appellate courts.

Death penalty rulings by state supreme courts are not the final word in some cases, but such appeals are important because they make appellate courts responsible for ensuring that capital cases and death penalty verdicts are as free from mistakes as possible. Unfortunately, as several well-publicized cases from a number of states have demonstrated, errors still occur and some innocent people are convicted of crimes they did not commit. A number of groups, such as the American Civil Liberties Union's Capital Punishment Project and the Death Penalty Information Center, have called for death penalty moratoriums around the country, but the majority of states still have death penalty statutes on their books.

SOURCE: Grisham 2006.

FEDERAL COURTS

Throughout this chapter, we note that there are a variety of courts at different levels of government in the United States. For most of us, if we have any contact with the courts, it is limited to courts at the local or possibly the state level. However, the federal courts of original jurisdiction also handle a large number of both civil and criminal cases. The jurisdictions of state and federal courts can be similar, but often they are very distinct. There can even be overlapping or concurrent jurisdiction. In this section we examine the following topics: (1) the basis for authority, (2) jurisdiction, and (3) structure of the federal courts of original jurisdiction.

The caseloads of federal courts are smaller than state courts, but the types of cases federal courts handle are important because they have an impact on our civil and criminal justice systems nationwide. In recent years, cases dealing with organized criminal activities (the federal Racketeering Influenced Corrupt Organization, or RICO, statutes) and civil rights violations directed at individuals and agencies in the criminal justice system have been especially important. Consider the recent conviction of mobster Whitey Bulger by a Boston-area federal jury. Bulger, accused of multiple homicides and various other criminal acts, was actually convicted under federal RICO statutes of racketeering and conspiracy. Bulger plans to appeal his conviction on the grounds that he was a federal informant and therefore immune from prosecution at the time of the alleged crimes.

Federal Trial Courts

Article III of the U.S. Constitution provides the basis for all of the federal courts' structures and jurisdictions. Article III, Section 1 says that "[t]he judicial power of the United States shall be vested in one supreme court and in such inferior courts as the Congress may from time to time ordain and establish." This means that the Constitution specifically establishes the Supreme Court of the United States and leaves the number, types, jurisdiction, and staffing of other federal courts up to Congress.

The outline established in the Constitution gives us two types of federal courts: **constitutional courts**, also called Article III courts, and **legislative courts**, established under Article I's powers granted to Congress (Carp and Stidham 1998). Our focus in this section is on Article III courts (the federal district courts), but we briefly discuss some of the legislative courts. A major difference between constitutional and legislative courts is that constitutional courts have only judicial powers, while legislative courts may exercise legislative and administrative powers (Abraham 1986: 148-149).

The structure and functions of the federal court system was a major topic of debate during the Constitutional Convention of 1787. Russell Wheeler says, "The very idea of a federal court system in addition to the existing state courts . . . was a source of vigorous opposition to the Constitution's ratification" (1992: 5).

One early political group, the **Anti-Federalists**, opposed a strong central government and were concerned that national courts "could become instruments of tyranny" (Wheeler and Harrison 1994: 2). As a result, the Anti-Federalists lobbied heavily for a limited federal judiciary. They proposed that state courts should handle most legal matters (see, for example, Wheeler and Harrison 1994). George Washington's political party at the time was known as the **Federalists**; they favored not only the establishment of a national Supreme Court but also a system of federal trial courts.

Eventually the Federalists won out, and in 1789, President George Washington signed one of the first pieces of legislation passed by Congress: "An Act to Establish the Federal Courts of the United States." This bill is often referred to as the **Judiciary Act of 1789**, and it contained several provisions that had an impact on the administration of justice early in our nation's history, many of which continue to have influence today.

At least four key elements among the Judiciary Act's provisions are relevant to our discussion. First, the bill provided for the creation of a federal court structure below that of the Supreme Court. Second, it created circuit courts with limited appellate jurisdiction. Third, it established the initial size of the Supreme Court as having a chief justice

Constitutional courts: federal courts created under Article III of the U.S. Constitution

Legislative courts: federal courts created under Article I of the U.S. Constitution granting such authority to Congress

Anti-Federalists: one of two original political parties in the United States; opposed a strong national government, preferring instead to allow the states to have broad political powers

Federalists: the political party of George Washington; supported a strong national government with broad political powers

Judiciary Act of 1789: one of the first congressional acts under the newly constituted United States; established the structure and jurisdiction of federal courts and created the offices of U.S. marshal, U.S. attorney, and attorney general

and five associate justices. Finally, it provided for the appointment of U.S. marshals, U.S. attorneys, and an attorney general, all to be chosen by the president.

The Federalists agreed to three compromises with the Anti-Federalists. First, the district courts and circuit courts were to be given limited jurisdictions. Second, no district or circuit boundary could cut across a state line. Third, the judges for these courts were to be chosen from the district or circuit within which they resided (Wheeler 1992: 5). This arrangement still exists today.

Throughout our nation's history, Congress has repeatedly modified the federal courts. The following sections highlight some of the legislative changes that define the jurisdiction and structure of today's federal courts.

Structure of the Federal District Courts

As Figure 7.2 shows, the current structure of federal courts in the United States can be illustrated in three tiers. The top tier is composed of the U.S. Supreme Court. The second tier contains the U.S. Court of Appeals for the Armed Forces and the 13 U.S. courts of appeals. These two levels of federal appellate courts are discussed later in

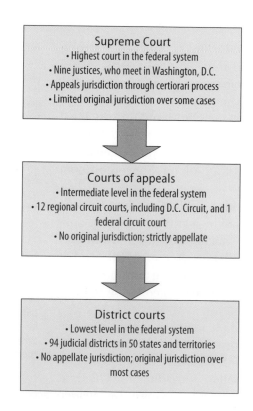

Figure 7.2
Federal courts: explaining the structure

Figure 7.3   Geographic jurisdiction boundaries of U.S. courts of appeals

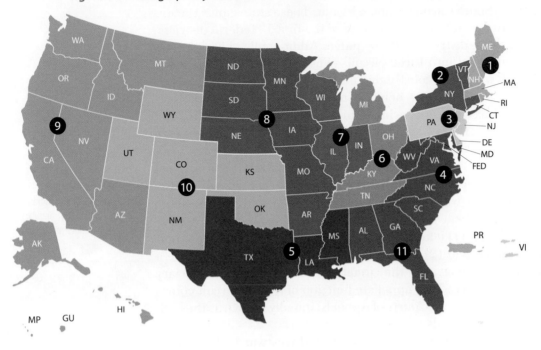

the chapter. Figure 7.3 shows the boundaries of the courts of appeals in the federal court system. Finally, there are 94 district courts and a group of specialized courts, including the Tax Court, U.S. Claims Court, Court of Veterans Appeals, and the Court of International Trade, below the Courts of Appeals. Congress originally created a number of these courts as legislative courts. However, the status of all of these courts—except the U.S. Tax Court, the U.S. Court of Military Appeals, and the Territorial Courts—has been changed to constitutional courts (Abraham 1986: 150).

In this section, we focus on the district courts. These courts are important because most federal cases never progress beyond this stage (Wasby 1988: 42). The district courts are the courts of original jurisdiction in the federal system, and they have both criminal and civil jurisdiction. Historically, however, the "primary trial court" designation for the district courts did not occur until passage of the Circuit Court of Appeals Act of 1891 (Wheeler and Harrison 1994: 18).

The federal court system has evolved slowly since the passage of the Judiciary Act on September 24, 1789, which initially outlined the structure of the federal court system. The first 11 states to ratify the Constitution were (alphabetically) Connecticut, Delaware, Georgia,

Maryland, Massachusetts, New Hampshire, New Jersey, New York, Pennsylvania, South Carolina, and Virginia. These states, plus the districts of Kentucky and Maine, constituted the first 13 federal districts, and each of these districts had one judge. Additionally, 11 of the districts were grouped into three circuits—Eastern, Middle, and Southern—in which a district court judge and two Supreme Court justices made up the circuit court bench. Originally the districts of Kentucky and Maine were not included in one of the three circuits, and the district courts there had both trial and appellate jurisdiction (see Wheeler and Harrison 1994: 5-8).

From 1789 to 1891, the U.S. federal circuit courts, the original federal courts of appeals, had a **circuit riding** operation, which was a holdover from the way many state courts had operated. Circuit riding by the federal judges, which took up to six months of the year, accomplished two things: (1) it kept the federal appellate courts close to their state court roots, and (2) it kept Congress from having to provide a separate group of judges for the circuit courts. The Federal Judiciary Act of 1891 transferred the appellate function of federal circuit courts to the newly created U.S. Courts of Appeals, initially known as the U.S. Circuit Courts of Appeals.

Circuit riding: the practice of judges to travel to several locations to conduct trials or appellate proceedings

As the nation grew and moved south and westward, the district court structure provided flexibility for expansion as well. There were 20 district courts in 1802, and there were 34 by 1837. The major problem area for the federal courts existed as a result of the circuit court and Supreme Court linkage. For instance, there were six federal circuits and six Supreme Court justices in 1802. By 1837, the number of circuits had increased to nine; the number of Supreme Court justices was also increased to nine to provide oversight for the new Eighth and Ninth Circuits (Wheeler and Harrison 1994). The practice of adding justices in response to the number of federal circuits eventually increased the Supreme Court to ten members in 1863. Some people—President Abraham Lincoln being one of them—criticized this approach to structuring the federal appellate courts (Wheeler and Harrison 1994: 12). From 1863 until 1870, there were fluctuations in the number of Supreme Court justices; Congress finally set the Court's size at nine, the number of justices that we have today.

Jurisdiction of the Federal District Courts

When the Federalists and the Anti-Federalists debated the nature of the federal courts, the issue of subject matter jurisdiction, particularly for the lower courts, generated a great deal of controversy. The Judiciary Act of 1789 initially gave federal trial courts jurisdiction in cases relating to admiralty, diversity of citizenship, the United States as a plaintiff, and federal crimes (see especially Wheeler and Harrison 1994: 6-7).

Admiralty cases, also known as maritime law, is "a broad body of law governing the transport of goods and passengers by water, the purchase and charter of vessels, the hiring and maintenance of officers and crew, the transportation of people and goods, the navigation of vessels, and the insurance of vessels, people, and cargo" (Sheppard 2012: 89). Since the United States was bounded by oceans and crossed by inland waterways, admiralty jurisdiction seemed especially important to the new national government. Very little controversy existed over federal courts exercising admiralty jurisdiction, and the district courts heard a number of these cases when they first were established (Wasby 1988: 42).

Admiralty:
cases dealing with maritime law or those related to legal matters occurring around or on waterways

However, both the Constitutional Convention and the First United States Congress wrestled with the question of **diversity of citizenship** jurisdiction. Article III, Section 2 of the Constitution says that federal courts shall have jurisdiction in cases involving "controversies between two or more states;—between a state and citizens of another state;—between citizens of different states;—between citizens of the same state claiming lands under grants of different states, and between a state, or the citizens thereof, and foreign states, citizens or subjects." Diversity of citizenship arises from "the diversity of citizenship of the plaintiffs from the citizenship of the defendants, in that the two parties . . . are citizens of different states of the union, citizens of different nation-states, or a foreign nation-state" (Sheppard 2012: 1453).

Diversity of citizenship:
constitutional questions relating to opposing parties from different states or those involving citizens of foreign countries

Diversity of citizenship jurisdiction concerned the Federalists for two reasons. First, since state judges were appointed by the legislatures in most instances, there was a concern that these judges would be influenced by the legislatures. Second, the Federalists were concerned about a possible bias in favor of in-state litigants over out-of-state litigants. No one knew for sure whether these two issues were likely to result or not, but they were real in the minds of many Federalist leaders.

Article III, Section 2 also provides federal court jurisdiction over "controversies to which the United States shall be a party." This seemed to cover both civil and criminal jurisdiction and appeared to have little potential controversy. It is important to remember, however, that when the Judiciary Act of 1789 was passed, there was relatively little federal statutory law (Wheeler and Harrison 1994: 6). This act left the state courts being responsible for many types of cases that later would become federal matters.

Basically, the U.S. Constitution establishes the types of cases federal courts may hear, but beyond the broad outlines provided for in the Constitution, Congress can further define federal court jurisdiction.

Take the example of diversity jurisdiction cases. In this area, Congress has determined that the amount in dispute must be greater than $75,000 (not including costs and interest); this amount was increased from $50,000 in 1996. Below this amount, state courts are to handle these cases.

Two additional factors need to be emphasized regarding federal court jurisdiction. First, the federal courts are limited by the Constitution to deciding "cases and controversies." Therefore, federal courts must be presented with actual disputes involving opposing parties who stand to win or lose; federal courts are prohibited from answering hypothetical questions or from issuing advisory opinions (see Abraham 1986).

Second, federal court jurisdiction is a somewhat fluid concept. Some jurisdictional elements are relatively fixed, but others have changed over time by court interpretations and congressional enactments to meet the needs of an ever-changing society.

Workload of the Federal District Courts

The typical federal district court case is heard by one judge in a jury trial rather than a bench trial. Historically, situations have arisen where three-judge panels have been used (see especially Wasby 1988: 47-48). Three-judge panels are typically composed of one U.S. appeals judge and two U.S. district court judges.

Beginning in 1903, three-judge courts were used to respond to requests for injunctions against the Interstate Commerce Commission; beginning in 1910, three-judge courts were used for injunctions against state laws; in 1913, this authority was extended to state administrative actions. In 1937, the use of three-judge courts was extended to injunctions against federal statutes.

One problem associated with the three-judge courts was that appeals of their decisions bypassed the courts of appeals and went directly to the U.S. Supreme Court, and these mandatory appeals overloaded the Supreme Court's discretionary docket. As a result, in 1976, Congress ended the use of three-judge courts in all cases except those involving legislative reapportionment, the Civil Rights Act of 1964 and the Voting Rights Act (Wasby 1988).

Table 7.1 shows the number of civil and criminal cases filed in the district courts for the 11-year period from 2001 to 2011, demonstrating what could be called the "normal" workloads of federal district courts. Two features of this table are especially important. To begin with, there are year-to-year variations, but the general trend is upward for both types of cases. Second, as is obvious, substantially more civil cases than criminal cases are filed annually in federal district courts. This section discusses both types of cases, along with bankruptcies.

Table 7.1	Criminal and Civil Cases Filed in U.S. District Courts, 2001-2011	
YEAR	CRIMINAL CASES	CIVIL CASES
2001	50,673	250,907
2002	55,219	274,841
2003	58,951	252,962
2004	59,496	281,338
2005	58,536	253,273
2006	56,532	259,541
2007	57,172	257,507
2008	61,026	267,257
2009	65,394	276,397
2010	66,693	293,352
2011	66,442	289,630

NOTE: The ending dates for all years except 2011 are September 30. The data for 2011 end on June 30.
SOURCE: Administrative Office of the U.S. Courts 2012a.

Civil Cases. The number of civil cases was fairly consistent between 2001 and 2011. There were three decreases from one year to the next: 2002-2003, 2004-2005, and 2006-2007. No single factor can be identified as contributing to these declines.

Criminal Cases. Table 7.1 reveals the number of criminal cases filed in the U.S. district courts from 2001 to 2011. Interestingly, the number of federal criminal cases declined from 2004 to 2005, and again from 2005 to 2006. However, beginning in 2007, the numbers began to increase once more. For the ten-year period from 2001 to 2010, there was a 24 percent increase in the number of federal criminal cases filed in U.S. district courts.

At this point it is important to note the influence of legislation regarding speedy trials and the processing of federal criminal cases. One provision in the Sixth Amendment to the Constitution says that "the accused shall enjoy the right to a speedy and public trial." In the earliest periods of our nation's history, and particularly in state cases, determination of a "speedy" trial largely was left to the discretion of trial judges (see the U.S. Supreme Court cases of *Klopfer v. North Carolina* (1967); *Barker v. Wingo* (1972)). However, in 1974, Congress passed the federal **Speedy Trial Act**, which gave speedy trials very specific meaning. Under the Speedy Trial Act, federal authorities essentially have 100 days from the time of arrest to bring a case to trial or face having the charges dismissed (18 U.S.C. Chapter 208). This includes 30 days from arrest to indictment or information and 70 days

Speedy Trial Act:
federal statute that provides for specific guidelines concerning the amount of time the government has to bring criminal cases to trial

Table 7.2 Federal Bankruptcy Cases, 2007-2012	
YEAR	NUMBER OF CASES
2007	695,575
2008	901,927
2009	1,202,503
2010	1,531,997
2011	1,571,183
2012	1,367,006

SOURCE: Administrative Office of the U.S. Courts 2012a.

from this date until trial. Some exceptions and exemptions can extend this time limit in specific cases.

Bankruptcy Cases.   As revealed in Table 7.2, the number of federal bankruptcy cases filed increased 55.7 percent from 2007 to 2011. Two other things are apparent in this table. First, the numbers of bankruptcies can be linked to the economic downturn that the United States has been experiencing. Second, while these numbers represent both personal and business bankruptcies, the overwhelming majority of bankruptcies in the United States—typically over 90 percent—are personal bankruptcies. These cases, along with the increase in criminal and civil cases, have contributed to the growing workload of federal district courts.

Federal Appellate Courts

The federal appellate courts are arranged in a two-tiered system, much like many state courts. In fact, it is safe to say that the federal courts provided the pattern that many states later adopted.

As noted earlier, Article III of the Constitution established the U.S. Supreme Court. The Supreme Court is *the* court of last resort in the United States. Nevertheless, the Supreme Court's decisions may be only one point in a circular process that can involve both the executive and legislative branches. For example, Supreme Court decisions like school desegregation (*Brown v. Board of Education* (1954)) depend on enforcement by the executive branch, and this enforcement can be slow or absent completely. Additionally, when federal and state laws are struck down as unconstitutional, Congress and state legislatures can pass new laws that meet the Court's original objections (see *Gregg v. Georgia* (1976)).

In addition to the U.S. Supreme Court, the U.S. Courts of Appeals were created very early in our nation's history, but their current structure and the practices they follow have developed over a long time period. The next section examines the structure and functions of the federal intermediate appellate courts.

U.S. Courts of Appeals

The official title for the intermediate federal appellate courts is the courts of appeals. However, many court observers and scholars continue to call them the circuit courts. This title is the result of the initial circuit riding practices of district court judges and Supreme Court justices who served on the various courts of appeals. The circuit court designation also continues to be used as a result of these courts being numbered and designated—by way of example, the Court of Appeals for the First Circuit (see Figure 7.3).

Like much of the rest of the federal judiciary, the Judiciary Act of 1789 created the circuit courts. Initially these courts were given limited appellate jurisdiction, and not until Congress passed the Circuit Court of Appeals Act of 1891 did these courts take on the functions now associated with them. In the Circuit Court of Appeals Act, Congress "shifted the appellate caseload burden from the Supreme Court to new courts of appeals, and, in so doing, made the federal district courts the system's primary trial courts" (Wheeler and Harrison 1994: 18).

Figure 7.3 provides a map outlining the federal courts of appeals jurisdictions. Presently, the federal court system has 11 numbered courts of appeals, plus an intermediate appellate court for the District of Columbia and one for the federal circuit (both of these are located in Washington, D.C.).

The intermediate courts of appeal hear most of the cases appealed in the federal system, and these cases include issues originally litigated in state courts but appealed to the federal district courts (like state prisoner habeas corpus petitions) and cases that originated in the federal district courts. Only a small percentage of cases are ever appealed, and most of these never go beyond the intermediate appellate courts. As Table 7.3 illustrates, in 2000, the U.S. Supreme Court had 8,965 cases on its docket compared with more than 54,000 appeals filed with the U.S. courts of appeals. By 2006, the Supreme Court's docket had grown to 10,256 cases compared with 66,618 cases filed in the U.S. Courts of Appeals (Maguire 2013). Generally, since 2006, the numbers of appeals for both types of courts have declined.

The federal courts of appeals for the various circuits meet in the following locations: Boston (First), New York (Second), Philadelphia (Third), Richmond (Fourth), New Orleans (Fifth), Cincinnati (Sixth), Chicago (Seventh), St. Louis (Eighth), San Francisco (Ninth), Denver

Table 7.3	Courts of Appeals and U.S. Supreme Court Cases on Docket, 2000-2010	
YEAR	COURTS OF APPEALS	SUPREME COURT
2000	54,697	8,965
2001	57,464	9,176
2002	57,555	9,406
2003	60,847	8,882
2004	62,762	8,588
2005	68,473	9,608
2006	66,618	10,256
2007	58,410	9,602
2008	61,104	8,966
2009	57,740	9,302
2010	55,992	—
2011	55,126	—

NOTE: Recent docket numbers for the Supreme Court are unavailable at this time.
SOURCES: Maguire 2013: tables 5.66, 5.67, 5.69, 5.71; U.S. Courts 2012.

(Tenth), and Atlanta (Eleventh). Three-judge panels normally decide these courts' cases, but in a small number of high-profile cases, all of the judges for a particular circuit may sit *en banc* (all together) to decide a case.

The U.S Supreme Court

The U.S. Supreme Court is much easier to describe than its state counterparts. There has been so much written about the Supreme Court and the justices who have served on the Court that it is difficult to summarize.

Article III of the U.S. Constitution provides the general authority for the Supreme Court, and Article III broadly outlines that there will be a Supreme Court and other courts that Congress may establish. It also defines federal court jurisdiction as including

all Cases, in Law and Equity, arising under this Constitution, the Laws of the United States, and Treaties made, or which shall be made, under their Authority;—to all Cases affecting Ambassadors, other public Ministers and Consuls;—to all Cases of admiralty and maritime Jurisdiction;—to Controversies to which the United States shall be a party;—to Controversies between two or more States;—between a State and Citizens of another State;—between Citizens of different States;—between Citizens of the same State claiming Lands under Grants of different States, and between a State, or the Citizens thereof, and foreign States, Citizens or Subjects.

Additionally, the Constitution says that the Supreme Court can exercise original jurisdiction in cases involving ambassadors, public ministers, and consuls, and those cases in which a state is a party. In all other cases, the Court exercises appellate jurisdiction.

Beyond Article III's broad guidelines, the Court's jurisdiction is somewhat vague. As a result, much of what the Supreme Court is today has developed from the personalities and predispositions of the men and women who have served on the Court (see Rehnquist 2001).

A key to understanding the Supreme Court's work is **judicial review**. The Supreme Court first asserted its authority to review acts of the president and Congress that appeared to be in conflict with the Constitution in the case of *Marbury v. Madison* (1803). Judicial review "is the power of a court to determine whether an act of government is an exercise of constitutional authority and to strike down that act if it adjudges it to be unconstitutional" (Stephens and Rathjen 1980: 13). Judicial review extends to acts of lower state and federal courts, federal and state legislatures, and executive officers at different levels, including those in administrative agencies, and it has been characterized as the "cornerstone of our constitutional system" (Stephens and Rathjen 1980: 13).

Judicial review: court authority to examine the acts of legislatures, the executive, administrative agencies, and lower-level courts to determine the constitutionality of their actions

The Constitution and Congress define part of the Supreme Court's appellate jurisdiction, but generally the Court sets its own judicial agenda. Two very clear examples illustrate the Supreme Court's control over its docket.

To begin with, currently most cases that are appealed to the Court come on **writs of certiorari**. The Supreme Court hears the discretionary appeals of certiorari when it asks the lower court to "send up the record" of the case for review. To accept a case on certiorari, four of the Court's nine justices must vote in favor of the writ to add the case to the docket; cases can be refused without explanation. Even when a case is accepted on certiorari, the Court may vote at a later time not to schedule the case for oral arguments and to drop it from the docket by noting that certiorari was "improvidently granted."

Writs of certiorari: discretionary appeals in which courts (especially the U.S. Supreme Court) ask lower-level courts to send up the record of a particular case to make a decision about whether it will be accepted for review

The Supreme Court's discretionary appellate process is also demonstrated by the relatively small number of cases decided each year. For example, in 2009, the Supreme Court had 9,302 cases on its docket and disposed of 8,133 cases. However, just 172 cases were decided on the merits, and only 81 were scheduled for oral arguments. This was down from a 1982 high with 282 cases decided on the merits and 175 cases scheduled for oral arguments (Maguire 2013). These numbers demonstrate something of the decrease in appeals heard by the U.S. Courts of Appeals and those reaching and decided by the U.S. Supreme Court.

Another interesting feature of the Supreme Court is that its term does not coincide with either the calendar year or the federal government's fiscal year (October 1 to September 30). While there is no exact starting date for the Court, its term always starts on the first Monday in October, and each term typically ends in late June or early July. Some of the justices stay in Washington for Court business, but most travel, complete non-Court legal writing (such as law review articles), and give speeches at law schools and professional conferences.

A relatively small number of people have served on the U.S. Supreme Court. Most members of the Court serve relatively long terms, with the longest-serving justice being William O. Douglas, who served 36 years, from 1939 until his retirement for health reasons in 1975. Since George Washington appointed the Supreme Court's first 6 justices, only 112 people have served in this capacity. Of this number, 2 (Thurgood Marshall and Clarence Thomas) have been African Americans, and 4 (Sandra Day O'Connor, Ruth Bader Ginsburg, Sonia Sotomayor, and Elena Kagan) have been women.

Finally, while the Supreme Court is the "court of last resort," as mentioned previously, it is not necessarily the final word on some issues. As one illustration, in the late 1800s, the Supreme Court ruled the personal income tax invalid since the Constitution provided that taxes must be levied among the states based on their populations (*Pollock v. Farmers' Loan and Trust Co.* (1895)). The result was the addition of the Sixteenth Amendment to the Constitution in 1913 that provided that "Congress shall have power to lay and collect taxes on incomes, from whatever source derived, without apportionment among the several States, and without regard to any census or enumeration."

The "checks and balances" element of our government allows Congress to pass legislation counteracting Supreme Court rulings, and the executive branch may ignore or choose not to enforce the Court's rulings. That being said, more than 200 years of our nation's history have added a great deal of symbolic authority and legitimacy to most Supreme Court decisions. As described in Box 7.4, however, not all Supreme Courts are equally supreme.

SUMMARY

Examining court structures and organizations in the United States can often be confusing and frustrating. There seem to be so many types of courts at all levels of government with such unique jurisdictions that it is difficult to make sense of the judicial landscape. However, certain features and characteristics allow a relatively easy summary of the courts.

Cities, towns, and townships establish local courts that handle the minor civil and misdemeanor criminal cases in the United States. People who have received a citation for a moving violation or a parking

---

Box 7.4   The Supreme Court of the United Kingdom: As Does the Child, So Does the Parent?

In Anglo-Saxon England, the kings were advised by the Witan, a political assembly of members of the ruling class, an idea that continued under Norman rule, following the conquest in 1066. Eventually, this body assumed greater legislative, judicial, and political roles, morphing over the centuries into first the *Curia Regis*, also known colloquially as the court of the king's bench and then, after 1236, as Parliament. This evolutionary body also became the House of Lords and the House of Commons, both of which functioned as trial and appellate courts. In 1399, the House of Commons ceased hearing appeals, effectively leaving the House of Lords as Great Britain's court of last resort.

The judicial functions of the House of Lords changed over the centuries. It tried its last peer of the realm in 1938. However, a key principle was that the Law Lords or judges, as select members of the House of Lords, could not review any act of Parliament. Since World War II, the work of the Appellate Committee of the House of Lords has been performed by the Lords of Appeal in Ordinary, a sitting body of highly qualified, full-time judges. Interestingly, appeals were not technically made to the House of Lords but rather to the Queen-in-Parliament, meaning that the Law Lords represented the entire nation.

Over the past 50 years, other social, legal, and historical developments have overtaken this committee, including the creation of the European Union, all of which have complicated the mission and scope of the Law Lords' work. To meet these and other pressing legal issues, Parliament created the Supreme Court of the United Kingdom in 2005; this body started work in 2009. The Court's jurisdiction is limited to the UK's three legal systems: England and Wales, Northern Ireland, and Scotland. Moreover, unlike the Supreme Court of the United States and other constitutional nations, the Supreme Court of the UK, like its predecessor, cannot overrule an act of Parliament. Consisting of 12 justices, all of whom are appointed by the monarch to lifetime tenure on advice of the prime minister, the court typically sits in a panel of 5, but panels of 3, 7, or 9 members are not uncommon. They also serve as members of Judicial Committee of the Privy Council, another of the UK's appellate courts. Justices are called lord or lady for life. Clearly, while the Supreme Court of the United Kingdom may initially appear to derive from its American cousin, it still retains much of its unique British characters and functions.

---

ticket are familiar with these courts. Most of the cases handled by local courts are disposed of quickly and often without attorneys representing either side. Local courts are typically informal, and fines are often levied against those who are found guilty (or who plead guilty) to violations. One of the criticisms of the inferior jurisdiction courts is they dispense "rough justice."

Although there are similar patterns of court organization, every state has its own unique court system; state courts may be organized into two, three, or more levels or tiers. Each state has at least one level of trial courts. Some states have two levels of these courts—one for minor civil and criminal cases, and another serving as the court of general trial jurisdiction for felonies and major civil cases. There can also be one or two levels of state appellate courts. The majority of states now have intermediate appellate courts in addition to their court of last resort. Most state courts operate with relatively little visibility or public scrutiny. However, sometimes high-profile cases, such as those involving George Zimmerman and Casey Anthony, will come along that allow the public to see what state courts do and how they operate.

Federal courts also may receive relatively little public attention, even considering the U.S. Supreme Court. Federal courts can have concurrent jurisdiction with the state courts over certain civil and criminal cases. Some issues, however, fall uniquely within the federal courts' jurisdiction. The Supreme Court's jurisdiction is broadly defined by the Constitution, and the U.S. Congress further defines the entire federal court system's specific jurisdictional boundaries. Whenever there is a vacancy on the Supreme Court and the president nominates someone to fill that vacancy public attention focuses on the federal courts. Often the news is filled with information on the confirmation proceedings conducted by the U.S. Senate, but most of the time the public is blissfully ignorant of the federal judiciary's judges and courts.

REVIEW QUESTIONS

1. Should each state maintain its own unique court system, or is there a reason (or reasons) to merge all courts into one national system?
2. Either through a library search or an online search, determine the number of levels in your state's court system. Does your state have specialized courts for civil and criminal cases? Does it have any other specialized courts?
3. Among the federal courts, what differentiates between constitutional courts and legislative courts? Is there a simple and clear distinction?
4. In what kinds of circumstances do state courts and federal courts have overlapping (concurrent) jurisdictions over certain kinds of cases? Give specific examples. Where would concurrent jurisdiction exist?
5. In reviewing the chapter, develop a list of the kinds of cases that can be heard by federal courts. What kinds of criminal cases are most likely to be heard in federal courts? What about civil cases?
6. Procedurally, federal courts cannot issue advisory opinions. Why would they take such a position?
7. Sometimes you hear people say, "I'll appeal this all the way to the Supreme Court." Is that likely to happen in most cases? Why or why not?

KEY TERMS

administrative office of courts (AOC)
admiralty
Anti-Federalists
bench trial
celebrated cases
chancery courts
circuit riding
constitutional courts
courts of appellate jurisdiction
courts of general trial jurisdiction
courts of limited jurisdiction
courts of original jurisdiction
courts of record
diversity of citizenship
Federalists
intermediate courts of appeal

judicial review
Judiciary Act of 1789
justices of the peace
legislative courts
local legal culture
magistrate judges
Missouri Plan

probate courts
problem-solving courts
pro se proceedings
Speedy Trial Act
trial de novo
wedding cake model
writs of certiorari

Trials and Trial Procedures

LEARNING OBJECTIVES

At the conclusion of this chapter, you should be able to:

- Explain the pretrial steps associated with processing criminal cases.
- Describe the jury selection process.
- Discuss the stages associated with criminal trials.
- Define the sentencing options available in criminal cases.
- Explain the process and bases for appeals.

INTRODUCTION

The American public is fascinated with the drama associated with criminal trials, and when there is a spectacular crime—like the 2012 movie theater shootings in Aurora, Colorado, or the 2013 Jodi Arias "fatal attraction" murder trial in Phoenix, Arizona—the case will draw national and even international attention.

A criminal trial represents the high point of criminal procedures in the United States, both for everyday citizens and for people who study courts and law. The truth, however, is that only a small percentage of the totality of criminal cases reach the trial stage in this country. The vast majority are resolved in a less formal, more routine manner through guilty pleas and, less often, other legal maneuvers, sometimes with explicit plea bargaining and sometimes without.

This chapter examines the events that take place before trials actually begin and follows that by considering the different steps that occur when there is a trial. Separate from the trial itself, the chapter also considers the process of jury deliberation and sentencing—including the range of sentencing options that are available to judges and juries. The chapter closes with a discussion of the grounds on which appeals can be based and the different types of appeals that are available to convicted criminal defendants.

PRETRIAL PROCEDURES

Arrest

Several preliminary steps must be completed before cases ever go to trial. We need to begin with the legal act known as an arrest to completely understand pretrial procedures. To begin with, the police can make an arrest with or without a warrant; however, it makes a difference whether the offense is a felony or a misdemeanor (Walsh and Hemmens 2008: 135). If police officers have a warrant, they can make arrests for either felonies or misdemeanors at any time. They can also make arrests for felonies without a warrant if the offense is committed in their presence or based on probable cause. **Probable cause** is an arcane legal idea that generally is taken to mean that there is "a reasonable amount of suspicion, supported by circumstances sufficiently strong to justify a prudent and cautious person's belief that certain facts are probably true" (Handler 1994: 431). In the present instance, a criminal act is believed to have taken place and a given person is believed to have participated in it. An example of a probable cause arrest would be one in which a citizen complainant flags down an officer and reports that a suspect has

Probable cause: belief that a crime has been committed and that a particular person is suspected of having committed the crime

been observed breaking into automobiles in a shopping center parking lot. If the officer subsequently spots an individual who matches the suspect's description, an arrest can be made without a warrant.

In misdemeanor cases, officers can make arrests with a warrant or when the offense is committed in their presence. In most other instances, they cannot make misdemeanor arrests. Some states allow police officers to make misdemeanor arrests for offenses they did not witness in a limited number of situations, such as shoplifting and domestic violence.

Once an arrest has been made, the next stage typically is to place the suspect into a police lockup for processing or to book the suspect into the local jail. The former arrangement is generally quite temporary, rarely more than a couple of hours, given that such facilities rarely have the needed infrastructure for longer stays, including toilets, beds, and food. To allow officers to continue their investigations, suspects may be detained prior to arraignment or booking for a limited time, and officers typically conduct custodial interrogations in jail-based interrogation rooms.

Right to Counsel

The Sixth Amendment to the U.S. Constitution provides, in part, that "[i]n all criminal prosecutions, the accused shall enjoy the right . . . to have the assistance of counsel for his defense." Traditionally, this right was attached to trials, especially in federal courts. It has been expanded by Supreme Court rulings to include state cases (*Gideon v. Wainwright* (1963)) and to any "critical stage" of the criminal process. Since eyewitness misidentification can occur during lineups and the effects of this misidentification can carry over to the trial, criminal suspects required to stand in a lineup may be entitled to representation by an attorney, especially after an indictment has been issued but before the trial takes place (*United States v. Wade* (1967); *Gilbert v. California* (1967)). Custodial interrogations also fall into the category of a critical stage. At this point, anything suspects say can be used in court against them. Therefore, when questioning moves from a general investigative line of inquiry to accusation, suspects have the right to have an attorney present (*Miranda v. Arizona* (1966)).

Bail

After booking and investigation have been completed, most suspects will be allowed to make bail. Stephen Michael Sheppard defines **bail** as a "[s]urety given as a pledge that a person will appear in court," and says that it is designed "to ensure the suspect does not flee or fail to appear in court at the time appointed" (2012: 226). A surety is anything

Bail:
the process of securing a person's release prior to the next court appearance

of value, such as money or property, that stands to be forfeited if the defendant flees the jurisdiction or fails to show up for trial. A **bond** is the actual surety posted to make bail, and often the two words appear together on signs or in telephone directories as bail bonds.

Depending on state laws and local legal practices, there are several ways that suspected offenders can post bail and leave confinement, at least until the trial. Being released on one's recognizance is the least restrictive way of making bail. In many instances, these are called OR bonds or ROR (for **release on recognizance**). ROR allows individuals to be released from custody by offering their word that they will appear for their court hearings. When you receive a traffic ticket and the officer asks you to sign it ("This is not an admission of guilt; it simply means you will appear in court on the date set"), this is actually a release on recognizance.

A second way of posting bail is with cash. Judges in some jurisdictions allow jails to post what may be called a "bail schedule." This allows suspects charged with routine offenses to know the amount of bail before they appear in court. If the judge sets a money bail, the suspect (or the suspect's friends or family) may be able to post the entire bail amount and secure the person's release. Under this approach, if the suspect makes all of the scheduled court appearances, the bail amount may be completely refunded unless the court deducts administrative costs.

The use of property bonds is a third way of posting bail. A number of states allow property owners to sign liens against their property if it is worth as much as the amount of bail set by the judge. The court can order the bail forfeited and the property can be seized as payment for the bail if the accused individual fails to appear for a hearing.

For many people, the most common way to post bail is by using a **bail bond company**. Bail companies are private businesses that provide services that benefit both the suspects and the courts. Suspects benefit by not being confined prior to their next court hearing, and the courts benefit by not having jails full of pretrial detainees that must be paid for by the county or other jurisdiction.

As an illustration, a judge might set money bail for a defendant at $5,000. If a bond company is contacted, it will sign a promissory note for that amount with the court in exchange for a customary 10 percent fee from the jailed individual. The fee could be any amount up to the face value of the promissory note. The fee may be increased from the normal amount in situations where there is concern about the person being a flight risk. Once the bonding fee has been paid, the bond company retains the fee as the cost of using this service, no matter what the outcome of the case might be. Whenever a suspect fails to appear in court, the judge can order the bail bond forfeited, and

Bond:
the surety (money or other property) posted to secure bail or pretrial release

Release on recognizance:
a type of pretrial release in which the accused offers his or her word through a signed document to return to court at the next scheduled appearance

Bail bond company:
a private, for-profit business that provides bonds to allow individuals to secure their release rather than having to wait in jail until the next court hearing

bonding companies will then contact bond agents (sometimes called **bounty hunters** or **skip tracers**) to track down the fugitive.

There is one final point about the bail process: Some states have altered the bail process to allow percentage deposits that can be posted with the courts. In these circumstances, the courts allow individuals waiting in jail to post a percentage of the bail in exchange for release instead of having to use the services of a bail bondsman. Consider the previous hypothetical example of the $5,000 bail. The court may charge 10 percent ($500) to secure the suspect's release. Once the case is concluded and the suspect shows up for all hearings, the court may deduct a certain percentage of the deposit (perhaps 10 percent, or $50) and return the rest to the accused. In effect, this process puts the courts in the bail bonding business.

Bounty hunters/skip tracers:
agents who seek a reward for recovering fugitives from justice

Initial Appearance

Sometimes serious misdemeanor and felony suspects cannot make bail; in these cases, an **initial appearance** will be scheduled before a judge or magistrate to review the charges, make sure the suspect is represented by an attorney, and decide whether a reduction in bail or a release on recognizance is appropriate. Most initial appearances occur shortly after the arrest, but generally they occur within 24 to 48 hours. The U.S. Supreme Court, in the case of *County of Riverside v. McLaughlin* (1991), said that initial appearances should take place without *undue delay*. Nevertheless, the Supreme Court recognized that weekends, holidays, and other circumstances might prevent the process from being completed quickly.

Initial appearance:
appearance before a judge or magistrate shortly after arrest; charges are preliminary at this point, and issues of bail and appointment of counsel are first addressed at this stage

Preliminary Hearing

Once the initial appearance is completed, the case will be scheduled for a **preliminary hearing**. These hearings often take place in a court of limited jurisdiction. During the preliminary hearing, the judge will once again inform the defendant of the allegations and criminal charges, and there will be a discussion of legal representation should the defendant not have an attorney present. If the defendant is represented by an attorney, there often follows a request to reduce bail. After the judge has disposed of these issues, and assuming the defendant does not waive the right to a preliminary hearing, the state will present an outline of its case, including some of its evidence. This can be a relatively rapid process, often consisting of the testimony of one or more police officers, perhaps an evidence specialist associated with the investigation, and some of the civilian eyewitnesses to the alleged event taking the stand in an effort to convince the judge that

Preliminary hearing:
a probable cause hearing that typically occurs before a case is referred to the grand jury

sufficient probable cause exists in the case that a crime has been committed and the defendant is involved in it.

Grand Jury

When the state is able to demonstrate probable cause to the judge's satisfaction, the case is bound over to the **grand jury**. All federal felony cases are heard by grand juries under the provision in the Fifth Amendment to the Constitution that states that "[n]o person shall be held to answer for a capital, or otherwise infamous crime, unless on a presentment or indictment of a Grand Jury." However, while this provision applies in federal cases, only about half of the states continue to use grand juries to determine probable cause for trial, and those that do not use grand juries employ a more thorough preliminary hearing process.

The grand jury is one of the least public and therefore least known and understood aspects of the entire criminal justice system. Two reasons explain why this is the case. First, the press and the general public do not have access to grand jury hearings because they are held behind closed doors. Second, unlike trial jurors, grand jury members are forever sworn to secrecy concerning the testimony and voting that occurs in the grand jury room.

Grand juries can vary in size from one state to the next, and they can be composed of 12 to 23 members. Grand jury members are summoned for service much as those who serve on trial juries, and they may meet daily or only periodically to hear cases during the time they are impaneled. Jurisdictions typically assign an assistant prosecuting attorney to serve as the grand jury's legal advisor. This individual will keep the grand jury on track and guide the witnesses as they appear to testify. When all of the testimony has been completed and it is time for the grand jury to vote, the prosecutor will be dismissed from the grand jury room. Box 8.1 presents a short history of grand juries and the functions they perform.

Another unique feature of grand juries is that unlike trial juries, grand jury decisions do not have to be unanimous. Many states require only an affirmative vote by two-thirds or three-fourths of the grand jury members to return a **true bill** or an **indictment**. An indictment "is a formal, written accusation against a person or persons or entity, authorized by the vote of at least a majority of a properly summoned grand jury, which must have found that there was sufficient evidence to amount to probable cause that the indictees had committed the crimes of which the indictment accuses them" (Sheppard 2012: 1295).

Some states use the **criminal information** document to bypass a preliminary hearing and grand jury process. The criminal information

Grand jury:
a group of citizens convened by a court to review cases presented by the prosecuting attorney to determine if there is sufficient probable cause for the case to move forward to trial

True bill:
a finding of probable cause by a grand jury (see also *indictment*)

Indictment:
the official accusation of a crime by a grand jury in which sufficient probable cause is found for a trial; also known as a true bill

Criminal information:
an alternative to grand jury indictment; an official accusation of wrongdoing filed by the prosecutor with the court

---

Box 8.1   Grand Jury Functions

Grand juries are part of our common law tradition dating back to King Henry II in 1166. From their earliest days, they were seen as a group of citizens who could protect the rights of individuals against malicious prosecution by the state. However, to fully understand grand juries, we must distinguish between their two primary functions: investigation and determining probable cause.

In many states, grand juries can be convened to determine whether a crime has been committed. The courts have used these types of investigative grand juries in cases involving organized crime and particularly high-profile cases, such as the New Orleans investigation of the assassination of President John F. Kennedy. Investigative grand juries can be particularly helpful to law enforcement authorities, but they also have been criticized for the breadth and scope of their investigations once they have been convened.

The second and most common function of the grand jury is to review cases presented by the prosecuting attorney to determine whether there is sufficient probable cause to send the case forward to trial. This function also has its critics. The prosecuting attorney's office presents its case to the grand jury (often through the testimony of investigating police officers); there is no presentation of the defense case (defendants and their attorneys are not present). Also, grand juries do not require a unanimous vote to return an indictment. Therefore, most cases result in indictments, and grand juries are accused of being "rubber stamps" for the prosecutor's office.

---

is "a pleading filed by an official in a criminal action that charges the defendant with a crime" (Sheppard 2012: 1308). In some situations, the criminal information document is only used with misdemeanor cases, though it may also be used with felonies, and it spells out the facts of the case and the substance of the government's accusations.

Arraignment

Once a grand jury indictment has been handed down or the prosecutor has filed the criminal information document, a trial court will schedule the case for an **arraignment**. During the arraignment, the judge may have to address the issues of counsel and bail once again. Additionally, the defense attorney (with or without the defendant being present) will be informed of the current charges alleged against the defendant. This is necessary at this point since the charges may have been adjusted up or down as a result of the grand jury hearing and indictment. The judge will also inform the defendant of the entire range of available due process rights. These include the right to a speedy and public trial, the right to confront the accusers in the case, and the right to be tried by a jury. Box 8.2 provides a brief overview of the issue of speedy

Arraignment:
a legal proceeding in which the accused is informed of the charges resulting from the grand jury indictment or similar process; the judge reviews the charges and addresses issues such as bail and legal representation at this point

---

Box 8.2   Speedy Trial

While the U.S. Constitution guarantees the right to a "speedy trial" for criminal defendants, it does not provide a definition of speedy trial. In the case of *Klopfer v. North Carolina* (1967), the U.S. Supreme Court said that the guarantee of a speedy trial was a fundamental right and applied this right to the states. However, at no point did the Court establish firm guidelines for what constitutes a speedy trial.

All of that changed in 1974 when Congress passed the Speedy Trial Act. This act requires an information or indictment within 30 days of arrest and a trial within 70 days after the information or indictment is issued. Either side can ask for a delay in the deadlines; if the judge grants the request, this allows more time to prepare the case. If no continuances are granted, the clock keeps ticking toward a trial date. Today, all states have similar speedy trial laws; deadlines vary from 90 to 180 days, during which the state must make every effort to bring the defendant to trial or face the possibility of having the charges dismissed.

---

trials. Finally, the judge will ask the defendant if he or she is prepared to enter a plea. The three options available to defendants are (1) not guilty (the court will enter this plea if the defendant stands mute and essentially refuses to give an answer), (2) guilty, and (3) *nolo contendere*, or no contest.

If the defendant pleads not guilty, the judge, usually through the court's scheduling clerk, will work with the prosecuting attorney's office and the defense attorney to set a mutually agreeable trial date. The original date may be changed if scheduling conflicts arise later or if the attorneys need additional time to prepare for the case. In the latter case, the defendant must waive his or her right to a speedy trial. In cases where the defendant enters a guilty plea, the judge will try to make sure that the accused is fully aware of the rights she or he is surrendering (including, in most cases, the right to appeal). When the judge is satisfied that the plea was voluntarily entered, a sentencing date will be set to allow the probation department to prepare a presentence investigation report.

Occasionally, the defendant chooses to plead *nolo contendere*, meaning that the accused individual does not contest the charges against him or her. The judge can treat a no contest plea like a guilty plea and set a sentencing date. Where the defendant does not want to go through the process of a criminal trial, but where there might be civil litigation pending, *nolo contendere* pleas may be entered. Since the defendant neither has pled guilty nor has been found guilty, the plaintiff cannot use this against the defendant in the civil proceedings. This means that defendants may employ no contest pleas as a tactical maneuver when they are facing other legal proceedings.

Nolo contendere: a plea of "no contest" that means that the defendant does not contest the charges but that allows the judge to impose a sentence as if there were a guilty plea

Plea Bargaining

It is important to reinforce the observation that the vast majority of criminal defendants in the United States never go to trial (Sanborn 2009). Typically, between 80 percent and 90 percent of the criminal cases in this country are disposed of with something other than a trial; this usually means a **plea bargain**. When there is overwhelming evidence facing them or they are unable for a variety of personal, financial, or other reasons to otherwise mount a reasonable and reasoned defense, some defendants simply plead guilty to the charges against them. Others actively participate in plea bargaining, directly or through their attorneys, with the prosecuting attorney's office (see Uphoff 2009). There are mixed feelings within both the criminal justice community and the general public about plea bargaining. Nevertheless, the U.S. Supreme Court has at least implicitly sanctioned it in a series of decisions (see, for example, *Bordenkircher v. Hayes* (1978); *North Carolina v. Alford* (1970); *Santobello v. New York* (1971)).

There has been a great deal of research on the nature of plea bargaining and the forces at work during the plea bargaining process that has resulted in several clear conclusions. First, the power in the plea bargaining process resides with the prosecuting attorney (Cole 2004; Heumann 2004). The prosecuting attorney's ultimate threat is that if the defendant does not accept the plea deal, then the case will be taken to trial; moreover, the prosecutor's office will expend every effort to get a conviction and go for the maximum sentence (see, for example, *Bordenkircher v. Hayes* (1978); Gershman 2009). When faced with the prospect of a long sentence or additional charges, many defendants will plead guilty.

Second, the "going rate," or what a case is really worth in terms of a jail or prison sentence or fine, is widely understood by members of the courtroom work group (Walker 2011). Given this widespread and shared sense of what to expect in a given courtroom, the defense attorney can state with relative certainty to a client to whom the prosecution has just made a plea deal agreement known whether the offer represents a "good deal." Case processing is expedited when all of the parties involved know and abide by the going rate.

Third, as a result of the judge's and the attorneys' knowledge of the going rate, the final deal offered by the prosecutor may not be significantly different than the outcome would have been if the case had gone to trial. However, there is always a degree of uncertainty—no matter how small it may be—for all parties in the trial process.

Fourth, as previously suggested, defendants are almost completely at the mercy of the prosecutor's office during the plea bargaining process. It is important to remember that defense attorneys are

Plea bargain: the agreement between the prosecutor and the defendant (defense attorney) that there will be a guilty plea in exchange for some type of leniency

sworn to protect the rights of their clients and to provide a vigorous defense. However, they often find themselves in the role of agent-mediator, trying to persuade the defendant (and sometimes the defendant's family) that a guilty plea is probably the best strategy for everyone involved (Uphoff 2009). Abraham Blumberg (2004) has said that when defense attorneys act in this capacity, it makes the practice of law a "confidence game."

The fifth conclusion we can draw is that the plea bargaining process is not simply bargaining over a plea. Actually, three different factors—the potential sentence, the seriousness of the charges filed, and the number of counts against the defendant—all come into play in the bargaining process. Eventually, the defendant is trying to achieve some amount of leniency; adjustments in any of the three elements can provide that leniency.

A sixth finding is that the judge may play a relatively minor role in the plea bargaining process. Some states prohibit judges from being directly involved in the negotiations, while other states allow or even encourage judges to be involved. Whatever the judge's role, as a result of the going rate, attorneys seldom agree to a bargain that is fundamentally unacceptable to the judge in the case.

Finally, most people inside and outside of the criminal justice system believe that plea bargaining exists because the courts face overwhelming caseloads. Researchers tell us, however, that courts of all sizes and in all types of locations dispose of about the same percentage of cases through plea bargaining (somewhere between 80 percent and 90 percent). This means that there must be factors other than caseload that promote plea bargaining. As a result, we must begin and end with the same assumption: With plea bargaining, everyone wins something. Prosecuting attorneys get a victory in another case, and this positive outcome helps their "batting average." Defense attorneys appointed to represent indigent defendants get rid of cases that they might not have sought in the first place. Public defenders get cases removed from their frequently large caseloads. Judges stay current with their dockets. Finally, in nearly every case, defendants receive some amount of leniency. Crucial to the entire process, however, is the fact that everyone involved in the process gets certainty. Both sides recognize that going to trial can be a risky and time-consuming proposition. Prosecutors and defense attorneys can exercise greater control over the outcome of their cases as a result of plea bargaining, rather than entrusting them into the uncertain hands of jurors.

Diversion

Before moving on to consider the trials themselves, we must acknowledge the role **diversion** plays in disposing of criminal cases. Diversion

Diversion:
removal of an accused person from the formal adjudicative process; often used with juveniles and minor or first-offense adult offenders

is said to occur when those with legal standing in the case agree to suspend further prosecution in favor of some other action. For example, a defendant who is profoundly incapable of participating in his or her own defense may be moved into the mental health system in lieu of prosecution, if only temporarily. Cases may be diverted prior to a trial (in the preadjudication phase), or they may be diverted after the trial (in the postadjudication phase); in either situation, moving the case out of the criminal justice process and into another legal or quasi-legal realm is viewed by many observers as a positive outcome.

Diversion is based on notions associated with sociological labeling theory—namely, that formal processing by the criminal justice system applies a label or stigma to a person and that this label has ongoing and lasting negative consequences. Therefore, many minor or first-time offenders (both juvenile and adult) may be diverted from the system in an effort to reduce the alleged stigma that might otherwise be attached to them. If diversion works—and sometimes that is a big if—these offenders will recognize the second chance they have been given and avoid further and more serious contacts with the criminal justice system.

TRIALS

Although the vast majority of criminal cases are plea bargained, a small fraction of cases in every jurisdiction end up on trial court dockets. Thus, while most people associate criminal trials as being at the very heart of the criminal justice system, they are relatively rare. This section examines the processes that occur once there has been a grand jury indictment or criminal information filed, through the trial itself.

After the accused has been through a preliminary hearing, has received a grand jury indictment, and has gone through an arraignment, that person is legally transformed from a suspect into a defendant. A few stages in the process must be completed before a defendant goes to trial. For example, most courts of general trial jurisdiction will schedule hearings to consider pretrial motions. Box 8.3 outlines some of the common pretrial motions that are filed in cases.

Privately retained attorneys often file a number of pretrial motions to demonstrate to their clients that they really are working on the case; it can also increase billable hours, leading to a bigger bottom line for the attorney. Court-appointed attorneys file pretrial motions but less often than privately retained attorneys. In any event, the judge dismisses many of these pretrial motions, and

---

Box 8.3   Pretrial Motions in Criminal Cases

Attorneys do not file pretrial motions in every case, but some of the common motions include:

- Motions for *nolle prosequi*, which are filed by the prosecutor and ask the court to dismiss some or all of the charges in the case
- Motions for dismissal of some or all of the charges
- Motions for a change of venue, meaning that there is a legal claim of potential or actual bias in the current court, and only by moving to a new (and often distant) court within the same legal jurisdiction can the defendant receive a fair trial
- Motions to sever charges, which request that the defendant be tried on one charge at a time when there is more than a single charge pending
- Motions to suppress witness testimony or physical evidence or confessions
- Motions for discovery, which are essentially attempts to learn what "cards" the prosecutor holds

SOURCE: Kamisar et al. 2008

---

one group of legal observers has said that pretrial motions result in case dismissals in fewer than 5 percent of felony cases (Kamisar et al. 2008).

Jury Trials Versus Bench Trials

Once the judge has disposed of the pretrial motions, a trial date will be set. Before that date arrives, the defendant can waive his or her right to a trial by jury and instead request a **bench trial**. The judge serves in a dual role for bench trials: both trier of fact and trier of law, effectively making the judge both judge and jury. Most major felony cases utilize the Sixth Amendment's guarantee that "[i]n all criminal prosecutions, the accused shall enjoy the right to a speedy and public trial, by and impartial jury of the State and district wherein the crime shall have been committed." However, like other provisions in the Bill of Rights, this section was originally applied solely to cases in federal courts. Eventually, in the case of *Duncan v. Louisiana* (1968), the Supreme Court applied this protection to state court proceedings as well.

Bench trial:
a trial conducted by a judge without the use of a jury

Assembling Jury Pools

Several events must take place before a jury can be selected. In most jurisdictions, the court clerk or some similar public official will assemble a master list of people who are eligible for jury service. Most states require that potential jurors must be at least 18 years of age, a legal resident of the jurisdiction, and not a convicted felon. States vary in the way they identify potential jurors, but many now assemble lists of potential jurors from property tax or voter registration rolls. Since not everyone owns property or is registered to vote, some states have started to add to their lists with driver's license registrations, stipulating a minimum age of 18.

When juries are needed for trials, the office responsible for sending jury summonses will identify a sufficient number of individuals from which to draw juries for a specified time period. Some jurisdictions require potential jurors to serve up to three months, while others have experimented with shorter periods of service to encourage more people to be willing to serve on juries. These latter states or counties may call people for jury duty for no more than one month, and some for even less time.

When an initial jury pool is created and summonses are served on eligible individuals, a survey instrument is often part of the notification process. These surveys address the issue of being excused from jury duty. Some states excuse any parent who has a child under a specific age, usually ten years; however, some excuse only mothers. Potential jury members also may ask be excused from jury duty for other reasons, but the list of acceptable ones is rather short (e.g., a chronic debilitating illness or injury, caregiving duties for an elderly parent, or scheduled surgical procedures). Where surveys are used, they are generally returned to the court officer, and excused members of the pool are notified prior to the reporting date; in other cases, those with excuses must bring them to court and present them as a form of testimony before the court.

Smaller pools of potential jurors are assembled from the **master list** of persons eligible to serve and ordered to report to the courthouse at a given time on a specific date. The groups who go through the jury selection process are called **venires**. Venires vary in size depending on the type of case; from the venire, the final group of jurors and alternates will be selected for a trial. The vast majority of states still use the traditional number of 12 jurors for felony cases, although some use 6 jurors for serious misdemeanors. The origin of the 12-person jury is something of a mystery, but the U.S. Supreme Court, in the case of *Williams v. Florida* (1970), labeled it a historical artifact and said that states may use 6-person juries in noncapital cases.

Master list:
the list containing the names of all persons eligible for jury service in a particular jurisdiction

Venires:
the pool of potential jurors from which a trial jury is chosen

Selecting Juries

The process of selecting a trial jury is known as the ***voir dire***, which means "to speak the truth." Most people assume that the attorneys for both sides are trying to pick a completely neutral jury. In truth, both the

***Voir dire*:**
"to speak the truth"; the process of questioning and selecting a trial jury from the larger pool of jury candidates

prosecution and the defense would like to have a jury favorable to its cause. The most-biased jurors for either side should be eliminated in the process of give-and-take questioning. In some courts, the prosecuting and defense attorneys are allowed to ask their own questions of the venire, but other courts require the attorneys to submit lists of potential questions for the judge to ask members of the jury pool. Common questions include: "Have you ever worked in law enforcement?" "Do you know any of the parties involved in this case?" "Have you seen, read, or heard anything about this case?" If the answer is yes to any of these questions, then there is often a follow-up question such as "Would that influence your verdict in this case?" In very complex or high-profile cases, potential jurors may receive a lengthy questionnaire prior to reporting for a specific venire, but it is quite unlike the one they received concerning reasons not to serve on the jury (Colquitt 2007-2008). Such questionnaires are composed of questions supplied by both the prosecution and the defense and are often reviewed by the judge. Attorneys on both sides review the juror answers and use them as part of the *voir dire* process as they search for unacceptable and acceptable jurors.

Once the *voir dire* has been completed, the judge and the attorneys may retire to the judge's chambers to discuss who is or is not acceptable to each side. In other jurisdictions, depending on practice and law, the striking or accepting of jurors occurs in open court. As a rule, both attorneys will have an unlimited number of exclusions for cause (or prejudice), although it may take some convincing for the judge to remove a potential juror. By contrast, both sides will have the same limited number of **peremptory challenges**. These "strikes" may be based on nothing more than an attorney's intuition about how a potential juror might vote. Attorneys may have from 6 to 12 peremptory challenges, depending on the nature of the case, and this allows them to remove potential jurors without having to state a cause. However, one significant principle that must be observed in peremptory challenges is that they cannot be exercised in a racially discriminatory manner (see *Batson v. Kentucky* (1986)).

Peremptory challenges: exclusion of potential jurors for no stated cause

Attorneys have many different orientations toward the jury selection process, with some considering it an art and others thinking of it as a science. There are even companies in the United States that can help in the "scientific" approach to jury selection in high-profile cases (Lieberman and Sales 2006). These firms can help well-to-do defendants pick the type of jury that would be most sympathetic to their cause. Whatever the attorney's orientation might be, there is a very strong belief that cases may be won or lost during the process of picking a jury. Box 8.4 discusses the process of using social science to aid in the jury selection process.

Box 8.4   **"Scientific" Jury Selection**

The notion of scientific jury selection in high profile cases began in the 1970s. However, it gained national attention with the O.J. Simpson murder trial in 1995 in California. In simplest terms, scientific jury selection refers to the use of social science methods (community surveys, questionnaires, and interviews) in order to help the defense pick the most favorable jury for its case. These methods are employed prior to a jury being selected to determine whether people of certain demographic characteristics are predisposed to vote a certain way on an issue. They are also used during the *voir dire* process itself to screen out (usually through peremptory challenges) jurors that might be unfavorable toward the defendant. Obviously, the application of social science techniques to jury selection is not used often (typically in "celebrated cases"), and it is used only by those defendants who have the economic resources to hire jury consultants. Therefore, the idea of such jury selection techniques and processes is totally foreign to the average criminal defendant.

The Opening Arguments

Once jury selection has been completed, both sides present their opening arguments. Prosecuting attorneys go first in opening arguments. It is at this time that both sides can give the jury a preview of their case. You sometimes hear attorneys describe opening arguments as a way of explaining to the jury their "theory" of the case or how they believe the crime was committed. After the defense has concluded their opening arguments, it is time to begin questioning witnesses.

The Case in Chief

In criminal matters, the burden of proof is on the prosecution. It must present its theory of the case, sometimes referred to as the case in chief. The prosecuting attorney orchestrates the presentation of evidence, which must be presented in court by a human witness—generally the person who collected or analyzed the physical evidence. This is circumstantial evidence, meaning the information's linkages to the case must be inferred as having a connection to a conclusion of fact. This would include most forensic evidence, such as DNA analysis of fluids found on the victim, fingerprints retrieved from a weapon, or lands and grooves from a spent bullet. Tying this forensic evidence to the offender may require additional, corroborating evidence that further links the evidence to the crime and the defendant. Direct evidence supports the conclusion without the need for an intermediate step and would include, for example, eyewitness testimony. However, testimony can be either direct, as in the case of a witness who indicates that the accused was the person who held up the bank, or circumstantial, as in the case of the person who saw the accused enter the bank, heard loud noises and saw the accused exit the bank with a bag labeled with the bank's name, which later was revealed to contain the holdup money. Whether witnesses are presenting circumstantial or direct evidence, the questioning of witnesses is crucial to both the prosecution and defense. This is especially true of the defense, as it is under no legal obligation to present an alternative theory of the facts as the defendant's case in chief. In most cases, the goal of the defense is to impeach or at least create reasonable doubt concerning the prosecution's case in chief.

Questioning Witnesses

The prosecution goes first in presenting its case in chief and questioning its witnesses, just like in presenting opening arguments. Whichever side calls a witness gets to do the initial questioning; this is known as **direct examination.** When the prosecution finishes questioning each of its witnesses, the defense has the opportunity to cross-examine the witness. If necessary, the prosecutor can ask questions on redirect, and both sides can go back and forth until they are satisfied that they have had their questions answered. It is important to note that questions asked on cross-examination and redirect must be related to information provided on direct examination, as they are for clarification or amplification only and not the introduction of new testimony, hence the often-heard challenge from the opposite number of the person asking the question: "Asked and answered, Your Honor."

Direct examination: the questioning of a witness in a trial by the attorney calling the witness

When the state rests its case, the defense may make a midtrial motion to the judge for a directed verdict of acquittal based on the fact that the state has failed to prove its case beyond a reasonable doubt. Although this is frequently done, it almost never works. Nevertheless, on rare occasions, the judge will agree with the defense motion and dismiss the charges.

Since in most cases the charges are not dismissed, the judge directs the defense to begin calling its witnesses, essentially laying out its case in chief, which may include alternative interpretations of the facts in evidence, new facts not yet in evidence, or cast doubt, thereby impeaching the testimony contained in the prosecution's case in chief. However, it is important to reiterate that the defense is not obligated to present a case. The state bears the burden of proof, and the defense can inform the court that it does not intend to call witnesses and will rest its case (this doesn't happen very often).

After the defense questions its witnesses, the prosecutor has an opportunity to cross-examine these witnesses. Once again, both sides have the chance to go back and forth until they have exhausted their questions, using the same provisions and limitations discussed for the prosecution's case in chief. When all of the questioning has been completed and both sides have rested their cases, the attorneys present closing arguments to the jury.

In the closing argument phase, the defense generally goes first, allowing the prosecution to have the "final word." At this point, defense attorneys will try to highlight for the jury any problems with the prosecutor's evidence and any inconsistencies that have appeared in the testimony by the state's witnesses, as well as emphasize the strength of the defendant's case in chief, if there is one. Finally, the prosecutor also will emphasize once again the strength of the evidence presented—including any inherent flaws in the defendant's case in chief or challenges mounted against the prosecution—and will encourage the jury to find the defendant guilty.

At the end of closing arguments, the judge will present the **charge to the jury** (sometimes just called jury instructions). Judges typically have a number of standard charges, including explanations of the state's obligation to prove guilt beyond a reasonable doubt. The judge also may instruct the jury to consider both what witnesses have said and what stake they might have in testifying in a certain way. Judges also ask the attorneys whether there are potentially special instructions that need to be provided. Special instructions are particularly important whenever there have been affirmative defenses like duress, entrapment, and insanity. After the jury instructions have been completed, the judge will dismiss the jurors, telling them to select a foreperson and begin the deliberation process.

Charge to the jury: instructions provided by the judge to the jury relating to the law and other considerations they must take into account in the process of their deliberations

JURY DELIBERATIONS AND VERDICTS

In every criminal case, the judge is faced with the decision of whether to sequester the jury. A **sequestered jury** is one in which the members are locked behind closed doors during deliberations (Levine 2009). In such situations, they are not allowed to go home until the trial has reached a conclusion and they have arrived at a verdict. In most cases, the courts make arrangements with local hotels to house sequestered juries, allowing jurors to be housed and eat together under the watchful eyes of court bailiffs.

Judges often use jury sequestration in high-profile and "celebrated cases" if "there is a reasonable likelihood of juror influence by the media or by other persons, if there is a chance of jury tampering, or if there is a chance of injury to a juror" (Sheppard 2012: 1493; see also Walker 2011). The judge will always warn jury members not to discuss the case with each other until all the evidence has been presented, whether or not sequestration is used. The judge will also emphasize to jurors that they are not to read anything or listen to or watch news reports about the case. The judge will normally err on the side of

Sequestered jury: a jury that is not allowed to return home at the end of court sessions each day but are housed in hotels under the watch and care of court bailiffs to prevent them from being exposed to prejudicial publicity concerning the trial

caution and order the jury to be sequestered if there is any question about the potential for prejudicial publicity.

Once the jury has been dismissed from the courtroom, it is somewhat difficult to know what goes on inside the jury room. Occasionally, jurors in high-profile trials, such as the trials of John Edwards, Jerry Sandusky, Jodi Arias, and George Zimmerman, speak openly once the case is concluded; jurors from other cases have even written books on their experiences. Nevertheless, we do know some of what happens during jury deliberations based on public reports and the results from jury experiments (see Kassin 2009).

For example, after electing a jury foreperson, many juries will almost immediately take a vote even before discussing the evidence in the case. Former jurors have said their perspective was that if all members are in agreement, there is no need to spend a lot of time rehashing certain issues. If they are not in agreement, then the deliberation process begins.

We also know, based on fragmentary evidence, that gender influences jury processes. Nonminority males with high-status jobs often are chosen to be the jury foreperson (Strodtbeck, James, and Hawkins 1957). This position is largely symbolic, but the foreperson may be able to direct the discussions and may have some power of persuasion in situations involving indecisive jurors. Males also tend to dominate jury discussions and deliberations, and they might intimidate jurors who are reluctant to convict, especially females (Strodtbeck and Mann 1956).

In some cases, jurors deadlock over a particular issue or over the entire verdict. In such situations, the judge can declare a **hung jury**. This outcome presents several options (Kassin 2009). There are cases in which the jury will send a message to the judge that they are deadlocked, and they may further report the results of the last vote taken. When this occurs, the judge can either send further instructions to the jury or clarify points that will help break the deadlock, or both. For instance, the judge might reach back into the original jury instructions and tell the jury once again that if they cannot reach a verdict on the original charge, there are lesser included offenses that might provide the jury with another option. This can happen in first-degree murder trials; often the result is that the jury finds the defendant guilty of second-degree murder or even manslaughter if those optional charges were included as lesser and included offenses.

The judge also might bring the case to a halt, dismiss the jury, and reset the case for a new trial date. Since the jury was not able to reach a verdict, this would not be double jeopardy. The charges also may be dismissed and the defendant released if the judge is convinced by an overwhelming jury vote to acquit.

As previously mentioned, the vast majority of states still use 12-member juries for felony cases, and most require unanimous ver-

Hung jury:
any jury that cannot come to a definite conclusion concerning the defendant's guilt or innocence

dicts. Nevertheless, the Supreme Court has upheld the use of smaller juries and has ruled that jury verdicts in noncapital cases do not have to be unanimous (see, for example, *Apodaca v. Oregon* (1972); *Johnson v. Louisiana* (1972); *Burch v. Louisiana* (1979); *Williams v. Florida* (1970)).

After the jury has reached a verdict, the foreperson will signal the bailiff from the room assigned to the jury for deliberations, and the judge will order all of the parties to reassemble in the courtroom. Usually, the foreperson will pass a written copy of the verdict to the judge, who will announce the verdict aloud. Occasionally, the defense attorney will ask that the jurors be polled individually in court to make sure this was the verdict they rendered, especially if there is some doubt about what the jury decided. Once this has been done, the judge will set a date for sentencing and order the probation department to prepare a presentence investigation report.

SENTENCING

Many court observers believe that sentencing is the most time-consuming procedure facing the courts. At the time of sentencing, it is important to consider a number of elements. First, depending on the jurisdiction, a legislative body has determined what it considers to be the appropriate punishment for each criminal offense. Second, within the context of legislative parameters, the judge may be given the responsibility for selecting the appropriate sentence, or this may be the jury's responsibility. This latter statement is especially true in death penalty cases, where juries serve as the both the trier of fact and the sentencing body (*Ring v. Arizona* (2002)).

Third, there is potentially a wide range of sentences in most criminal cases. At the most lenient end of the punishment continuum are probation, fines, and community service. In some cases, judges use these three sanctions in combination with each other. The middle level of punishment severity includes sentences that require periods of incarceration from a few days up to one year for misdemeanors (even more in some states) and from one year or more to life imprisonment for felonies. The ultimate punishment, of course, is the death penalty, which now can be imposed by 36 states and the federal government (Snell 2011).

At least four additional factors must be taken into account in sentencing. First, a number of states still impose **indeterminate sentences,** where the legislature has set a minimum and maximum period of possible confinement. As an example, the least-serious felonies may have sentences of not less than one year and not more than five years in a state prison. However, with indeterminate sentencing, it is important

Indeterminate sentences: statutory sentences that provide for a range of punishment in which the judge imposes the sentence, but the actual time served is determined by the paroling authority

to note that once the judge imposes the sentence, the state parole board will determine the actual time served. In contrast with indeterminate sentencing, some states have adopted **determinate sentences**. Determinate sentences impose a specific amount of time to be served by the inmate, such as five years; the release date is based on the sentence minus any accumulated **good time credits**.

A second factor that enters into the sentencing equation is the question of **concurrent** versus **consecutive sentences**. The judge can impose concurrent sentences and allow multiple sentences to be served simultaneously. This usually means that the actual sentence is determined by the most severe crime of which the defendant is convicted. Consecutive sentences, by contrast, allow judges to "stack" prison terms one on top of the other. This can make the convicted offender serve all or a large part of one sentence before beginning the next sentence. In this way, judges can increase the time served, sometimes significantly.

A third sentencing element involves the use of guided sentences. The state of Minnesota pioneered **sentencing guidelines** beginning in 1983 (see, for example, Knapp 1984; Knapp and Hauptly 1989), sentencing guidelines and other forms of guided sentences (such as **presumptive sentences**) define for judges the appropriate sentences for each crime. Most sentencing guidelines systems use a two-dimensional sentencing grid like that illustrated in Figure 8.1. These grids are based on the present offense along with the defendant's criminal history. This means that factors such as age, race, socioeconomic status, drug use, and employment history are not considered relevant in most guided sentencing systems. In fact, the reduction of judicial discretion and sentencing disparities is one of the major justifications for implementing sentencing guidelines.

The fourth sentencing consideration involves the imposition of **mandatory sentences** (Parent et al. 1997). Currently, all states and the federal government have some form of mandatory sentences. These range from mandatory prison terms for certain drug or weapons offense convictions to habitual offender laws that require long prison terms, sometimes without parole, for those with three or more felony convictions. The U.S. Supreme Court has upheld the constitutionality of virtually all of these laws (see, for example, *Rummel v. Estelle* (1980)). The most famous of the habitual offender laws are those with the label "three strikes and you're out," used in California and some other states. For example, offenders convicted under California's three-strikes law are given prison sentences from 25 years to life. Like other challenges to habitual offender laws, the Supreme Court has upheld the constitutionality of the three-strikes laws (see *Ewing v. California* (2003); *Lockyer v. Andrade* (2003)). We return to the issue of three-strikes law in Chapter 9.

Determinate sentences: sentences provided for by statute that are of a fixed length in terms of months or years; sentence reductions are often limited to the accumulation of good time credits

Good time credits: sentence reductions accumulated by prison inmates for good behavior and treatment program participation

Concurrent sentences: multiple sentences imposed by the court that can be served at the same time

Consecutive sentences: multiple sentences imposed by the court that must be served one after the other

Sentencing guidelines: statutory provisions that consider the present offense and the offender's criminal history in determining the appropriate sentence to be imposed by the judge

Presumptive sentences: the normal or typical sentence that should be imposed based on the stipulations provided for in statutes or sentencing guidelines

Mandatory sentences: sentences that must be imposed by a judge as a result of conviction of a certain offense

Figure 8.1   Minnesota Sentencing Guidelines Grid

Presumptive sentence lengths are in months. Italicized numbers within the grid denote the discretionary range within which a court may sentence without the sentence being deemed a departure. Offenders with stayed felony sentences may be subject to local confinement.

SEVERITY LEVEL OF CONVICTION OFFENSE (Example offenses listed in italics)		CRIMINAL HISTORY SCORE						
		0	1	2	3	4	5	6 or more
Murder, 2nd Degree (*intentional murder; drive-by-shootings*)	11	306 *261–367*	326 *278–391*	346 *295–415*	366 *312–439*	386 *329–463*	406 *346–480[2]*	426 *363–480[2]*
Murder, 3rd Degree Murder, 2nd Degree (*unintentional murder*)	10	150 *128–180*	165 *141–198*	180 *153–216*	195 *166–234*	210 *179–252*	225 *192–270*	240 *204–288*
Assault, 1st Degree Controlled Substance Crime, 1st Degree	9	86 *74–103*	98 *84–117*	110 *94–132*	122 *104–146*	134 *114–160*	146 *125–175*	158 *135–189*
Aggravated Robbery, 1st Degree Controlled Substance Crime, 2nd Degree	8	48 *41–57*	58 *50–69*	68 *58–81*	78 *67–93*	88 *75–105*	98 *84–117*	108 *92–129*
Felony DWI	7	36	42	48	54 *46–64*	60 *51–72*	66 *57–79*	72 *62–84[2]*
Controlled Substance Crime, 3rd Degree	6	21	27	33	39 *34–46*	45 *39–54*	51 *44–61*	57 *49–68*
Residential Burglary Simple Robbery	5	18	23	28	33 *29–39*	38 *33–45*	43 *37–51*	48 *41–57*
Nonresidential Burglary	4	12[1]	15	18	21	24 *21–28*	27 *23–32*	30 *26–36*
Theft Crimes (Over $5,000)	3	12[1]	13	15	17	19 *17–22*	21 *18–25*	23 *20–27*
Theft Crimes ($5,000 or less) Check Forgery ($251–$2,500)	2	12[1]	12[1]	13	15	17	19	21 *18–25*
Sale of Simulated Controlled Substance	1	12[1]	12[1]	12[1]	13	15	17	19 *17–22*

☐ Presumptive commitment to state imprisonment. First-degree murder has a mandatory life sentence and is excluded from the Guidelines under Minn. Stat. § 609.185. See Guidelines section 2.E. Mandatory Sentences, for policies regarding those sentences controlled by law.

▨ Presumptive stayed sentence; at the discretion of the court, up to one year of confinement and other non-jail sanctions can be imposed as conditions of probation. However, certain offenses in the shaded area of the Grid always carry a presumptive commitment to state prison. Guidelines sections 2.C. Presumptive Sentence and 2.E. Mandatory Sentences.

1. 12[1] = One year and one day
2. Minn. Stat. § 244.09 requires that the Guidelines provide a range for sentences that are presumptive commitment to state imprisonment of 15% lower and 20% higher than the fixed duration displayed, provided that the minimum sentence is not less than one year and one day and the maximum sentence is not more than the statutory maximum. Guidelines section 2.C.1-2. Presumptive Sentence.

SOURCE: Minnesota Sentencing Guidelines Commission 2014: 73.

APPEALS

The nature and processes of appeals will vary depending on whether the cases are misdemeanors or felonies. Misdemeanor convictions normally occur in the courts of limited jurisdiction, and these typically are courts of nonrecord (that is, they do not keep verbatim transcripts); therefore, misdemeanor appeals normally go to general trial jurisdiction courts, the next-higher courts in the local jurisdiction. This means that there will be a **trial de novo**, or an entirely new trial. By contrast, as Chapter 7 discusses, felony convictions go to the courts of intermediate appeals, in court systems where they exist, or directly to the courts of last resort (see Kamisar et al. 2008).

A number of U.S. Supreme Court cases are cited throughout this book. These cases help us understand the nature of criminal appeals in the United States. The remainder of this section examines some of the issues related to appeals. These issues include the reasons on which appeals can be based, the numbers of cases appealed, the legal mechanisms for appeal, and the results of appeals.

Trial de novo:
a new trial; when cases are appealed from limited jurisdiction courts to general trials courts, they must be tried all over again in a de novo process

The Reasons for Appeals

We must begin this section by noting that "the right to appeal is limited to the right to have an appellate court examine the record of the trial proceedings for error. If error is found, the appellate court either may take definitive action—such as ordering that the prosecution be dismissed—or it may set aside the conviction and remand the case for a new trial" (Allen and Kuhns 1985: 19). That is, an appeal, if it is to result in a new trial or dismissal of charges, must be based on a matter of law, the misapplication of which threatens the quality of justice in this specific case. Potentially exculpatory evidence, in and of itself, may not be sufficient for an appeal, unless, for example, the prosecution kept such evidence hidden from the defense at the original trial. Additionally, relatively few cases are appealed. There are numerous reasons for this. The primary reason is that appeals must be based on errors of law, not errors of fact. In most cases, decisions or actions by the judge overseeing a trial will result in an appeal being filed. As previously noted, the judge is the trier of law, while the jury is the trier of fact.

Some of the most common errors of law are ineffective assistance of counsel, false testimony or coerced confessions, admission of illegally obtained physical evidence, improper jury instructions (see Steele and Thornburg 2009), sentencing errors, improper prosecutorial arguments, or plea negotiation errors (see King, Cheesman, and Ostrom 2007). Judges must ensure that the state obtains a conviction by a fair process and, as Supreme Court Justice Sutherland emphasized, the prosecutor may "prosecute with earnestness and vigor—indeed he should do so. But, while he may strike hard blows, he is not at liberty to strike foul ones" (*Berger v. United States* (1935)).

The Numbers of Appeals

A relatively small number of felony convictions and even fewer misdemeanor convictions handed down in the United States are appealed each year. Chapter 7 presents some of the numbers associated with federal and state trial and appellate courts. For example, in 2010, there were 12,797 criminal appeals from U.S. District Courts to the U.S. Courts of Appeals, nearly 30 percent of 43,737 total cases on the docket (Maguire 2013). By comparison, in 2004, there were 1,078,920 state felony cases terminated and 240,531 criminal appeals filed in state appellate courts, slightly more than one in five of the case total (Schauffler et al. 2006). Thus, appellate courts handle far fewer cases than trial courts.

The Legal Mechanisms for Appeals

There are several legal mechanisms that convicted offenders can use to file appeals, but the most common mechanisms fit into the categories of **mandatory** or **automatic appeals** and **discretionary appeals**. Mandatory appeals involve those cases in which the courts are obligated to provide a review once there has been a conviction and an appeal has been filed. An example of such an appeal would be cases involving death penalty sentences. Most states require that these cases are automatically appealed to the court of last resort for mandatory review.

Mandatory appeals: cases that must be heard (by constitutional mandate or statute) by an appellate court

Automatic appeals: cases such as those involving death penalty sentences that do not depend on filing an appeal by the convicted person, but instead are sent for review to the appropriate appellate court

Discretionary appeals: appeals over which appellate courts have complete freedom of choice whether to accept

State statutes provide for some mandatory appeals, but often they result from either state or federal constitutional provisions. On the one hand, in 2004, state intermediate appeal courts disposed of 127,973 mandatory appeals, and state courts of last resort disposed of another 24,631 (Schauffler et al. 2006). On the other hand, in 2004, there were 30,578 state intermediate courts of appeals and 57,349 state supreme court discretionary petitions (Schauffler et al. 2006). Appellate courts can accept or reject discretionary appeals, and the appellate numbers from 2004 show that intermediate state appellate courts primarily handle mandatory appeals (by about four to one) and state supreme courts primarily handle discretionary petitions (by about two to one). Thus, state supreme courts have a greater ability to set their own docket.

Convicted offenders, especially those serving prison sentences or facing the death penalty, still can apply for postconviction relief even after their state appeals have been exhausted. By moving the cases from the state courts into the federal courts, offenders can pursue two mechanisms for federal postconviction relief: **writs of habeas corpus** and **civil rights actions**. Habeas corpus, which is taken from the Latin phrase *habeas corpus ad subjiciendum*, literally means "you should have the body for submitting." Such writs are normally filed in federal district courts and ask that the state be required to demonstrate why a prison inmate's incarceration is lawful and justified. Habeas corpus petitions challenge the essence of incarceration, meaning that if prison inmates are successful in their claims, they may have their convictions reversed, resulting in release from incarceration. As a result, appeals involving habeas corpus petitions have been called "turn 'em loose suits."

Up until the 1970s, habeas corpus petitions were the primary mechanism of postconviction for many state prison inmates, then civil rights actions increased significantly. However, as a result of congressional limitations on prison appeals in the mid-1990s, habeas corpus appeals once again have increased in number and civil rights claims have decreased (see, for example, Mays and Winfree 2014: 309-313).

The most commonly cited federal civil rights statute is the Civil Rights Act of 1871, frequently identified by its statutory citation, 42 U.S.C. §1983, and commonly called Section 1983 suits. Section 1983 suits can be directed at police officers for violations of suspects' civil rights; they also can be aimed at corrections personnel.

Civil rights actions are different from habeas corpus petitions in that they do not question the basis of an inmate's incarceration but instead contest the conditions under which inmates are confined (Mays and Winfree 2014). Civil rights actions ask for equitable remedies or monetary damages when they challenge police use of unnecessary or excessive use of force with suspects.

Writs of habeas corpus: to "have the body"; a legal document for appeal that requires the state to come forward and to establish why an offender's conviction is legitimate and why incarceration should be continued

Civil rights actions: legal actions (particularly in federal courts) alleging that certain protected rights of an individual or group have been violated, particularly under color of law

The Results of Appeals

Once an accused offender has been convicted and files an appeal, what happens next? This is a basic question, and often the answer is not much. Most appeals never make it past the first level of review, and even fewer result in the outcome desired by the person filing the appeal. By one estimate, state and federal appeals are only successful in 10 percent to 20 percent of cases (see Kamisar et al. 2008), and postconviction appellate success (habeas corpus and civil rights cases) is even worse. About 2 percent to 4 percent of these cases result in relief being granted (Collins 1993; Kamisar et al. 2008). Although the public may focus on highly publicized cases of inmates winning lawsuits against a state or on those of wrongfully convicted persons, in reality most of the people convicted of crimes in the United States receive the sentence the judge imposed and serve their period of probation or prison sentence with no further action being taken by the courts. Therefore, while appellate review is symbolically important, it has very little practical impact on most criminal cases.

SUMMARY

This chapter outlines the criminal process from arrest to bringing that person to trial as a long and complicated process. There are many processing stages, and multiple criminal justice actors are involved. Even before getting a case to trial, numerous decisions must be made and actions must be taken. When the police arrest and book a suspect, the issue of bail must be addressed. For those individuals who cannot make bail, there will be a jail stay until an initial appearance can be scheduled.

After the initial appearance, the judge will set a date for a preliminary hearing to determine if there is sufficient probable cause to move the case to the next stage. The prosecutor usually presents just enough of the case to convince the judge that there is probable cause to move the case forward.

Just over half of all states routinely use grand juries to hear felony cases. The grand jury decides once again whether there is probable cause to take the case to trial. It is important to remember that only the prosecution presents its case, and indictments or true bills can be handed down on a fractional vote of the grand jury members. Indictments are formal accusations on which trials proceed and allow the trial courts to set a date to hold an arraignment on the indictment.

The arraignment addresses bail and representation by counsel, and perhaps for the first time, the defendant will be asked to enter a plea. After the arraignment has been concluded and all pretrial motions filed and dispensed with, the judge will set a trial date.

Once again, relatively few cases in the United States make it to trial. Some have the charges dismissed, but in most cases, the prosecutor and the defense attorney reach a plea agreement demonstrating the defendant's willingness to plead guilty in exchange for some type of leniency. For many people, plea bargaining remains something of a "necessary evil." In reality, the "going rate" (Walker 2011) allows the courtroom work group to process cases in a routine and speedy manner. For most criminal cases, there is little dispute over the facts. This allows the courtroom work group to dispose of those cases quickly and move on to cases where the issues are unresolved.

While trials remain the hallmark of the U.S. justice system, they are somewhat rare. Jury selection and opening arguments from the prosecutor and defense attorney take much of the time in the trial's initial stages.

The state begins the trial by presenting its case. After the state's case is concluded, the defense attorney may ask the judge for a directed verdict of acquittal or present its case. It is important to remember that the defense does not have to present a case at all since the burden of proof rests with the state.

After both sides have completed their cases, the judge gives the jury instructions to help guide their deliberations. Some juries are allowed to go home, whereas others may be sequestered. When a verdict is reached, the jury returns to the courtroom, and the verdict is announced.

From this point, the judge will request a presentence investigation report from the probation office, and the probation officer will recommend community supervision or incarceration. In most jurisdictions, the judge imposes the appropriate verdict, but in other jurisdictions—especially in capital cases—the jury may decide the verdict.

The trial process is concluded with the filing of appeals. The defense has the opportunity to file an appeal if it believes there have been errors of law and that these have negatively influenced the verdict in the case. Relatively few criminal convictions are appealed, and most of those never make it beyond the first appellate review. A few convictions will be overturned, and new trials will be ordered, but most convictions stand as imposed.

REVIEW QUESTIONS

1. Define and explain the purposes of bail. What are some of the ways available to make bail?

2. The average person knows very little about what grand juries are and what they do. Explain the functions that grand juries serve. Do a little library or online research to find out if your state requires grand jury indictments.

3. Who seems to benefit from plea bargaining and how? Are there multiple beneficiaries? Does plea bargaining promote justice or not? Explain.

4. Explain the jury selection process. What are the attorneys trying to achieve? What does that mean about who survives the questioning by both sides?

5. The use of peremptory challenges is somewhat controversial. Take a position on either side of this proposition: Attorneys should not be able to remove potential jurors for no stated cause.

6. In a couple of cases from the 1970s, the U.S. Supreme Court said that the use of less-than-unanimous jury verdicts was constitutional. Would you support the use of less-than-unanimous verdicts in your state?

7. Sentencing guidelines limit the amount of discretion a judge may exercise. Is it appropriate for legislatures and sentencing commissions to have this kind of authority, or does this impose on the notion of judicial independence?

8. Why does the public believe that appellate courts are turning criminal defendants loose in large numbers? What shapes this public perception?

KEY TERMS

arraignment
automatic appeals
bail
bail bond company
bench trial
bond
bounty hunters
charge to the jury
civil rights actions
concurrent sentences
consecutive sentences
criminal information
determinate sentences
direct examination
discretionary appeals
diversion
good time credits
grand jury
hung jury

indeterminate sentences
indictment
initial appearance
mandatory appeals
mandatory sentences
master list
nolo contendere
peremptory challenges
plea bargain
preliminary hearing
presumptive sentences
probable cause
release on recognizance
sentencing guidelines
sequestered jury
skip tracers
trial de novo
true bill
venires
voir dire
writs of habeas corpus

Issues in the Judiciary

LEARNING OBJECTIVES

At the conclusion of this chapter, you should be able to:

- Explain the methods for providing indigent defense.
- Discuss the methods for choosing and disciplining judges.
- Define the notion of judicial independence.
- Explain recent sentencing reform efforts.
- Discuss the notion of wrongful convictions and the reasons for such convictions.
- Understand the role the death penalty plays in the sentencing process.

INTRODUCTION

There is no end to the possible issues facing the courts in the United States, and this chapter deals with nine of these issues. For the sake of brevity, we address the issues that seem to be the most critical today and the ones that are likely to persist far into the future. Some of the dilemmas deal with attorneys and juries, while others focus on judges, including the ways in which they are chosen, retained, and disciplined. Others deal with the courts' broader legal environments. Three areas of substantial interest are sentencing reforms, the persistence of wrongful convictions, and the death penalty. After reading this chapter, you will understand the difficult tasks facing courts in this country and some of the difficult circumstances under which they labor.

ADEQUATE INDIGENT DEFENSE

The U.S. Constitution's Sixth Amendment provides, in part, that "[i]n all criminal prosecutions, the accused shall enjoy . . . the assistance of counsel for his defense." Like much of the Constitution and its amendments, the Sixth Amendment's implications for and direct application to criminal matters was not all that clear in the 18th century, and it would take more than a century and a half and several court decisions before its reach was fully understood, if then. Specifically, until the 1960s, the general understanding of this provision was that it applied only to federal courts and federal cases and that if you could afford an attorney, you could have one, but only at your personal expense. As the U.S. Supreme Court decided in the case of *Gideon v. Wainwright* (1963), the right to counsel applied to state felony cases in addition to those dealing with the death penalty (which had been addressed in *Powell v. Alabama* (1932)). This meant that states were obligated to provide attorneys for **indigent defendants**, or those persons who could not otherwise afford them. The right to counsel was extended further earlier in the processing of suspects when the Supreme Court said that individuals facing police **custodial interrogations** also had to be informed of their right to counsel (along with the right to remain silent) before questioning could begin (*Miranda v. Arizona* (1966)).

These and other Supreme Court decisions left states scrambling for ways to provide adequate indigent defense. The numbers of such cases are somewhat difficult to determine, but one observer has noted that indigent defendants represent between 48 percent and 90 percent of the felony defendants nationwide (Worden 2009: 385). The Bureau of Justice Statistics has reported that 66 percent of federal court felony

Indigent defendants: criminal defendants who cannot afford their own attorneys

Custodial interrogations: police interviews of suspected criminals in which the person being questioned is not free to leave

defendants and 82 percent of state court felony defendants qualified for indigent representation (Harlow 2000). Our review of this important topic includes the most common methods of indigent representation—appointed attorneys, public defenders, and contract defenders—along with a few other methods that are occasionally encountered.

Appointed Attorneys

The most widely used system for providing indigent defense involves **court-appointed attorneys** (DeFrances and Litras 2000). Nineteen states and 60 percent of U.S. counties use this method. These tend to be among the most rural and least populous jurisdictions; state and local governments provide funding for attorneys who are appointed by judges on an as-needed basis (DeFrances 2001).

> **Court-appointed attorneys:** lawyers assigned by judges to represent indigent defendants based on a court-maintained list of eligible attorneys

The methods for assembling the list of possible attorneys for appointment vary from state to state, but judges typically use one of two systems. First, judges can take volunteers for appointment in indigent cases. These often are lawyers who are just beginning their practices or those with declining practices (for health reasons, for example). Most jurisdictions pay a flat fee for serious misdemeanor cases and a slightly higher fee for felony cases. Court appointments under this approach provide a steady but modest income for attorneys starting a legal practice or those struggling to keep their practice.

A second method for creating lists of attorneys for appointment involves using a list of all attorneys in the local bar association, with the expectation that each will receive one or more appointments at some time. An expanded list such as this means that a lucky criminal defendant might get the top criminal defense lawyer in the county, while an unlucky one might draw an attorney whose practice is principally in real estate law (see *United States v. Cronic* (1984)).

Whatever method the courts use, there are two significant issues with this approach. First, state and local governments struggle to fund appointed indigent representation systems, and some states run out of funding for appointed attorneys before the end of their fiscal years (Spangenberg and Beeman 1995). As Box 9.1 suggests, using pro bono attorneys is one answer, but not all attorneys participate at the level suggested by the American Bar Association. The same issue exists about the adequacy of counsel if, for example, a defendant draws a "free" attorney whose specialty is divorce and the case involves an aggravated DWI felony charge. Second, many financially successful attorneys are reluctant to take low-fee cases since such cases reduce their earning potential. Occasionally, in misdemeanor cases, judges must appoint an attorney on the spot for a case that is about to be called. Obviously, this means the lawyer is totally unprepared and

> ### Box 9.1 Pro Bono Publico: Is It Always in the Public Good?
>
> The Latin term *pro bono publico* literally means "for the public good." It is used in the legal profession in cases where attorneys donate their time and expertise to assist individuals, such as indigent criminal defendants, who otherwise would not be able to afford their services. The American Bar Association suggests that attorneys provide at least 50 hours per year of pro bono services (although not necessarily for criminal defense work). The ABA uses two categories to classify pro bono work by attorneys: "*Category 1* pro bono is defined as direct legal representation provided to persons of limited means or organizations that support the needs of persons of limited means for which no compensation was received or expected. *Category 2* pro bono is defined as any other law-related service provided for a reduced fee or no cost (without expectation of fee) to any type of client, not including activities performed to develop a paying client or anything that is part of paying job responsibilities" (2013: vi).
>
> In 2011, 36 percent of the attorneys surveyed reported providing at least 50 hours of Category 1 pro bono services, 26 percent donated 20 to 49 hours, 18 percent contributed 1 to 19 hours, and 20 percent reported no pro bono work. In terms of the broader Category 2, 68 percent reported contributing some pro bono work in 2011.
>
> As with any type of nonpaying legal services, there are three major limitations. First, the clients may not believe they are getting anything of value and that they do not have a choice of attorneys. Second, severe time constraints can be imposed by work and family obligations for many attorneys. Finally, the attorneys who are contributing their time may not have the particular expertise that would be desirable in a given case. Nevertheless, it seems that some legal assistance, especially for indigent criminal defendants, is better than none at all.

SOURCE: American Bar Association 2013.

may never have met the defendant prior to the case beginning. Thus, the issue may not be legal representation but *adequate* legal representation.

Public Defenders

The indigent defense method that covers the largest segment of the U.S. population is that of **public defenders**. The first public defender's office was established in Los Angeles County, California, on January 9, 1914 (Los Angeles County Public Defender's Office 2012). One hundred years later, all states but one—Maine—employed public defenders in 957 separate public defender offices (Langton and Farole 2009: 1). Public defenders are salaried governmental employees and the counterpart to prosecuting attorneys. This means that their pay does not vary no matter how many cases they handle. The position of assistant public defender is often taken by recent law school graduates as a way to earn a living and get practical experience, especially in a courtroom and at plea negotiations.

Public defenders: publicly funded attorneys who represent indigent defendants

As Figure 9.1 shows, 23 states have state-operated public defender systems employing more than 4,300 attorneys. In 2007, these offices processed almost 1.5 million cases, with each attorney averaging 88 felony cases, 147 misdemeanor cases, and three appeals. Additionally, 26 states have county-funded public defender offices, and 11 states have offices with mixed state and county funding. In 2007, county-based public defender offices employed nearly 13,000 attorneys who processed almost 4.3 million cases. On average, the attorneys in these offices each were responsible for 106 felony cases, 164 misdemeanor cases, and two appeals (Langton and Farole 2010).

Currently, public defender offices are located in 1,144 counties (slightly more than one-third of all counties) and represent about 70 percent of the U.S. population. This means that public defender offices tend to be found in large, urban counties. In fact, 90 of the 100 most populous counties in the United States have a public defender's office (DeFrances 2001; DeFrances and Litras 2000). There are at least five problems associated with indigent defense by public defenders (Burnett 2010; Langton and Farole 2010). First, public defenders often are not held in high regard by many criminal

Figure 9.1   Twenty-three states with state public defender programs in 2007

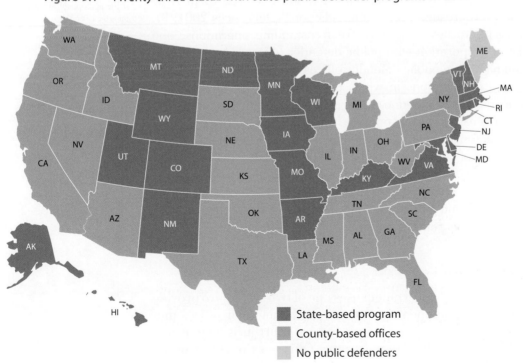

defendants, as there is a fairly strong perception that "you get what you pay for." This was once expressed in a cartoon showing two prison inmates. One asks the other, "Did you have a lawyer when you went to court?" The second one responds, "No, I had a public defender." Second, as is true of all indigent defense systems, public defender offices tend to be understaffed and overworked. Each assistant public defender typically carries a heavy caseload of both misdemeanor and felony cases. Third, public defender offices, as suggested above, may be staffed by some of the least experienced attorneys. This creates a problem for the more senior staff who must handle their own cases and mentor those who are new to the practice of law. Fourth, public defender offices tend to have high turnover rates as assistant PDs gain experience and move on to more lucrative (and sometimes less stressful) positions in private law firms. Finally, public defender offices receive far less money overall and per case than does the opposing prosecutor's office.

Contract Attorneys

Another common method for providing indigent defense is through **contract attorneys**. A report by the Bureau of Justice Statistics says that contract attorneys include "[n]onsalaried, private attorneys, bar associations, law firms, consortiums or groups of attorneys, or non-profit corporations that contract with a funding source to provide court-appointed representation in a jurisdiction" (DeFrances 2001: 3). Some contract attorney programs are freestanding operations, and others exist in cooperation with public defender offices. The programs that operate alongside public defender offices often are responsible for overflow cases or situations in which the PD's office is handling one codefendant and needs someone else to represent another codefendant.

Contract attorneys: lawyers who represent indigent defendants based on annual contracts awarded by the courts or the appropriate funding agencies

Contract defense programs operate in 11 states, and normally funding agencies ask for bids annually. To request bids, the courts must estimate the number of defense hours that will be needed, and the agency, firm, or organization that submits the lowest acceptable bid wins the contract. Contract attorney programs operate much the same as appointed attorney and public defender programs in most other aspects. They have the same strengths and many of the same weaknesses.

Federal Defenders

For its part, the federal government uses one of two systems to provide counsel for indigent defendants. Federal public defender offices mirror the U.S. attorney's offices in most federal court jurisdictions and are directly funded by the Administrative Office of the U.S. Courts. A second model is the community defender, an organization that

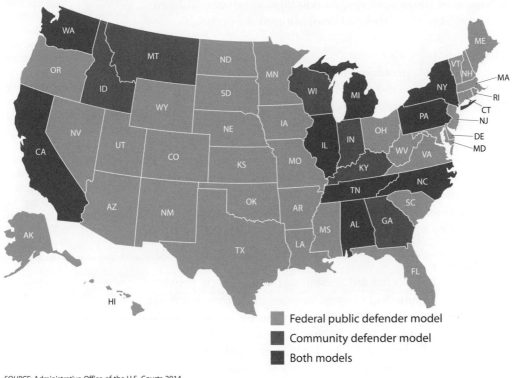

Figure 9.2 Federal defenders across the nation

Federal public defender model

Community defender model

Both models

SOURCE: Administrative Office of the U.S. Courts 2014.

receives federal grant money and acts more independently from the federal courts than the federal public defender offices; however, in neither case do the lawyers or their offices work on behalf of the federal government (Administrative Office of the U.S. Courts 2013).

As represented in Figure 9.2, the federal public defender office is the most common model, operating as the sole federal defender system in the District of Columbia and 35 states; it is found alongside the community defender model in another 9 states. The community defender model is the only federal public defender system operating in 6 states. Seven contiguous states—Colorado and Wyoming; North and South Dakota; and Massachusetts, New Hampshire, and Rhode Island—share the same district offices, each of which in each case uses the public defender model.

Other Methods of Representation

The three methods of indigent defense already discussed cover most of the indigent defense in the United States. However, at least three other systems appear periodically: **voucher systems**, **legal aid societies**, and **legal clinics**. Not all of these options provide legal service to indigent criminal defendants, but they should be mentioned nevertheless.

Voucher Systems

Once again, a persistent problem associated with court-appointed attorneys (especially public defenders) is the perception that they are not highly trained and skilled at their craft. A way around this problem is to give indigent criminal defendants a voucher that allows them to pick their own attorney (Smith 1991). A voucher system gives the accused person a piece of paper saying the court will cover legal expenses up to a certain amount. The individual must then find a lawyer willing to take the case on that basis. While vouchers address one deficiency of the public defender system, they still limit the amount that can be earned, just like appointed attorneys.

Legal Aid Societies

Many large U.S. cities have legal aid societies. These groups provide legal assistance to low-income individuals. In most instances, legal aid societies deal only with civil matters; however, some provide assistance for serious misdemeanors and, at times, even felonies.

Legal aid societies depend on attorneys donating a certain amount of time annually to assist low-income persons. For instance, an attorney might give 40 hours per year to the legal aid society and, in return, get a tax deduction for a charitable contribution (of course, charged at the lawyer's normal hourly rate). (See Box 9.1.)

Legal Clinics

In addition to legal aid societies, cities with law schools may have access to legal clinics. Much like low-income medical clinics, legal clinics allow second- and third-year law students to handle minor civil and perhaps minor criminal cases under the watchful eye of law faculty. This gives the students real-world, practical experience and helps those individuals who otherwise could not afford legal services.

Again, these three methods of legal representation are generally limited to civil matters. There are some exceptions, however, and these depend on the agency or organization and the local legal culture.

JUDICIAL SELECTION AND QUALIFICATIONS

The United States is unique among the world's nations in the methods used to select its judges. In most European countries, judges are appointed and viewed as civil servants. They are trained for their

Voucher systems: the method of indigent defense whereby criminal defendants are provided a form worth a certain amount of money that allows them to hire their own attorney

Legal aid societies: groups of attorneys who donate time to represent individuals who cannot afford to pay for legal representation

Legal clinics: courses offered by law schools that allow second- and third-year students to gain practical legal experience under the supervision of clinical professors

positions while they are in law school, and most have never been practicing attorneys. By contrast, in the United States, there are several paths to becoming a judge; this section considers three of those paths: appointment, election, and merit selection.

Appointing Judges

When discussing appointing judges in this country, one group in particular comes to mind: federal judges. Article II, Section 2 of the U.S. Constitution provides, in part, that the president "shall nominate, and by and with the advice and consent of the Senate, shall appoint judges of the Supreme Court, and all other officers of the United States." This means that the president has the authority to nominate people to fill all vacancies for federal judges. These people must then go through a lengthy background check and screening process conducted by the FBI and eventually the Senate Judiciary Committee. All candidates who pass this screening are voted on by the full U.S. Senate and, if confirmed, appointed to the position for life (during good behavior). This means that, once appointed, federal judges hold their positions somewhat insulated from the world of partisan politics. The reality, however, is that politics is very much a part of choosing federal judges and never far from the decisions they are called on to make.

Not only are federal judges appointed, but also there are certain situations where state judges can be appointed. However, for state judges, this is the exception rather than the rule. Most of the appointments of state judges are **interim appointments**, meaning that whenever there is a vacancy—for example, by the death or resignation of a state judge—the governor usually has the constitutional power to appoint someone as a judge until the normal process for filling the vacancy can be employed. Interim appointments for state judges are meant to be temporary solutions to prevent backing up court dockets and delaying other court business.

Interim appointments: the temporary appointment of someone to the office of judge until the normal process of judicial selection can be employed

Electing Judges

Popular election is the most common method of selecting state and local judges in the United States. Early on in our nation's history, practically all judges were appointed, but during Andrew Jackson's presidency, the so-called "long ballot" became popular (Meador 1991). Under this practice, virtually every state and local office was filled by election, part of the movement historians call Jacksonian democracy. Andrew Jackson had little formal education when he was elected president, and he felt that the "common man" should have a chance to hold public office, rather than government being run by political (and formally educated) elites. This idea spurred the election of judges at the state and local level under one of two systems: partisan elections and nonpartisan elections.

Partisan Elections

Partisan elections are what most people think of when they think of elections in the United States. In a partisan election, candidates' names appear on the ballot and are identified with a particular political party. Eight states use partisan elections to choose appellate court judges, and 19 states use partisan elections to fill some or all of their trial court vacancies (Rottman and Strickland 2006: 25-27, 33-37).

The supposed advantage of partisan elections is that voters get a say over who their judges will be. If the voters feel a candidate is unqualified, they can simply vote for someone else. Additionally, voters can "unelect" judges who do not seem to be doing their jobs. However, at least two significant problems are associated with judicial election systems. First, most voters know little about the candidates for judicial offices. Researchers who study judicial elections say people take cues from the candidates' last names, political party affiliation, gender, and incumbent status. In some cases, voters simply do not vote for judicial candidates at all. Even when people do vote for a given judicial candidate, it is difficult to say that voters are making informed choices based on qualifications, and they routinely return incumbents to office (Webster 1995).

The second problem associated with electing judges is fund-raising. Candidates for judicial positions must raise campaign funds just like other political candidates. Quite often it is the case that individual lawyers, law firms, and corporations that could have business before the courts are major contributors to judicial election campaigns. For example, the American Judicature Society, the leading court-reform organization in the United States, found that "[i]n 2005-2006 44% of the contributions to state high court candidates came from business groups, and 21% came from lawyers" (American Judicature Society 2008: 5). This does not necessarily mean that judges will be influenced by such contributions, but the Annenberg Public Policy Center found in one study that more than two-thirds of respondents believed that "raising money for elections affects a judge's rulings to a moderate or great extent" (American Judicature Society 2008: 5).

Nonpartisan Elections

One way of combatting overt partisan politics is through the use of **nonpartisan elections**. In nonpartisan elections, voters may know which political party a particular candidate belongs to, but there is no political party identifier for the candidates on the ballot. Four-

Partisan elections: election of judges in a process where the candidate's political party affiliation appears on the ballot (see also *nonpartisan elections*)

Nonpartisan elections: election of judges by a process in which the candidate's political party affiliation does not appear on the ballot (see also *partisan elections*)

teen states use nonpartisan elections for their appellate judges, and 17 states use nonpartisan elections for one or more types of trial court judges (Rottman and Strickland 2006: 25-27, 33-37).

In nonpartisan elections, both media coverage and bar association endorsements play prominent roles. However, as Webster notes, "far from being an improvement upon partisan elections, nonpartisan elections are an inferior alternative to partisan elections because they possess all of the vices of partisan elections and none of the virtues" (1995: 26). Other judicial scholars maintain that nonpartisan elections have the lowest level of accountability among all methods of judicial selection (Bonneau and Hall 2009). Thus, while several state and local jurisdictions employ nonpartisan judicial elections, there is very little evidence that this is a superior way of choosing judges.

Merit Selection

As a result of dissatisfaction over electing judges in the United States, the American Judicature Society has championed the **merit selection** system. Merit selection was first introduced in Missouri in 1940, and some people still refer to it as "the Missouri Plan" (Watson and Downing 1969). The American Judicature Society (2013) has strongly endorsed this approach to judicial selection and describes the system as "[t]he process by which judicial applicants are evaluated by a nominating commission, which then sends the names of the best qualified candidates to the governor. The governor appoints one of the nominees submitted by the commission" (American Judicature Society 2008: 6).

When there is a vacancy in a merit selection state, the statewide judicial nominating commission will solicit nominations and applications from people interested in the job. From the pool of potential candidates, the commission will select a small group of names (typically three) to be forwarded to the governor. Some states allow the governor to reject the final list if written justifications are given, but in most instances the governor will choose one of the names and appoint that individual on an interim basis. At the next general election, the appointee must run for election and can be opposed on the ballot. However, once a judge is elected for a regular term of office, subsequent elections are on a **retention ballot**. In simple terms, in retention elections, judges run unopposed, and a retention ballot allows voters to choose between yes-or-no options over whether to keep judges in office. States may require a simple majority for retention, or they may require a higher percentage. Whichever is used, judges in merit selection systems are routinely retained in office.

Merit selection:
a method of judicial selection that combines elements of appointment with those of retention elections

Retention ballot:
the method used to select judges in merit selection systems once the judge has been elected to office; retention ballots present voters with a yes-or-no choice about whether the judge should be retained in office

Currently, 21 states use merit selection for some or all of their appellate court judges, and 13 states use merit selection for some or all of their trial court judges (Rottman and Strickland 2006: 25-27, 33-37). Thus, states are more likely to use merit selection for appellate courts than trial courts.

In concluding this section on judicial selection methods, several key points must be emphasized. First, there is no perfect system for choosing judges. As long as we are selecting candidates from the human race, we are doomed to live with human deficiencies. Second, every system has some political element associated with it. Since the courts are part of the political system in the United States, there will be political considerations in any way we select judges. Third, while no system is capable of selecting perfect judges (whatever that means), we do know that systems involving some element of appointment are more likely to pick women and minorities than systems relying on elections (Brown 1998).

Judicial Qualifications

Judicial qualifications have long been debated in our nation's history. Essentially, this issue breaks down into two questions: (1) should judges be required to possess a law degree, and (2) if they have a law degree, how much experience beyond the degree should be required?

Lawyer or Nonlawyer Judges?

The United States has a long tradition of nonlawyer (or lay) judges. In fact, when many colonies and the early states selected **justices of the peace**, these judicial officers often were not required to be educated in the law. Justices of the peace were part of our English legal heritage; in some communities, these individuals served on a full-time basis, while in others they served part-time. Today, only Arizona, Delaware, Louisiana, Montana, and Texas have retained justices of the peace. Many states that once had this office have converted justice of the peace courts into magistrate (or similar) inferior courts (Rottman and Strickland 2006).

At least 27 states still have courts that do not require judges to be trained in the law. Most of these are courts of limited jurisdiction, such as magistrate's court or municipal court. For example, there are magistrate's courts in 12 of New Mexico's 13 judicial districts. The judges elected to these courts must meet the minimal qualifications for any elected office in the state (at least 18 years of age, no felony conviction, and able to read and write English), but they are not required to have a law degree—or any college degree for that matter.

Justices of the peace: a judicial office that we inherited from England; these are elected judicial officers who preside over limited jurisdiction courts (especially traffic cases)

Jurisdictions that retain nonlawyer judges somewhat adhere to Andrew Jackson's philosophy about democracy and elected offices. While there has been some movement to abolish these positions over the years—or to require a law degree—states that still have lay judges seem fairly content to remain with this tradition (see Courtney 2009).

Three basic questions remain relative to lay judges. First, shouldn't we expect some previous legal experience from the judges who preside over our courts, even the inferior jurisdiction courts? Second, if these judges do not possess law degrees, where and when will they get trained? Obviously, on-the-job training is not the preferred way to prepare judges. Third, does the use of nonlawyer judges cast all judges in a negative light, especially when they do things that bring negative publicity to their courts? While some nations have moved away from the practice of using lay judges, Box 9.2 shows that some continue the practice.

Degree Plus Experience?

In addition to the question of whether judges should have a law degree, there is a question about how much legal experience beyond the degree

---

Box 9.2 Lay Judges Around the World

Most other nations do not use the jury system that we do. In fact, many European and Central and South American nations use multi-judge courts with panels of judges. Typically one of these judges is a civil servant professionally trained in the law; this judge is joined by two or more citizens who may be called lay judges or "assessors." Convictions require only a majority vote, but usually the lay assessors defer to the professionally trained judge's opinion. Nations like Germany, England, Wales, and Japan continue to use lay judges, often buttressing them by employing tribunals of three judges, one of whom is a professional. For example, in 2004, Japan passed a law (that took effect in 2009) requiring citizen participation as lay judges, much as citizens are called for jury duty in the United States. Routinely four *sai-ban-in* (or lay judges) sit with three professional judges to decide cases. If there is little dispute over guilt, the panel is composed of four lay judges and one professional judge.

In Germany, community groups submit nominations for the office of lay judge, and municipal selection committees screen the nominees. While there are some exceptions, most cases in Germany are tried before panels composed of lay and professional judges. Research has shown that most of the lay judges are middle-age men of some social standing in the community.

England and Wales have a long history of lay judges, dating back to the first justices of the peace (a tradition carried over to the United States). Today, these judges are called magistrates and sit in three-judge panels to hear less-serious criminal cases. One of the three magistrates is designated the chairman, and while all of the judges have an equal vote, only the chairman speaks for the court.

SOURCES: Casper and Zeisel 1972; Courts and Tribunals Judiciary, n.d.; Levin and Tice 2013.

is desirable. In other words, would someone who just graduated from law school and passed the bar exam be an appropriate candidate for judge?

States vary in their requirements for judicial office, but the clear trend is to require general trial jurisdiction and appellate court judges to have not only a law degree but also a certain number of years of experience as a licensed and practicing attorney. The requirements range from two years (Kentucky, Montana, and Oklahoma) up to ten years (New Jersey and New York). The most common numbers seem to be five to six years since admission to the bar. Therefore, it is safe to say that most state court judges will need to have both a law degree and some amount of legal experience.

JUDICIAL DISCIPLINE AND SANCTIONING

One of the unfortunate realities of the American judiciary is that there are unfit people serving as judges. Some were unfit before they were selected, and their deficiencies were unknown or not well known; others became unfit while serving on the bench. In these cases, states (and the federal government) have designed different mechanisms for disciplining judges and, if necessary, removing them from the bench. This section briefly examines two of the most common methods.

Impeachment

Federal judges and some state judges must be impeached to be removed from office. Stephen Michael Sheppard says that **impeachment** is "[a]n accusation against an official that the official should be removed from office. Impeachment is the accusation against an officer of government, that for some specified reason the officer is not fit to continue in office and should be removed" (2012: 1258). For federal judges, the U.S. House of Representatives must bring articles of impeachment against a federal judge based on "treason, bribery, or other high crimes and misdemeanors." The U.S. Senate then serves as the body trying the case and must vote with a two-thirds majority to remove the judge from office. To shield federal judges from the political whims of the day, impeachment is a deliberately cumbersome process. In fact, in the history of the United States, only 15 federal judges (including Samuel Chase, an associate justice of the Supreme Court) have had articles of impeachment brought against them, and four (including Chase) were found not guilty. The other 11 resigned or were removed from office (U.S. Senate, n.d.).

It is important to recognize that state judges may be impeached as well. There is no central repository of information on the number of

Impeachment:
the formal process of removing an unfit public servant (including judges) from office as a result of official misconduct; used with federal and some state judicial systems

state judges that have been impeached, but undoubtedly that number is relatively small. As the next section shows, given the tendency to reelect judges (even those who should not be reelected) and the difficulty of impeachment, states have turned to other mechanisms for judicial discipline and removal.

Judicial Conduct Commissions

The states have a variety of mechanisms for disciplining judges or removing them from office including recall elections and failure-to-retain elections. There are also **judicial conduct commissions**. California created the first state judicial conduct commission in 1960. This body was established to receive complaints of unethical or illegal behavior by state judges (Frankel 1991). Many states have followed California's example and created similar bodies known as judicial discipline committees, judicial qualifications committees, or judicial performance committees. In some states, the state supreme court operates these organizations; in others, they are independent boards (Rottman and Strickland 2006: 56-59).

Whatever the title, judicial conduct commissions are charged with receiving and investigating allegations of misconduct by judges. If an investigation finds that there is substance to the charges, the judicial conduct commission may be empowered to impose sanctions itself, or it may recommend to the state supreme court that sanctions be imposed. Discipline can range from warnings, written reprimands, and suspension from duties for some period of time. In the most extreme cases, the state supreme court may be authorized to remove erring judges from the bench and prohibit them from ever holding judicial office again.

Judicial conduct commissions: investigative bodies that are constituted to receive allegations of misconduct on the part of sitting judges; they may be empowered to impose disciplinary actions, or they may make disciplinary recommendations to the court of last resort

JUDICIAL INDEPENDENCE

A continuing concern for the judiciary is the issue of **judicial independence**. Judicial independence "means that in deciding cases judges are free from control by the executive and legislative branches of government as well as from control by the popular will of the moment. In other words, judges act free of extrajudicial controls in determining the facts, ascertaining and enunciating the law, and applying the law to the facts to arrive at decisions in cases" (Meador 1991: 59-60). The American Judicature Society (2012) has established the Center for Judicial Independence; part of its mission is to prevent removal "from the bench judges who have issued unpopular rulings."

Several elements are related to judicial independence that cause this to be an ongoing concern for the courts. First, since the founding

Judicial independence: the idea that the judiciary should be insulated from undue political influence from the executive and legislative branches of government

of our nation, we have had three supposedly coequal but independent branches of government: executive, legislative, and judicial. This is the basis for the notion of "checks and balances" and dates to the time of the ancient Greeks, although Montesquieu formulated the modern version in the 18th century. In reality, the judicial branch of government has always been the "least equal" of the three. The Founding Fathers viewed the courts as wielding neither the sword (of the executive branch) nor the purse (of the legislative branch). This means that the courts are dependent on legislatures to fund their operations, to establish the appropriate number of judgeships, and to define jurisdictional parameters. The courts are also dependent on the executive branch to enforce their orders involving issues such as school desegregation (see *Brown v. Board of Education of Topeka* (1954)). This means that the courts are not entirely the masters of their own domains.

Second, in our system of democracy, we strive to balance independence of action with accountability on the part of government officials. Thus, we want to give judges the freedom to carry out their jobs without political interference, but we also want them to be answerable to someone. These two opposing forces create a dynamic tension that continues as judges strive to be uninfluenced by forces outside of the courts while still operating in legal, political, and social spheres.

CONTINUED USE OF JURIES

As discussed in Chapter 8, jury service is a direct way for citizens to observe and interact with the courts. For most citizens, the possibility of jury duty is considered a civic duty, even though many do all they can to get out of it. Nevertheless, the way cases are tried and the jury decision-making process remain under scrutiny by many who study the courts. Perhaps it is best to begin this section with a discussion about how we try cases in the United States versus the systems used in most other nations.

In the United States, we provide the opportunity for jury trials in all felony cases and in serious misdemeanor cases (see *Duncan v. Louisiana* (1968)). As Chapter 8 also discusses, relatively few criminal cases actually go to trial in this country, but of those that do, most defendants choose to have a jury trial. Therefore, jurisdictions continuously struggle to assemble a sufficient jury pool for the cases that must be tried. Thus, we can say that trial court operations often revolve around assembling and selecting juries. At one time or another, most American adults have received a summons for jury duty. Some look forward to participating in this important process, but others ignore the summons (potentially facing a charge of contempt of court) or try to get the judge to dismiss them from serving. Small business owners, mothers of small children, and others in similar situations might face a hardship by being required to serve on a jury. However, most people who seek being excused do so because it is inconvenient.

This leaves us with a question: Since the jury system in the United States is cumbersome and expensive, shouldn't we just eliminate it altogether? More than likely, the overwhelming response would be no. People don't want to serve on juries, but they don't want the jury system eliminated either. For the time being, it seems likely that most states will retain jury trials, based on either constitutional protections or legal traditions. Nevertheless, the time may have come when we can ask: Should we eliminate jury trials?

SCIENTIFIC EVIDENCE IN THE COURTS

The use of scientific evidence in the investigation of crimes and the identification of criminals can be traced to the late 1800s and early 1900s. Examples include Cesare Lombroso's categorization of Italian prisoners based on unusual "body anomalies" and his concept of the "criminal man," along with various body measurements pioneered by Alphonse Bertillon as a means of classifying prison inmates, the eventual acceptance of fingerprinting, and most recently, DNA profiles.

With each of these new scientific advancements, trial and appellate courts were faced with the issue of when and under what circumstances "scientific evidence" should be allowable as valid, reliable, and admissible. Some investigative techniques such as ballistics, serology (analysis of bodily fluids), fingerprints, and shoe and tire marks eventually gained acceptance as admissible forms of scientific analysis. Other types of analysis—such as polygraph exams, bite marks, and hair analysis—have been rejected outright or limited by some courts.

The twentieth century saw an explosion in the use of scientific techniques in criminal investigation and identification. Eventually, the courts had to develop a standard for the acceptance or rejection of each new procedure. One of the most widely used early tests was the *Frye* test, based on a decision by the U.S. Court of Appeals for the District of Columbia in *Frye v. United States* (1923). The six-paragraph decision dealt with the introduction of expert testimony relating to changes in systolic blood pressure related to the detection of deception (with polygraphs). In its opinion, the court said:

Frye **test:**
a test applied by the courts to determine the validity of certain forms of scientific evidence

Just when a scientific principle or discovery crosses the line between the experimental and demonstrable stages is difficult to define. Somewhere in this twilight zone the evidential force of the principle must be recognized, and while courts will go a long way in admitting expert testimony deduced from a *well-recognized scientific principle or discovery*, the thing from which the deduction is made must be *sufficiently established to have gained general acceptance* in the particular field to which it belongs. The Court went on to write in *Frye* that blood pressure, as measured by polygraphs, had not yet achieved that standard and was disallowed. (Emphasis added)

State and federal courts continued to use the *Frye* test until 1993, when the U.S. Supreme Court decided *Daubert v. Merrell Dow Pharmaceuticals, Inc.* Since the decision in *Daubert*, most courts have used a two-pronged test relative to expert testimony and scientific evidence. Under the *Daubert* test:

Faced with a proffer of expert scientific testimony under Rule 702, the trial judge must make a preliminary assessment of whether the testimony's underlying reasoning or methodology is scientifically valid and properly can be applied to the facts at issue.

Cross-examination, presentation of contrary evidence, and careful instruction on the burden of proof, rather than wholesale exclusion under an uncompromising "general acceptance" standard, is the appropriate means by which evidence based on valid principles may be challenged.

Thus, for the introduction of new scientific testing techniques like DNA analysis, the courts must consider more than just the principle of "general acceptance" in deciding whether to admit expert testimony related to scientific analysis.

SENTENCING REFORMS

From the 1970s through the 1990s, almost no issue was more challenging to the judiciary than that of sentencing reforms. Every state undertook some alteration of its sentencing system—some large and some small—beginning in the 1970s and continuing into the new millennium. This section examines some of the major reforms that states (along with the federal government) implemented and what we know about the effects of these reforms.

For the first three-quarters of the twentieth century, the states and the federal government relied on **indeterminate sentencing systems**, in which the legislature determined the sentence range, judges imposed the sentences, and a parole board or similar body determined the actual length of time served. As an example, a convicted felon

Indeterminate sentencing systems: prison sentences that fall within a minimum and maximum range; release from prison is determined by the process of parole based on some fraction of the sentence imposed

might receive a sentence of one to ten years; however, as a result of parole rules, he or she could serve less than one year and probably would serve no more than two or three years at the most.

This trend brought about two types of criticisms of discretionary parole. First, conservatives felt that discretionary parole demonstrated a "soft on crime" approach and that offenders were not being required to serve the sentences they received. The phrase "a slap on the wrist" often was used to describe the fact that most criminal sentences were not severe. Second, liberals sometimes decried the fact that *discretionary* parole was, in fact, *discriminatory* parole. As a result, minority inmates and those with few economic resources and little in the way of community support systems were likely to serve longer sentences on average than nonminority and more well-to-do inmates.

As a result of criticisms from both ends of the political spectrum, states began to reevaluate their sentencing systems. The outcome was sentencing changes that fell into three categories: determinate sentences, guided sentences, and harsher sentences. The remainder of this section considers each of these sentencing changes.

Determinate Sentences

Determinate sentences altered the way penal sanctions were handed down. Under determinate sentencing systems, rather than convicted offenders being given a range of punishment (one to ten years), they were given a specific amount of time to be served (for example, 36 months). Beginning with California and Maine in the mid-1970s, many states moved toward determinate sentencing while at the same time restricting or eliminating discretionary parole (Hughes, Wilson, and Beck 2001; Mays and Winfree 2014: 64-65). There were two principal reasons for the movement toward determinate sentences. First, these sentences were designed to require inmates to serve most of the sentence that the court imposed. Second, these sentences removed some discretion from sentencing judges, and the ultimate result should be more uniform sentences.

Determinate sentences: court-imposed sentences of specific duration or length

Even with alterations to the parole system, determinate sentences still generally allowed early releases. In most states, inmates left prison early as a result of **good time credits**. Good time credits could be accumulated for good behavior while incarcerated, or they could be earned through participation in drug and alcohol counseling, educational programs, job training, or life skills training. In some systems, inmates could earn as much as a one-day credit for each day served, effectively cutting their sentences in half. With this approach, when an inmate's good time credits equaled the remainder of the sentence to be served, a mandatory release would be in effect.

Good time credits: sentence reductions for prison inmates based on good behavior and treatment or program participation

Table 9.1 **Total State and Federal Prison Inmate Population, 2000–2012**	
YEAR	NUMBER OF INMATES
2000	1,391,261
2001	1,404,144
2002	1,440,144
2003	1,468,601
2004	1,497,100
2005	1,527,929
2006	1,569,945
2007	1,598,245
2008	1,609,759
2009	1,617,970
2010	1,612,395
2011	1,598,783
2012	1,571,013

SOURCE: Carson and Golinelli 2013: 2.

A sentencing system that included good time credits had its critics as well. Beginning with passage of the Sentencing Reform Act of 1984, the federal government began the **truth-in-sentencing** movement and used its financial influence to encourage states to follow suit (Sabol and McGready 1999). For federal offenders, truth-in-sentencing meant they must serve at least 85 percent of their sentence before being eligible for release. In contrast with state inmates, who might earn good time credits of a day for each day served, federal inmates could earn a maximum of 54 days of good time credit per year.

The net effect of changing from indeterminate to determinate sentencing (along with truth-in-sentencing) has been an average increase in the sentences inmates serve in both state and federal prisons. This increase in average sentence length has also contributed to the increase in the number of prison inmates nationwide. Table 9.1 shows something of the increase in the nation's prison population for the years 2000 to 2009 but also illustrates the decrease in prison populations (largely a result of California's movement to reduce its number of inmates) since 2010.

Truth-in-sentencing: shorthand for the requirement that prison inmates must serve a substantial portion of their sentences (often 85 percent) before they are eligible for release

Guided Sentences

With determinate sentencing came the development of guided sentences. As discussed in Chapter 8, Minnesota pioneered sentencing guidelines in the 1980s, and other states (and the federal government, for a time) followed suit. Guided sentences are designed to do several things. First, guided sentences are designed to reduce sentencing disparities and impose similar sentences on similarly situated offenders; this is *sentencing uniformity*. Second, as a by-product of the process, guided sentences limit judges' discretion in sentencing. Third, some states (Minnesota, for example) link sentencing guidelines to state prison capacity. This means that sentencing guidelines are intended to keep prison populations at or near the levels that existed when the guidelines went into effect.

States have taken different approaches to guided sentences. In some—like Minnesota—the guidelines are mandatory, and judges are bound by them, with limited exceptions. The exceptions must fit into a category known as "manifest justice," which requires a substantial justification for departure from the established guideline. Other states—such as Maryland and now the federal government—use voluntary guidelines by which judges can choose to follow the prescribed sentence or depart and craft an individual sentence. Obviously, voluntary guidelines are more likely to result in a lack of uniformity.

The movement toward sentencing guidelines has been slow but steady. At the end of 1999, 18 states had some sentencing guideline system in place, 4 states had them pending, and 3 states were studying whether to create guidelines. A study by the National Institute of Justice gives a useful summary: "Guidelines have proven to be more than a fad; they have left a lasting imprint on sentencing policy, practice, and thought in the United States" (Lubitz and Ross 2001: 1). However, criminal justice system personnel have not universally embraced guided sentences. Under sentencing guidelines, judges have lost the most in terms of the sentencing discretion they traditionally exercised. By contrast, prosecuting attorneys have gained discretion in that they can manipulate the present charge as well as a defendant's criminal history (not taking previous crimes into account) to move the presumed sentence into another square on the sentencing grid. This enhances the prosecutor's ability to alter the "going rate" and exercise more leverage in the plea bargaining process.

Harsher Sentences

As a general rule, since the 1970s, criminal sentences can be described in terms of more of everything. More behaviors have been labeled criminal, resulting in what has been called the "crisis of overcriminalization" (Kadish 1967). Additionally, we have sentenced more people to prison, and most of them to more time than they might have served in the 1950s or 1960s (Hughes, Wilson, and Beck

2001). The result is that by the end of 2011, 6.97 million adults in the United States (1 out of every 34 adults) were under some form of correctional supervision (Glaze and Parks 2012). Nearly 4 million people were on probation, and another 2.2 million were in either local jails or state or federal prisons.

While it is possible that there are simply more criminals in the United States today than 30 or 40 years ago, we cannot discount the effect of harsher sentences on probation, prison, and parole populations. Three influences seem noteworthy. First, the use of **mandatory sentences** or mandatory minimum sentences is unprecedented. Presently, all states and the federal government have established some type of mandatory sentences for certain offenses, especially drug or weapons crimes (Parent et al. 1997). This trend means that at sentencing, the judge has no option but to sentence the now-convicted person to a prison term.

Mandatory sentences: sentences that a judge must impose upon conviction of a specified crime

Second, some states now have habitual offender statutes. These laws stipulate that after the conviction of a certain number of felonies, the state can file separate charges against a defendant for being a habitual offender. Conviction of this charge can bring an additional prison sentence, such as 99 years or life imprisonment. Perhaps the most famous (or infamous, depending on your view) of the habitual offender laws are the so-called "three strikes and you're out" statutes, first developed in Washington and California (see, for example, Dodge, Harris, and Burke 2009). In California, conviction of any three felonies (not just violent or personal crimes) as well as certain serious misdemeanors termed "wobblers" can result in prison sentences of 25 years to life. There have been challenges to such laws, but the U.S. Supreme Court has ruled in *Ewing v. California* (2003) and *Lockyer v. Andrade* (2003) that penalties such as these are not excessive and do not constitute "cruel and unusual" punishments (see Mays 2012: 237-238).

A third trend in harsh sentencing is the sentence of life without the possibility of parole (LWOP). States have developed LWOP sentences in addition to or as an alternative to the death penalty (Mays and Ruddell 2012). Traditionally, life sentences in many states meant something other than natural life. For example, in New Mexico a life sentence is interpreted as 30 years in prison. Therefore, LWOP sentences mean that offenders will now spend the rest of their days behind bars. This has presented some problems, especially in cases involving offenders under the age of 18. As a result, the U.S. Supreme Court ruled in the case of *Graham v. Florida* (2010) that LWOP for adolescent criminals not convicted of homicide offenses constituted unreasonably harsh punishment. Nevertheless, several states still have the option of LWOP for juveniles convicted of homicides and for adults convicted of certain other crimes, and this may become the alternative to the death penalty for more states in the future.

WRONGFUL CONVICTIONS

Wrongful convictions may be the most serious problem with which the judiciary struggles. Simply put, if we cannot trust the courts to convict the guilty and acquit the innocent, then who or what can we trust?

The problem of wrongful convictions began to surface in the late 1980s and early 1990s with the increasing use of DNA testing (Huff, Rattner, and Sagarin 1996; Scheck, Neufeld, and Dwyer 2000). Several different reasons have been raised for the occurrence of wrongful convictions in all types of cases. While there may be as many reasons for wrongful convictions as there are people who are wrongfully convicted, this section examines five of the most common reasons: eyewitness mistakes, false confessions, the use of jailhouse snitches, prosecutorial misconduct, and the ineffective assistance of counsel (see Mays and Ruddell 2008: 187-209). A sixth reason—problems with scientific analysis of evidence (or "junk science")—has been discussed previously.

Eyewitness Mistakes

There is a substantial body of research establishing the unreliability of eyewitness testimony in criminal cases (see Cutler and Penrod 1995; Fradella 2007; *United States v. Wade* (1967)). There are many reasons for eyewitness misidentification. Some have to do with the stress associated with being a victim of or a witness to a crime. Others are related to the physical surroundings of the event, such as crowds or little to no lighting. There is also evidence that crime victims of one race have a difficult time accurately identifying perpetrators of another race (Loftus 1996; Rutledge 2001). Police procedures, such as those used in photo and physical lineups, also can contribute to victim or witness misidentification.

Another element of this problem is that identification mistakes made early (such as during a police lineup) tend to become unquestionable identifications later in the process (such as at trial). Therefore, police and prosecutors must take care to ensure that the eyewitnesses correctly identify suspects to prevent costly trials resulting in wrongful convictions, false imprisonment, and time-consuming appeals.

False Confessions

When the issue of false confessions is raised, the average person usually asks, "Who would confess to a crime they did not commit?" The answer is that occasionally people do confess to crimes of which they are innocent and for many reasons. For example, some people confess after lengthy police interrogations. They may be told, "Things will go easier if you just confess," and sometimes they do. Also, police departments routinely encounter "false confessors" whenever a particularly notorious crime has been committed. These individuals may be seeking notoriety or have psychological problems that compel them to take the blame for something they did not do.

To counter this problem, most police agencies will be cautious about releasing information associated with especially spectacular crimes. They will withhold information known only by the perpetrator as a check against false confessions.

Jailhouse Snitches

One of the most troubling sources of wrongful convictions is the use of what are known as jailhouse snitches. In simplest terms, a **jailhouse snitch** is an inmate who is willing to testify against another inmate in exchange for leniency by the police or prosecutor. When an inmate expresses such willingness, the police will place a suspect in the cell with the potential snitch and instruct the snitch to listen for incriminating statements about what was done. The movie *The Shawshank Redemption* contains a scene where one prison inmate overhears another prison inmate confessing to the murder supposedly committed by Andy Dufresne (the central character played by Tim Robbins). This was a case of innocently overhearing an incriminating statement, but in many cases jailhouse snitches prompt a confession or falsely testify to having heard a confession that never occurred. Again, all of this happens to receive leniency in the cases for which the snitches are being held.

Jailhouse snitch: prisoners who are willing to inform on other prisoners to receive leniency from the prosecuting attorney or court; one of the major sources of wrongful convictions

Prosecutorial Misconduct

Almost as troubling as the use of jailhouse snitches is the issue of prosecutorial misconduct. In a classic article, Bennett Gershman (2009) asked why prosecutors misbehave. The simple answer is that it works, and there is limited recourse against prosecutors who commit misconduct. Courts have long held that prosecutors are virtually immune to suit for the way in which they conduct their business; the U.S. Supreme Court case of *Miller v. Pate* (1967) demonstrates something of the win-at-all-costs approach to prosecuting cases. In this murder case, the prosecuting attorney introduced into evidence a pair of men's underwear with a red stain. The implication to the jury was that this was blood, when, in fact, the stain was paint. On appeal, the Supreme Court overturned the conviction, noting that the prosecuting attorney had "deliberately misrepresented the truth" to the jury.

In *Miller*, the Supreme Court referred to Justice Sutherland's statement in the case of *Berger v. United States* (1935) that the prosecutor "may prosecute with earnestness and vigor—indeed, he should do so. But, while he may strike hard blows, he is not a liberty to strike foul ones." As a result of this principle, the U.S. Supreme Court accepted the case of *Pottawattamie County, Iowa, et al. v. McGhee et al.* (2009) to determine whether prosecutors could be sued civilly for a wrongful conviction and imprisonment as a result of obtaining false testimony in the criminal investigation and then using that testimony during the trial. The parties to this case settled before the Supreme Court could make its decision, but the case nonetheless reinforces the idea that prosecutors are not completely immune from suit for their actions.

Ineffective Counsel

A final source of wrongful convictions is ineffective assistance of counsel. The Sixth Amendment to the Constitution provides that criminal defendants have the right to assistance of counsel for their defense. However, having an attorney and having a competent attorney may be two different matters. For example, in the case of *United States v. Cronic* (1984), "[t]he court appointed a young lawyer with a real estate practice to represent [the defendant], but allowed him only 25 days for pretrial preparation, even though it had taken the Government over four and one-half years to investigate the case." In deciding this case, the Supreme Court held that Cronic failed to demonstrate specific errors his attorney made; thus, representation by the counsel in this case was adequate.

Recently there have been high-profile cases in which appointed attorneys have slept through part of the proceedings or appeared in court intoxicated. In such cases, wrongful convictions are more likely to occur, and some of these cases have resulted in substantial prison sentences for those wrongfully convicted.

In concluding this section on wrongful convictions, there are several key points worth noting:

- Most of the people convicted of crimes—either from trials or plea bargaining—are factually and legally guilty.
- The amount of cases involving those wrongfully convicted is almost impossible to know, but the estimates range from as low as 1 percent to as high as 10 percent to 20 percent; whatever the figure is, this represents an unacceptable number.
- Most of the wrongfully convicted are sentenced to prison terms; however, some are sentenced to death and the prospect of executing an innocent person is a specter that hangs over the entire criminal justice system (Grisham 2006).

The next section deals with the death penalty specifically because it is the one punishment that cannot be reversed once it is carried out.

THE DEATH PENALTY

This chapter ends with a discussion of one of the most controversial aspects of judicial business: capital punishment, or the death penalty. In many ways, this discussion is tied to two previous issues: the use of scientific evidence in courts and wrongful convictions. While there does not seem to be any resolution to positions by the two sides on this issue, the divide between those who favor capital punishment and those who are opposed to it seems to be narrowing.

The United States inherited its tradition of executions from England, where most crimes were felonies and most felonies called for the death penalty (Banner 2002: 5-23). The Founding Fathers and the framers of the Constitution must have assumed that there would be the death penalty in this country since the Fifth Amendment to the Constitution provides that no person shall be "deprived of *life*, liberty, or property, without due process of law" (emphasis added).

Among the nations of the world, the United States is one of 58 (and the only Western democracy) that still executes its citizens (and those of other nations). The trend worldwide has been to eliminate the death penalty, and the number of death penalty states in this country is declining. However, most states still have the death penalty on their books, and public opinion polls show that a majority of Americans express some sympathy toward the death penalty.

Nevertheless, public support has been waning over the past two decades, and the number of executions has generally declined from the modern high of 98 in 1999. Table 9.2 shows the number of people on death row in the United States as of 2011, Table 9.3 shows the number of executions carried out by state in 2011, and Table 9.4 shows the number of executions in the United States by year since 1977.

One final issue must be addressed in closing the discussion of the death penalty: executing offenders who were under the age of 18 at the time of their crime. Early in our nation's history, children and adults were treated much the same legally (see Gardner 2009; Mays and Winfree 2012). Beginning with the juvenile court's founding in 1899, most children were treated less harshly than their adult counterparts, but there were exceptions. Every state had provisions under which it could try juveniles as adults. This meant that the most serious juvenile offenders faced the possibility of adult punishments, including prison and execution. A series of Supreme Court cases—including *Eddings v. Oklahoma* (1982), *Stanford v. Kentucky* (1989), and *Thompson v. Oklahoma* (1988)—said that states could execute offenders for murders committed by youngsters under the age of 18, but the Court emphasized that age should be a mitigating factor and those below the age of 16 should not be considered for the death penalty. However, that changed when the Court decided the case of *Roper v. Simmons*

Table 9.2   Number of People on Death Row in the United States, 2011

JURISDICTION	NUMBER
California	705
Florida	393
Texas	301
Pennsylvania	207
Alabama	196
North Carolina	158
Ohio	142
Arizona	130
Georgia	96
Tennessee	87
Louisiana	87
Nevada	81
Oklahoma	63
Mississippi	57
Federal government	56
21 other jurisdictions	323
Total	3,082

SOURCE: Snell 2013: 1.

Table 9.3   Number of Executions in the United States by State, 2011

STATE	NUMBER
Texas	13
Alabama	6
Ohio	5
Georgia	4
Arizona	4
Florida	2
Mississippi	2
Oklahoma	2
Missouri	1
Delaware	1
South Carolina	1
Virginia	1
Idaho	1
Total	43

SOURCE: Snell 2013: 1.

Table 9.4 Executions in the United States by Year, 1977-2011			
YEAR	NUMBER	YEAR	NUMBER
1977	1	1995	56
1979	2	1996	45
1981	1	1997	74
1982	2	1998	68
1983	5	1999	98
1984	21	2000	85
1985	18	2001	66
1986	18	2002	71
1987	25	2003	65
1988	11	2004	59
1989	16	2005	60
1990	23	2006	53
1991	14	2007	42
1992	31	2008	37
1993	38	2009	52
1994	31	2010	46
		2011	43
Total			1,277

SOURCE: Snell 2013: 14.

(2005), in which the majority held that "evolving standards of decency" dictated that the death penalty not be imposed on those under 18 years of age, even for murder. The result has been that states have increasingly turned to the use of life without parole for juveniles convicted of very serious crimes (see Mays and Ruddell 2012).

SUMMARY

This chapter considers several difficult issues that confront the courts in the United States. Most of these are lingering issues, and easy solutions do not seem on the near horizon. A continuing issue concerns providing attorneys for the large number of indigent defendants. There are also a host of questions dealing with how we choose judges and what their qualifications should be, along with how we should sanction judges who fail to perform their duties. Such questions highlight the difficulty of maintaining an independent judiciary while at the same time holding judges accountable.

Trials also present challenges to the judiciary. Should we continue to use the citizen-juror model, or should we move to a European-style "professional" juror or lay assessor model? And what about the use of scientific evidence in courts? How do we decide what is really scientific and the degree to which new scientific techniques should be allowed as evidence?

Finally, two of the most significant issues confronting the courts have to do with wrongful convictions and the related concerns associated with the death penalty. Nothing undermines the integrity of our judicial process like highly publicized cases of defendants who were wrongfully convicted, and no judicial system can easily withstand the criticism that would result from a wrongfully convicted person being executed.

REVIEW QUESTIONS

1. What are some of the ways by which we can provide indigent defense? Does one of these systems seem superior to the others? Explain your answer.
2. Is there "one best way" of choosing our judges? What system does your state employ? If you had the choice, would you choose another system?
3. Could a judge be ineffective but not really misbehaving? Is it easy to know whether judges are doing their jobs? How can we know, and what can we do about it?
4. Take a pro or con position on this proposition: The jury system in the United States is inefficient and ineffective. Provide a justification to support your position.
5. Scientific evidence must meet the standards of reliability and validity. What is meant by these terms? Is it possible that a particular scientific analytical technique could be both reliable and valid and still be inadmissible in court? Explain.
6. Compare and contrast indeterminate sentences and determinate sentences. What has

been the trend over the past 40 years in the United States? Which system does your state use?
7. Sentencing guidelines are said to promote uniformity and decrease sentencing disparities. Are there unintended consequences of using guided sentences? Explain your answer.
8. The chapter discusses five of the most common reasons for wrongful convictions. Which among these five reasons is likely to be the most common? The least common? What, if anything, can be done to minimize wrongful convictions?
9. Does your state have the death penalty on its books? If not, when was it eliminated? If so, for which crimes is it applicable? Take a poll among your classmates, giving them the following three options: (1) I'm in favor of the death penalty under appropriate circumstances, (2) I'm completely opposed to the death penalty, and (3) I can't decide where I stand on the death penalty. How does your professor stand on this issue?

KEY TERMS

contract attorneys
court-appointed attorneys
custodial interrogations
determinate sentences
Frye test

good time credits
impeachment
indeterminate sentencing systems
indigent defendants
interim appointments
jailhouse snitch
judicial conduct commissions

judicial independence
justices of the peace
legal aid societies
legal clinics
mandatory sentences
merit selection

nonpartisan elections
partisan elections
public defenders
retention ballot
truth-in-sentencing
voucher systems

PART IV

Punishment and Community Reentry

Probation and Community Corrections

LEARNING OBJECTIVES

At the conclusion of this chapter, you should be able to:

- Explain how probation began in the United States.

- Understand how probation conditions form the foundation of community
  sentences as an alternative to incarceration.

- Describe how restitution, fines, and community service can be used
  to financially compensate victims and help the community.

- Identify community corrections programs that are used for intensive
  supervision and treatment.

INTRODUCTION

In Chapter 8, you learned that during each individual offender's sentencing, a judge considers what the law says must be done together with what the judge feels is best for the offender and the community. While substantive law mandates that some crimes, particularly those of a heinous or violent nature, require offenders to be sentenced to prison, it also allows judges some flexibility on other offenses, typically those related to theft, property destruction, or drugs and alcohol. The decision to incarcerate someone, even for a temporary period of time, sends a message that the crime itself is either so serious that it deserves punishment of this magnitude or that the offender's pattern of behavior over time has not changed despite other forms of punishment or treatments that have been tried without altering behavior. To sentence a person to some other criminal sanction sends an altogether different two-part message: (1) this crime is less serious than one warranting incarceration, and/or (2) this person will best be served—and will not pose a serious threat to community—by his or her conditional return to that community. For most misdemeanor and felony crimes, judges allow defendants to remain at liberty in the community. This is in lieu of incarceration, according to the defendant's ability to follow certain conditions and with minimal risk to the community or the victim. Regardless of the court's choice, once a judge decides on a sentence, the corrections system is responsible for carrying out that court order for each individual offender. This chapter introduces and discusses **probation** as the most common correctional sentence (Glaze, Bonczar, and Zhang 2010) and identifies other common ways that individuals serve correctional sentences in lieu of incarceration.

More than 5 million offenders are currently serving at least a portion of their sentence in the community. As this chapter discusses, there is a wide array of programmatic choices available that can be added to a probation term so that probation functions as a foundation for **graduated sanctions**. Graduated sanctions allow additional supervision or treatment conditions to be added to an initial term, and/or some terms of supervision can be lengthened, depending on the behavior of the probationer.

Probation: community supervision of a convicted offender in lieu of incarceration under conditions imposed by a court for a specified period, during which it retains authority to modify those conditions or to resentence the offender if he or she violates those conditions

Graduated sanctions: aimed at probation and parole violators, these are more restrictive community supervision or treatment conditions added to an initial probation or parole term

HOW PROBATION BEGAN

Probation began in the United States in the 1840s. At about the same time, critics were beginning to question the effectiveness of the penitentiary and were already looking for more humane alternatives (the next chapter discusses the history of the penitentiary). Most criminal courts already allowed defendants to be released on their own recognizance to avoid unnecessary pretrial detention. Some courts allowed the accused to go free if the court received monetary payment as a form of collateral for good behavior, similar to modern-day bail. Less-serious cases would be **filed**, which meant that the case was neither dismissed nor adjudicated; it was simply laid to rest without judgment. Judges had the ability to mitigate punishment by sparing some offenders from the penitentiary, but there was no formal supervision alternative other than filing or dismissing the case.

Filed case:
a case for which an indictment is held in abeyance with neither a dismissal nor a final judgment because the judge determined that a prison sentence was too harsh and no other options existed at that time

John Augustus

The development of probation supervision is credited to a Massachusetts business owner named John Augustus. Augustus made his living making and selling shoes in downtown Boston; he was also devoted to helping people in trouble. Once his shoe business became successful enough that he had employees running the shop, Augustus frequently visited the Boston municipal court to observe people and social problems (Jones 2005). At that time, the court allowed some defendants to be released on recognizance if they had support from a third party, called a **surety**; in other cases, the defendant had to be bailed out. The surety was held responsible for the defendant's conduct until the next court appearance.

Surety:
an individual who agrees to become responsible for the debt or pretrial behavior of a defendant should the defendant fail to attend the next court appearance

As defendants were brought into court, Augustus interviewed them and sponsored the most motivated first-time offenders. He assured the court that the defendants would return for their sentencing hearings in return for the court releasing the defendants to him instead of jailing them. Augustus had a number of defendants living under his roof and was able to help many find permanent homes and secure employment. By 1858, with his business in financial trouble and his health failing, Augustus was forced to stop supervision. After nearly two decades, Augustus and his group of volunteers made a difference in the lives of 1,152 men and 794 women, but his good deeds did not go unnoticed. Massachusetts enacted laws to make pretrial supervision a permanent part of court proceedings in line with the newly developed indeterminate sentencing laws (Jones 2005). By the mid-1940s, the corrections system became a place to treat "sick" inmates as a part of the **medical model**, and every state used pretrial supervision and probation as an alternative to incarceration. Probation work was no longer voluntary or merely supervisory. Rather, a **casework** approach evolved by which the probation officer became a specialized career populated by social workers and counselors who acted as therapists working individually with offenders (Wodahl and Garland 2009). During the same time that the casework approach became more accepted, mentally ill clients were deinstitutionalized from the mental health system to criminal justice.

Medical model:
the notion taken from medicine that crime is an illness that can be cured

Casework:
a community-supervision philosophy that allows an officer to create therapeutic relationships with clients through counseling and behavior modification, assisting them in living productively in a community

From Mental Health System to Criminal Justice System

In the 1960s, experts acknowledged the harmful effects of long-term mental health institutionalization for persons who no longer posed a danger to themselves or others. Because of significant advances made in psychotropic medication, people with mental illnesses could have more control and stability over their daily lives without the need for being institutionalized. The Community Mental Health Center (CMHC) Act of 1963 established federal funding to operate outpatient mental health centers to treat eligible persons who were released from state hospitals. While some CMHCs were funded, most funds were later used for Vietnam War efforts. Existing CMHCs were overwhelmed and limited in the clientele they accepted. As the mental health system became more privatized, CMHCs tended to prioritize service for people with health insurance. Indigent and uninsured persons with mental illness were increasingly served, and occasionally supervised, by a system *outside* of the mental health profession—namely, the criminal justice system.

At the same time that persons with mental illnesses were entering the corrections system, probation services became overwhelmed with more clients for whom each individual officer was responsible. This left probation officers with less time to treat social problems like alcoholism, drug addiction, and mental illness. These problems were contracted through other community agencies outside of criminal justice, to which offenders were referred.

The mid-1980s brought the latest iteration in the ongoing war on drugs, the victims' rights movement, and a stronger emphasis on public safety. Probation officers were chiefly responsible for surveillance, monitoring offender fee payments and restitution to victims. **Intensive supervision probation** was popularized by limiting freedom of movement and minimizing access to treatment. A heavy surveillance tactic with little treatment benefit proved to be a mistake when research showed that probationers were being revoked and sent to jail only to occupy valuable space that should have been reserved for offenders who are dangerous to the community. Jails became overcrowded with probationers who did not necessarily commit crimes—they simply did not follow the conditions of their probation.

By 2000, the philosophy of probation supervision, among other factors, had to change. One of the major philosophical changes was the basic approach to probationer supervision. Probation departments began to use **neighborhood-based supervision**, which divides supervision areas into smaller jurisdictions so that an officer is assigned to supervising offenders in a single zip code rather than throughout the entire city. This allows probation officers to learn one particular neighborhood and to become more visible in the community, make more

Intensive probation supervision:
a form of probation used in the 1980s that stressed intensive monitoring, close supervision, and offender control with little treatment benefit

Neighborhood-based supervision:
a probation supervision strategy that emphasizes public safety, partnerships with other community agencies, getting out of the office, and supervision by zip code

home visits, and engage community groups as partners in offender supervision, a topic to which this chapter later returns. More generally, probationary programs began to expand services to first-time and nonviolent offenders, imposing less restraint on freedom for a lower cost than jail or prison. Today, these programs are collectively known as **community corrections**.

Community corrections: a nonincarcerative sanction in which offenders serve all or a portion of their sentence in a community

WHY USE COMMUNITY-BASED CORRECTIONS?

Community corrections programs allow the offender to avoid incarceration by living and working in the community under court-ordered supervision. Community supervision is designed to correct law-breaking behavior by imposing certain restrictions and requiring offenders to become more responsible by establishing new habits and routines. For example, community correction programs are more likely than prison to require that an offender work, go to school, complete community service, pay restitution, and enroll in some sort of treatment program. The offender can retain positive family ties and continue to support dependent children, if necessary. This ensures the offender remains a taxpayer, not a tax burden. It also ensures that children are not punished for the criminal actions of their parents.

Another benefit of community-based sanctions is that with the offender living at home there is an immediate cost savings to taxpayers over housing expenses incurred in jail or prison. Offenders who live at home can avoid the violence, corruption, and stigma that accompany incarceration. When an offender lives with other family members, his or her supervision status can sometimes intrude on the privacy that others enjoy in the same household. For example, other family members might also be restricted from possessing alcohol or firearms at their own home if that condition is court-ordered for a probationer or parolee. Perhaps the greatest general problem with community corrections sentences is the chance that an offender may commit another offense or in some way jeopardize the safety of another that could have been averted—or delayed—through incarceration. It is impossible to predict with 100 percent certainty whether a given offender will harm someone else in the future. However, we do know that the benefits of keeping an offender in the community far outweigh the risk to public safety.

Preadjudication Probation

Probation forms the foundation of most community-based sentences and may be used in two main ways: (1) in the early stages before a conviction or (2) after the court imposes a sentence of probation for a misdemeanor or felony conviction. In both the juvenile and adult justice systems, when probation is used before a conviction, it is typically known as **diversion** or **deferred adjudication**. This means that the police have detected an individual wrongdoing, and the defendant goes to court on the charges and agrees to complete probation in exchange for the court dropping the charges without a conviction. For adults, the charges still remain on the record, but the outcome is listed as a deferred adjudication, which is understood *not* to be a conviction. Juveniles who successfully serve a period of nonadjudicated (or informal) probation are likely to qualify to have their record of this incident permanently sealed (Mays and Winfree 2012).

A defendant who does not successfully abide by the conditions of diversion supervision may be ordered back to court for resentencing on the original charges. This condition remains in force for individuals who commit new crimes after diversion is over—up to five years later in some jurisdictions or longer in others. In this case, the former charge can now become a conviction that can be used against the defendant as a prior misdemeanor or felony sentence and will remain permanently on that person's record.

Deferred adjudication/ diversion: an offering made by a court to a defendant during the preadjudication stage to allow the defendant to complete community supervision and/or a community-based treatment program; successful completion results in dropped charges and no formal conviction

Post-Adjudication Probation

Probation is also used as a formal sentence following a plea of guilty or conviction for a misdemeanor or felony crime. In this situation, a convicted offender is subjected to community supervision under court-imposed conditions for a length of time according to the offense severity and completion of all court-ordered conditions. Judges have some discretion, but they are generally guided by statutes when deciding whether to impose probation and how long a probation term will be. Often, the probation sentence is less than if the offender were sent to prison. When deciding whether probation is appropriate for a pending felony crime, judges rely primarily on a defendant's criminal history and courtroom demeanor. With indeterminate sentences, in which judges have more discretion, judges also consider all relevant information contained in a **presentence investigation report** that details a defendant's childhood, family background, employment history, community ties, and ability to pay. Probation works the same in the juvenile and adult justice systems by being the most commonly used disposition for offending behavior. Figure 10.1 shows that probation is used in six out of ten cases of adjudicated delinquents.

Presentence investigation report: a summary report submitted to the court after a defendant's plea of guilty for a felony in which a sentence is recommended based on the totality of the defendant's situation and ability to handle probation

What Does a Person on Probation Have to Do?

As you have learned so far, community supervision has some pretty significant advantages. So what is being on probation like? The fol-

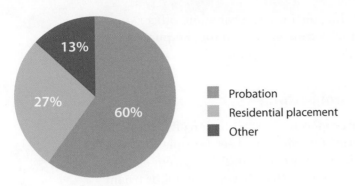

SOURCE: Livsey 2012: 1.

Figure 10.1
Community sentences for adjudicated juveniles

lowing is a typical list of 12 **standard conditions** that most offenders are required to follow. They include restrictions on some freedoms but also include many responsibilities and obligations.

Standard conditions: conditions imposed on all probationers or parolees regardless of their offense

- Maintain full-time employment and/or full-time school attendance.

Freedom of movement and associations is restricted:
- Report to the assigned probation officer as required.
- Remain within the city or county jurisdiction at all times. Going outside the jurisdiction, even momentarily, requires advance permission.
- Advance permission is required before changing employment or moving a residence.
- Advance permission is required before associating with anyone with prior felony convictions.
- Promptly inform the probation officer of any contact with law enforcement.

Possession/use of certain items is restricted:
- Firearms or any other dangerous weapons are not permitted, and you cannot be in the immediate vicinity of guns or dangerous weapons.
- Use or possession of controlled substances or dangerous drugs is not permitted unless preapproved with a medical doctor's prescription.
- Alcohol use is not permitted if you are under supervision for an alcohol-related offense.

Right to privacy is restricted:
- Allow the probation officer access to the home and workplace at reasonable times.
- Allow the warrantless search of self, vehicle, or premises if the supervising officer has reasonable grounds to believe that evidence of a violation will be found.

- Submit to drug or alcohol testing. A probation officer may supervise the collection of a urine specimen for the purpose of drug testing.

Juvenile Probation in School Settings

Like with adults, juveniles must report to their probation officer and be subjected to searches and testing for substance use. Juveniles are also required to attend school, among other conditions. For juveniles, probation in school settings has become an effective way to monitor truant and delinquent youths during and after school. First, with the probation officer at the school, getting access to school records, peers, and observing youths is crucial. Traditionally, most probation officers are located in a different area of the city and have a hard time getting access to attendance records, grades, and progress reports. They also have little knowledge about peer groups, which is the most significant part of a youth's life (Alarid, Sims, and Ruiz 2011b).

Second, a child on probation still needs to meet with his or her probation officer but must rely on someone else for transportation. A child should not be expected to rely on friends or public transportation. Having a probation officer at the school also eliminates the need for parents to miss work hours to drive their child to appointments with probation officers. Third, statistics show that much juvenile delinquency is committed *during* school hours, whereas alcohol and drug use is more frequent on the weekends (Soulé, Gottfredson, and Bauer 2008). Juvenile probation officers meet with youngsters during or after school. Their offices are within one of the school buildings, and they can act preventatively about potential problems with peers or in the classroom (Alarid, Sims, and Ruiz 2011a). This can lead to fewer incidents of school bullying, fewer days of missed classes, and reduced school misbehavior.

Special Conditions and Community Corrections Programs

As you have learned, probation represents the foundation of most community sentences for adults and juveniles. Adults on probation must contribute to the household with full-time employment or some combination of work and school. Juveniles on probation live with family members at home and are expected to attend school and abide by curfew. Other than the list of 12 standard conditions previously discussed in this chapter, many offenders are subjected to **special conditions** that may be ordered by a court and are unique to that offender's particular circumstances or category of offenses.

Special conditions: conditions of probation or parole tailored to fit the offense or the needs of an offender

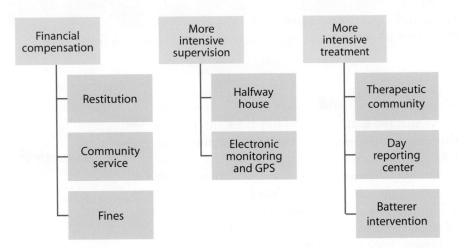

Figure 10.2
Special conditions of community corrections sanctions

Figure 10.2 shows three different functions of special conditions that are incorporated into community corrections programs. First, it is recognized that offenders should financially compensate victims and/ or society wherever and whenever possible. Thus, restitution, community service, and fines were developed to address those needs. Other special conditions seek to reduce recidivism through increased surveillance, which is accomplished through residential community corrections facilities and home confinement, both enforced by electronic monitoring or GPS depending on the nature of one's conviction. A third reason for special conditions relates to the offender's "specific problems" that are revealed by the instant offense or the presentence investigation. Such conditions could require the offender to obtain community-based services such as mental health evaluations and classes dealing with domestic violence, substance abuse, and driving. We address all three of these punishment strategies and provide examples of community-based programs that meet each special condition.

COMMUNITY CORRECTIONS PROGRAMS THAT FINANCIALLY COMPENSATE

The financial compensation for crimes committed can include one or more of these special conditions as ordered by the court:

- If there is a victim, pay restitution as ordered by the court.
- Complete any court-ordered community service.
- Pay all court fines.
- Remain current on monthly probation supervision fees.

- Support dependents, including keeping current on any child support obligations.

Restitution

Crime victims deserve payment for tangible losses they incurred from the crime itself, and it is expected that offenders pay back the victims for those losses. **Restitution**, or compensating crime victims, has come a long way since the 1980s and earlier, when victims were rarely if ever compensated. The burgeoning victims' rights movement broadened the use of restitution to include offenders who went to prison and those who owed back child support. Restitution also became mandatory in felony crimes of violence, sexual offenses, and property offenses (Dickman 2009). Restitution amounts are based on tangible losses, such as the replacement value of stolen or damaged property and expenses the victim incurred as a result of the crime. Payment of restitution is dependent solely on the offender's financial assets and/or means to pay through employment. A more affluent offender with a good job will be more likely to be able to pay than someone who has little or no employment history. Inability to pay restitution in full or in a timely and regular fashion is common in such situations and does not constitute a reason to revoke probation as long as the offender is trying to pay as much as possible.

Victims of violent crimes who incur substantial losses can be compensated through the state **victim compensation fund** if the attorney general or chief prosecutor for the state or commonwealth agrees to go forward with the prosecution they agree to prosecute. Potential losses incurred from an aggressive assault may include emergency room bills, lost income from missed days of work, mental health counseling sessions, physical rehabilitation, and moving expenses (Office for Victims of Crime 2010). Expenses incurred vary by type of crime and individual victims' circumstances, such as whether the victim paid for child care during court sessions (many courts do not allow children), or whether the victim traveled long distances for court.

Community Service

Community service provides an option for judges to require the offender to perform unpaid labor for the general good of the local community. The idea behind labor performance is the symbolic need for character building and so the offender can give back in some way to individuals or organizations that are most in need of help such as a charity or a nonprofit organization. In a sense, community service offsets what the offender may have taken from the community in terms of

Restitution:
court-ordered payment by an offender to a victim to cover tangible losses that occurred during or following a crime

Victim compensation fund:
a fund managed by the state attorney general's office and subsidized through offender fees that dispenses financial assistance to victims of violent crime

Community service:
unpaid labor on behalf of the public to compensate society for harm done by an offense

time, resources, and energy. Community service is a common sentence used in drunk-driving cases (Klein 1997).

As a character-building exercise, most community service involves outdoor labor and is performed in supervised groups, such as picking up roadside litter, emptying trashcans at city parks, removing graffiti in public places, or sweeping sidewalks. Some community service is individualized to an offender's talents or skills and may include tutoring, mentoring, or being a classroom aide. A third type of community service attempts to change offenders or make an impression on them through the less fortunate, such as working at a food bank or serving soup in a shelter for the homeless. Some jurisdictions allow judges to sentence drunk drivers to perform low-skill activities such as janitorial work in an alcoholism treatment facility, a hospital emergency room, or the county morgue.

The number of hours must be commensurate with the seriousness of the crime. Many states now have guidelines for judges, given that community service hours can substitute for jail time, such as performing 30 days of community service (240 hours) in lieu of serving 90 days in jail (Klein 1997). The U.S. Supreme Court allowed community service to substitute for unpaid restitution and fines if the defendant could not afford to pay (*Bearden v. Georgia* (1983)) but left the decision up to the individual state or jurisdiction.

Fines

A monetary **fine** may be one of the most common and oldest forms of punishment known in the world. European examples of monetary compensation to the victim or the state date back to at least the wergild of 6th century's Franco-Germanic Salic Law, which established the value of a human life, with some lives worth more than others, and every piece of property. Over the millennia, fines have become one of the most often used forms of punishment around the world; however, the way the fine is used in the United States today is quite different from many other countries. American judges tend to use fines as the sole means of punishment for less serious offenses such as traffic violations, city ordinance violations, and petty misdemeanors. For felonies, fines can be an additional sanction appended to probation, intermediate sanctions, and incarceration, but they are not required. The only exception is that the federal system requires that a fine be assessed for all felony offenses if the court chooses not to impose either restitution or community service. Fines for state offenses can be added to a probation term and paid in installments, but because of the probationer's many other financial responsibilities, fine collection in full is unlikely. Many states allow unpaid fines to be subjected to interest,

Fine:
a monetary penalty imposed by the court that is statutorily defined by severity of the offense committed

surcharges, and penalties (Beckett and Harris 2011). A fine can also be added to a prison term, but its enforcement is difficult when the prisoner is indigent and not working. When imprisoned, if a fine is not paid, that cannot be held against prisoners if they have no means to pay the fine.

Fines tend to serve only punitive purposes, as they do not fulfill a rehabilitative or reintegrative component (Beckett and Harris 2011). Unlike restitution and community service (or their historical precedent, the wergild), fines in most of the United States are *not* assessed by the amount of loss from the crime but by statute in which the amount of the fine is fixed no matter what the financial situation is of the offender. The fixed fine creates a situation of financial hardship for those less well-off than for wealthy offenders. Since a disproportionate number of offenders in criminal justice are financially strapped or indigent, the American Bar Association has consistently opposed the use of fines. In contrast, throughout parts of Scandinavia and other nations in Europe, the day fine, also called the unit fine, imposes a fixed number of days of net income received by the convicted person, again based on a fixed schedule available to the court. For example, a minor offense may result in a ten-day fine. If the offender earned 20 euros a day, the fine would be 200 Euros, but if he or she earned 200 euros a day, the fine would be ten times greater. Much like income tax for all citizens, the day fine represents a progressive rather than regressive burden for convicted persons.

Failure to pay a fine when incarcerated is handled typically through contempt proceedings or the civil court. However, the courts do *not* allow people to be held in contempt if they are unable to pay a fine because they are incarcerated. So, if a fine is paid at all, it would have to be before or after the incarceration period.

Another problem with fines is the possibility that the money used to pay it originated from someone other than the offender, such as a family member or friend who loaned or gave the offender the money. While courts approve added surcharges and penalties to late fine payments, doing so makes it *less* likely that an offender can pay the fine in full. Instead, courts have been more successful if they mandate community service in lieu of the unpaid fine.

COMMUNITY CORRECTIONS PROGRAMS FOR INTENSIVE SUPERVISION

You may consider probation to be rather intrusive, especially after reviewing the conditions typically associated with it. However, there is an even more intrusive and intensive form, not surprisingly called intensive probation supervision. Intensive supervision entails even more frequent contact between a convicted offender and the supervision officer, and greater restrictions on the probationer's liberty, such as curfews and unscheduled home visits. In theory, more supervision may sound like it could increase public safety, but in reality it doesn't—it only seems to increase the likelihood that officers will discover that an offender is behaving in a way that violates probation supervision rules—not criminal conduct per se, but less serious forms of behavior (Wodahl and Garland 2009).

Until recently, **correctional boot camps** would have been a main part of intensive supervision for probationers and parolees. However, boot camp programs, as implemented in the corrections system between 1982 and 2010, were found to be ineffective at reducing long-term recidivism and were too expensive to justify keeping them open. As a result, boot camps have all but disappeared from the correctional scene. Instead, we present examples of two community-based programs that have been shown to be successful: residential community correctional facilities and electronic monitoring/global positioning systems.

Residential Community Corrections Facilities

Halfway houses began in the mid-1800s and were operated by faith-based and other nonprofit organizations as a way to help recently released prisoners with temporary housing and clothing. The goal was to help ex-convicts meet their most immediate needs with food and shelter until they found a stable job that would allow them to live independently. Early halfway houses gave clients everything they needed and allowed them to save the money they made from a job.

Halfway houses changed dramatically in the 1960s and 1970s to include a formal graduated sanction option for probation violators. Today, halfway houses are also known as **residential community correction facilities (RCCFs)** and have no bars or surrounding razor wire. RCCFs are virtually all privately owned and operated and contract with federal, state, and local governments; they often provide services in freestanding houses in gentrified neighborhoods or as community-based facilities near commercial districts. At the federal level alone, as of 2014, there are 172 residential reentry facilities (Federal Bureau of Prisons, n.d.); thousands more exist for county and state probationers who are juveniles or adults.

Unlike the generous (and free) assistance that earlier halfway houses provided in the 1800s, contemporary halfway houses now charge daily rent to all residents to help subsidize the cost of food and shelter. The primary goal for today's RCCF resident is to obtain

Intensive probation supervision:
a form of probation with the most restrictions and monitoring for offenders thought to be at the highest risk of recidivism

Correctional boot camp:
a 90- to 180-day program modeled after a military-style regimen designed to instill discipline, respect, and teamwork in younger offenders ages 14 to 24; treatment programs are secondary in importance

Residential community corrections facilities (RCCFs):
a community sanction in which a convicted offender lives at a corrections facility and must be employed, but can leave the facility for a limited purpose and duration if preapproved

full-time employment and complete all court-ordered treatment, but it seems that the financial expectations decrease the money clients can save for independent living once they are discharged from the RCCF. When not working, residents complete household chores, attend court-ordered drug-treatment programs, and submit to random drug and Breathalyzer tests.

Most RCCFs slowly increase a client's leisure time that can be spent outside of the facility using a system of privileges or levels. The privileges depend on employment status, the amount of time without a disciplinary infraction, and the amount of money saved. Advance permission must be obtained to leave for any reason, including work, religious services, treatment, and family visitation passes. Daytime leisure visits to a family member's home are allowed, provided the client returns first to the facility to check in after work. Clients out on leisure time must be available by phone at all times and must produce receipts to verify their whereabouts. Clients who receive a disciplinary report for misconduct or who fall behind on making rental payments to the facility will lose privileges. According to one of the authors' experience (Alarid) working at an RCCF, the most successful residents were the ones who worked as many hours as possible or were able to secure a good-paying job.

Electronic Monitoring and GPS

As our society becomes more mobile, reliance on technological advancements to track movement in the community has increased, using **electronic monitoring (EM)** and **global positioning systems (GPS)**. EM actually began in the 1970s for offenders who were court-ordered to **home detention**. EM uses radio frequency signals that transmit from a device worn around the offender's ankle to a receiver located inside the offender's home. The receiver is connected to a landline telephone and can detect the offender's whereabouts from 250 to 500 feet.

Two types of home-based systems have been used: the continuous signal transmitter and random calling. The continuous signal transmitter sends signals to the receiver as long as the offender stays in range. Once the offender is out of range (more than 500 feet from the landline telephone), the signal is lost and the date and time of the loss is recorded. The second type of home-based system randomly calls the offender's residence; the offender must verify his or her identity by inserting the ankle (or wrist) transmitter into the receiver.

In either case, the activity of each 24-hour period is automatically sent in the middle of the night to a central computer via the phone lines (similar to the way a fax is transmitted). The next morning, a community supervision officer examines the printouts from the night

Electronic monitoring (EM):
a correctional technology used in intensive supervision probation, parole, day reporting, or home confinement that uses radio frequency waves to track an offender's whereabouts via a separate transmitter and receiver connected to a landline phone

Global positioning system (GPS):
a correctional technology that uses satellites to track an offender's whereabouts via a combined transmitter, receiver, and microprocessor

Home detention:
when defendants or offenders are restricted to staying at home, with permission to leave only for work, court dates, or court-ordered treatment

before to determine if the offender had permission to leave when the signal was lost. When enforced with EM, home detention affords greater control over an offender's physical whereabouts, but not the offender's behavioral activities. Additionally, the early systems were not foolproof. Still, they provided versatility for people who lived in an RCCF or anywhere other than a jail.

Offenders today are still monitored by EM units that transmit radio frequency signals, except that verification can be done by voice, video, and/or fingerprint scan. As GPS technology has become less expensive, more offenders are being monitored using an additional GPS tracking unit that is paired with a cellular phone. Monitoring offenders through GPS works similarly to the way a cell phone operates—that is, through the use of satellite towers that register the precise location of an offender in the community. The only difference here is that unlike a cell phone, an offender must wear his or her device at all times and can never turn the device off. The location of the offender is registered once every few hours for passive systems or once every 10 to 15 minutes for active GPS systems. If the signal is not received when it should be, a computer sends a report of the violation to a central computer. GPS units now have the transmitter and receiver combined into a single unit. A computer chip inside the unit also allows the probation officer to program in places where the offender is not allowed, such as near a victim's house or near a school. The main drawbacks to GPS technology are loss of GPS signal and cost. There are also battery issues, such as relatively limited battery life, and they must be constantly recharged using a mobile charger or a charging base station at home.

Most prior evaluations of EM using moderate- to high-risk offenders are methodologically weak and as a result, it is only possible to determine the independent contribution that EM or GPS had on reducing recidivism using a small number of studies (Renzema and Mayo-Wilson 2005). One such study showed that offenders on both continuous signal EM and on GPS were less likely to be revoked for technical violations and new crimes than offenders on home confinement without any EM device (Padgett, Bales, and Blomberg 2006).

COMMUNITY CORRECTIONS PROGRAMS FOR INTENSIVE TREATMENT

Courts routinely order that offenders enroll in a wide array of treatment program to address deficits, challenges, or problems that have a direct relationship to their current offense or why they continue to return to the criminal justice system. Rehabilitation is a term often used to refer to efforts intended to increase an offender's skill set to make him or her more independent and/or competitive in today's job market. These skills can include learning basic computer skills, GED education, learning a trade, or financial management. Increasing one's skill set helps offenders find employment, so they can in turn help pay for the treatment they must complete. The two most common community-based treatment programs that offenders might have to complete are related specifically to substance abuse problems or anger management issues. In either case, the offender must participate at his or her own expense if the court deems it necessary and related to the offense.

Treating Offenders with Drug Problems

Drug use and criminal behavior are no doubt related in a significant way, although the exact causal nature of this relationship—which one causes the other—is difficult to specify with any scientific accuracy. Nationally, about 70 percent of all convicted offenders have a drug or alcohol dependency problem (Karberg and James 2005). Dependency is identified as a situation in which individuals who committed a crime to support a drug habit or who were under the influence of drugs or alcohol when they committed their crime. Of course, the degree of dependency (occasional, moderate, or severe), length of use, and the types of substances vary greatly, and so does the type and length of treatment. There are surprisingly *few* existing treatment programs to help offenders in the corrections system. It is estimated that 1.5 million people who are arrested each year have drug/alcohol dependency or substance abuse problems. Of this number, only about 55,000 juveniles and adults are treated through court-ordered programs such as **drug court** (Bhati, Roman, and Chalfin 2008). Juvenile drug courts benefit greatly from parental involvement throughout treatment. Researchers found that parental involvement also contributes to increasing their children's completion rates, which, in turn, decreases youth recidivism (Alarid, Montemayor, and Dannhaus 2012). Other options exist to treat offenders with substance abuse problems, including community-based residential drug treatment programs and day reporting centers, discussed below.

Day Reporting Centers

A **day reporting center (DRC)**, also called a day custody program, is a nonresidential alternative to incarceration that blends high levels of control with the delivery of specific services that offenders need. Officials in Connecticut and Massachusetts initially adopted the idea in the 1990s from England. By the mid-1990s, more than 20 states used this model (Parent and Corbett 1996); today, it is estimated that over two-thirds of the states authorize some form of the day reporting system. While there is no universally agreed definition, DRCs are typically used

Drug court:
a treatment program for drug dependency in which a judge, prosecutor, defense attorney, and probation officer use a team-based approach to monitor the progress of offenders through biweekly courtroom visits and behavior modification strategies

Day reporting centers (DRCs):
nonresidential programs typically used for defendants on pretrial release, for convicted offenders on probation or parole, or for probation or parole violators as an increased sanction; services are provided in one central location, and offenders must check in daily

as a "graduated sanction" for probationers who violate conditions of supervision, most commonly for drug use, but who need to be in a treatment program or kept in the community.

Clients live at home but report to the DRC daily during the work-week and attend classes such as anger management and cognitive behavior modification. Only some states have DRCs. For example, Georgia has 14 DRCs throughout the state, with each DRC servicing up to 100 high-risk/high-needs offenders with substance abuse problems. DRC participants do not have a job during the first 30 to 45 days of the program, as they are involved in a wide array of services, including intensive substance abuse treatment, cognitive restructuring, moral reconation therapy, drug testing every other day, adult basic education, and 40 hours of community service in each phase. Beginning with the second phase, they are approved to begin looking for employment but continue to attend treatment at the DRC. A six-month after-care component follows the on-site phases. DRCs are currently revising their risk assessment and classification schemes to more fully embrace evidence-based practices (Kim, Joo, and McCarty 2008). A more recent controlled experiment of DRCs for prison releasees, however, revealed that participants did more poorly on release than did members of the control group (Boyle et al. 2011). DRC participants were more likely to use drugs and commit new crimes at higher rates than other recent parolees. The researchers recommended that other community-based services that cost less than DRCs be used to help parolees. Indeed, DRCs may be more effective if used as alternatives to *incarceration* rather than as alternatives to community-based options.

Residential Drug Treatment Programs

Offenders on probation who have severe addictions may require a longer period of intensive treatment than day reporting centers can provide. Residential drug treatment facilities, otherwise known as **therapeutic communities (TCs)** focus on long-term treatment of about 6 to 9 months followed by 6 to 12 months of aftercare (Alarid and Webster 2013). TCs are voluntary, so many people who try this program but do not complete it must be resentenced by the courts. A TC is a highly structured, confrontational, and emotionally exhausting experience with the goal of getting the client to admit the excuses and justifications they use to keep drinking and using drugs, recognizing how drug use has stunted their emotional development, and learning how to replace drugs with a new way of life (Alarid and Webster 2013). The individual and group sessions may be led by recovering addicts who have been through a TC and have remained clean and sober. For individuals who complete drug treatment, recidivism and

Therapeutic communities (TCs): peer-led confrontational-style drug treatment for severe drug addicts

drug use are significantly less than those who drop out or even for offenders who complete just outpatient treatment (Bhati, Roman, and Chalfin 2008).

Treating Assaultive Offenders

Domestic violence and assault are other common offenses in which offenders receive community-based correctional sentences. In the past, domestic violence victims were lucky to obtain a temporary restraining order (also known as an order of protection), but the offender was often not arrested or convicted of wrongdoing. At times, the restraining order would only lead to more violence. With the recognition that domestic violence is a serious and repeated form of abuse and control over another person, arrest policies changed, victim services increased, and child support payments were better enforced. In the late 1970s, courts began to mandate that batterers convicted of domestic violence complete a batterers' intervention program while on probation. Couples counseling was just not effective. Instead, 26 to 52 session programs were developed just for the assaultive individual to learn problem-solving techniques without resorting to violence. All treatment programs require that abusers take responsibility for their actions and for the solution to change their behavior, which include developing listening skills and healthier ways to express their emotions no matter how other people around them act. The other goal of the treatment is for abusers to overcome the secrecy and deception for which they have managed to convince themselves that the victim is at fault (North Carolina Domestic Violence Commission 2013).

Evaluations of batterer intervention programs found that between 22 percent and 42 percent of participants dropped out. About 65 percent of batterers who completed treatment had no further incidents of violence between six months after completion and up to three years (Rothman, Butchart, and Cerda 2003). However, the intervention must be at least 12 weeks and preferably closer to 52 weeks for maximum benefit. Intervention programs of only eight sessions were simply not effective. Along with treatment, the use of electronic monitoring or GPS is advisable to know the offender's whereabouts while on probation. This, in turn, can decrease the tendency for stalking and increases victim protection.

LEAVING PROBATION AND COMMUNITY CORRECTIONS: SUCCESSFUL VERSUS UNSUCCESSFUL OUTCOMES

Probation officers must enforce the conditions of the offender's court sentence. After initial sentencing and if a probationer shows improvement, judges may shorten the length of probation. About 65 percent of probationers in the United States successfully complete supervision or are discharged early (Glaze, Bonczar, and Zhang 2010).

Probation officers must keep current with every single individual assigned to them. This includes bringing any new crimes or rule violations to the court's attention. If an offender commits a new crime while under correctional supervision, that **legal violation** goes through the courts just like a new arrest. Prosecutors sometimes agree to forgo prosecution of the new crime in exchange for offenders having their probation revoked and being sent to prison for the original crime (for which they were initially placed on probation). Committing crimes on probation varies by jurisdiction, and occurs between 10 percent and 16 percent of the time (Alarid and Webster 2013; Gray, Fields, and Maxwell 2001).

Legal violations: when an offender commits a new misdemeanor or felony while being supervised on probation or parole for another offense

It is more common for probationers to commit **technical violations,** which include ignoring standard conditions such as changing residence, quitting a job, or leaving the city limits without first obtaining the probation officer's permission, or special conditions such as failing to participate in court-ordered therapy or treatment. Other technical violations are more serious, such as getting behind on restitution or fee payments or not showing up for appointments with the probation officer. In all of these cases, the offender's failure to follow through with court-ordered conditions will eventually lead to consequences. The probation officer will begin by issuing verbal warnings, which escalate to written warnings. Should the offender continue to neglect his or her responsibilities, the probation officer must report the infractions to the court, which then recommends a course of action, ranging from retaining probation with modifications, resentencing to a different graduated community sanction, or completely revoking probation.

Technical violations: multiple rule violations that breach one or more noncriminal conditions of probation or parole that may result in revocation

A very real challenge with all the court-ordered conditions is that sometimes the numerous financial obligations and new responsibilities become too overwhelming for offenders. Offenders may feel they are being asked to do too much at one time, and they might not be allowed to phase in the responsibilities slowly. Researchers have found that while fair and consistent sanctions are important for noncompliance, positive reinforcements are more important than additional punitive sanctions to offender success (Wodahl et al. 2011). Rewards can include verbal praise, certificates, fee reductions, curfew removal, special visits, and good time. If offenders are only told about the negative things such as how much they still owe, they will get discouraged faster and know that failing to meet these obligations means that they will be incarcerated. However, individuals on supervision also know that once they are incarcerated, many of their community obligations will simply vanish.

A second challenge is the lack of options that many jurisdictions have to deal with people who fail on probation. Jails have traditionally served as the first place for revocations, which makes sense *if* a probationer has committed a new felony. Once probationers are incarcerated, they may be delayed in jail by as long as six months because of preexisting case backlogs.

Successful models—exemplars—do exist. Given that most people who fail on probation have committed technical violations relating to drug use or failing to report to their probation officer, courts in Hawaii have decided to try a different approach to failure. The Hawaii Opportunity Probation Enforcement program (known as the HOPE program) focuses only on people who have had multiple incidents of drug use and/or no-shows on probation, in the hopes of decreasing this behavior without any new arrests. HOPE begins with the judge issuing verbal warnings, followed by the probationer being issued a color (red, blue, green, yellow, etc.). Probationers call a hotline every morning to find out the color of the day; if their color is selected, they must provide a drug test that same morning. If they refuse to provide a sample or fail a drug test, they are arrested and immediately go to court that same day, where the judge modifies the probation sentence. The modification includes a weekend in jail. HOPE has resulted in a general improvement in probationer behavior and a roughly 50 percent decrease in revocations and new arrests (Hawken and Kleiman 2009).

THE FUTURE OF COMMUNITY CORRECTIONS

Community corrections programs are definitely here to stay, as they not only provide a cost-effective alternative to incarceration but also are a legitimate sentence in their own right. But critics caution that the legitimacy of community corrections is threatened when revocation rates get too high (Wodahl, Ogle, and Heck 2011). One solution would then be to keep revocations as low as possible by first having options on what to do with an offender who has a pattern of technical violations before suggesting revocation to a court. Departmental policies and practices aimed at graduated sanctions allow for predefined responses to certain behaviors, such as drug use, terminating employment without permission, failure to attend treatment, or failure to report to the supervisory officer.

Another idea for lessening the possibility of technical violations is to decrease the number of rules and conditions—keeping only the ones that are deemed the most necessary and directly tied to recidivism risk and/or criminogenic factors. For example, while it is necessary to forbid alcohol use for DWI offenders on supervision, it may be excessive to require that condition for *all* offenders, and so on.

Another idea for improvement is to ensure that technical violators of probation do not contribute to jail overcrowding. There are at least two solutions. First, expedite the revocation process by holding regular court hearings for probationers. The preliminary hearing should be held within 24 hours of arrest unless the offender requests more time to prepare his or her case for revocation. A second solution might be to build separate probation violator units to allow a short stay if necessary of a few days to a few months before the offender is rereleased to the community. In that way, that offender never occupies space in jail or prison unless a new crime is committed.

In closing, the challenge of community corrections in the future is to use appropriate services and treatment regimens for each individual that eventually translates into permanent behavior change. Ultimately, the hope is that each person will no longer return to the criminal justice system and can become successful despite his or her conviction.

SUMMARY

Probation as it is known today was brought about by criticisms that penitentiaries were not accomplishing their stated purpose of reforming the offender and that suspension of sentence without supervision was not a satisfactory alternative to incarceration. Building on the foundation laid by criminal court judges, John Augustus was instrumental in developing the practice of modern-day probation. With the deinstitutionalization of the mentally ill and as the mental health system became more privatized and less accessible, indigent persons with mental illness were increasingly treated and supervised by the criminal justice system.

Community supervision corrects law-breaking behavior by imposing certain restrictions and requires offenders to become more responsible by establishing new habits and routines. Upon completion of a period of diversion supervision, an offender will not have a formal record of conviction. If an offender on diversion supervision does not comply with the conditions, a formal sentence ensues.

Standard conditions of probation include maintaining full-time employment or school-restricted freedom of movement and associations, restricted possession/use of firearms, and restricted privacy. For juveniles, probation in school settings has become an effective way to monitor truant and delinquent youths during and after school.

Offenders should financially compensate victims and/or society whenever possible through restitution, community service, and fines. Other special conditions seek increased surveillance through residential community corrections facilities and monitoring through landline telephones or satellites. Individualized community-based treatment is specific to the offender's problems, such as with drug and alcohol dependency or lack of emotional control and being assaultive. Patterns of technical violations are more common than committing new crimes while on probation. Graduated sanctions and a guideline matrix to help community corrections officers with making revocation decisions more consistent are among the suggestions for decreasing revocation rates. Fair and consistent sanctions are important for noncompliance, but positive reinforcements and treatment are more important than negative and threatening sanctions to overall offender success.

REVIEW QUESTIONS

1. What are some of the reasons that led to the expansion of community corrections over time?
2. What do you believe is the main goal of probation today? What if the probationer is subject to intensive probation supervision? Justify your answer.
3. What are some of the problems with revocation, and how can the problems be remedied? Have you thought of other solutions that were not mentioned?
4. What other examples of intensive supervision can you give?
5. Other than substance abuse and assault, is there another common form of community-based treatment that offenders might be required to attend?
6. Boot camps are an intermediate sanction of the past. Do you think they will ever resurface again? Justify your answer.
7. What is the future of electronic monitoring and GPS?

KEY TERMS

casework
community corrections
community service
correctional boot camp
day reporting center (DRC)
deferred adjudication
diversion
drug court
electronic monitoring (EM)
filed case
fine
global positioning system (GPS)
graduated sanctions
home detention
intensive probation supervision
legal violation
medical model
neighborhood-based supervision
presentence investigation report
probation
residential community correction facilities (RCCFs)
restitution
special conditions
standard conditions
surety
technical violations
therapeutic communities (TCs)
victim compensation fund

Institutional Corrections

LEARNING OBJECTIVES

At the conclusion of this chapter, you should be able to:

- Trace the history of incarceration from its roots in medieval Europe to the invention of the penitentiary in the United States.
- Understand how American prisons developed differently for men and women and according to region of the country (North vs. South).
- Outline the differences between jails and prisons.
- Explain how prisoners are classified according to security level.
- Summarize the issue of why juveniles are in secure facilities with other juveniles compared to with other adults.

INTRODUCTION

In the United States, nearly 7 million people—representing 1 in 34 adults—are under some form of correctional supervision. Figure 11.1 shows that this number includes 4 million people on probation, 2.2 million inmates incarcerated in jails and prisons, and 853,000 parolees. Chapter 10 discusses how probation remains the most frequently used correctional punishment; Chapter 13 examines parole as a method of prisoner reentry. The current chapter explores institutional corrections, including its origins and evolution. What becomes evident in this chapter is that long-term prison incarceration is used in the United States at a significantly higher per capita rate than any other nation in the world. The United States imprisons about 700 people out of every 100,000 living within its borders; this rate is even higher for young men and persons of African American or Latino descent.

The correctional system population peaked in 2008 at 7.3 million people before steadily declining over the next three years because of states' economic problems and being unable to afford high levels of incarceration. Despite the economic downturn, correctional spending remains one of the largest line items in most states' budgets, accounting for a national total of more than $173 billion every year. The money spent on corrections is fourth highest after education, health care, and transportation (Vera Institute of Justice 2010).

How did the rates get so high, and why do we continue to spend so much money in this way? To understand fully how we got to this point, we must first introduce the basic concepts and then discuss the history of the penitentiary, including the methods of punishment in various parts of the world before its invention and the differences in how U.S. corrections developed compared to other countries in the world.

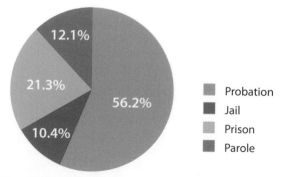

Figure 11.1
Status of adults on correctional supervision

SOURCE: Adapted from Glaze and Parks 2012.

Jails, prisons, youth detention centers, and private facilities make up various types of **institutional corrections**, all which have the primary goal of depriving a person of his or her liberty and various freedoms as part of the criminal sentence. The second reason these facilities exist is to keep individuals separated from society at large and to protect others, at least temporarily, while the individual offenders receive help for their deficits and recognize the error of their ways so they can make different choices in the future.

In brief, **jails** incarcerate both pretrial detainees who have not been convicted and individuals convicted of crimes for which they will be held less than one year. Prisons are long-term institutions for convicted felons who are serving sentences of more than 12 months. Prisons traditionally have been known as penitentiaries and reformatories because of their focus on different goals over time. Most prisons are public facilities, but this chapter discusses how and why some correctional facilities have become owned and operated by private companies. Finally, youth facilities are separate residential placements within the juvenile justice system. Some juvenile facilities are secure lockdowns and others allow youths to freely move about. We begin our look at institutional corrections with an overview of the history of punishment.

Institutional corrections: a sanction in which incarcerated offenders serve their sentence away from the larger community in a jail or prison institution

Jails: short-term confinement facilities where pretrial defendants are held pending court hearings or convicted persons serve less than one year

THE HISTORY OF INSTITUTIONS OF PUNISHMENT

As Chapter 1 explains, ancient Middle Eastern communities (including areas that are now called Israel, Egypt, Syria, Iraq, and Iran) punished offenders primarily with death, corporal or physical punishment, fines, and exile. The purpose of corporal punishment was to publicly humiliate the offender and to inflict physical pain by beating and mutilation (Spierenburg 1995). Common methods of a death sentence included stoning, crucifixion, decapitation, strangulation, and pouring hot molten lead down the perpetrator's throat.

The earliest record of prisons dates back to 2050 B.C.E., when Egyptian pharaohs forced offenders into hard labor building pyramids. Imprisonment was also documented as a form of punishment for unpaid fines and as a place of detention as early as 399 B.C.E. in ancient Greece, according to Plato's work *Apology* (Peters 1995). Most early prisons, however, were temporary holding cells until corporal or capital punishment was carried out. Interestingly, in Rome (400 B.C.E.), male heads of households could incarcerate members of their own household for short periods as a disciplinary measure if needed. Real Roman criminals awaited their fate at the Tullianum, later named the Mamertine prison, and those who offended the emperor were sentenced to fight—or more often just be eaten by—exotic animals at the public Colosseum (Peters 1995).

Monastery Prisons in Medieval Europe

In Europe, laws and punishments developed around the church, particularly when Christianity was legalized. Bishops assumed judicial roles for when members of their congregations committed behaviors considered to be immoral. Bishops were tasked with defining ways to achieve penance as the way to salvation, and church courts rejected death and mutilation if at all possible. Instead, isolation in a disciplinary cell (the Latin term *carcer*) within the monastery was enforced for immoral behavior committed by monks and nuns. Immoral monks were subjected to hard labor, beatings, and restricted diets of bread and water.

By the 12th century, accusations as a common procedure reverted into an inquisitional method, which was more of a fact-finding hearing through interrogation, written evidence, and professional judges. In the mid-13th century, England began constructing prisons for behaviors that the king deemed offensive. Punishments were severe and "ranged from shaming display—the pillory, mutilation, branding, public stocks, and ducking stools—to severe and aggravated capital punishments—hanging, drowning, burning, burial alive, or decapitation—and any of these could be preceded by the infliction of torments before the execution itself" (Peters 1995: 35). Other than England, other European countries had prisons that more closely resembled dungeons. For example, France and Italy were known to have constructed special inquisitorial prisons for the investigation of suspected heretics, for which torture was used to help the fact-finding process (Spierenburg 1995). The French also built the Chatelet and the Bastille as royal custodial dungeons, a practice for which the Tower of London was also employed in England before, during, and after the reign of Henry VIII. The idea was that the ruling nobility housed other nobles who threatened their hold on power. Offenders were generally offered exile or, if they refused or returned unbidden, internal exile in a royal dungeon. After all, if the ruler executed someone of equal rank, what was to stop someone else from killing them in turn? Medieval German towns and principalities also used prisons as a midrange sentence between fines and death (Peters 1995).

Facilities other than dungeons were used to store or warehouse European convicts through the early Enlightenment period. One main difference was that these facilities were initially built for another purpose and happened to house convicts if space was available or if the facility was no longer being used for its original purpose. Facilities such as monasteries, convents, abandoned military barracks, hospices, and insane asylums were used to house convicts. In some places, convicts were kept all together in one large room and rarely separated by sex or age, so safety was a concern, as was keeping inmates from escaping. As

Box 11.1 Creative Forms of Incarceration

From the founding of its first colony in North America, England and later Great Britain transported convicted felons as forced colonists, a practice called **penal transportation**. Early on, this practice was undertaken at the expense of the offender or the ship owners in whose ships they sailed. In 1718, the British Parliament passed the first Transportation Act, which allowed convicted prisoners to be sent to the colonies for seven years; moreover, should they attempt to return, a death sentence awaited them. Beginning in 1776, when American colonies declared their independence, the British were denied access to their former colonies as destinations for prisoner transportation ships. Since Britain still needed a place to send prisoners, the government began converting dilapidated merchant and naval ships, known as **hulks**, into floating prisons that were attached to the shoreline. Prisoners left the hulks during the day to work, but poor hygiene standards contributed to one in three prisoners dying out of the 8,000 convicts who experienced this form of imprisonment. The hulks were used temporarily until British sea captains could find another transportation destination. In 1787, transportation resumed, this time to Australia, until 1870, when Great Britain finally ended the practice entirely.

Penal transportation: the removal of convicted criminals to a remote location where they were forced to work as indentured slaves and laborers as their sentence

Hulks: old English ships that were no longer seaworthy and were tied to the shore to be used as temporary prisons during the late 1700s

Box 11.1 suggests, some of these nations had to resort to new and creative means of securing a growing number of offenders—and, in the case of colonial powers, populate distant lands with settlers, even reluctant ones.

European Punishment in the 1700s

Repeat offenders were banished or, for the most serious offenses, were sentenced to public execution, usually by hanging. By this time, formerly small villages were now bustling cities, and public humiliation punishments became less effective. Even public executions did not seem to have the intended deterrent effect, as they turned into events where people attended to have fun and show admiration for the soon to be executed (Spierenburg 1995). By the 1870s, England and most other European countries—with the notable exception of France, which held its last public guillotining in 1939—ended the practice of public executions.

Punishment during this time involved forced labor on French galley ships and naval arsenals, German and Swiss chain gangs, and workhouses. Workhouses, also called "bridewells," were correctional institutions for convicted persons of lower socioeconomic status who were forced into labor for 10- to 12-hour days. Women prisoners spun and wove canvas and linen, while male prisoners pulverized logs to produce colored dye for the material. The work was so taxing that when criminals from middle- and upper-class families were sentenced, the families demanded that their kin be sent to a private prison to be spared from forced labor. Gradually, the idea of penal servitude and hard labor was replaced by imprisonment. Among those who influenced this change was Jonas Hanway, who authored a book in 1776 called *Solitude in Imprisonment*, in which he advocated a separate system of reformation through religious influences (Spierenburg 1995).

At that same time in another part of England, newly appointed sheriff John Howard was shocked to see prisoners in his jail without food or proper bedding because they could not afford to buy food from their jailer (McGowen 1995). Over the next decade, Howard visited institutions all over Europe to see what other countries were doing. He was impressed with the order and adequate sleeping arrangements that prisoners had in Amsterdam, and how they worked and attended religious services. At the Hospice of St. Michael, Howard was quite taken with the monastic philosophy of doing penance in seclusion. He returned to England and published *The State of Prisons in England and Wales*. This book was the foundation on which Great Britain passed the Penitentiary Act in 1779, which permanently improved jail conditions by ruling that jails must:

- Be safe, sanitary, and subject to regular inspection
- Abolish the fee system and provide prisoners with food, clothing, and bedding
- Separate inmates by gender and age and provide solitary confinement, silence, and labor

As the next section shows, these principles later helped influence the development of correctional facilities in the American colonies.

18TH- AND 19TH-CENTURY CORRECTIONAL PUNISHMENTS IN THE UNITED STATES

Capital punishment, fines, banishment, and the same types of corporal punishments discussed earlier in this chapter were used in colonial America well into the 18th century. Before the American Revolution, long-term incarceration and hard labor were offered only as alternatives to corporal punishment. However, prisons were disorderly, and riots and escapes were common. New concerns arose that the social institutions (families, churches, schools, and community) within this new America, with its freedoms and openness, were losing leverage and stabilizing influences, thus a new institution was necessary (Rothman 1995).

Inventing the Penitentiary

Keeping people in jail until they could pay their fine was finally agreed to be an ineffective solution, so new forms of social control were discussed. Pennsylvania's Benjamin Rush and other Quaker reformers began examining how to make jails more sanitary, safer, and places where people could make positive changes to their lives. A new penal code was passed in 1786 that included solitary confinement and hard labor. The Walnut Street Jail in Philadelphia was the first correctional facility that was transformed from a diseased and desolate dungeon atmosphere to one that encouraged reformation. There was even a new housing unit built to keep the most hardened criminals in solitary confinement (Rothman 1995).

The Pennsylvania System

Penitentiaries were built exclusively for long-term incarceration, based on the idea that prisoners—the penitents—were to reflect on their misdeeds in solitude to achieve change. This strategy of being separate and silent, although first started at the Walnut Street Jail, later became popularly known as the **Pennsylvania system** because of the location of Eastern State Penitentiary in Philadelphia. In 1829, Eastern State began to accept felony inmates, and visitors came from all over the world. High outer walls lined the ten acre perimeter, with towers at each corner and one tower in the middle above a central rotunda. Eastern State was originally designed to house 450 inmates within seven cell blocks. Each cell block was like a long straight hallway with cells positioned on each side. The seven hallways radiated out from a central rotunda and were known as a radial or wagon wheel floor plan. For its time, Eastern State became the most expensive and state-of-the-art prison in the world. Each cell door had a small slot in the middle that opened from the outside to fit a food tray. Every 8-by-18-foot cell had a skylight for natural light, plumbing, sewage system, centralized heat, and individual exercise yards outside back door. Although prisoners worked in their cells making shoes and chairs, production was slow and not very lucrative. Inmates left their cells only for medical attention, and when they did, masks and blindfolds prevented them from talking and knowing the prison layout.

These practices soon had the disastrous and unintended consequences of social withdrawal, depression, mental health problems, and even suicide. These poor results, coupled with the expense of housing inmates in single cells, caused critics to rethink the Pennsylvania system design and to seek other ways of incarcerating convicted offenders.

Penitentiary:
an institution for correctional punishment that emphasized punishing the mind over the body so that inmates could reflect on their misdeeds and repent

Pennsylvania system:
an early system developed in Philadelphia that emphasized complete silence and solitary confinement day and night

The Auburn System

The Auburn prison opened in 1817 in Auburn, New York, initially using the "separate and silent" idea from the Walnut Street Jail, but this idea was abandoned after only six years (long before Eastern State Penitentiary even opened) because the inmates experienced the same kinds of mental health problems. Instead, at Auburn, inmates were locked in their cells at night but were allowed to work and eat together, in silence, during the day. Inmates worked in factories on the prison grounds and produced goods that could later be sold by the state for profit. Silence was enforced through routines of flogging, lockstep marching, and prohibitions against eye contact (Rothman 1995). Order, discipline, and routine became known collectively as the **congregate system**.

Congregate system: an early system developed in Auburn, New York, that emphasized lockstep marching, factory work, and eating with other prisoners in silence

The Auburn prison was designed and built very differently from Eastern State. Instead of cells facing one another and built like wheel spokes, Auburn cells were built back-to-back, about five stories high, so they occupied less room. The cells were smaller and occupied by two inmates instead of only one. A catwalk or narrow ledge with a railing was built along the front of each cell.

Eventually, the Auburn or congregate model was adopted in states across the country because it was more cost effective and turned a profit in some states. Even Eastern State Penitentiary officially abandoned the Pennsylvania system by 1913 and finally closed its doors in 1971.

Post-Civil War Reformatories in the North

The silence, order, and discipline of the original congregate system significantly declined following the Civil War, when prisons became unruly and brutal places. New immigrant groups from Ireland in particular were sent to northern prisons, and there was increased interest in having penitentiaries serve an entirely different purpose. In the northern states, penitentiaries emphasized education and vocational training so that inmates were better prepared for their eventual return to the community. Prevailing ideas included allowing prisoners to earn their freedom through self-improvement and learning new skills, with a reduced emphasis on manual labor. Some 20 years before this period in prison evolution, the **marks system**, a behavioral management tool aimed at giving inmates credit for good behavior, was successfully tried at Norfolk Island in Australia by superintendent Alexander Maconochie. The marks system (discussed in more detail in Chapter 13) had been successfully replicated in Ireland and other parts of the world, and support for it began to emerge in the United States.

Marks system: a behavioral modification system developed by Alexander Maconochie that emphasized earning daily points through good behavior, which reduced time from the sentence

Indeterminate sentences were used with fixed minimum terms, and eventual release was dependent on whether a parole board believed the prisoner had been reformed. Thus, some correctional facilities built during this time period became known as **reformatories**. The first reformatory opened in 1876 in Elmira, New York, to carry out the progressive ideals of Maconochie and Zebulon Brockway. Brockway advocated using indeterminate sentences in the courts as a mechanism to encourage rehabilitation and to allow the corrections system the flexibility to release inmates early or to keep them longer if warranted. Brockway also stressed the importance of separating prisoners by sex, age, and seriousness of offense. Most of the existing custodial, fortress-style penitentiaries were converted into men's reformatories with less successful results because true reformation was difficult in a more oppressive building built for security and safety. Female offenders did not escape unnoticed in this movement toward a new correctional ideal, as Box 11.2 shows.

Reformatories:
the label given to prisons in the mid- to late 1800s that emphasized indeterminate sentences, treatment programs, good time, and parole

Post-Civil War Leasing in the South

Northern and southern states differed on a number of issues with respect to philosophies of punishment, means of production, and ideas about involvement of centralized government. First, southern states in this era had a long history of using harsh punishments, including corporal and capital punishments; moreover, southerners generally believed such punishments to be more effective than treatment and reformation. Today, southern states still tend to favor longer terms of incarceration and retain the use of the death penalty when compared

---

Box 11.2   Women's Reformatories

There was an emerging interest in treating women differently from men by having separate reformatories for women. Prison reformers such as Elizabeth Fry and Dorothea Dix were instrumental in making prison conditions for women more humane in the 1800s. In the United States, women targeted for the reformatories were Caucasians convicted of misdemeanors, while African American women were relegated to custodial prisons or segregated from white women. Women's reformatories were built as small cottages so that the female prisoners could receive domestic training to become good housewives. The skills thought to be important at the time included cooking, cleaning, gardening, and sewing. While reformatory life was certainly better than being sexually victimized and neglected in the custodial prisons, the reformatories failed to adequately prepare women to be independent.

SOURCE: Zedner 1995.

to northern states (Snell 2014). Secondly, in the antebellum South, the economies of most southern states were largely agricultural. There was a traditional reliance on slave labor in the South, whereas northern states had more factories and industries and employed European immigrants (Walker 1988; Weiss 2001). Finally, southern states seemed to favor localized control over state- or federal-based criminal justice systems. In corrections, county jails were favored over spending money to build centralized state prisons.

After the Civil War, most southern states were left in financial ruin. There was a shortage of male labor because of huge losses in combat and from disease; moreover, the unemployment of newly freed African Americans surfaced as a new problem. It has been observed that many people who were forcibly exploited by slavery before the Civil War continued to be marginalized by new laws that made vagrancy and loitering prison-eligible offenses (Walker 1988; Weiss 2001). Imprisonment quickly replaced slavery in the South as prisoners provided the same plantation labor they were doing before. For example, Louisiana, Mississippi, and Texas purchased thousands of acres of farmland and former plantations where prisoners worked for the state. In addition, because of the labor shortage, state prisoners were also **leased** to private contractors to build roads and bridges, lay railroad track, and perform other public construction work for which the state provided the labor (prisoners), the immediate supervisory personnel (guards), and the supplies.

Leased prisoners: prisoners provided by the state government as cheap labor to private contractors; the private contractors in turn provided food and clothing to the inmates

The state profited from the labor in two ways: The state maintained control of a ready supply of cheap labor rather than hiring workers from the general population, and the mobile labor camps provided a substitute for building new prisons. During the leasing period, correctional officers were poorly trained and provided with horses and guns to prevent inmates from escaping. Officers and inmates alike had bad food and slept in mobile tent camps that moved from location to location. Their living and working conditions were brutal and abusive. When reformers sought to end leasing, the taxpayers prevented change as long as possible. The leasing system officially ended 70 years later with the Great Depression, when labor unions contested using prisoner labor over union labor for large contracts (Walker 1988).

Eventually, each state developed its own prison system. Most states called their prison system the Department of Corrections, but there are some variations to this name. This department is responsible for the punishment of all state felony crimes eligible for incarceration. Today, there are nearly 1,200 state prisons and several hundred federal prisons across the United States (Stephan 2008).

CORRECTIONS IN THE 20TH CENTURY

At the turn of the 20th century, the United States experienced significant social, political, and legal changes. Prisons were noisy places to live, full of sights and smells that few who have not visited one could fully appreciate, and like their 19th-century predecessors, they included bone-crushingly monotonous daily routines. They became known as "big houses" because they held between 2,500 and 4,000 people at a time (Rotman 1995). Among the changes occurring at this time were the creation of the Federal Bureau of Prisons and the dissemination of new ways of thinking about criminal behavior.

Federal Bureau of Prisons

In 1891, in direct response to the growing number of inmates serving correctional sentences for committing federal crimes, Congress authorized three federal penitentiaries. McNeil Island was the first to open on the West Coast, near the state of Washington, followed by a maximum-security U.S. penitentiary (USP) in Leavenworth, Kansas, and a USP to the southeast in Atlanta, Georgia. The Federal Bureau of Prisons (BOP) was established later, in 1930, through a central office situated in Washington, D.C., to standardize prison conditions (Rotman 1995). The BOP is chiefly responsible for the care and custody of offenders serving time for federal offenses, such as bank robbery, international drug trafficking, securities fraud, counterfeiting, and immigration violations.

The BOP has since grown to more than 200,000 prisoners incarcerated in 116 institutions (28 of which are for females), 22 residential community corrections facilities, and 9 jails. Because of deteriorating building conditions, Leavenworth and Atlanta are no longer maximum security, having been downgraded to medium-security institutions. The McNeil Island prison closed in 2011 and is now vacant, but the Washington Department of Corrections is considering purchasing the land and building from the federal government for renovation (Langeler 2013).

Criminal Behavior as More than Just Choice

Around the same time that the Federal BOP was getting organized, people began thinking differently about criminal behavior. Over the next 30 years, social science disciplines such as psychology and sociology developed in higher education to better understand human behavior. Sociologists and psychologists believed that criminal behavior was more than just a matter of bad or deliberate choices. The prevailing belief was that youthful delinquency and adult criminal behavior were influenced by micro and macro factors pertaining to economic, sociological, psychological, and even biological reasons concerning why people may commit crimes. Criminological theories were developed that started to explain various forms of crime and criminality. In the corrections arena, progressives advocated for treatment reforms and prison programming that tried to fix the root of the problem for wayward youths and adult inmates.

Rehabilitation

These ideas gave rise in the 1930s to the view that crime was like a social disease, and criminals were like patients who could be cured of their crime sickness through methods like psychotherapy, shock therapy, education, and other social programs that raised families out of poverty. Termed the **medical model**, this way of thinking presented criminal behavior as a pathological condition to be diagnosed and treated. Rehabilitation programs addressing a wide variety of social problems were initiated throughout the prison system, particularly following World War II, and prisoners had a wide range of choices available to improve their lives. The rehabilitation era lasted well into the 1970s, with prisons being viewed as places where inmates could receive help and reintegrate as productive societal members.

Medical model: a philosophy that dominated from 1930 to the 1960s that assumed crime was caused by biological and psychological conditions that required treatment

Throughout the 1960s, crime became even more politicized than it had been in the past. Indeed, there were bipartisan demands—and congressional hearings and reports—for the federal government to take the lead in combating crime. National crime surveys were developed and field-tested throughout the late 1960s. These political and scientific efforts culminated in the Omnibus Crime Control and Safe Streets Act of 1968, which created a multitude of programs, including the U.S. Department of Justice's Law Enforcement Assistance Administration (what is today the Office of Justice Programs), all intended to drive down crime and improve what scholars, politicians, and practitioners alike began to call the criminal justice system. The subject of crime and punishment became a major political platform item in the 1968 presidential election between candidates Hubert Humphrey and Richard Nixon. Nixon's "get tough" stance contributed to his winning the election by a close margin. Crime and punishment seemed to become more political and to infiltrate the media's attention and all future elections from that point forward.

"Get Tough" Era

The medical model fell out of favor in the 1970s with concerns about sentencing disparity as some people were released much later than others who committed the same crime. In addition to these concerns about sentencing, there was a perception that rehabilitation did not work, and there was less willingness to offer treatment programs (Martinson 1974). While this perception about rehabilitation was unfounded, the general view about what worked with rehabilitation was misunderstood and poorly communicated. At the same time, the law and order montage of Nixon's political platform continued to transform public perceptions about criminals and drug users as a threat to public safety and about what is right, just, and moral. Nixon's actions eventually paved the way for President Ronald Reagan to commit funding for federal law enforcement to wage the official war on drugs in the 1980s (Dufton 2012).

Eradicating the causes of crime was simply replaced with punishing criminals, and especially drug users, who were seen as morally bankrupt as criminals. Sentencing laws in many states became harsher for drug crimes and also restricted judicial discretion in sentencing. Beginning with Maine in 1976, some state parole boards were abolished and early release from prison decreased. By the 1990s, these changes in sentencing and parole caused serious crowding problems in the nation's prison system. States had already begun financing new prison buildings to keep up with the growth, but the growth far outpaced the bed space. Starting in the late-1970s, some states came under federal mandates to solve crowding problems, and most states were still building new prisons in what seemed like a never-ending race. Prison populations continued to increase throughout the 2000s with no end in sight, until 2008, when the nation experienced significant economic problems from which many states failed to recover. In 2011, a report by the Global Commission on Drug Policy declared:

> The global war on drugs has failed. When the United Nations Single Convention on Narcotic Drugs came into being 50 years ago, and when President Nixon launched the US government's war on drugs 40 years ago, policymakers believed that harsh law enforcement action against those involved in drug production, distribution and use would lead to an ever-diminishing market in controlled drugs such as heroin, cocaine and cannabis, and the eventual achievement of a "drug free world." In practice, the global scale of illegal drug markets—largely controlled by organized crime—has grown dramatically over this period. (4)

At the current time, about half of all federal offenders are in prison for drug offenses, a decrease from over 60 percent just a few years ago. Drug trafficking has a longer average sentence (78 months) compared with the average (54 months) for federal prisoners as a whole (La Vigne and Samuels 2012). In the federal system over the past few years, the number of drug offenders has been replaced by a crackdown in immigration-related offenses.

CORRECTIONAL FACILITIES TODAY

Jail Operations

Jails today have not changed much from their original purpose of housing pretrial detainees and convicted offenders. About half of all jails in the United States are quite small and lack resources. The building itself may have space to detain up to 100 people at once. Only the most populous metropolitan areas have jails large enough to hold more than 1,000 people. Large jails, such as Los Angeles County in California and Riker's Island in New York City, tend to have services and problems similar to that of prisons.

Jails are often operated by city or county law enforcement agencies. About six states operate all jails and prisons through the state department of corrections. In addition, nine federal detention centers in large metropolitan areas are operated by the Federal Bureau of Prisons (West, Sabol, and Greenman 2010).

Chapter 8 discusses the pretrial process that occurs between arrest and arraignment. County jails serve as the primary institution responsible for accepting individuals who have been suspected of committing a crime but may pose a danger to themselves or others. Jails also accept new defendants in felony and misdemeanor cases but will later bond out 95 percent of defendants, as only 5 percent are denied release (Cohen and Kyckelhahn 2010). Even though most qualify for release, nearly four in ten felony defendants remain in jail because they are unable to afford the bond amount, while the other six who qualify are released on an ROR or bail. Qualifying for release is based on a number of factors at time of arrest, including history of failure to appear at previous court dates, severity of current charges, other outstanding warrants, whether on active community supervision such as probation or parole, and evidence of employment, school, and/or community ties.

Pretrial release from jail is conditioned on the defendant's agreement that he or she will return for the next court appearance. Some defendants are released but supervised in the community by the jail under a specific program such as electronic monitoring, home detention, community service, and work release (Minton 2013). The important point here is that although they are supervised by the jail, these defendants are *not confined* inside the jail. Most defendants who get released on bond or on pretrial supervision return to court without incident.

Positive pretrial behavior can indeed lead to a probation sentence or a reduced prison sentence. However, about 18 percent of released defendants get rearrested for a new offense while they are on pretrial release for a felony (Cohen and Kyckelhahn 2010). Pretrial release allows defendants to maintain their employment and family obligations while assisting in the preparation of their defense, so the benefits of pretrial release definitely outweigh the risks.

In addition to offering fewer treatment alternatives than prisons, jails house a more varied population with a wide range of legal statuses and security needs. Other than pretrial detainees who are held pending arraignment, trial, or sentencing, jails also keep inmates temporarily for other agencies or other states that are experiencing overcrowding. These inmates are called **transfers** and include people who are under the jurisdiction of the military, the federal system, or another state. Within their own jurisdiction, jails also admit people who have had their probation, parole, or bond revoked (Minton 2013).

Jail Classification

Defendants and convicted offenders who will remain in jail longer than 72 hours are typically assessed for an appropriate residential placement within the facility. This is called **classification**, and its primary function is to ensure not only that the inmate's housing unit assignment within the jail will be safe enough for that individual but also that each person in that unit will get along with others around him or her. The facility's classification unit employs experienced full-time staff who interview each new or returning inmate to determine the best possible placement, considering factors outlined in Figure 11.2, such as conviction status (pretrial detainee, transfer, or convicted), severity of current charge, prior jail/prison institutional conduct, gang affiliation, and enemies within the system. Special management concerns include any situation that may be a major disruption to the facility, such as an attempted escape or suicide. Another management concern is any personal characteristics that may cause someone to be victimized within the institution, such as major psychological, physical, or developmental impairments.

Prison Security Levels

Both the federal and state systems have security levels that define, structurally speaking, how secure the building and perimeter is, and secondly, how much movement each prisoner has inside.

First, inmates in a **minimum-security prison** have earned their way there and therefore get the most freedom and privileges. Also, prisoners who are within two years of their release date may qualify for a new classification, including into a minimum-security facility. In the federal system, minimum security applies to prison camps. The facility's

Transfers:
inmates who are en route to another facility within the state or are housed temporarily in a particular jail or prison for another jurisdiction such as the military, the federal system, or another state

Classification:
the process of assigning an inmate to a facility, housing unit, and/or work assignment based on the security risk he or she poses and the treatment needs defined by prior history and the current crime

Minimum-security prison:
prison with a custody level that dictates more freedom of movement inside and outside the perimeter; for convicted offenders who have earned a good disciplinary record with few acts of misconduct while incarcerated and/or for first-time nonviolent offenders

Figure 11.2
Sample custody
assessment scale

Score points for each question and sum the results at the end.

Q1 Attempted/completed escape from a medium or maximum facility   _____ points
    0 = No
    7 = Yes

Q2 Most severe current charge (whether convicted yet or not)   _____ points
    0 = Misdemeanor
    1 = Nonviolent felony
    2 = Drug felony
    4 = Violent or sex-related felony

Q3 Most severe prior offense   _____ points
    0 = Misdemeanor
    1 = Nonviolent felony
    2 = Drug felony
    4 = Violent or sex-related felony

Q4 Failure to appear in court or walkaways from minimum facility   _____ points
    1 point for each FTA or walkaway

Q5 Institutional disciplinary history   _____ points
    0 = No infractions or unknown
    1 point for every three minor infractions
    1 point for each major infraction

Q6 Current age   _____ points
    −1 = 55 and over
    0 = 25-54
    1 = 24 and younger

TOTAL of Q1 through Q6:   _____ points
    0–3 = Minimum
    4–6 = Medium
    7 and above = Maximum

Special management concerns (check all that apply)
    ☐ Gang affiliated   ☐ Developmental disability
    ☐ Suicide risk   ☐ Medical concerns or physical impairment
    ☐ Major psychiatric problems   ☐ Protective custody

SOURCE: Compilation of multiple jail classification instruments.

outside perimeter either has no fence or one that is an unimpressive barrier. The well-kept grounds may look like a college campus. The housing units are often dormitory-style in appearance, and inmates have their own key.

Prisoners at a **medium-security prison** are not allowed to leave the institution's grounds, but they have more freedom within the prison perimeter itself as they move around within their dormitory housing, work assignments, recreation yards, and chow halls. Medium-security perimeters are enclosed with chain-link fences topped by razor wire and either electronic sensors or a security vehicle that patrols the outside perimeter.

For **maximum-security prisons** built before the 1940s, the most distinguishing features from the outside are high stone walls that go

Medium-security prison: prison with a custody level that dictates that the perimeter is more secure than minimum security but less secure than maximum security; prisoners are not able to leave the perimeter but have a fair amount of free-dom inside the perimeter

Maximum-security prison: prison with a custody level that dictates a secure perimeter, with limited freedom of movement inside the perimeter

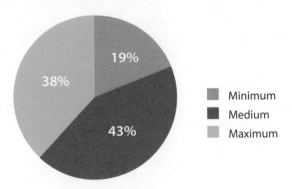

SOURCE: Stephan 2008.

Figure 11.3
Prison security levels

deep into the ground with six **pickets**, four of which are located at each corner of the wall and one at each front and back entrance. New prisons are not built with these walls. In more contemporary maximum-security units, the perimeter has two fences topped with razor wire. In between the two fences is either coiled razor wire or a lethal electric fence. Prisoners are housed in single or double cells, and time out of the cell is structured and controlled with passes for a specific purpose. Security takes priority over rehabilitation, so fewer treatment and work programs are present than in minimum- or medium-security facilities. Figure 11.3 shows that most prisons in the United States are either medium or maximum security.

Pickets:
perimeter tower structures reaching 50 to 100 feet high, located at the corners of maximum-security prison walls or fences and near the entrance

Jails as Maximum-Security Buildings

Jails tend to be built near the courthouse so that pretrial detainees can be easily transported to their court appearances. However, most jail buildings are *not* surrounded by perimeter walls or fencing because they are typically located at or near city hall or the police or sheriff's department. This makes it necessary for the jail building itself to have enough layers of security within it (via reinforced steel doors and **sally ports**) equivalent to a maximum-security building. As a maximum-security institution, there is very limited inmate freedom of movement inside and virtually no outside recreation facilities because of limited space. Large jails in metropolitan areas are built between 5 and 15 stories high, with the only outside recreation area on the building's roof. Security needs will always take priority over rehabilitation, so jails offer inmates few treatment and work programs. Compared to prisons, which actually offer more activities and freedom of movement, jail inmates spend most of their existence within a small, enclosed podular housing unit.

Sally ports:
contained areas inside a jail or prison that separate key entrance and exit points; the area has two doors, and one must be closed before the next door can be opened

Federal Correctional Complexes

Since the late 1990s, the federal system has tended to favor construction of federal correctional complexes (FCC), which include two or more correctional facilities of different security levels at one location. For example, FCC Butner in North Carolina has two federal correctional institutions (FCI) that are medium security, an FCI that is low security, and a medical facility. FCC Tucson in Arizona has a high-security U.S. penitentiary (USP) in which inmates are not allowed to work or hold jobs because of security concerns. Next door to USP Tucson is a medium- and minimum-security institution that creates a mobile inmate workforce who can go to work inside the high-security prison. FCCs are also beneficial for correctional officers and treatment staff, who can have career mobility without relocating.

Supermax or Secure Housing Units

Prisons at the highest security level are known as **supermax** or secure housing units. A supermax facility can be a separate housing area within a maximum-custody facility, or it can be an entirely separate facility. In both cases, inmates at this level are isolated from the general population of prisoners and from each other at all times. Inmates assigned to supermax facilities are believed to pose an ongoing threat to other prisoners and correctional officers. These threats include attempted or completed escape from a maximum-security facility, confirmed gang membership, or violent behavior while incarcerated such as assaulting correctional staff and/or killing other inmates.

The first supermax prison was the U.S. penitentiary in Marion, Illinois. USP Marion became a supermax prison because of an unforeseen incident that happened in 1983. Two correctional officers were stabbed to death on the same day by two different inmates. At that time, USP Marion was maximum security but then went into permanent lockdown status immediately following the murders. The federal BOP decided to replace USP Marion by constructing a brand new supermax penitentiary in Florence, Colorado. Interestingly, the federal BOP includes its supermax prison under its administrative category, formally calling it USP Florence-ADX. ADX Florence was built to house inmates who needed special protection because of their notoriety or their aggressive or lethal behavior while incarcerated. Included among their number is a long list of foreign and domestic terrorists, spies, gang leaders, and drug kingpins, including Al-Qaeda operative Ramzi Yousef, shoe bomber Richard Reid, Oklahoma City bomber Terry Nichols, Centennial Olympic Park bomber Eric Rudolph, former FBI agent and spy Robert Hanssen, Tijuana cartel leader Francisco Javier Arellano Felix, and Aryan Brotherhood cofounders Barry Mills and Tyler Bingham.

Arizona has what might be one of the few supermax units for juvenile offenders. The unit has 20 cells as part of a larger unit, which also houses adult death-row inmates and mentally ill adults.

Supermax: the highest level of custody that dictates that prisoners are kept in solitary confinement and are taken out of their cells in constraints and in a controlled fashion with extra staff

However, youths are kept away from all other adult inmates and other juveniles. The youths are allowed to spend three hours per day on their education, locked in separate cages within a common educational area. During these three hours, the youths can converse with an instructor to prepare themselves for the GED test, take limited vocational courses, or finish a book report that is required of them every two weeks. Providing educational opportunities to youths is required, and the cages at least allow youths to see and talk to others, as well as learn as a group (Austin, Johnson, and Gregoriou 2000).

JUVENILE CORRECTIONAL PLACEMENTS

Most juveniles who are adjudicated delinquent receive a disposition of probation or deferred adjudication. Like with adults, the number of juveniles in secure placements has decreased over the past few years because fewer juveniles have been arrested. Still, about one in four juveniles is placed out of his or her family home in a residential setting such as a group home, wilderness camp, or a longer-term secure facility (Hockenberry, Sickmund, and Sladky 2011). Group homes and wilderness camps tend to be smaller, privately operated community-based facilities. The facilities are generally not secure, which means that juveniles are supervised but not locked into their rooms at night. Escapes or walkaways are strongly discouraged; too many escapes may result in the juvenile judge altering the juvenile's placement to a secure lockup. Despite these countervailing pressures, some occupants sneak out at night. The group homes are residential facilities but provide a more homelike setting for gender-specific programming. Group homes accommodate juveniles who are dependent and neglected by their parents, or who have committed delinquency offenses (Sedlak and Bruce 2010).

Secure Placements

Some youths are held temporarily in county detention centers until their cases are adjudicated and disposed. Detention centers function much like adult jails. For adjudicated cases that receive a disposition, a small percentage of delinquents end up in a secure locked facility that is designated for youths who have committed a felony offense and/or who have been adjudicated as delinquent but pose a danger to the public or themselves. These larger, publicly operated facilities lock juveniles into their rooms at night and are more likely to use restraints or even solitary confinement if necessary. Solitary confinement for juveniles is for a shorter period of time, since juveniles have more difficulties with social isolation, lack of patience, and the concept of time. For example, a 14-year-old status offender started a fight with another girl in a New York juvenile facility, and the aggressor was placed in solitary confinement for 14 days. The court ruled that this period of time violated the Eighth Amendment of the Constitution—it was simply too long under the circumstances (*Lollis v. New York State Department of Social Services* (1971)).

About 70 percent of residential facilities are large training schools operated by the county or state, and most occupants are boys between the ages of 15 and 17. Secure institutions are located in remote areas of the state, and family visits occur less often than in community-based group homes (Hockenberry, Sickmund, and Sladky 2011). The cost of these placements also varies between $115 per day per person for a typical group home to $162 for a secure training school (Deitch 2009).

Juveniles in Adult Facilities

Normally, when juveniles and adults must be housed in the same facility, juveniles must be separated from adults by sight and sound. However, when youths are transferred or waived to adult court, these requirements are quite different. Waived youths still have the right to be safe from violent and aggressive inmates, and prison staff have an "obligation not to act with deliberate or reckless indifference" if they know that someone is vulnerable (Austin, Johnson, and Gregoriou 2000: 13). However, waived youths (some as young as 13) are also treated the same as adults, so the sight and sound requirement no longer applies. About one-third of the nearly 5,000 youths in adult prisons spend most of their sentence alone or in a protective custody situation, having limited contact with other vulnerable inmates (see Table 11.1). Twenty-one states house juveniles directly with adults, while 17 states and the District of Columbia provide separate housing units for transferred/waived youth until they reach age 18. At that point, they are mainstreamed into the adult population (Austin, Johnson, and Gregoriou 2000).

Juveniles, even those waived to adult court, still have the opportunity for release from prison. Recently, the U.S. Supreme Court ruled that juveniles may no longer be sentenced to life without parole, whether the crime is for a felony (*Graham v. Florida* (2010)) or a homicide (*Miller v. Alabama* (2012)).

Juveniles in secure facilities still attend school and are entitled to receive services for learning disabilities, mental illness, and developmental disabilities. In general, lower courts have ruled that juveniles should receive some level of treatment or programming that allows them to correct their behavior (Austin, Johnson, and Gregoriou 2000). However, the U.S. Supreme Court has never addressed the issue on whether juveniles have the constitutional right to treatment.

Table 11.1 **Characteristics of Juveniles Waived to Adult Prisons**	
CHARACTERISTIC	PERCENTAGE
Gender	
Male	96.4
Female	3.6
Age	
13-14	0.2
15	2.7
16	17.6
17	79.5
Race/ethnicity	
African American	55
Caucasian	26
Hispanic	14
Other	5
Offense of conviction	
Person	57
Property	21
Alcohol/drugs	13
Other	9
*Housing type within 21 adult prisons**	
Dormitory	51
Single cell	30
Double cell	19

* Does not include the juveniles housed in juvenile facilities until age 18.
SOURCE: Austin, Johnson, and Gregoriou 2000.

PRIVATE PRISONS

When a person is sentenced by a municipal court for a misdemeanor, by a state district court for a state felony, or by a federal district court for a federal offense, the government takes primary responsibility for the care and custody of inmates who are incarcerated in any jail or prison within the United States. Thus, the corrections system is primarily a publicly operated enterprise. However, some correctional facilities are owned and/or operated by private businesses and/or large conglomerate companies that contract with state and federal government.

A **private correctional facility** is operated by a nongovernmental entity that enters into a contract with federal or state authorities to provide security, housing, and/or treatment programs to offenders. The contract ultimately outlines the responsibilities and conditions

Private correctional facility:

a correctional facility that is operated by a nongovernmental entity that enters into a contract with federal or state authorities to provide security, housing, and/or treatment programs to offenders in exchange for fees

the private business must follow, and in exchange, the government pays the business a certain amount of money depending on the services provided and the number of inmates within the facility. When the government enters into a contract with a private business to build a facility or to manage a state-owned facility, the government remains, first and foremost, responsible for the care and custody of inmates; the government now becomes the monitor of the privately provided services (Stolz 1997).

Since the business is doing this to make a profit, it willingly agrees to provide the services but is interested in minimizing its costs as much as possible while at the same time keeping its facility full so that payment maximizes profits. Not only do private businesses incarcerate state and federal prisoners using its own employees, but also some companies design and construct new facilities much faster than the government can.

The latest figures indicate that about 130,000 prisoners are held in privately operated corrections facilities (West, Sabol, and Greenman 2010), but that number is not evenly distributed across the United States. Private facilities are used most often by the federal system for immigration and customs enforcement, with more than 34,000 inmates in private facilities. The presence of private corporations is welcomed in southern and western states such as Texas (19,000 inmates), Florida (9,800), California (9,000), Oklahoma (6,000), Georgia (5,100), and Tennessee (5,100), where privatization first began in the 1980s.

Privatization became a popular alternative when government resources decreased or became too restricted for the rate of growth that correctional systems across the country experienced during the 1980s and 1990s. This alternative existed in states that were either particularly punitive or experienced a great deal of prison overcrowding and were looking for expedient solutions to the problem (Selman and Leighton 2010). Private corporations and nongovernmental associations such as the American Correctional Association (ACA) became involved in and influenced the correctional policy-making process within certain states. For example, the president of the ACA in the mid-1980s was one of the cofounders of Corrections Corporation of America, now one of the largest private prison companies in the world (Stolz 1997). Box 11.3 examines two of these large private correctional providers. Other founding members of private prison companies were former directors and other high-level administrators of the Federal Bureau of Prisons.

Since much criminal justice legislation is introduced by a small number of prominent and influential state legislators, correctional privatization did not seem to attract the attention of interest groups until after its passage (Stolz 1997). This pattern of expansion, however, did

---

Box 11.3 Private U.S. Correctional Providers Are Going Global

GEO Group, Inc. and Corrections Corporation of America are two of the largest private correctional providers in the world. Both companies are so large and profitable that company shares are publicly traded on the New York Stock Exchange. The main focus of the GEO Group is on adult correctional facilities throughout the United States and expanding into Canada, England, South Africa, and Australia. The company boasts a total of 95 facilities holding up to 72,000 inmates and employing 18,000 staff. Of the 95 facilities, GEO maintains 13 residential and 4 nonresidential juvenile facilities. GEO also owns Abraxas Youth and Family Services, among other smaller companies. GEO recently expanded into the electronic monitoring and global positioning system market with its recent purchase of BI Incorporated. (See http://www.geogroup.com.)

Corrections Corporation of America (CCA) designs, constructs, and manages correctional facilities in 16 states. With its main office in Nashville, Tennessee, CCA employs about 17,000 staff in more than 60 facilities that are designed to hold over 90,000 inmates. CCA also owns a company called TransCor America, which provides inmate transportation services. (See http://www.cca.com.)

---

not exist in all states. About 18 states still do not have private prison facilities. The main concern with privatization is that private corporations with shares that are traded on the stock market are accountable to their shareholders for earning a profit and *increasing* their revenue, which is only going to occur if more people, not fewer, go to prison. Thus, from an ideological standpoint, private prison companies are interested in maintaining the drug war, increasing sentence lengths, and detaining undocumented immigrants, all of which contribute to the demand for prison beds (Hall 2013).

Another open question with private facilities is whether existing laws have adequately considered when a private company in one state leases its facility to a government in another state. For example, inmates from another state who escaped from private facilities in Texas could not be prosecuted for escape because laws related to this issue applied only to Texas inmates. Further questions relate to whether private companies who contract with the government are subject to the public access of information through open records and public information acts or if they are able to operate without public disclosure.

Most private facilities were built as medium- or minimum-security facilities, designed to accept prisoners in good physical health, who have an adequate behavioral record while incarcerated, and who lack severe problems associated with mental illness or disabilities. Essentially, private facilities can choose the general type of prisoner they wish to accept, and they are interested in prisoners who will minimize their costs. The ideal prisoner is someone who is serving a sentence of two years or less, does not cause a disciplinary problem or destroy property, and has minimal medical needs. The other way private prisons save money is by paying their entry-level staff lower wages and/or offering fewer benefits compared with state and federal facilities in the same area (Selman and Leighton 2010). However, prisoners within U.S. correctional facilities seem to be one population whose industry *cannot* be moved overseas. The future of privatization, therefore, seems to be one of continued expansion in two directions: first, within U.S. borders and with inmates under the jurisdiction of Immigration and Customs Enforcement and, second, in territories and countries throughout the world in a global industry.

SUMMARY

The U.S. incarceration rate per 100,000 people is the highest in the world. While there has been some decrease over the past few years, correctional spending remains high. Jails incarcerate both pretrial detainees who have not been convicted and individuals convicted of crimes for which they will be held less than one year. Prisons are long-term institutions for convicted felons who are serving a sentence of more than 12 months.

England's Penitentiary Act of 1779 improved jail conditions throughout England, abolished the long-standing fee system, and made jails safer. The act also significantly influenced the conditions of correctional facilities in the United States. The penitentiary was invented for punishing the mind over the body, so that inmates could reflect on their misdeeds in silence and solitude and repent. The Pennsylvania system was developed in Philadelphia and emphasized complete silence and solitary confinement as a means to achieve repentance or penance inside a penitentiary. Prisoners in this situation developed depression and mental health problems. The congregate system was developed in Auburn, New York, to rival the Pennsylvania system because of differences in opinion about how to achieve change. The Auburn or congregate system emphasized lockstep marching, factory work, and eating with other prisoners in silence, but they were in the company of other prisoners. The Auburn system was eventually adopted over the Pennsylvania system because it was more cost effective and produced fewer mental health problems.

In the northern states, penitentiaries emphasized education and vocational training so that inmates were better prepared for returning to the community. Following the Civil War and at times throughout our history, incarceration has been linked with the economy and the labor market. The southern states are an example of this with the leasing system that developed out of perceived necessity and labor shortages.

Understanding criminal behavior became possible through the disciplines of biology, psychology, and sociology, which led to rehabilitation programs and the medical model. This model fell out of favor in the 1970s with claims that rehabilitation did not work. Simultaneously, crime and punishment became part of a more conservative political platform, which began a law-and-order approach that led to the war on drugs in the 1980s. Jails today incarcerate both pretrial detainees and persons convicted of crimes. All jails are maximum-security units. Prison custody levels vary between minimum, medium, maximum, and supermaximum, depending on the risks each prisoner poses within the prison walls and their risk to outside society.

Juveniles are most commonly sentenced to probation. Of adjudicated youths who are placed out of the home, some juveniles are placed in community-based group homes and wilderness camps. Other youths are placed in secure facilities such as training schools and closed treatment facilities.

Private correctional facilities can provide services for less money, but costs are reduced by paying staff less than public sector employees for doing the same work. Large private corporations are accountable to their shareholders for earning a profit and increasing revenue, which is ideologically at odds with attempts to reduce crime and the use of incarceration.

REVIEW QUESTIONS

1. Why were penitentiaries created in the United States, and what differentiated them from previous forms of punishment?
2. What were the major advantages and disadvantages of the Pennsylvania system compared to the Auburn system?
3. Is long-term isolation effective? In what way, or why not?
4. How has mass imprisonment been linked with the economy and/or the labor market over time? Provide examples.
5. What led to the collapse of the medical model and rehabilitation era in the 1970s?
6. What led to the influence of private prison companies in the 1980s?
7. What advantages and disadvantages does privatization create in the corrections industry? Should the United States be involved in correctional privatization? Defend your answer.
8. Given where we are now, what direction is the correctional system likely to take in the future?

KEY TERMS

classification
congregate system
hulks

institutional corrections
jails
leased
marks system
maximum-security prison

medical model
medium-security prison
minimum-security prison
penal transportation
penitentiaries
Pennsylvania system

pickets
private correctional facility
reformatories
sally ports
supermax
transfers

Living and Working in Prison

LEARNING OBJECTIVES

At the conclusion of this chapter, you should be able to:

- Explain elements of prison life, including learning prison norms, emphasis on race/ethnicity, and the use of slang to communicate meaning.
- Trace the history of the prisoners' rights movement and the court cases that later defined prison conditions from the 1960s to the present time.
- Understand why prisoners use violence and gangs as an informal method of power and control.
- Compare and contrast women's prisons and men's prisons.
- Describe the function of security and treatment staff relative to correctional goals.

INTRODUCTION

What would it be like to be incarcerated in prison? When most people think about this question, they rely on popular TV series such as *Orange Is the New Black* or on movies such as *Stone, Felon, Animal Factory,* or *The Shawshank Redemption*. Prisons are largely depicted as violent and tense places riddled by gangs, such as in *American Me,* and unethical correctional officer behavior, as illustrated by *Prison of Secrets*. A recent television series titled *Locked Up* shows a more realistic view of prisons in the United States and abroad. This chapter examines research and firsthand accounts about what life in prison might be like, whether prison really is different from the outside world, and why people find it hard to reintegrate into society.

PRISON SUBCULTURE

As a correctional punishment, the prison experience was intentionally meant to deprive lawbreakers of property, relationships, and certain freedoms. In his book *The Society of Captives,* Gresham Sykes (1958) argues that the "pains of imprisonment" were more humane than the brutality of physical, corporal punishment or the death penalty. Sykes identified the five main deprivations of incarceration:

- Liberty: Prisoners lose the physical freedom of movement. Prisoners are confined from outside society and are also controlled within the institution itself.
- Autonomy: Inmates are not allowed to make their own decisions and are forced to become dependent on the system for their existence. The individuality of each prisoner is stripped away to depersonalize them—they are given a number, a uniform, and strict regulations prohibiting jewelry or other personal items.
- Security: Involuntary association with other violent, predatory, and unethical people causes ongoing anxiety and fear of harassment, bullying, and attacks in public view as others see how individuals respond.
- Goods and services: The amount and brand names of material goods are strictly limited in number and type so that inmates live with the bare minimum.
- Relationships: Relations with family, friends, and associates on the outside weaken with limited contact; normal sexual relationships become nonexistent.

These losses became known as the **deprivation model**. This model suggests that inmates will try to circumvent and work around these

Deprivation model: the theory that prisoners get around the formal rules to circumvent the pains of imprisonment and make their experience more pleasurable

deprivations as much as possible to make their time in prison more bearable. For example, Sykes argues that a demand for black market goods was still present despite the deprivation of goods and services, so inmates would do all they could to fulfill the demand by bringing in items that they could use or sell. This underground and illegitimate economic system is known as the **sub rosa economy**. These items were in short supply compared to demand, so the prices for black market goods were more expensive. Stephen Lankenau (2001) discusses how cigarettes are a lucrative item in the black market. On the outside, a pack of cigarettes might be $6 or $7 a pack, but in prison a pack will cost $100 to $200.

Sub rosa economy: the underground and black market economic system of inmate supply and demand

The other way inmates will attempt to fill demand is through homemade products, using supplies and parts available within the prison itself. For example, homemade prison alcohol known as "hooch" can be made by fermenting fruit or potato skins with water or fruit juice in a container for a few weeks. If left undiscovered by prison staff, the fermentation process will eventually break down the naturally occurring sugars in the fruit and potato skins and turn them to alcohol. A tattoo gun can be made using a ballpoint pen, black "ink" from melted-down rubber, a needle from a piece of a razor blade or thin wire, and a tiny motor built from spare parts removed from electronics equipment.

Sykes also argues that inmates temporarily engaged in same-sex relations because of the deprivation of heterosexual relations. While some of Sykes's points have merit, John Irwin and Donald Cressey (1962) argue that the prison subculture could not have developed purely from deprivations alone. Some of the behaviors in prison resulted from how people lived on the street before they came to prison. Some of the prisoners merely brought these same ways of life into the prison. This line of thought is called the **importation model** and also has merit for why some inmates who used drugs or joined a street gang continue their drug habit or continue being a gang member while in prison. When you think about each of the elements of prison life throughout this chapter, keep in mind whether it more closely fits the deprivation model or the importation model.

Importation model: the theory that prisoner behaviors are present on the streets in outside society and are brought into the prison

Adjusting to Prison

Imagine the following scenario: A bus of 50 new inmates has just pulled up to the back entrance of a reception and diagnostics prison unit. The inmates get off the bus and are corralled into a large room, where they are instructed as a group to line up, remove all their clothing and personal property, and place it in bags marked with their names. They are then instructed to turn in their property while it gets cataloged, and they are issued a receipt for its contents. This property is not given back until they finish their sentence or are paroled early from the institution. Each inmate is then issued a department of corrections number that he must commit to memory.

The next stop is undergoing a strip search to ensure that no weapons or unlawful items have been brought into the prison. Following the search, they must use delousing powder and then shower; they are also issued a uniform that may or may not be the right size. The next stop is the barber chair, where their hair is shaved completely off, including all facial hair. The last stop for the first day is a temporary housing assignment, where all the new inmates will live. There, each person is issued a bar of soap, a toothbrush, tooth powder, a razor, a washcloth, towel, and a book of rules. The new inmates remain locked up for the next week while they are pulled out in small groups to complete diagnostic testing, such as a psychological exam, intelligence test, reading and writing test, and medical exam. They also have to demonstrate that they know the official rules on what behaviors are not allowed and the penalties for each infraction if written up by a correctional officer.

For someone who has never been to prison, this scenario is very intimidating and discomforting. It takes some time to adjust to having no privacy and being told what to do and when to do things. Being institutionalized means not having to make decisions about what to wear or what to eat. It also means giving up control over things that most of us take for granted, such as what channel to watch on television or the room temperature and electricity. Activities such as eating, sleeping, and working become routine since everything is done in groups. Having a regular schedule is more efficient to feed, shower, and move large groups of people in an organized and orderly fashion.

Some people feel like prison is the worst place to be, but for others, going to prison may have actually saved their lives. Some people use their time in prison to get clean from alcohol and drugs and reflect on how they can change the course of their lives. They take advantage of treatment opportunities such as Alcoholics Anonymous and join Bible study groups to increase their spiritual connection. Some prisoners remain or become physically fit and become a part of an organized athletic team that plays handball, basketball, or flag football. These groups are important to help self-development and keep prisoners busy. Other people spend their time sleeping or becoming involved in illegitimate ways to make money through the sub rosa economy.

Inmate Code of Conduct

Most days in prison can be described as monotonous, dull, and boring. However, prison inmates as a group have shown that they do not follow rules well, do not associate well with others, or both. Prisoners have thus worked against the institutional routine by long ago developing their own informal rules, language, economic system, and groups that exhibit a strong influence on life in prison (Santos 2004). These different norms, values, and beliefs are part of an unwritten **inmate code** that is enforced by other inmates. One important thing to remember is that the inmate code varies in strength and influence according to the custody level of the prison. The inmate code will be weaker in minimum-security units and stronger in maximum-security prisons.

When did the inmate code of conduct start? You may recall from the last chapter that penitentiaries in the mid-1800s enforced complete silence, lockstep marching, and striped uniforms. They had strict rules and were known to use corporal punishment to keep inmates in line. Even with mandatory silence, prisoners would still communicate with each other through gestures and sign language. As a result, the silence rule eventually went away since it was impossible for prison staff to stop inmates from communicating with one another. Very little is known about prison life in the early 1900s except that an informal code did exist, there was a deep division between inmates and staff, and prison conditions had more deprivations.

While prisons are now more populated with younger prisoners who are convicted of drugs and individuals involved in gang behavior, the inmate code has remained fairly constant over time and is remarkably similar in prisons throughout the world (Sykes and Messinger 1960; Winfree, Newbold, and Tubb 2002). The deep chasm between inmates and correctional officers remains. The code includes the following maxims for male prisoners:

Inmate code: the unwritten and suggested behaviors that inmates live by to make doing time easier

- Don't interfere with inmate interests. Allow everyone to get the most pleasure and the least amount of pain in their own way from the prison experience.
- Be loyal to other convicts. Never rat or snitch.
- Never steal from or exploit other cons.
- Mind your own business and do your own time. Don't complain about the daily irritants.
- Show courage even when challenged by another inmate. React with aggressive behavior. Don't weaken by asking for protective custody.

More contemporary prison observers believe that convicts, as a group, are less unified than in the past. Inmates have been known to talk to correctional officers and to steal from one another and exploit each other in the name of profit and power. The old-time convicts view this kind of behavior as unacceptable. These convicts see themselves as a dying breed and believe that they are quickly being replaced by a younger generation that lacks respect for others.

Prison Slang

Prison argot is the language, slang, and physical gestures used to communicate meaning in prison. Most of these terms tend to be labels that are considered by today's standards to be racist, prejudicial, and derogatory toward women (Encinas 2001). The language used also supports how race/ethnic identification, associating with one's own racial group, and toughness become the primary means of defining the prison experience for men (Alarid 2000). Prison argot also helps us understand what types of behaviors are valued in prison. It seems that prisoners have a hierarchical structure that values the use of violence at the top. Individuals who are perceived as weak, such as snitches or people who have been convicted of a sex offense against a child, fall to the bottom of the hierarchy (Carceral 2004). Most prisoners fall somewhere in the middle: They do not challenge the norms; they go along with them and try to do everything they can to avoid trouble, harassment, and violence (Terry 2003). Going along with prison norms for men who are doing longer sentences means severing emotional ties with those outside prison and "getting into the life" by participating in illegal behavior such as trafficking drugs, contraband, and other goods that are not allowed in prison. For others, it means joining a prison gang.

Prison argot:
the slang terms, symbols, and gestures that comprise inmate prison communication

Snitches:
inmates who overidentify with correctional officers or who are perceived to be informing on other prisoners

Contraband:
items that inmates are not allowed to have in their possession

Race Relations and Riots

In the 1960s, the influence of the civil rights movement outside prison and increasing numbers of political prisoners among the African American population began to shape race relations within prisons. The Black Panther Party was influential, for example, in San Quentin State Prison in California. Prisoners became aware of racial inequality and inconsistent treatment when Caucasian prisoners were getting treated better than African American and Hispanic prisoners. Prisoners also realized that correctional officers encouraged racial unrest as a way to control the prisoner population from taking over the prison. Groups such as the Vice Lords, Latin Kings, and the Black Guerilla Family began as political groups to address these social issues. While some prisoners staged large-scale protests and hunger strikes, prisoners in other parts of the country organized large-scale riots where they forcibly took over the prison to bring media attention to prisoner treatment and to try to change conditions.

One of the more famous riots occurred in New York's Attica Correctional Facility in September 1971. The riot occurred because of unfair treatment of prisoners and racial discrimination (Wicker 1994). This riot lasted nine days, and after a series of negotiations, ended in disaster and as a national embarrassment. Law enforcement ended the riot by storming the outer walls and using tear gas. The situation ended with 39 deaths—29 inmates and 10 correctional officers—all caused by bullets linked to law enforcement weapons. The only officer who died at the hands of prisoners was one who died three days later from head injuries when he had his keys taken away (Wicker 1994). Since the 1970s, prison riots have decreased as prison administrators and researchers have learned more about what causes riots and how to prevent them.

Rise of Prison Gangs

The political groups quickly realized that money could be made through involvement in trafficking and trading contraband and weapons. The Vice Lords, Latin Kings, and the Black Guerilla Family, among other groups, began to overlap their illegitimate behavior in prison with community activism on the outside.

Prison administrators in California and Texas began to notice that prisoners of Hispanic descent formed groups based on ethnicity that seemed to be tied into conflicts between Latino prisoners from Southern California (the Mexican Mafia) and Latino prisoners from Northern California (La Nuestra Familia), who seemed to be more rural and agricultural. Both groups wanted to seize a piece of the action to make money. At the same time, the groups provided protection from being victimized by outsiders (Irwin 1980). Caucasian inmates responded to the perceived threat by forming the Aryan Brotherhood and by allowing outlaw motorcycle clubs to recruit from within. As the numbers of gang members increased and became a perceived threat, the numbers of new gang groups became problematic by the 1980s. The groups were racially segregated, loyal, and bound by strict adherence to a constitution that demanded the use of violence for control and to earn respect. Many prison gang members had to shed blood in some way (through fighting someone else, taking a beating by members of their own gang, or killing another rival member) to be accepted into the gang. Membership was for life, and once accepted in, there was no getting out, or the consequences could be death.

Prison gangs preyed on weaker inmates and exploited correctional officers and weaknesses in the security system all in the name of profit and ultimate power. For individuals who were raised in impoverished areas, where the school systems and communities were blighted and employment opportunities were nonexistent, being a gang member became a way to earn money, respect, and brotherhood both inside prison and in the neighborhoods outside prison.

Currently, states like California, Texas, New York, Florida, Illinois, and Wisconsin have significant problems with prison gangs, where it is estimated that about one in four male inmates and one in ten females are confirmed prison gang members or are in some stage of recruitment into the gang during imprisonment (Knox 2005; Winterdyk and Ruddell 2010). Females are less likely to join gangs in prison, and gangs are less of a security threat problem in women's prisons. Less than 4 percent of female inmates are recruited during imprisonment, and 6.3 percent of female prisoners were gang members before imprisonment (Knox 2005). In total, that translates to an estimated 500,000 security threat group members currently in jail and prison throughout the United States.

To combat the gang problem in these states, units known as **security threat group (STG)** teams surfaced in the 1990s when gang activities were determined to pose a threat to the security of the institution itself and to the safety of staff and inmates. STGs apply to all prison gangs as well as more than 1,000 other groups, such as outlaw motorcycle clubs, militias, Asian gangs, and organized crime groups—all requiring constant monitoring by specially trained officers known as gang intelligence officers (Winterdyk and Ruddell 2010).

Security threat group (STG): a collective group of confirmed gang members who pose a threat to institutional safety and security

Gang Intelligence

Gang intelligence officers collect information on suspected gang members using specific identifiers such as tattoos, hand signs, clothing colors, and associates. The thinking here is that inmates who are being recruited into a gang or who are already in a gang will only hang around confirmed gang members (Knox 2005). Once active STG members are identified, prison officials place restrictions on them, such as removal from the general prison population, restriction from certain job assignments, or reclassification to a higher-custody level. Some states, such as California and Texas, place confirmed gang members in administrative segregation for the remainder of their prison terms (Winterdyk and Ruddell 2010). Despite prison administrators' best efforts to control STGs, prison gangs have shown no signs of decreasing in power or number in prisons throughout the United States.

For inmates who do not wish to join a prison gang, one common intermediate step for many inmates is to join a "**crew.**" A crew is a more loosely affiliated clique that exists for backup protection but does not have the same loyalty expectations as prison gangs. A crew does *not* engage in trafficking drugs and contraband for profit but will only serve as backup if one of its members is called to fight (Terry 2003).

Crew: an informal group of friends who provide support and backup when necessary but are not members of a prison gang

Inmates become social outcasts if they elect not to assimilate fully; they eventually become targeted and harassed for their perceived weakness. To avoid harassment and getting targeted, the outcast becomes afraid to leave the confines of his cell and becomes known in prison argot as a **cave dweller**. In the worst cases, some prisoners are so often harassed or targeted for rape that they must request protective custody.

PRISONER RIGHTS

Prior to the 1960s, very few rules and regulations existed about the way prisoners should be treated. Prisoners were considered "slaves of the state," and judges did not want to interfere, so they steered clear of prison wardens and administrators, who were allowed to decide their own prison conditions. This era was known as the **hands-off period**.

Hands-Off Period

The lack of court involvement caused a rift and vast differences across the country in how much training staff received and in the quality of prison conditions. At several prisons in southern states, there were fewer correctional officers for the number of prisoners because the state wanted to minimize the amount of funding it provided. Instead of paying staff to supervise prisoners, some states turned to other prisoners to supervise each other. Until the early 1980s in Texas, correctional staff walked the halls and prevented inmates from escaping, but control of the inside of each housing unit was through the **building tender system**, which involved handpicked inmates who were provided with extra privileges in exchange for keeping order in the general prison population through whatever means necessary. At that time, prisoners lost nearly all of their rights upon conviction and experienced brutality from ill-trained guards and violent building tenders (Colvin 1997).

Judicial Activism

As political prisoners and civil rights group members were incarcerated for behavior outside the walls, they asserted themselves to change conditions inside the walls. One of the benefits of this action was that the courts reinterpreted Section 1983 of the civil rights statute to apply to prisoners whose rights had been violated (Call 1995). Secondly, the U.S. Supreme Court interpreted the **due process clause** of the 14th Amendment to incorporate most clauses from the first ten amendments to all people, including convicted prisoners. One exception was grand juries, which have not been mandated on the states. The due process clause became a catchall phrase by which a number of cases applied. With these two changes, the gates opened and waves

Cave dweller:
an inmate who is afraid to leave his or her cell because of perceived or actual victimization from other inmates

Hands-off period:
the era prior to 1964 when courts refused to become involved in prisoner rights cases and left prison administrators to decide their own prison conditions

Building tender system:
the warden's use of handpicked inmates to control the larger inmate population in exchange for special privileges

Due process clause:
a section of the Fourteenth Amendment of the U.S. Constitution that provides general guidelines as to when rights must be provided to individuals when issues relevant to life or liberty are at stake

of prisoner lawsuits flooded the federal courts over the next 15 years, from 1964 to 1979. The courts ruled on many issues that gave inmates rights in a number of areas, such as the right to medical care, the right to court access, the right to religious materials, the right to be informed about why good time credits were being taken away, and protection against cruel and unusual punishment. Inmates do not have to suffer actual harm; they only have to show that conditions in the prison or deliberate indifference of another exposed the inmate to unreasonable risk that was linked to a necessity of life, such as food, water, and safety (Call 1995).

The Court established a balancing test in *Pell v. Procunier* (1974), whereby the prison's legitimate need for safety and security generally outweighed some constitutional rights previously afforded to inmates. In this case, prohibiting inmates the right to speak with journalists did not interfere with the First Amendment freedom of the press when balanced against the importance of keeping the entire prison population safe and secure. As a result, court cases after 1974 tended to further limit inmate rights in other areas, such as privacy, the type of mail received, and transfer to administrative segregation. Inmates were also subjected to cell searches, double bunking, and cavity searches if necessary for the safety and security of the institution (Call 1995). Table 12.1 summarizes some of the main prisoner rights cases that the U.S. Supreme Court decided between 1964 and the 1990s.

Between the mid-1980s and 2005, most prisoner cases decided by the U.S. Supreme Court involved constitutional issues, such as those emanating from the due process clause of the Fourteenth Amendment; the Eighth Amendment's prohibition against cruel and unusual punishment; the First Amendment freedoms of association, expression, and religion; and the Fourth Amendment's protections against unreasonable searches and seizures (Smith and Corbin 2008). Other cases are considered statutory in nature because they involve issues in prison in which the Court further defines federal statutes such as Section 1983 of the Civil Rights Act, the Prison Litigation Reform Act, and various federal appellate rules of criminal or civil procedure. The trend over the past few years (and probably continuing into the future) has tended toward upholding legal protections for prisoners with limitations. If any changes are to occur, Christopher Smith and Anne Corbin (2008) predict that it will be statutory rather than through the U.S. Constitution.

Internal Grievances

Federal courts are one way to address systemic problems, but they are not the only way. Every prison has procedures to address any grievances internally. Prisoners complain about all kinds of issues, but

Table 12.1 **Examples of Cases That Affected Prison Conditions**	
CASES FAVORING PRISONER RIGHTS	**CASES LIMITING PRISONER RIGHTS**
Cooper v. Pate (1964): State prisoner could bring a Section 1983 lawsuit alleging his religious freedom rights had been violated.	*Meachum v. Fano* (1976): No due process required when an inmate is transferred to a higher-security prison for disciplinary or administrative reasons.
Johnson v. Avery (1969): Prisons must allow prisoners with help to prepare post-conviction petitions, such as a jailhouse lawyer (another inmate).	*Baxter v. Palmigiano* (1976): In a prison disciplinary hearing, an inmate cannot exercise privilege against self-incrimination, and refusal to answer questions can be used against the inmate.
Younger v. Gilmore (1971): Prisons must provide inmates with access to an adequate law library.	*Bell v. Wolfish* (1979): Cell searches can be conducted without the inmate present. Body cavity searches of inmates are permitted after contact visits. Inmates may not receive packages from outsiders, except for books directly from the publisher. Double celling is not unconstitutional.
Procunier v. Martinez (1974): Prisons cannot censor outgoing mail unless they provide an inmate notification and proper due process (hearing, notice of charges, etc.).	
Wolff v. McDonnell (1974): Prisons must provide inmates with proper due process if good time credits are taken away.	*Turner v. Safley* (1987): Prohibiting inmates from corresponding with inmates at other prisons is constitutional.
Estelle v. Gamble (1976): Prisons must provide inmates with adequate medical care.	*Whitley v. Albers* (1986): A prisoner who has been harmed by a staff member must prove that the official acted maliciously and sadistically for the purpose of causing harm toward that individual.
	Wilson v. Seiter (1991): With regard to general conditions of confinement, inmates must show that prison officials acted with "deliberate indifference" to a basic need.

some of the more common complaints concern the prison in which they are classified, where they are assigned to live or work, unfair officer treatment, food quality, and confiscated property that is now missing. The process begins with a written complaint and the request for a hearing by the inmate. At the hearing, the inmate has basic due process rights, such as the right to a neutral hearing officer (typically an experienced committee), the right to present evidence on his or her behalf, the right to challenge evidence to the contrary, and the right to have the decision in writing. Overall, the grievance process has greatly reduced violence and riots. The courts now require that prisoners first exhaust their administrative remedies through fully addressing their complaint with all levels of the internal grievance committee before filing a lawsuit, so this is an important step in easing pressures on the courts.

PRISON BEHAVIOR

A great deal has changed since the 1960s to make doing time more fair and less brutal. What most people don't realize is that changing prison conditions also benefitted correctional officers and treatment staff, who can now work in safer places. Today's prison officials face an enormous set of regulations and challenges on a daily basis. The Eighth Amendment requires officials to keep prisoners safe from hurting themselves or others. At the same time, working in a prison is like working in a pressure cooker—the potential for violence is always present, but no one knows just exactly where and when the place may explode. This section discusses interpersonal violence between two people, larger group disturbances, and inappropriate sexual behavior.

Interpersonal Violence

Inmate violence from prison staff has significantly decreased but has not completely dissipated. Figure 12.1 shows that two-thirds of all assaultive behavior happens between two inmates, while the remaining involves an inmate against a staff member.

Most inmates fear other prisoners and gangs more than staff. New inmates are tested to see their willingness to fight and to see who their friends are, or if they are loners. Threats and harassment are perhaps the most common forms of assault, but these are undocumented in official statistics. Inmates also underreport cases of physical assault and sexual assault/rape out of fear of being labeled a snitch (Santos 2004).

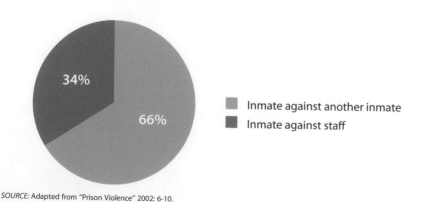

Figure 12.1
Inmate assaults

34%

66%

■ Inmate against another inmate
■ Inmate against staff

SOURCE: Adapted from "Prison Violence" 2002: 6-10.

Group Disturbances

While riots are rare, **disturbances** are the most documented because they involve small groups of inmates. Disturbances occur a few times per week in maximum-security prisons and once every few months in minimum-security correctional facilities. Most disturbances occur in areas where inmates greatly outnumber officers by as much as 50 inmates or 100 inmates to every 1 officer. These areas include the prison recreation yard, dining hall, dormitories, and dayroom. Most disturbances end within minutes when the prison is locked down, and prison staff always remains in control. Causes of disturbances are most commonly from small groups of inmates who fight each other because of gang rivalries, gang initiation, or retaliation. Disturbances can also involve property damage, such as when inmates purposely stop up the plumbing in their toilets, set a fire, or refuse a staff order ("Prison Violence" 2002: 11-14).

Violence is clearly concentrated in higher-security units, where the inmates live in an environment that encourages violence to create a reputation, bully or harass as a show of power, impose fear when necessary to avoid being victimized, and settle problems without staff (Carceral 2004). Inmates who are unwilling to fight end up paying someone else for protection (taking out a prison life insurance policy), pay a toll or tax to use the prison yard, or are permanently prohibited by the inmates in power from using certain toilets, sinks, telephones, athletic equipment, or even sitting in certain chairs.

Disturbances: short-term chaotic events involving a small group of inmates in which correctional staff maintain control

Inappropriate Sexual Behavior

Sexual behavior of any kind while incarcerated is prohibited, including sexual harassment, indecent exposure, or sexual acts. Before 2003, there were few negative consequences resulting from engaging in sexual acts. The lack of consequences existed for a number of reasons. First, the general consensus at the time was that rape and sexual harassment were just part of being in prison. Correctional officers either ignored the behavior, or at most, ordered the inmates to stop, but rarely issued any disciplinary reports. In some prisons, staff members were reportedly engaged in sexual relationships with inmates without fear of repercussion. In fact, correctional staff committed more incidents of sexual abuse in prisons than did other inmates (Beck and Hughes 2005). Inappropriate relationships between inmates and staff were primarily initiated by inmates to exploit staff members to bring in contraband, to create problems and disruptions, or to create an emotional bond in hopes that it may lead to sex (Worley, Marquart, and Mullings 2003). The 1996 movie *Prison of Secrets* was based on real events that took place at a California women's prison. After the inappropriate sexual relationships were exposed, 20 correctional officers quit, and 3 correctional officers were prosecuted for sexual misconduct.

The rate of sexual assault and rape ranged widely, as some incidents were measured over the past year while others were measured across the entire period of incarceration, and many studies included small samples (Gaes and Goldberg 2004). There was indeed acknowledgement that a problem existed, particularly if sexual coercion and harassment was included, since that behavior seemed to be quite common among prisoners (Alarid 2000; Hensley, Castle, and Tewksbury 2003). Prisoners who were targeted for sexual assault by their fellow inmates tended to be first-time felons who were loners and might have had some sort of disability or mental illness (English, Heil, and Dumond 2010). If a victim was targeted for rape, a small group of inmate perpetrators acted as lookouts and intentionally caused a disturbance in another part of the prison to draw the officers' attention away from the rape.

The **Prison Rape Elimination Act (PREA)** was passed at the federal level in 2003 to address this problem in a number of ways. First, the act enforced zero tolerance and prosecution for perpetrators of sexual misconduct and rape. Staff who had any type of relationship with an inmate (sexual or nonsexual) faced grounds for termination and additional criminal charges. Second, the act provided resources and model programs in which states could establish guidelines to protect prisoners from sexual assault and rape. These resources included appointing a designee at each jail and prison in the United States where rapes could be reported and investigated. Third, PREA mandated victim access to counseling and protective custody housing. Fourth, correctional officers were trained on the new law. Finally, the act called for research to accurately measure the incidence of sexual assault and rape in U.S. correctional institutions. A national commission was set up to develop more permanent standards, which were ultimately passed in 2012. These standards implemented all parts of the original act and included provisions for educating prisoners and flagging known perpetrators and victims during the classification process (Thompson, Nored, and Dial 2008). State departments of corrections have until 2014 to comply or risk losing prison funding.

Using more accurate measurement techniques and larger samples of youths and adults, the average annual incidence of sexual victimization is 4.4 percent in prisons and 3 percent in jails. Incidents ranged widely from less than one percent to almost 20 percent based on inmates who said that an incident happened to them at least once within the past 12 months. Of the 88,500 calculated incidents every year, only about 10 percent were actually reported (Beck, Harrison, and Guerino 2010)—roughly about 6,200 in adult facilities and 2,800 in

Prison Rape Elimination Act (PREA):
a federal act passed in 2003 to prosecute predatory inmates and staff who commit sexual assaults and to protect sexual assault victims in prisons

juvenile facilities nationwide. Most incidents of sexual assault are not reported because of victim fear and lack of evidence.

WOMEN'S PRISONS

As Figure 12.2 shows, women make up only 7 percent of the prison population, while 93 percent of inmates are men. As a result, women have had a harder time getting recognized for their specific needs given their small numbers. Rosemary Gartner and Candace Kruttschnitt (2004) compared doing time in the 1960s to 30 years later at the same California prison and found that even though the philosophy had become more punitive and less rehabilitative over time, the way prisoners perceived staff members and other inmates were more similar than different. Women still face the same problems. For example, female prisoners are more likely than male prisoners to have experienced childhood sexual abuse, neglect, and domestic violence. So, treatment programs should be aimed at helping women heal from past abuses and how they can prevent future family violence.

Gender-Specific Needs

Women are more likely than men to need job skills training and financial knowledge to live independently. In the past, prison programs focused on providing only male inmates with skilled labor opportunities. In today's world, the structure of family life has drastically changed. The majority of women will return to the community as primary caretakers of dependent children and single heads of household. This situation makes garnering enough education and skills to earn a livable wage to support dependents equally important for women and men.

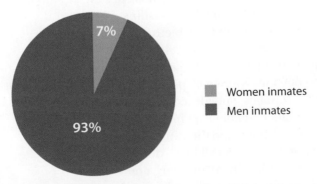

Figure 12.2
Gender composition of incarcerated prisoners

Women inmates
Men inmates

SOURCE: Adapted from Sabol, West, and Cooper 2009.

Women's prisons are different from men's prisons, so the inmate code is also different. The first difference is that women prisoners tend to interact more casually with correctional officers, as well as with other women inmates for help and support. Men tend to keep problems to themselves while incarcerated because sharing problems is considered to be a weakness. As a result of knowing each other's problems, women were more likely to use this information to create drama through gossip and rumor mills (Pollock 2002). Women seem to associate with each other in more mixed-race groupings, and there is less of a need to join a prison gang or group for protection. Assaults, when they occur, were less likely to involve deadly weapons and less related to racial/ethnic tension. The causes of most female inmate-on-inmate assault were jealousy, sexual pressuring, and unreciprocated attention. In general, women's prisons are much less violent places than men's prisons (Alarid 1996).

Friendships and Pseudofamilies

About 75 percent of women in prison have one or more dependent children under the age of 18. Most women prisoners defined themselves primarily by their roles as mothers, so the separation from their children exacts a significant toll on their self-esteem and stress level while incarcerated (Alarid and Vega 2010). Ironically, women prisoners receive fewer visits from their children than men who are incarcerated. This is because women's prisons are usually in a more remote area of the state, making visitation more difficult for families (Christian 2005). Secondly, when men are incarcerated, women take more time and effort to make the trip with their children to visit father, spouse, or boyfriend. When women are incarcerated, the children are often cared for by their grandparents or father, none of whom treat visitation with the same priority (Mumola 2000).

The fact that women are more physically isolated from the outside world means that social support plays an important role inside women's prisons. Close friendships of a few people were the most prevalent type of relationship found in women's prisons. Friendships were used as a coping mechanism and as way to solve problems. Socializing in larger group settings is also important for about 40 percent of women as a way to deal with the emotional loss of their children and close family relationships from the outside. Known as **pseudofamilies**, these groups function the same as families outside of prison. Most families were matriarchal in that an older female role model becomes the center of the family, or the household head, and the younger females become her adopted daughters. They may even call her "Mom."

Another type of pseudofamily is headed by a "mother" and a "father," with the "father" as a woman posing in a masculine role and

Pseudofamilies:
a make-believe family structure composed of women inmates who are not related to each other

involved in a sexual relationship with the mother. This family structure occurred less often and was less permanent as women sought out new relationships. Generally, matriarchal family structures seemed to share commissary, persuade members into compliance, and protect each other from predatory inmates (Alarid 1996).

WORKING IN PRISON

Correctional facilities are one of the few places in society in which people are held against their will for a specific amount of time decided by the courts. Not only does this create resentment, hostility, and anger, but prison operations also rely on resentful and hostile prisoners to do most of the work without getting paid.

People who work in prison are categorized according to three types. First, there are correctional officers, who are the foundation of prison security and considered by inmates to be the police of the prison. Second, treatment staff is made up of people involved in the rehabilitation and self-improvement of inmates. The third group is administration, which is composed of the leadership, as well as all the clerks, accountants, and purchasing employees who are required to track incoming and outgoing supplies, as well as inmate money that family members wish to send.

Security Staff: Correctional Officers

As the courts have gotten more involved in prison conditions, learning about correctional law has become more important for **correctional officers (COs)**. COs are tasked with enforcing correctional law, prison policies, and ensuring a safe and secure prison for inmates, other staff, visitors, and the general public. To carry out these goals, COs are the first to respond to all incidents. They are involved in pat-down searches, cell searches, and seizures of contraband. COs have daily contact with the same prisoners for months or even years, so interpersonal skills are critical. But relationships between inmates and officers are *not* like they are portrayed in movies such as *The Green Mile* or *Dead Man Walking*. Getting too personal or starting a relationship with an inmate not only is inappropriate and cause for termination but also may involve criminal prosecution (Worley and Worley 2013).

Working in a prison is certainly a difficult job, especially when staff members are greatly outnumbered and there are limits as to the kinds of rewards and punishments that can be granted to inmates. Many people mistakenly believe that prisons are run by sheer force. In reality, prisons run smoothly when the officers obtain prisoner cooperation. In some ways, there is give and take between officers and

Correctional officers (COs):
institutional staff whose primary responsibilities are enforcing correctional law, prison policies, and ensuring a safe and secure facility for inmates, other staff, visitors, and the general public

inmates. If the officer agrees to relax some of the minor rules, then there is an informal agreement that inmates won't give the officer a hard time. The officer must be careful about which rules to relax (e.g., time on the phone or overlooking when inmates pass notes called "kites") and which rules are important to keep "by the book," such as pat-down searching for contraband or intervening in a fight.

Relaxing rules can be distinguished from unprofessional behavior. COs must refrain from sharing personal information about themselves and not accept anything from inmates. Inmates look for signs of weakness and vulnerability in staff, such as relationships, habits, and finances. Staff who are in financial trouble, are perceived as too empathetic or nice, are unattached to a significant other, or are unhappy in marital relationships are prime targets for inmates. New COs in particular are tested just like new inmates to see how they respond. To be respected, a professional CO must be firm, fair, and consistent. COs knows that their main job is to prevent disturbances, assaults, and escapes and to protect treatment staff.

A final quality for a good CO is to avoid letting personal biases interfere with how inmates are treated post-conviction and to remember that the corrections system is designed to carry out the court's sentence—not to administer more than the necessary punishment. COs are frequently asked what they think about the crimes that the inmates around them have committed. A common response is similar to one that a captain once gave to a student visitor who asked that question during a facility tour. The captain said, "Most of us do not know and don't want to know. Although the files are available to us on their crimes if we want to go and look it up, our job is to treat everyone the same regardless of what they have done to get themselves in here."

Treatment Staff

Another important part of prison life is the treatment staff. Figure 12.3 shows the occupations of treatment staff who are responsible for prisoners' health, well-being, and self-improvement. Treatment staff members participate with inmates in redirecting their lives and maintaining themselves through their prison sentence. The same rules of professionalism that apply to correctional officers also apply to treatment staff.

Education programs in prisons are targeted at prisoners who dropped out of school or are unable to read or write. Literacy programs are primarily designed to teach prisoners how to read and write at a level so they can apply for jobs and qualify for basic employment. For prisoners who can read and write but did not graduate from high school, general equivalency degree (GED) preparatory classes are

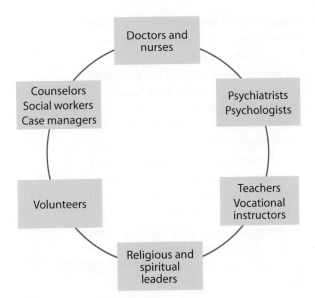

Figure 12.3
Occupational titles of prison treatment staff

offered in math, social studies, English, or reading comprehension to inmates who may be ready to take the GED within one year. The federal prison system requires inmates to earn their GED prior to release. This is an important policy because research shows academic and vocational programs lead to more employment opportunities, which in turn leads to reduced recidivism (Visher, Winterfield, and Coggeshall 2005). Prisoners who want to pursue higher education must apply to distance learning classes and pay the same tuition and fees as every other student. Face-to-face higher education classes are rarely offered in prison. Vocational classes are offered to inmates with good disciplinary records, so they must earn their way into classes in welding, automotive repair, and computer drafting, for example.

Prisoners with mental health problems are seen by psychologists and psychiatrists, who monitor their medications. A psychological interview is completed at intake or within the first 24 hours of institutionalization. Prisoners are not allowed to keep psychotropic medications in their cells; they must line up in the "pill line," where a nurse distributes the correct medication and dosage to each inmate. The next chapter discusses the issue of mental illness in the corrections system in more detail.

Medical Treatment

The treatment staff also includes doctors, nurses, and dentists. When the government incarcerates someone, the system must also care for them, and this includes addressing their medical needs. Jails and prisons provide all the basic health care services that an average clinic does, including examinations, diagnostic testing, and treatment. While prisoners are not allowed to abuse the system, and many are charged a co-payment for an office visit, staff cannot deny medical treatment to the indigent. In fact, staff can be held legally accountable for failing to treat medical conditions or ignoring requests to see a doctor (*Estelle v. Gamble* (1976)). The right to mental health treatment has the same standards as medical or physical health (*Bowring v. Godwin* (1977)).

As prisoners serve longer sentences, they will be older when and if they ever get out. During their sentence, they may contract communicable diseases such as HIV, along with cancer, heart disease, and diabetes. As prisoners age, they will require wheelchairs, walkers, and hospital beds, which is something that most people fail to consider when they chant the "lock 'em up" mantra. Next to paying prison staff, health care is the second most expensive part of a prison sentence for taxpayers.

Substance Abuse Counselors

Counselors, social workers, and other community volunteers lead group therapy sessions, such as parenting classes, anger management, and **substance abuse treatment**. The format that most of these sessions take is cognitive-behavioral in nature, which links thinking errors and patterns to a change in behavior. One interesting issue concerning substance abuse treatment is that, unlike mental health and medical health, prisoners have no constitutional right to drug treatment (*Marshall v. U.S.* (1974)). Prisons are *not* obligated to provide the treatment. Following the *Marshall* decision, many substance abuse treatment programs closed down. The treatment programs that remain open are not subject to any standards or regulations. According to Roger Peters and Marc Steinberg (2000: 91), the Substance Abuse and Mental Health Services Administration Center for Substance Abuse Treatment has recommended guidelines:

Substance abuse treatment: nonresidential or residential treatment of drugs and/or alcohol in different phases depending on the client's severity of addiction

- Standardized screening and assessment approaches
- Matching to different levels or types of treatment services
- Individual treatment plans
- Case management services
- Use of cognitive-behavioral/social learning and self-help approaches, including interventions that address criminal beliefs and values
- Relapse prevention services
- Self-help groups (AA, NA)
- Use of therapeutic communities
- Isolated treatment units
- Drug testing

- Continuity of services, including linkages to parole and community-based treatment services
- Program evaluation
- Cross-training of staff

There are many different types of substance abuse treatments, depending on the client's level of addiction and needs. Treatment varies from 12 weekly drug education classes up to 18 months of intensive, full-time residential therapeutic communities that emphasize peer confrontation and accountability and development of prosocial behaviors to replace previously addictive behaviors. Each intensive program has various phases or levels in which a recovering addict progresses. Most programs accept inmates with no history of violent crimes or no history of institutional violence and with enough time on their sentence to complete the program. In-prison therapeutic communities are successful in reducing drug use, relapse, and future recidivism (Pelissier, Motivans, and Rounds-Bryant 2005; Turley et al. 2004).

Spiritual Development

An important part of self-improvement is spiritual development. Some prisoners are ignored or even criticized for finding religion in prison, but it seems to serve a positive function of increasing acceptance and self-esteem. The courts have required that as long as there is a prisoner who practices a bona fide religion, and as long as it does not violate institutional security and safety, then elements of that religion or faith can be practiced. These elements include a place to worship, dietary needs, observance of religious holidays, access to religious books and materials, and access to a chaplain, rabbi, or other spiritual leader, even if it is on a part-time basis. Some chaplains are assigned to one or more prisons on a full-time basis, while less-practiced denominations have volunteers and advisors who come in from the outside. In general, religious programs help prisoners adjust to prison life and reduces disciplinary infractions.

In conclusion, the power structure of prisons has shifted largely from prison staff to prison gangs. While security measures have gotten better and treatment staff have been able to target what works in a more effective manner, violence and fear are still present as most prisoners try to navigate their way and do their time without getting victimized. The inmate code of conduct is not as strong today compared to years ago; nor is the code as strong in minimum-security compared to maximum-custody facilities. Prisoners serving two years or less can usually resist the pressures of the prison environment and avoid joining a gang. Individuals with longer sentences in maximum custody find it difficult to remain connected to the world outside and succumb to their situation to make their life easier (Santos 2004). Individuals who get fully "into the life" and leave the outside world behind become **prisonized** such that they have fully accepted and adopted the prison value system as their own. Long ago, Donald Clemmer (1966) cautioned that once individuals become prisonized, they find it much more difficult to fully adjust back into society as a law-abiding citizen.

Prisonized:
state in which prisoners identify with and have fully adopted the convict code of conduct over the conventional value system outside prison

SUMMARY

This chapter discusses various elements of prison life from the point of view of new prisoners and how they learn prison norms and behaviors through language and gestures to communicate meaning. Deprivation and importation theories are identified as explanations for why institutional life in prison or jail is so stressful and involves a high level of violence and necessity to be connected in some way to other prisoners.

The five main deprivations of incarceration are goods and services, liberty, autonomy, security, and relationships. The deprivation model suggests that prisoners will try to circumvent the pains of imprisonment by getting involved in gangs, same-sex relationships, and the sub rosa economy to make their post-conviction sentence more bearable. The importation model suggests that prison life is an extension of street life for the disproportionate number of prisoners who are already involved in drugs and gangs before coming to prison.

Drug-involved prisoners and prison gangs have a strong influence on the inmate code, economic system, and level of violence within each prison unit. Once gang intelligence officers identify gang members with tattoos, hand signs, clothing colors, and associates, the confirmed member can be reclassified to a higher-security prison.

This chapter also discusses prisoner rights and why conditions in jails and prisons must be kept to a certain standard. Court involvement in correctional law began with the hands-off approach, and then judges became active in extending prisoners' rights beginning in the 1960s and continuing through the 1970s. Courts are still involved in overseeing prison conditions, but the trend over the past three decades has turned toward restriction of prisoner rights. As a result of an increase in prisoner rights and prison law development, prisons have become safer, regulated, and more consistent places to do time compared to before the 1960s.

Women's prisons are less violent, less influenced by gangs, and have a less strict inmate code and a higher tolerance of racial mixing and pseudofamilies than men's prisons. In men's prisons, violence, when it occurs, takes the form of interpersonal assault, group disturbances, and sexual assault/rape.

Prison staff is composed of three groups of individuals. First, correctional officers are involved in the security and safety of inmates. Second, treatment staff are tasked with the rehabilitation and well-being of prisoners. Finally, administrative staff are responsible for the prison's operations, bookkeeping, and leadership.

REVIEW QUESTIONS

1. When you think about each of the elements of prison life in this chapter, which ones more closely fit the deprivation model, and which are linked to the importation model?
2. How has the inmate code of conduct changed over time?
3. What purpose does the sub rosa economy serve in prison life? Can the black market be controlled?
4. Do prisoners have too many rights, not enough rights, or just enough? Defend your position.
5. Has the court's active move toward governing prison conditions made prison safer or made it more difficult for gangs to rise to power?
6. How has prison violence changed over time?
7. Has the Prison Rape Elimination Act reduced prison rape? What else could be done within prison settings to decrease rape?
8. Other than the gender differences already mentioned in the chapter, what other differences do you think there might be between doing time in men's and women's prisons?
9. Are there lessons that we can learn from women's prisons that could be applied to men's prisons to make them less violent?
10. Would it be more effective to combine custody and treatment staff roles together, such that correctional officers are also involved in rehabilitation? Support your answer.
11. Should convicted prisoners with drug problems have a right to drug treatment?

KEY TERMS

building tender system
cave dweller
contraband
correctional officers (COs)
crew
deprivation model
disturbances
due process clause
hands-off period

importation model
inmate code
prison argot
prisonized
Prison Rape Elimination Act (PREA)
pseudofamilies
security threat group (STG)
snitches
sub rosa economy
substance abuse treatment

Issues in Corrections

LEARNING OBJECTIVES

At the conclusion of this chapter, you should be able to:

- Explain why racial/ethnic disproportionality exist in corrections and how racial disparity affects the larger community.

- Summarize why women commit crime and what is being done in the corrections system to treat female offenders.

- Understand why more persons with mental illnesses enter the corrections system and what is being done to respond to the problem.

- Trace the origin of parole and the issues prisoners face when they leave prison to reenter the community.

- Analyze the degree to which imprisonment deters crime and reduces overall recidivism.

317

INTRODUCTION

Studying criminal justice is about studying the law and how the system works through the police, courts, and corrections. Another important part of learning more about the corrections system is to understand and become more sensitive to human behavior and the kinds of issues the corrections system currently faces. This chapter examines five important issues in corrections that are germane to more fully understanding who is in the corrections system and why they return:

- Racial/ethnic disparities in prison
- Gender and correctional treatment
- Persons with mental illnesses in the corrections system
- Leaving prison and community reentry
- Effects of imprisonment: deterrence and recidivism

RACIAL/ETHNIC DISPARITIES IN PRISON

Students of criminal justice have often wondered whether people incarcerated in jails and prisons are truly proportionate by race/ethnicity. In other words, if we compared the percentage of different racial or ethnic groups in the United States, would that breakdown be similar to or different from the race/ethnicity percentages in the corrections system? If you answered "different," you are (unfortunately) correct.

Figure 13.1 shows that men and women of African American and Latino descent are disproportionately overrepresented in the prisoner population compared to their percentages in the larger community. However, the difference is especially pronounced for African Americans, who have an imprisonment rate more than six times higher than whites and nearly three times higher than Hispanics (Bales and Piquero 2012).

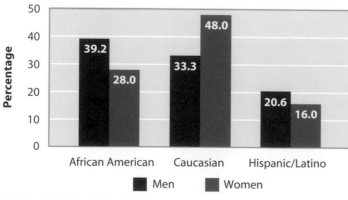

Figure 13.1
Racial/ethnic composition of incarcerated prisoners

SOURCE: Adapted from Sabol, West, and Cooper 2009.

About one in three African American men will serve prison time at some point in their life, while incarceration will affect one in ten Hispanic men and only 6 percent of Caucasian men. Why is it that persons of color disproportionately occupy jails and prisons? The answer to this question is quite complex and differs, of course, individually on a case-by-case basis. However, the overall picture can be explained by a combination of historical factors, extent of criminal involvement, discrimination, and drug sentencing policies that together contribute to this difference.

Historical Factors for Adults

While prisons are used for the punishment of violent crimes and as a way to separate people who intentionally harm others, incarceration has also been used historically as a social control mechanism for certain groups. For example, immediately following the Civil War, many people of African American descent could not find anyone who would hire them. At the time, fear and social stigma were associated with helping newly freed slaves. At the same time, there was a labor supply shortage and an agricultural economy that was in financial ruins from the war. Freed slaves who stayed in the South were intentionally arrested and incarcerated for minor offenses (vagrancy, loitering). They picked cotton on prison farms as inmates instead of as slaves on private farms owned by Caucasian families. Ironically, most of the land that the states purchased was from former private plantation owners. At the time, prisoners were considered slaves of the state, so very little had actually changed in the lives of many people. Abuses of the system continued with regard to the Southern states' widespread use of the convict leasing system from the 1880s to the 1930s, where African American inmates were forced into cheap labor to rebuild vehicle roads and railroads (Walker 1988). While the leasing system was formally abolished during the Great Depression, perceptions that many people held about criminalized African Americans as a group have remained.

War on Drugs

The subject of race/ethnicity in the corrections system was not given much attention until the 1980s, after the Sentencing Reform Act of 1984 allowed for incarceration to be used as the primary response to drug possession, sales, distribution, trafficking, and manufacturing. In 1989, President George H.W. Bush officially declared the latest chapter in the nation's long "war on drugs." While the most recent drug war did disrupt some major kingpin activity, law enforcement efforts targeted small-time drug dealers primarily from low-income, urban areas. Enforcement of the Sentencing Reform Act contributed to a significant increase in prisoners incarcerated for drug offenses, from 25 percent in the early 1980s to 60 percent by 1995. Figure 13.2 shows that the number of drug offenders in federal prisons since then has slightly decreased each year but not by much. As of 2011, 51 percent of all federal prisoners remain incarcerated for a drug crime.

Drug sentencing policies were different not only for different types of drugs (such as marijuana vs. heroin), but also for different forms of the same drug. The best example of this discrepancy was the crack versus powder cocaine difference. A person who sold 10.6 pounds of powder cocaine would be sentenced from ten years to life in prison in the federal system. That same penalty applied to offenders who were convicted of selling less than two ounces of crack cocaine. Given that crack cocaine was commonly sold by African American and Hispanic offenders and powder cocaine was most often sold by Caucasian offenders, the penalty was arguably unfair and affected each race/ethnic group differently.

The U.S. Supreme Court agreed that mandatory drug sentences are unfairly weighted when it ruled in 2007 that federal judges would no longer be legally required to follow the federal sentencing guidelines as they relate to the powder and crack cocaine disparity. The U.S. Sentencing Commission was then able to permanently reduce the disparate sentences for future offenders and retroactively for offenders who had already been sentenced under this regime. Sentence lengths were apparently reduced for nearly 20,000 federal prisoners (Radosh 2008).

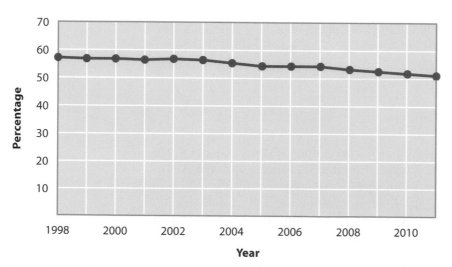

Figure 13.2
Percentage of federal offenders sentenced for drug offenses, 1998-2011

SOURCE: Compiled from Bureau of Justice Statistics Federal Criminal Case Processing Statistics tool at http://bjs.ojp.usdoj.gov/fjsrc.

People of Hispanic descent have also experienced a great deal of hardships and discrimination within the criminal justice system. Research revealed that Hispanics were sentenced more harshly than either Caucasians or African Americans in the federal system (Steffensmeier and Demuth 2000) and in various states, including North Carolina (Brennan and Spohn 2008), Florida (Spohn and Holleran 2000), and Pennsylvania (Steffensmeier and Demuth 2001). Most recently, detention and incarceration has been used to limit movement of undocumented immigrants.

Disproportionate Minority Contact in the Juvenile System

Juvenile institutions originally had both reformatories designed to treat and rehabilitate youths and workhouses, which were more like adult prisons. It seemed that reformatories existed for Caucasian youths adjudicated as delinquent, whereas African American youths were sent to workhouses. Like with adults, not much attention was paid to this issue until 1988, when the Coalition for Juvenile Justice submitted a report to Congress expressing explicit concern that too many children of Hispanic and African American descent were being institutionalized in residential facilities (Soler and Garry 2009). This report drew national attention, and Congress appropriated money to address this issue, which became known as **disproportionate minority contact (DMC)**. DMC became a primary concern in the juvenile justice system, where the overrepresentation problem was substantial but has since improved; however, there is still much room for improvement. More than 25 years later, African American or Hispanic children account for 20 percent of the U.S. juvenile population but make up over 50 percent of juvenile violent crime arrests, more than one-third of adjudicated delinquency cases, and more than half of youths in residential placement facilities (Knoll and Sickmund 2010; Puzzanchera 2009; Sedlak and Bruce 2010).

Disproportionate minority contact (DMC): a movement that began in the 1990s to reduce the overrepresentation of juveniles of African American and Hispanic descent in the juvenile justice system

Racial Stereotyping and Cultural Insensitivity

A number of factors have been suggested that together contribute to minority youth overrepresentation. DMC begins with media representation of racial stereotypes and how race/ethnicity and crime are constantly linked where there is a heavier focus of minority suspects and white victims. This view continually contributes to public perceptions (Soler and Garry 2009). Another issue is neighborhood conditions of disadvantage youths, such as less than adequate school systems with high dropout rates. Related to this issue is the lack of after-school programs and athletics to give students an outlet between the time school ends and parents return from work. In low-income areas, parents must work more than one job and do not have time to transport kids to activities because they must work. In turn, this limits parents' ability to supervise their children.

When school and lack of supervision are tied to possible racial stereotyping and cultural insensitivity by people in authority, certain actions of youths may be scrutinized more closely when occurring in one neighborhood as opposed to another, more affluent area. Police, for example, may be more likely to stop and question youths who may stereotypically look like gang members more often than other youths. Increased police contact results in a greater likelihood of arrest for both juveniles and adults. Studies investigating the phenomenon called "driving while black" (or "driving while brown") support a view of racial bias toward minorities in decisions to search, but that effect was mediated by criminal history (Tillyer 2012).

Differential Involvement in Some Crimes of Violence

Another view suggests that while young males across all racial groups engage in criminal offenses in their teens and early twenties (as suggested by self-reported data), African American males engage in more violent felony offenses and continue offending behavior for a longer duration than males of other racial groups (McNulty and Bellair 2003). When it comes to crimes of violence, there is less discretion in arrest decisions, and incarceration is a more likely outcome. This difference in rates of violent crime is supported by official arrest records, which also show African Americans' higher involvement in violent crimes. This may account for some of the reasons there are so many black men in prison (Harris et al. 2009). But the difference in violent offending patterns alone cannot explain why there is also a difference for property and drug crimes. Even after carefully matching similar cases with one another based on current offense, previous criminal history, age, gender, and sentencing year, one study found that between 1994 and 2006, racial bias existed. All else being equal, African American individuals were *still* more likely to be incarcerated than whites or Hispanics (Bales and Piquero 2012).

How Incarceration Affects the Community

The numbers of young men and women who have done time has had a profound effect within Latino and African American communities, both on breaking the cycle of crime and experiencing significant future change. The incarceration experience itself significantly affects the potential for individuals to move up the economic ladder. Included within this are lost wages during the time spent incarcerated as well as decreased chances for finding regular employment upon exiting prison (Ramakers et al. 2014). Incarceration affects not only the individual but also dependent children of the incarcerated person who have experienced the temporary (or sometimes even permanent) loss of a parent. The loss children experience may contribute to problems at school, depression, or involvement in delinquency.

Most people who are released from prison return to a community that has been decimated by a lack of job opportunities near where they reside, unreliable public transportation, and a dearth of good schools because of a low tax base and little to no political influences. Many working-class communities experienced a similar shift across the United States when manufacturing businesses that offered positions to people with limited education chose to relocate overseas. Smaller service-related businesses that remained could not compete with larger, more centralized chain stores, so the smaller businesses closed, leaving a gaping hole in many communities that may now have only a convenience store and liquor store surrounded by public housing, vacant buildings, and overgrown lots. These disparities, in turn, ultimately reinforce some people's stereotypes about dangerousness and who is perceived to be a criminal.

GENDER AND CORRECTIONAL TREATMENT

Both the juvenile and adult criminal justice systems were initially designed for males because they were (and still are) the largest population of offenders. Girls who ran away from home were historically institutionalized to protect them from abusive and dysfunctional family members. Thus, the juvenile justice system subjected girls to harsher sanctioning than boys for similar offenses; this became an issue of **sentencing disparity**.

Adult women who broke the law and were sentenced to a term of incarceration were neglected and relegated to attics and back rooms of men's prisons. When adult institutions for females were built, women were treated differently than men and had access to rehabilitation programs that taught them the virtues of being a "good" woman; of paramount importance was learning how to cook, clean, sew, and, of course, have good table manners. Eventually, as women's roles changed in the larger society and with the realization that women were also primary caretakers, heads of households, and lived longer than men, women needed more marketable skills that would allow them to compete for jobs. With that change in perception, correctional rehabilitation programs themselves had to change.

sentencing disparity:
a type of injustice that occurs when individuals are sentenced differently for the same crime

Why Do Women Commit Crime?

As researchers have learned more about why juvenile girls and adult women commit offenses, program administrators are better able to design programs to help. We know for sure that as girls and boys mature and develop in different ways, so too do their experiences differ with respect to delinquency and crime. At an early age, girls face specific risk factors at higher levels than boys that also seem to negatively affect their later involvement in delinquency and crime. While boys face more peer pressure than girls, girls are more likely to have experienced repeated and prolonged sexual or emotional abuse by family members and acquaintances. Sexual and emotional abuse leads to depression, suicidal thoughts, low self-esteem, and substance abuse as a coping mechanism. According to Polly Radosh, "Whether the representation of abused women in the prison population is related to more persistent or more serious abuse than other abused women, whether they are less able to cope with the abuse, or whether the response system has differentially failed them is not clear" (2008: 175).

Another gender difference is that girls are more likely to be faced at an earlier age with decisions about pregnancy, reproductive problems, and prematurely dropping out of school. Teen pregnancy can affect future employment opportunities and development of marketable skills. Is it any coincidence that women in the criminal justice system have previously experienced many of these issues as girls and that these issues have never been dealt with?

Another reason some women commit crime is that they overidentify with a significant other who overruns her sense of self, who she is, and what she will or will not do. Many women become overly influenced by the actions of their mates, making poor choices and failing to establish healthy boundaries because they are being abused, because they haven't learned how to be independent, or both. All of these situations lie at the root of most women's paths to criminal activity. Previous experience does not absolve legal responsibility for how people behave, but it can explain why people commit crime and, more important, what can be done to stop the cycle of crime.

Treatment Programs for Women

One way of stopping the cycle is to expose girls to **gender-specific programs** such as that described in Box 13.1. Gender-specific programs help females address childhood abuse and feelings of anger and depression. They can also help women develop better coping skills in the company of positive female role models who can help reinforce a positive female identity. Gender-specific programs also help adult women with living independently, parenting skills, and establishing

Gender-specific programs: correctional treatment programs for women that address trauma linked to substance abuse

---

Box 13.1   Helping Women Recover

For some women who have experienced extensive emotional trauma, going to prison represents the first "safe place" they have experienced away from an abusive situation. Very few women-only programs exist as treatment while incarcerated. One example of a gender-specific program is called Helping Women Recover. This program is based on the premise that women's substance abuse in most cases is directly tied to earlier childhood physical, sexual, and emotional trauma. Addiction is viewed as a disease brought on by lifestyle choices (the use of alcohol or drugs in response to trauma) and the environment (unhealthy relationships, stress, etc.). The recovery process first teaches women how to feel emotionally and physically safe. Then, women are empowered to connect with positive and nurturing

people and, at the same time, establish boundaries with or avoid unhealthy relationships. To cognitively interpret and respond to an experience, a method called ORID is used and consists of the following steps:

1. *Objective:* obtaining facts through observation
2. *Reflective:* expressing emotional reactions to the event or experience
3. *Interpretive:* assessing the meaning and impact of the event, its significance or usefulness, and its value
4. *Decisive:* identifying actions or decisions in response to the experience

Women ultimately learn how to respond behaviorally in different ways than through the use of alcohol or drugs.

Source: Covington 1999.

---

boundaries in relationships. The most successful programs are women only (as opposed to mixed gender) because the power dynamics are quite different. Girls and women who have been repeatedly victimized by men need a safe place to heal and slowly reestablish their lost trust in males. Once women enter the criminal justice system, the workers within that system have a responsibility to find solutions to help women find a different path (Radosh 2008).

PERSONS WITH MENTAL ILLNESSES IN THE CORRECTIONS SYSTEM

Chapter 10 introduces how mental health deinstitutionalization in the 1960s created a need in the community to serve persons with mental illness. The situation has gotten significantly worse, such that America's jails and prisons have become our nation's largest mental hospitals. This section delves further into this important topic and discusses how and why mental health currently affects the corrections system in such a significant way.

Before deinstitutionalization, it was quite easy for a husband to commit his wife, for a parent to commit a child, or for a police officer to commit a perfect stranger. Commitment periods were indefinite, according to when people felt better or were ready to go home. Some people became institutionalized and became fearful of being released. Others wanted to go home but were kept against their will for a longer time than necessary. By the mid-1970s, institutionalizing people in state mental hospitals became more difficult when the courts applied new commitment standards requiring a civil commitment hearing and also requiring that the person show evidence of being an immediate and serious danger to themselves or to others. At the same time, state-funded treatment cutbacks led to the privatization of community mental health centers (CMHCs) and created a situation where the CMHCs served only people with health insurance because the centers could get reimbursed for the treatment they provided (Slate, Buffington-Vollum, and Johnson 2013).

The socioeconomic gap widened over time so much that indigent and uninsured persons with mental illness were increasingly served by the criminal justice system—but only after they decompensated or their situation became dire and their need serious enough to where they became a danger to themselves or to others.

How or Why Does a Person Mentally Decompensate?

Mental illness is thought to be a result of a chemical imbalance in the brain, of a deficiency and/or an excess of certain neurotransmitters such as dopamine and serotonin. The type of mental illness that a person has is largely determined by the type and amount of brain chemicals already present and a person's coping ability to handle stressful situations. The biological component is a tendency to be a certain way and runs in families. So mental illness has both a biological component that can predetermine certain tendencies and a behavioral component that is determined by one's environment.

When a person mentally decompensates, symptoms of the mental illness come to the surface and become very evident, usually in response to a triggering event or a series of stressful situations. With some people, their thinking often becomes disconnected and irrational; others may be prone to mood swings; a third group may become psychotic and fearful because they see or hear things that aren't really there. Some people can even trigger these kinds of episodes through the continual use or abuse of certain drugs and alcohol, which can affect people in different ways.

A person who becomes prone to continued episodes can show signs of unclear or even irrational thinking. The difficulties of street life, the tendency not to comply with medication dosages, and the problems associated with impaired mental functioning often result in displays of eccentric behavior. Acting in an odd way, such as yelling loudly while running down the middle of a busy street is not criminal per se, but this kind of behavior places homeless mentally ill people in direct conflict with societal norms. As a result, they are frequently involved with the criminal justice system. In many states, unless individuals are suicidal or homicidal, state hospitals will not admit them without a series of tests and court hearings.

When Does Mental Illness Start?

The mainstream accepted understanding of mental illness is that it manifests itself from a biological predisposition in combination with environmental factors. Some individuals are born with a chemical imbalance in the brain or with certain personality factors or tendencies to develop mental illness. Individuals who are mentally ill usually have other family members who also suffer from the same illness, and that biological predisposition is passed through the genes. However, many **serious mental illnesses** (e.g., bipolar disorder, schizophrenia, major depression, obsessive-compulsive, and other anxiety disorders) also become apparent when environmental stressors increase, such as during the passage to adulthood when people begin to work full-time, go to college, start a family, and live independently. Some people are more capable of handling stress or pressure than others, and this difference may be tied to how the brain is hardwired.

Serious mental illness: disorders of the brain that affect thinking and behavior and that are identified by the Diagnostic and Statistical Manual of the American Psychological Association

About 17 percent of jail inmates suffer from a serious mental health problem that requires medication. Box 13.2 includes examples of questions that may be asked to screen people for possible mental health problems.

People with long-standing mental health problems at early ages are more likely to have lived in a foster home or juvenile institution. As adults, people with mental health issues who also end up in jail are less likely to hold a job and more likely to have been homeless in the year before their incarceration (James and Glaze 2006).

Mentally ill people are often more of a danger to themselves than to others. The biggest problem is that our nation's jails were not designed as mental health facilities, yet there are more individuals with mental health problems in jails than there are in the mental health system itself. Arthur Lurigio believes that the disproportionate number of mentally ill persons within the criminal justice system is a combination of residential instability, living in "impoverished environments that exert pressures on them to become engaged in criminal behavior," and "punitive crime control policies and the war on drugs" (2011: 13, 11). This situation certainly seems to be a common one for other groups of people already mentioned in this chapter.

| Box 13.2 | **Mental Health Screening Questions (Yes/No Responses)** |

1. Do you get annoyed when friends or family complain about their problems? Or do people complain that you're not sympathetic to their problems?
2. Have you ever tried to avoid reminders, or to not think about, something you experienced or witnessed?
3. Some people find their mood changes frequently—as if they spend every day on an emotional roller coaster. For example, they might switch from feeling angry to depressed to anxious many times a day. Does this sound like you?
4. Have there ever been a few weeks when you've felt like you were useless, or sinful, or guilty?
5. How much of the time do you feel depressed most of the day? *(Yes = depressed mood most of the day or more than half the time)*
6. Do you find that most people will take advantage of you if you let them know too much about you?
7. Have you ever been troubled by repeated thoughts, feelings, or nightmares about something you experienced or witnessed?
8. Have you ever been in the hospital for non-medical reasons, such as in a psychiatric hospital?

SOURCE: Ford and Trestman 2005.

Only one in six jail inmates with a mental health problem received treatment since their admission to jail (James and Glaze 2006). Instead of treatment, it is more often the case that a person with a mental illness who ends up in the criminal justice system will be convicted and serve jail time. Common offenses that mentally ill people are arrested for include traffic violations, disorderly conduct, trespassing, minor property crimes, drug possession, and assault (Etter, Birzer, and Fields 2008). Mentally ill offenders often receive sentences up to four times longer than regular inmates for the same crime (Gonzales and Davak 2006).

Correctional System Responses to Persons with Mental Illness

Community-based centers and jail diversion programs used in conjunction with **crisis intervention teams** seem to be the best option for mentally ill offenders. Diversion programs combine community correctional supervision with mental health treatment without the stress of the jail environment. Crisis intervention teams consist of a social worker and a police officer who are specially trained in interacting with persons with mental illnesses. The team is able to more effectively communicate and gain compliance with a person who may be in crisis, such as a person who is having a panic attack or may be suffering from post-traumatic

Crisis intervention teams:

teams that include a specially trained social worker and police officer who work together to respond to dispatched police calls when the perpetrator may be showing signs of mental distress or has a history of mental illness

stress disorder. The goal of the team is to offer clients supervision and treatment services without spending undue time in jail. The defendant can also receive help for addiction/substance abuse, housing placement, and medication regimens, which are common needs with this population (Matejkowski 2011). Within 72 hours of arrest, clients can enter the program through referrals from police, the magistrate court, or the county jail. In partnership with the mental health court judge, these centers can supervise individuals until their next court date. Diversion from jail to community-based services has reduced the number of days in jail and has also reduced offending behaviors and arrests in the 12 months after their diversion from the prior 12 months (Alarid and Rubin 2013; Case et al. 2009). Up to this point, we have discussed why various groups of people enter prison or become incarcerated in disproportionate numbers. The next section examines the ways inmates get out of prison, as well as the challenges that prisoners face when reentering the community.

LEAVING PRISON AND REENTERING THE COMMUNITY

Prison sentence lengths vary considerably for each individual, but about 95 percent to 97 percent of prisoners will leave prison at some point in their lives. About one in five will leave prison after serving the maximum time on their sentence. Once this happens, the prisoners have no obligations to report to anyone for post-release supervision. This is known as **unconditional release**. The ex-felon is simply free to go.

Most prisoners are released under some form of post-release supervision in the community. **Supervised mandatory release** is the most common form and includes the automatic release of inmates after serving a certain percentage of time in prison (e.g., 85 percent) or once the maximum prison sentence has been completed. The release date is dictated by law rather than by a committee. Post-release supervision is for a certain period of time (usually one to two years). This form of release came about as a way to equalize the release dates based solely on amount of time served and not according to the vote of a politicized parole board. Prior to mandatory release, most states relied on the experience and judgments of a **parole board**, whose members are appointed by the state governor. All parole boards review the case files of eligible prisoners, and in some states, they meet face to face with the prisoner. If the board members agree that a person should be released on parole, they set a future parole date. The next sections trace how parole began and why many states switched over in the 1980s from discretionary parole to mandatory release.

Unconditional release:
when a prisoner leaves a correctional institution after completing his or her entire sentence behind bars and there is no period of post-release supervision

Supervised mandatory release:
legislatively defined release from prison once a prisoner has completed the mandatory minimum time on his or her sentence

Parole board:
a politically appointed group that meets regularly to review files of prisoners who are eligible for early release

History of Parole

Parole began on the other side of the world in a place called Norfolk Island, which was British-owned and is located off the coast of Australia. Norfolk Island was the British Alcatraz, because it was known to house the most violent and incorrigible prisoners. During the mid-1800s, the inmates were subjected to severe beatings and harsh physical labor (Morris 2002). Captain Alexander Maconochie was hired to keep the prisoners in line. Instead, he created and tested a behavioral modification system called the marks system. Prisoners who remained out of trouble and fully participated in work and education programs were credited with a single tally every day they complied. Marks could be removed for disciplinary violations or refusing to participate in labor. Once an individual prisoner accumulated enough marks, he was released early from the island (Morris 2002). When word got back to England that Maconochie had also abolished corporal punishment and chain gangs, he was fired and replaced with a different superintendent who resumed the beatings and severe discipline.

The important point of Maconochie's four-year experiment (1836-1840) was that it worked to change the behavior of even the most incorrigible prisoners, who were able to obtain a ticket-of-leave and obtain freedom. While under a ticket-of-leave, releasees were expected to keep the police informed of their whereabouts but were not under any formal supervision. Some prisoners chose to remain on Norfolk, residing and growing crops on the other side of the island.

Maconochie's efforts also drew attention from other prison superintendents, such as Sir Walter Crofton, director of the Irish prison system. Crofton developed a system of increasing privileges known as the **Irish system**. Prisoners under the Irish system began their first three months in solitary confinement and were not allowed to work or comingle with the general population. During months four through ten, inmates were still subjected to solitary confinement but were allowed to work. After the tenth month, the inmate was transferred to the general population and could begin earning marks, which would eventually earn his or her release.

Irish system: mid-19th-century system credited to Sir Walter Crofton that emphasized reformation and increased freedom over time

Parole in the United States

Superintendent Zebulon Brockway adopted the ideas of Maconochie and Crofton at his new prison institution in Elmira, New York. In 1876, Brockway implemented an indeterminate sentence and encouraged positive behavior through sentence reductions via good time. Citizen volunteers supervised inmates released early from Elmira. A secondary but important effect of early release, Brockway found, was that it was easier to control the prison population size by releasing some prisoners early to make room for new arrivals. Parole had the effect of increasing prisoner conformity to prison rules, was an incentive for prisoners to rehabilitate themselves, and could be used as a population-reduction strategy. After the indeterminate sentence and parole had been successfully implemented at Elmira, they became the dominant philosophy with the courts and correctional systems throughout the United States.

Indeterminate sentencing left the release date open to the parole boards, who then decided when a prisoner was rehabilitated. The parole board recognized that people change at different rates; some were in transition faster than others and required less time, while others who were more reluctant to change served longer sentences. Prisoners soon realized that they had to convince the parole board that they had been rehabilitated and show evidence of classes they completed and certificates earned. By the mid-1970s, there was widespread concern that with recidivism rates increasing, parole boards might not really know who had genuinely changed and who was just trying to "play the game" to convince the board to get released. With an unknown release date, some offenders spent many more years behind bars than their crimes warranted and it became a question of fairness. It was thought that parole boards were ill equipped to make prison-release decisions since many of the parole boards at that time were composed of political appointees with little knowledge of or experience in dealing with convicts.

Another criticism centered on a perceived lack of effectiveness of prison treatment programs. In 1974, Robert Martinson published a short piece in the *Public Interest* to communicate his disdain for prison as a sanction. Instead of readers being convinced of his cause, the media focused on Martinson's criticisms of prison treatment programs. Martinson concluded, "With few and isolated exceptions, the rehabilitative efforts that have been reported so far had no appreciable effect on recidivism" (1974: 25). Even though Martinson later recanted those statements, the damage had already been done. It seemed that the Martinson study (which was now termed "the Nothing Works study") was used by conservative policy makers as evidence that we needed to get tougher on prisoners and remove prison treatment programs, which was the exact opposite of what Martinson had originally intended.

Change to Determinate Sentencing

In the 1980s, many states revised their sentencing laws and began using a new philosophy of sentencing called determinate sentencing (defined in Chapter 9) or a combination of indeterminate and determinate sentencing. You may recall that the new sentencing policies include mandatory minimums, three-strikes laws, and sentencing guidelines. Some states, such as Minnesota, used determinate sentencing for all felony crimes, while nearly half of all states used determinate sentencing for violent crimes or crimes against a person and retained the use of parole for nonviolent crimes. The federal correctional system and states that had decided to use determinate sentencing for all felony crimes eliminated their parole boards and replaced parole with supervised mandatory release. Mandatory release is still a form of community supervision, but it is based on the percentage of time served instead of whether a prisoner has been rehabilitated. Generally speaking, states that decided to eliminate their parole boards also eliminated any chance of reducing their prison populations through early release. Thus, determinate-sentencing states experienced a huge influx of prisoners who were required by statute to remain in prison until their time was served. A small number of determinate-sentencing states later had to reinstate discretionary release because the prisons became too crowded.

In the wake of the Martinson (1974) article, indeterminate sentencing states that retained parole boards established minimum standards for board members. In the 1980s and 1990s, parole boards began to use quantitative scoring instruments to help them assess future risk. Assessment tools helped the parole board to become more objective in their decision making. Factors that the parole board considers include current offense, prior record, conduct while incarcerated, and participation in treatment programs where applicable.

Parole Supervision

Once the parole board decides the inmate is ready to be released, a field officer will visit the residential address where the parolee will be living to check that the address is legitimate. The field officer also ensures that the individuals at this address agree to have the former felon living with them and agree to have a parole officer visit their home and conduct searches if necessary. Sometimes there are other stipulations, such as no weapons in the home or no consumption of alcohol or drugs by *anyone* at the address where the parolee is living. As you are probably thinking right now, might this infringe on the other individuals in the household? Having a parolee (or probationer) living at another individual's home does indeed limit the actions of everyone living at that address, and for that reason, some family members refuse. If parolees have nowhere to live, they can be sent to a homeless shelter or halfway house to secure more permanent living arrangements.

Once offenders are released from prison, they must report to their assigned parole officer within 24 hours. At that first visit, the rules and conditions are explained, and the offender must sign the **parole agreement/order**. Parole conditions are nearly identical to those for probationers (see Chapter 10 for a list of probation conditions). In fact, parole is so similar to probation in how it is implemented that many jurisdictions have simply assigned both probation and parole clients to the same officer. Of course, parolees will naturally be supervised more intensely than probationers because they pose a higher risk, but the foundation of supervision and documentation is the same. Both parolees and probationers spend an average of between one and two years on supervision.

Parole agreement/ order: terms and conditions set by the parole board to which the parolee agrees during the first meeting with his or her parole officer

Parole Revocation

A parole officer is responsible for monitoring offender behavior, and for documenting technical violations. When the number of technical violations becomes excessive, a parole officer can choose to file a revocation with the parole board. If the parolee commits a new crime, a parole officer must automatically report this to the parole board, which makes the final decision on whether to return the parolee to prison or some other community-based sanction. Options that parole boards consider include day reporting centers and halfway houses or other residential community facilities. If incarceration is inevitable, some states limit the amount of time that can be served for a revocation. For example, Kentucky parole officers can decide, without going through a formal revocation proceeding, to incarcerate a technical violator for up to 30 days per every 365-day period on parole (Vera Institute of Justice 2010).

Formal revocations require that the parolee have a two-stage hearing. First, the preliminary hearing notifies the parolee of the charges and allows the parolee time to put together a defense and witnesses. Most parolees are incarcerated and unable to freely contact witnesses, so many parolees waive the preliminary hearing and proceed straight to the revocation hearing. During the revocation hearing, the Supreme Court said in the case of *Morrissey v. Brewer* (1972) that a parolee is entitled to:

1. Written notice of the charges
2. Disclosure of evidence against him or her
3. The opportunity to be heard in person and to present witnesses and evidence

4. The right to confront and cross-examine witnesses against the parolee
5. A neutral and detached hearing body
6. A written statement after the hearing as to the evidence relied on and reason(s) for revoking parole

Since parole is a privilege and not a right, a parolee is not provided with an attorney or a jury, and there is no privilege against self-incrimination. In effect, parolees must defend themselves and must answer all questions posed to them during the revocation hearing.

Because of the cost and time in filing and proceeding with revocations, parole departments have favored graduated community-based sanctions for technical violations and incarceration for new crimes. Parole departments also recognize the importance of increasing the quality of each visit rather than have each experience filled with negativity and fear. This means that parole officers are being trained more in how to establish rapport, how to increase motivation with their clients, and how to use positive reinforcement with rewards and incentives.

DOES INCARCERATION WORK?

With the millions of dollars spent on our correctional system every year, we should be asking ourselves if what we are spending is worth it. Are we achieving what we had hoped?

Deterrence Versus Incapacitation

The theory of deterrence suggests that a punitive response to crime will serve as an example to keep others from committing crime. It also suggests that those who endure the incarceration experience will learn from their painful mistakes and pursue a different course in the future. The theory of incapacitation says that keeping identified criminals behind bars will prevent those who are most dangerous from committing crimes in the community, but only while they are incarcerated. Both theories suggest that more prisons will ultimately reduce crime. But do these theories really work this way in practice?

The answer to this question is complex because no two states are exactly alike—each state, in effect, has its own correctional system. Some states have a low incarceration rate (per 100,000 population), but when they choose to incarcerate someone, the prisoner will serve a long sentence, most likely for a violent crime. States such as Hawaii, New York, Massachusetts, and Wisconsin tend to practice an incapacitation strategy (Spelman 2000). Other states, such as Alabama,

Georgia, Mississippi, and North Carolina, have a high incarceration rate, where many people have the prison experience, but judges give shorter sentences in hopes of maximizing deterrence. To muddy the waters a bit more, some states have more flexible release policies with indeterminate sentences, while others are more rigid with automatic releases based on determinate sentences (Spelman 2000). But when asked this question in a more general way, Michael Tonry (2004) provided persuasive evidence that severe punishment has had little effect overall on decreasing crime rates.

Recidivism

A primary goal in the correctional system seems to be minimizing offenders' recidivism while under supervision and changing the course of their lives after supervision ends. Research has compared felons who were sentenced to prison with those sentenced to probation. Those who had been incarcerated experienced a greater likelihood of recidivism in the future than those who were sentenced to probation (Freiburger and Iannacchione 2011; Spohn 2007; Spohn and Holleran 2000). Also, the length of time spent in prison did not seem to make a difference with respect to recidivism. Recidivism rates were the highest with young, single male prisoners who were convicted of a drug offense, had an untreated drug addiction, and had several prior convictions (Spohn 2007; Spohn and Holleran 2000). By contrast, drug treatment has been shown to be effective if used with people who have the desire to change.

Where does that leave us with respect to the correctional system? For one, we cannot build our way out of the prison problem. No matter how many people we incarcerate, punishment alone is not the answer. Despite recent declines in the prisoner population, the United States continues to use incarceration as a response to crime more than most other countries in the world. We must rethink our punishment strategies and combine them with treatment modalities that work for long-term solutions.

SUMMARY

This chapter examines five important issues in corrections including racial/ethnic disparities in prison, gender and correctional treatment, persons with mental illnesses in the corrections system, community reentry after a prison sentence, and the longer-term effect of imprisonment with respect to deterrence and recidivism.

Racial/ethnic disproportionality in prison can be explained by a combination of historical factors, differences in the extent of involvement in violent crime, system discrimination, and drug sentencing policies that together contribute to this difference. Disproportionate minority contact became a priority when the National Coalition for Juvenile Justice brought to congressional attention the disproportionately high number of children of Hispanic and African American descent being institutionalized in residential facilities.

Part of the explanation for more African American males in prison is that this group engages in more violent felony offenses and continues offending behavior for a longer time than males of other racial groups, so incarceration is more likely to be the outcome. Racial bias still exists in the system. When crime seriousness is equalized, African American individuals were *still* more likely to be incarcerated than whites or Hispanics.

Women have different pathways to criminal behavior than men: They become involved as victims of sexual and/or emotional abuse, which leads to substance abuse, or they become involved in relationships with men who are involved in criminal activity. Correctional treatment for women should address issues of trauma, neglect, and empowerment.

Mental illness manifests itself from a biological predisposition combined with environmental stressors. The presence of a disproportionate number of mentally ill persons within the criminal justice system is a combination of residential instability, living in impoverished environments that exert pressure to become engaged in criminal behavior, and punitive crime control policies. Community-based centers and jail diversion programs are the best option for mentally ill offenders because they combine supervision with mental health treatment without the stress of the jail environment.

Captain Alexander Maconochie created and tested a behavioral modification system called the marks system on Norfolk Island. This same system was successfully used in Ireland by Sir Walter Crofton and in the United States by Zebulon Brockway. Parole was the primary method of release from an indeterminate sentence. Parole helped to increase prisoner conformity to prison rules, it was an incentive for prisoners to rehabilitate themselves, and it could be used as a population-reduction strategy. Following the criticism of correctional treatment programs, many states revised their sentencing laws to determinate sentencing and abolished parole boards. Formal parole revocations require a preliminary hearing followed by a revocation hearing, where the parolee is afforded minimal due process rights.

The final topic was whether incarceration had a deterrent effect. While each state in the United States has different laws, severe punishment without treatment has had little effect overall on decreasing crime rates. The length of time spent in prison did not seem to make a difference with respect to recidivism. Recidivism rates were the highest with young, single male prisoners who were convicted of a drug offense, had an untreated drug addiction, and had several prior convictions. Reduced recidivism has had more success with cognitive-behavioral treatment than with prison alone.

REVIEW QUESTIONS

1. What potential solutions do you have for reducing the number of minority juveniles in residential facilities?
2. Would the solutions to reduce minority representation for juveniles be the same for adults? Why or why not?
3. What kinds of gender-specific programs might be the most helpful for women, given their previous experiences?
4. Why do people with mental illnesses end up in the corrections system?
5. What challenges might there be to incarcerate someone with a mental illness?
6. What alternatives to incarceration might be most beneficial for the mentally ill who can work?
7. What reentry challenges do people face when they first leave prison?
8. If you were a parole board member, what kinds of questions might you ask to ensure the prisoner is ready to be released?
9. Would you support building more prisons to increase the prison population if (hypothetically) you knew that for every 1,000 more inmates you put in prison, crime rates would go down by 0.5 percent?
10. Given the known research on prison and deterrence discussed in this chapter, what other creative ways to reduce crime might you suggest?

KEY TERMS

crisis intervention teams
disproportionate minority contact
gender-specific programs
Irish system
parole agreement/order
parole board
sentencing disparity
serious mental illness
supervised mandatory release
unconditional release

PART V

Criminal Justice in the 21st Century

CHAPTER 14

The Future of Criminal Justice: Making Sense of It All

LEARNING OBJECTIVES

At the conclusion of this chapter, you should be able to:

- Appreciate the complexities of the possible questions and answers that confront the future of criminal justice in the United States.

- Understand why a global perspective is necessary to frame these questions and develop adequate answers.

- Describe what it is about the criminal justice system's possible futures that interests you and why.

- Make better sense of the connections between the seemingly disparate parts of the nation's criminal justice system.

341

INTRODUCTION

As should be apparent by now, the administration of justice in the United States is a major and complex enterprise involving tens of millions of offenders and hundreds of thousands of criminal justice system personnel, along with annual expenditures that run into the billions of dollars. In closing our examination of crime, criminals and justice, we first provide a brief general review of six selected components of the system, followed by a single topical issue related to each element that is likely to continue being problematic for decades to come. We also frame this discussion in terms of each of the topical issues and the notion of globalization.

According to Nayef Al-Rodhan and Gerard Stoudmann, **globalization** is "a process that encompasses the causes, course, and consequences of transnational and transcultural integration of human and non-human activities" (2006: 2). Globalization is important because the distances between nations and continents are shrinking, not only with respect to the time it takes to move about them but also in terms of the interdependence among the nations of the world (Larsson 2001). This chapter reviews six areas about which there is a great deal of consensus as to their relevancy in the 21st century as domestic and global issues.

Globalization: the interconnectivity of modern life around the world, including all aspects of culture, from industry and economics to crime and justice

MAKING SENSE OF GLOBAL CRIME

Globalists make two main distinctions between types of crimes, differences that frame our understanding about which ones are likely to come to the attention of the U.S. criminal justice system. As Mangai Natarjan (2005) observes, **international crime** refers to criminal activities that threaten world order and security. Crimes against international law include offenses such as crimes against humanity, war crimes, and genocide.[1] Such crimes are of little significance to the administration of justice in the United States, no matter how heinous they may be. Perhaps the only time that the U.S. criminal justice system must deal with such acts is when a person accused of them resides inside the nation's borders, meaning that some agency with the appropriate jurisdiction is called on to detain or arrest the suspect, pending extradition and transport to another legal jurisdiction. That entity may be the nation where the crimes allegedly were committed or the International Criminal Court in the Hague, a permanent judicial body established in 2002 by the Rome Statute, of which there are currently 122 signatories. All of the cases tried in the first decade of the ICC's existence have involved nations from Africa (International Criminal Court, n.d.).

International crime: criminal activities that threaten world order and security; includes crimes against humanity, war crimes, and genocide

The second form is **transnational crime**, which is crime than spans the boundaries and laws of two or more nations. Philip Reichel (2008:

Transnational crime: "ordinary" crime (i.e., not international crime) that spans the boundaries and laws of two or more nations

44-59) suggests that nine transnational crimes are important to criminal justice practitioners worldwide. Box 14.1 summarizes these crimes. The key difference to keep in mind is that international crime is generally viewed by the world at large as a threat to international social order and even world peace (e.g., waging war as a crime against humanity), whereas transnational crime may not even be a crime in the country where the activity originates or through which the criminals pass on their way to the target nation, where the activity is clearly a crime. For the act to be a transnational crime, two of the affected nations must classify some aspect of the activity as a crime.

Box 14.1 Globalized Justice: Transnational Crime

The following lists nine forms of transnational crime:

- **Cybercrime** ranges from attempts to extort or otherwise defraud victims of money via unsolicited e-mails on the Internet to sophisticated computer hacking of bank and electronic funds transfer records. Thanks to the Internet, nearly all such acts are transnational crimes since most communications that travel on it spend some time—if only a millisecond—in another nation. Some nations in Eastern Europe and Africa are infamous as sources of computer-based fraud attempts.

- **Corruption and bribery of public officials, party officials, and elected representatives** must involve the officials of one nation and legal residents of a second one. Not all nations around the globe define this activity criminal or see it as a serious problem, although even in those nations, corruption and bribery of persons in public life threaten the legitimacy of the government itself and erode confidence in public institutions, including the police and courts.

- **Illegal drug trafficking** goes far beyond the economic concerns associated with such activities. There are also collateral damages that include health risks, such as deaths, hepatitis, and AIDS/HIV, as well as erosion of confidence in social and political institutions intended to protect citizens from criminals. As previously mentioned, the drugs in question must be illegal in at least two of the nations affected by the trafficking activities for it to be transnational crime.

- **Money laundering** occurs whenever someone in one nation engages in activities intended to hide the origin or destination of funds or negotiable monetary instruments with someone in another nation. "Dirty" money enters at one end of the process, and "clean" money comes out the other end. In the past, money-laundering investigations were limited to the proceeds of illicit activities; however, in recent years, the focus has broadened to include financially linked activities deemed in support of criminal actions, including terrorism and corruption.

Cybercrime/computer crime:
any criminal activity that requires or employs the use of a computing device; may also use various communications networks, including the Internet, in their commission

Corruption:
dishonest or fraudulent behavior by a person in power; often involves bribery

Bribery:
an act that generally involves the exchange of something of value (e.g., money) for someone to do something

Illicit drug trafficking/ illegal drug trade:
global black market or illegal economy that cultivates, manufactures, distributes and sells drugs that are subject to lawful governmental control

Money laundering:
crime that occurs when one party engages in activities intended to hide the origins or destination of funds or negotiable monetary instruments

(continued)

Box 14.1 Continued

- **Sea piracy**, defined as the apprehension, boarding, and robbery of vessels and/or persons at sea, has declined since the early 2000s. However, the statistics on piracy reflect reported incidents, and there is reason to believe that many ship owners simply take care of the matter "off the books," meaning they pay off the pirates and do not report them through official channels.
- **Crimes against cultural heritage** occur when someone illegally obtains archeological or artistic objects that are part of a nation's cultural legacy and transports them to a second nation. Such crimes are common in times of armed conflict. We know little about the theft of art and cultural objects.
- **Human organ trafficking** is a growing transnational crime, whether they are obtained legally or illegally.[2] In this area, it is clearly a case of supply and demand; the supply of legally obtained human organs cannot keep up with the demand for them, and crime is often one result.
- **Trafficking in persons** is the transportation of human beings, usually for the purposes of involuntary servitude or slavery, across international boundaries.[3] Sex trafficking is a form of human trafficking. These activities are sometimes confused with human smuggling, which rarely involves the level of deception or coercion associated with human trafficking. To cloud the issue further, some "migrants" may think that they are being smuggled, only to discover when they arrive at their destination that they have been trafficked or sold into virtual slavery.
- **Terrorism** is the use of unlawful actions to achieve sociopolitical ends. Terrorism includes acts of violence, whether by a weapon of mass destruction or a handgun; it could be an economic act, such as cyberattacks on a nation's business infrastructure; it could be a symbolic act, such as hacking a government website or strategically placing graffiti supporting the overthrow of the duly constituted government. One person's terrorist, however, could be someone else's freedom fighter or revolutionary.

Sea piracy:
the apprehension, boarding, and robbery of vessels and/or persons at sea

Crimes against cultural heritage:
the theft of art and other cultural objects that are considered part of a nation's patrimony or property left to the nation by its forbearers

Human organ trafficking:
the for-profit, commercial trade in internal human body organs for transplantation

Trafficking in persons:
the transportation of human beings, usually for the purposes of involuntary servitude or slavery, across international boundaries; generally involves coercion or deception at some point

Terrorism:
a violent act or series of acts that is intended to instill high levels of fear, intimidation, and anxiety in the general population or to influence public policy or effect changes in government; can involve assassination, warlike activities, mass destruction, or kidnapping

SOURCES: Ambagtsheer and Weimar 2012; Arnold 2005; Financial Action Task Force 2013; Frulli 2011; Hippen 2008; International Chamber of Commerce 2013; Liss 2003; Livingstone 2002; Loughman and Sibery 2012; National Heritage Board of Poland 2011; United Nations Global Initiative to Fight Human Trafficking, n.d.; United Nations Office on Drugs and Crime 2013; Wall 2007.

Focal Issue: International Cooperation

The international crime picture comes from many sources. Three are worthy of review. The first is the senior member of the international crime-fighting community, the **International Criminal Police Organization**, better known as **INTERPOL**. Established in 1923, INTERPOL's primary goal is to provide technical and informational

International Criminal Police Organization (INTERPOL):
a treaty-based organization consisting of 190 member nations dedicated to the suppression and reduction of crime on a global scale

support to its 190 member nations, which include the United States, where the FBI headquarters in the District of Columbia is the contact agency. As Article 2 of its constitution states, INTERPOL seeks "[t]o establish and develop all institutions likely to contribute effectively to the prevention and suppression of ordinary law crimes." Included in these ordinary law crimes are all nine of the key criminal activities, as well as crimes against children, firearms crimes, environmental crimes, pharmaceutical crimes, vehicle crimes, and illicit goods trafficking and counterfeiting. One of its better-known activities is fugitive investigations, which include so-called INTERPOL red notices that can help member nations locate, arrest, and detain wanted persons.

Also at the international level is the **United Nations Office on Drugs and Crime (UNODC)**, an entity that is part of the United Nations. Established in 1997, UNODC is a partnership between the UN Drug Control Programme and the Centre for International Crime Prevention; it is headquartered in Vienna, Austria. UNODC includes as topical areas all nine of the transnational crime areas, as well as international firearms trafficking, wildlife and forest crimes, fraudulent medicines, HIV/AIDS, and general crime prevention (see United Nations Office on Drugs and Crime, n.d.).

Finally, beyond its participation in INTERPOL and UNODC, the U.S. government, through the State Department operates the Bureau of International Narcotics and Law Enforcement Affairs (INL) as a conduit to participating nations that receive a broad range of crime-fighting services and related information. INL maintains a presence in embassies worldwide and participates in the International Law Enforcement Academy training centers around the globe, the latter intended to strengthen participant nations' criminal justice systems. Its overall focus is the reduction of international drug trafficking and transnational crime. INL works toward these goals through a broad agenda that includes synchronizing efforts of various U.S. law enforcement agencies. The bureau also provides technical support to partner nations, defined as those countries that have signed formal agreements with the U.S. State Department.

Effective transnational partnerships are essential for any nation that seeks to protect its homeland from either domestic or international terrorists. Both types of terrorist groups have close associations with organized crime groups. Trafficking routes, whether the cargo is drugs or people, are the same routes also followed by terrorists of all stripes. Terrorists commit crimes, including all forms of trafficking and sea piracy, to finance their agendas and instill terror. This is a new world, and if the student of criminal justice is to understand fully the nature of crime and justice, a global perspective is not a value-added component; it is a necessity. Hence, throughout this textbook, we have embedded international examples of criminal justice polices,

United Nations Office on Drugs and Crime (UNODC): located in Vienna, Austria, and dedicated to assisting the UN in combating interrelated issues of illicit trafficking in and abuse of drugs, crime prevention and criminal justice, international terrorism, and political corruption

practices, and procedures to give you a sense of what globalization means for criminal justice in the 21st century.

MAKING SENSE OF JUSTICE

In the first chapter of this book, you learned that there are several ways to define justice. Furthermore, two people can look at the same socio-legal situation and disagree over whether justice exists. Take the shooting of Trayvon Martin by George Zimmerman. The facts were clear: Zimmerman shot and killed Martin. What was in dispute was whether Zimmerman was criminally liable for the shooting. After the Florida jury returned a not guilty verdict for Zimmerman, there were intense arguments around the country over whether justice was really served in this case. Fundamentally, the differences in perspective can result from race, age, gender, and socioeconomic status. They can also result from disagreements over the particular philosophy that guides the administration of justice in the United States.

For a just society to function, fundamental processes must operate and be directed at a common goal. These are the forces that shape a nation's responses to crime and criminals, as reflected in its justice system. What is it, we must ask, that a society's formal legal mechanisms and processes wish to achieve? Is it sufficient to punish and exclude offenders so that they serve as examples for others who might consider engaging in similar acts? Such motivations might have sufficed when communities were far simpler or when the intra-societal differences were minimal. However, in a complex, multilay-ered nation, pushing people to the fringes may more or less perma-nently exclude them from engaging in the mainstream of society. This may ultimately create a situation that threatens the stability of the whole society. For example, convicted felons often lose the right to vote, may not hold certain jobs, or find themselves excluded from certain entitlement lists for life. Again, look back at the disproportion-ate minority contact issues discussed in earlier chapters if this idea does not resonate with you. Moreover, how do we balance the rights of the various interest groups in a society? How do we guarantee civil liberties and associated freedoms in the post-9/11 world? It is no easy task to balance the fundamental values of a democracy with the very real concerns of safety and security, both from internal and external threats.

No one said this was an easy exercise. Go back to Chapter 1 if you doubt that is the case. Consider the history of the justice apparatuses that we have reviewed in this text. What did justice mean in ancient

Mesopotamia? What did in mean in ancient Rome or Greece? How did the rulers of a small village in medieval France or England view their role in defining justice for those under their power? What was the meaning of justice in ancient China before the rise of its powerful ruling families? What did justice look like when blood or marriage linked everyone in a community? These are more than rhetorical questions. Answers to them may inform our search for a guiding philosophy of justice for the 21st century.

So many questions, so few answers. What is clear, however, is that there is a groundswell movement throughout the nation that is questioning the philosophy of retributive justice and its accompanying system of punitive harm. We need something else, claim the experts. What could that be? Is some agency, somewhere in the world, already addressing the issue?

Focal Issue: Searching for a 21st-Century Guiding Philosophy

As discussed previously, one of the oldest philosophies associated with punishment is that of retribution, or punishment for the sake of punishment. During the first part of the 20th century, retribution fell out of favor and was replaced with "modern" approaches to deal with accused and convicted offenders, including treatment and rehabilitation. However, beginning in the 1980s, a neo-retributionist movement began in the United States; once again, it became popular to take the stance that "if you do the crime, you do the time."

The result of this get-tough orientation—combined with the "just deserts" approach (see Fogel 1975)—was that sentences were lengthened, more people were sent to prison, and the costs associated with punishment spiraled upward. Funding at the federal level increased to add 100,000 new police officers to departments at all levels throughout the United States. State and local governments also increased the capacities of prisons and jails to accommodate the expanding offender populations. The result has been that we have created an expensive justice system that we cannot sustain forever at this level based simply on costs alone.

Therefore, as we move toward the middle of the 21st century, people of all political persuasions—Democrats and Republicans, liberals and conservatives—are advocating a different approach to crime. The new catchphrase is that rather than being tough on crime, we need to be "smart on crime." While that phrase does not tell us about the particular policies we might pursue, it does recognize that continually getting tougher does not seem to work in terms of reducing crime and controlling costs. This means that the future of the justice system in the United States is likely to emphasize the continued partnerships between the police and the community, reparations for crime victims, holding offenders accountable, and providing former offenders with the skills and abilities they need to live productive lives. These skill sets focus primarily on increasing employment opportunities, enhancing coping strategies for conflict resolution, and reducing drug and alcohol dependence. Interestingly, offender accountability and victim reparation are among the elements associated with the balanced and restorative justice (BARJ) approach for juveniles (Office of Juvenile Justice and Delinquency Prevention, n.d.).

Whatever philosophy we pursue and whatever label we put on it, public safety is at the foundation of the justice system. However, the United States clearly is looking for solutions to crime and criminality that are both effective (producing the desired outcome) *and* affordable. No one knows for sure what that will look like, but the next decade is likely to produce a new or newly packaged guiding philosophy for the administration of justice in this country. However, we have gained a sense from other nations as to how restorative justice models operate, including the two examples provided in Box 14.2.

MAKING SENSE OF POLICING

We find the origins of policing in the use of what were essentially military forces or auxiliaries to maintain social order in emerging city-states and extended empires. No longer could the populace "police" itself. Rather, what the community needed was a professional force, regulated by the state that could provide safety, protect commerce, and create a sense of stability and peace. The fact that the police often first served their masters and then the people was not lost on either the police or those being policed. For more than 5,000 years, the individuals who policed a given geopolitical area were largely an extension of the local government, responding to its needs, and often serving a paramilitary function, sometimes fully militarized in time of war. Only in the past 1,000 years or less, and then mainly through its ties to the civil government of England and eventually Great Britain, did the practice of a nonmilitary police emerge. Thus, the police have served and continue to serve both civilian and military functions in most historical and contemporary societies.

Some critics view the police in the United States (and perhaps around the world) as being reactionaries with strong ties to the status quo. Studies of the personality types working in policing show a strong

Box 14.2   Globalized Justice: Restorative Justice Practices in the United Kingdom

As previously observed (Box 1.1), restorative justice (RJ) is one of the oldest models of justice practices and one of the most resilient, as it has resurfaced not just as an anthropological anomaly in studies of Stone Age people living in the 21st century but also as a viable alternative to other more repressive models of justice. The theoretical basis of RJ is **reintegrative shaming**, a practice that emphasizes working with crime victims or their families, offenders and, where possible, their families, and other representatives of the community, to achieve agreement on the best way to move the offender back into the community. **Disintegrative shaming** makes examples of offenders (e.g., deterrence) or makes them pay for their crimes (e.g., just deserts), thereby pushing stigmatized offenders to the fringe of society and beyond.

RJ practices can begin as early as the beginning of justice processing—at detention or arrest (restorative policing) or prior to prisoner reentry (restorative corrections). The UK has embraced RJ at both ends of the spectrum. Some 33 different police agencies across the UK have adopted RJ-based practices for handling many types of offenses. Initially limited to minor offenses for youths and adults, recent changes have extended the practices to serious offending by persistent offenders. The idea is to engage the public, in this case the local community, with the police in determining the proper approach to take when confronted with certain "qualified" offenses and offenders. The specific approach ranges from conferences and mediation sessions to referrals to specialized policing teams trained in RJ principles and practices or other specialists inside or outside the formal justice system. To many who objectively view restorative policing, it seems like community policing meets problem-oriented policing with an overarching framework based in RJ and reintegrative shaming.

At least seven prisons in England and Wales employ RJ programs as a means of increasing victim empathy in offenders and changing offenders' behavior and causing them to take responsibility for their actions. These prison-based programs, called supporting offenders through restoration inside (SORI), have shown mixed but generally positive outcomes for inmates. SORI is a useful adjunct program, particularly as a means of supplementing existing efforts to manage inmates during their incarceration.

Reintegrative shaming: public and private practices that focus on offender rehabilitation within a supportive and engaging community that assists in various processes designed to receive the offender back into the community

Disintegrative shaming: public and private practices that label and stigmatize offenders, making their reentry into society difficult if not impossible

SOURCES: Beech and Chauhan 2013; Lofty 2002; Paterson and Clamp 2012; Winfree 2009.

tendency toward authoritarianism, political conservativism, and cynicism, while it has long been debated whether this is a case of recruitment or socialization.

Since the mid-1970s—principally with the advent of the Law Enforcement Assistance Administration—police agencies at all levels of government have experimented with different ways to enforce the laws, maintain order, and keep the peace. These efforts have included team policing, neighborhood foot patrols, community-oriented policing, problem-oriented policing, and intelligence lead policing. Some pundits have characterized these practices as the search for the "next big thing." Nevertheless, as the next section demonstrates, the increasing militarization of policing in the United States has erected a barrier that makes it difficult for police agencies to engage some elements of the public in low-key, nonthreatening ways.

Focal Issue: The Militarization of Policing

Critics characterize police agencies as paramilitary organizations (Auten 1981). The fact that officers wear uniforms and hold military-style ranks influences that characterization, as well as the common practice of arming the police and the authorization to use deadly force. However, the reality is that the police are a *part of the public*, not *apart from the public*, and the paramilitary characterization presents as many problems as it does solutions. Nevertheless, several factors have had a profound effect on the increased **militarization of the police** (Balko 2013; Shank and Beavers 2013).

Militarization of the police: the movement to make civilian police departments more like military units in their looks and operations

Initially, there was the influence of the Law Enforcement Assistance Administration (LEAA) in the late 1960s and early 1970s. LEAA contributed to increased training by police agencies as well as the purchase of specialized equipment. The result was that many departments created tactical units called **special weapons and tactics** squads, or simply SWAT teams. These operational units continued to develop during the next 30 years. However, the terrorist attacks of September 11, 2001, fundamentally changed police operations in the United States.

Special weapons and tactics (SWAT): military-style tactical units used by police agencies for situations such as barricaded armed suspects and hostage taking

Even prior to the 9/11 attacks, the National Defense Authorization Act of 1997 allowed the Department of Defense to donate surplus military equipment (such as armored personnel carriers) to local police departments. Between 1997 and 2012, the Department of Defense donated $4.2 billion worth of equipment to local agencies. Following the 9/11 attacks, the federal government created the Department of Homeland Security by pulling together the federal law enforcement functions of several agencies formerly located in the Department of Justice, Department of the Treasury, and various other cabinet departments, such as transportation (see also Chapter 5). The Department of Homeland Security began providing state and local police departments with funding to fulfill the "homeland security" mission that the nation had undertaken. Many of those local and state policing agencies began to create homeland security divisions within their own organizations as well. From its inception until 2012, the Department of

Homeland Security provided $34 billion in grants to local police departments as part of its counterterrorism effort. Overall, the result of this funding and these efforts by the federal government has been an increasingly military orientation by local law enforcement agencies. Moreover, as Box 14.3 reveals, this is a concern shared around the world.

Box 14.3   Globalized Justice: International and Domestic Implications of Police Militarization

Two ideas are central to this discussion: militarism and militarization. "Militarism" refers to an ideology or orienting philosophy toward problem solving that endorses the use of military-based power, hardware, technology, and operations. By the term "police militarization," we mean the application of the weapons of war, supplemented by the tactics of warriors, to civilian police officers.

Police in Africa and parts of Asia have long had close ties to their nation's military. Paramilitary policing units around the world are the remnants of colonialism, when the local police and colonial army historically worked in concert to control an often unruly and independence-minded populace. Today such practices are viewed as possible threats to both liberty and the **rule of law** generally and police-community relations in particular. In developing nations, paramilitary policing is seen as a double-edged sword, having the potential to be used to repress the citizenry yet necessary to instill discipline and unity in an otherwise disorganized and unprofessional police force. In Europe, critics of police militarization see it as part of a growing pattern of racial and ethnic intolerance aimed at controlling an emerging power group, people of color. Critics view the prospects of a militarized police with some trepidation and concern.

Concern about "warrior policing" is increasingly common in the United States. Consider the recent standoff in Nevada between a local ranching family and their supporters on one side and the Bureau of Land Management and other federal police officers on the other, both sides heavily armed. The legal elements of the confrontation aside, this event presented the specter of an armed encounter that more resembled a scene from rural Afghanistan or Iraq than rural America. Consider too the deadly incident between Albuquerque, New Mexico, police officers and a homeless mentally ill man whose "crime" was illegal camping. This caught-on-camera incident strongly suggests that the police acted more like a fire team in Fallujah than a SWAT team in Albuquerque. In 2010, local and federal police agencies deployed SWAT teams 45,000 times and conducted 80,000 "no knock" raids on citizens' homes. "**Swatting**," a practice whereby an anonymous call falsely alerts the police to a barricaded suspect or shooting incident in progress that requires a SWAT team, has also become a nationwide problem. The presence of heavily armed, military-trained police is likely to result in more deadly confrontations between citizens and their police.

Rule of law:
an elusive international principle of law that is generally taken to mean that no one is above the law, that the law must clearly specify what is a crime and how guilt must be determined, and that all actions of government must be open and transparent

Swatting:
a practice whereby an anonymous call falsely alerts the police to a barricaded suspect or shooting incident in progress that requires a SWAT team

SOURCES: Dansky and Solon 2013; Domanick 2014; Federal Bureau of Investigation 2008; Kraska 2007; Linke 2010; Simon 2013; Tanner and Mulone 2012.

MAKING SENSE OF JUDICIAL DECISION MAKING

In some ways, the U.S. courts lag behind the other criminal justice system components in terms of funding and research efforts. Police and correctional organizations garner much more of our attention. Nevertheless, we depend on the courts to ensure that justice ultimately is done in criminal cases. Whenever the public learns about persons wrongly accused or wrongly convicted of crimes, trust and confidence in the justice system drops.

Focal Issue: Wrongful Convictions

Throughout our nation's history, there have been cases of individuals wrongfully convicted of crimes, some more notorious than others. However, from the end of the 20th century into the first two decades of the 21st century, there has been increasing emphasis on the issue of **wrongful convictions**. A variety of factors contribute to our understanding of wrongful convictions. The Innocence Project, begun in 1992 by Barry C. Scheck and Peter J. Neufeld, focused the nation's attention on the issue (Innocence Project, n.d.a). To date there have been 317 post-conviction exonerations based on DNA evidence testing alone. The Innocence Project has been involved in about one-third of these cases (Innocence Project, n.d.b). This section explores some of the key factors contributing to wrongful convictions.

Wrongful convictions: situations in which an innocent person is convicted of a crime or in which a person is convicted despite insufficient evidence

One of the primary sources of wrongful convictions is mistaken identification by individuals who are victims of or witnesses to crimes. Research over the past three decades has demonstrated the unreliability of eyewitness identification, and this continues to be a problem (Wells 2006; Wells et al. 1998). Several factors account for eyewitness misidentification. For example, the stress of a criminal incident, such as an armed robbery or rape, can cloud witnesses' perceptions about the suspect's age, height, weight, and even race. Furthermore, research has demonstrated that eyewitness identifications by persons of one race to those of another race are tremendously inaccurate. There are a variety of explanations for this, but researchers continue to find that this is an issue (see, e.g., Bothwell, Brigham, and Malpass 1989; Michel et al. 2006).

A second cause for wrongful convictions is that some people falsely confess to having committed a crime. While this may sound strange, there appear to be a number of reasons people are willing to confess to crimes they did not commit (Leo and Ofshe 1998). Included among the reasons for false confessions are (1) police coercion during custodial interrogations, (2) emotional or psychological deficiencies in some individuals who display a strong need for approval or to please those in authority, and (3) individuals who seek to gain the notoriety that may result from being associated with a particular high-profile crime.

A third source of wrongful convictions—and one that is particularly troubling—is the use of **jailhouse snitches.** Some accused criminals seem to make it a practice of "overhearing" others confess to crimes while they are housed together in jail. If you have read the book or seen the movie *The Lincoln Lawyer,* you are aware of at least one fictional portrayal of this problem (Connelly 2005). Jailhouse snitches are accused criminals housed in jail cells with others accused of crimes. They may be willing to testify in court to conversations they had or overheard of an incriminating nature in exchange for leniency from the police or the prosecutor. In cases involving jailhouse snitches, the police and prosecutor may be willing to let a "little fish" go in order to catch a "bigger fish."

The use of jailhouse snitches is made even more troublesome by the fourth source of wrongful convictions: police and prosecutor misconduct. There have been several high-profile wrongful conviction cases attributed to police misconduct, prosecutor misconduct, or both. The state of Illinois at one point suspended executions of death row inmates as a result of evidence that Chicago police officers had wrongfully charged a number of individuals or had withheld evidence of the innocence of some suspects (Babwin 2013; Dardick 2013). In fact, in 2003, Illinois governor George Ryan commuted the death sentences of 115 offenders and pardoned 4 others as a result of some of the allegations of misconduct by agents of the justice system (see Bonczar and Snell 2005).

One of the most obvious cases of prosecutorial misconduct came to light in the U.S. Supreme Court case of *Miller v. Pate* (1967), in which a prosecutor showed the jury a pair of men's underwear with a red stain on it and inferred that it was the victim's blood when, in reality, the red stain was paint. As Justice Potter Stewart, writing for the Court's majority and overturning the defendant's conviction, said, "More than 30 years ago, this Court held that the Fourteenth Amendment cannot tolerate a state criminal conviction obtained by the knowing use of false evidence. There has been no deviation from that established principle. There can be no retreat from that principle here." Nevertheless, there continue to be cases of prosecutorial misconduct today for one very simple reason: it works (Gershman 2009). In virtually all cases, there are no repercussions for prosecutors who act inappropriately in criminal prosecutions.

The fifth factor contributing to wrongful convictions is ineffective assistance of counsel. Since the U.S. Supreme Court decided the case of *Gideon v. Wainwright* (1963), indigent defendants have had the right to court-appointed attorneys at the state's expense in all felony cases. However, having an attorney and having a *competent*

Jailhouse snitches: individuals who are housed in jail with other accused criminals and who might testify against them for leniency by the police or prosecuting attorney

attorney—especially in complex death penalty cases—are two different matters. In the Supreme Court case of *United States v. Cronic* (1984), the majority said that to establish ineffective assistance of counsel, the convicted defendant must establish (1) that there was a specific error committed by the attorney and (2) that the error was directly related to the conviction. While these two criteria sound relatively simple, this is a substantial and almost insurmountable hurdle for most accused offenders to overcome.

Finally, advances in science have provided both solutions and problems in the area of wrongful convictions. In terms of solutions, perhaps no scientific innovation has had a greater impact on the field of criminal justice than the use of DNA evidence (Dale, Greenspan, and Orokos 2007). DNA evidence has exonerated people wrongfully accused of crimes at the time of trial, and it has also been used to release from prison those wrongfully convicted, even years or decades later (Innocence Project, n.d.a).

Nevertheless, mishandled evidence can lead to miscarriages of justice, as can the use of "junk science," or largely invalid scientific evidence (Huber 1993). As the U.S. Department of Justice observed, the use of junk science in criminal cases "has resulted in findings of causation which simply cannot be justified or understood from the standpoint of the current state of credible scientific or medical knowledge" (1986: 39). In the case of junk science—such as hair analysis and bite marks—the consequences go beyond monetary judgments. Junk science has convicted innocent people or defendants who might be guilty but against whom no other physical or testimonial evidence exists. Well-established science may not hold the answer. For example, consider drug testing, a long-used method to determine whether a substance was a specific legally controlled substance or something else. Even here, mistakes can happen, as the public learned in 2012 when errors by one lab technician placed in jeopardy hundreds and perhaps thousands of drug-case convictions (Rogers 2012).

What is critical to remember about expert testimony is that the presiding judge, generally holding a separate hearing or outside the presence of the jury (if one is present), decides whether to allow admission of such testimony at trial. The key element is whether the scientific community accepts the analytical technique or procedure and whether it is beyond the "ken" or knowledge of the average person to comprehend without the expert's guidance. Next, the court must be satisfied with the witnesses' expertise in the area. As a rule, experts—those who present the technical evidence at court—are granted status as expert witnesses based on prior testimony in court or on the basis of training or work experience. Once qualified as an expert, courts often stipulate to that expertise, allowing them to testify without additional examination by either side. Box 14.4 shows that the problem of wrongful convictions is not confined to the United States.

MAKING SENSE OF CORRECTIONS

The corrections component of the criminal justice system has become a large and expensive enterprise for the states and the federal

---

Box 14.4   Globalized Justice: Wrongful Convictions

Apparently, no legal system is free of wrongful convictions. Overzealous prosecutors—those who seek a conviction at the expense of the truth—also work in civil law nations, as well as those following English common law. An inquisitorial system is prone to wrongful convictions, as is an adversarial system, although some legal experts argue that the former, with more strict guidelines as to the search for "objective truth," make fewer such errors. For example, the Swiss justice system emphasizes evenhanded investigations of facts, and, except for minor cases, will not convict based solely on a confession. When wrongful convictions occur, they appear to be for minor offenses that receive fewer legal resources.

Two other forces can be at work behind the scenes creating wrongful convictions. First, **moral panics**, situations in which reported events are blown out of proportion and even misrepresented by the media or other agents of government, can play a role in generating a societal demand for immediate justice in high-profile cases. This was the situation from the 1980s through the early 2000s across several continents when suspected organized rings of child-abusing daycare workers were convicted and sentenced to lengthy prison terms. Appellate courts reversed the convictions when it became apparent that many of these charges were false. Second, political systems can use the justice system for their own ends, as was often the case in socialist nations before the fall of communism in Eastern Europe. Courts in post-Soviet-era Poland, for example, decided that politically inspired convictions could be undone simply by finding the defendants not guilty, essentially declaring invalid decisions rendered during the repressive Stalinist regime. The trick, discovered the Poles, was to establish a legal system and social culture that did not accept such practices in the future.

Legal experts uniformly agree that errors of this nature are unlikely to disappear. The intent may not even be to subvert the justice process. The pressure to convict suspects of crimes is omnipresent, irrespective of the legal system in which the investigation or trial occurs. The legal community, then, must be vigilant in policing against such mistakes by regular and vigorous review of questionable convictions, which has led to the creation of Innocence Projects worldwide.

Moral panic: an emotive sense or feeling expressed in the general public about a specific issue or concern that threatens fundamental values within the community where is it expressed

SOURCES: Huff and Killias 2008; Innocence Project, n.d.c.

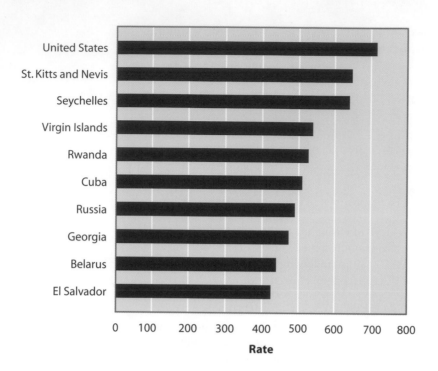

SOURCE: Adapted from Walmsley 2013.

Figure 14.1
Incarceration rate (per 100,000) in countries throughout the world, 2013

government. Corrections and punishment costs account for more than $173 billion per year at the state and local levels. The amount spent on the corrections system is the fifth costliest endeavor for U.S. tax-payers, behind defense, education, health care, and transportation (Vera Institute of Justice 2010). Prison populations that continued on an ever-increasing spiral upward for over four decades have resulted in the United States having the highest incarceration rates in the world. Figure 14.1 shows the nations with the most prisoners per 100,000 citizens. As of 2013, the United States imprisoned 716 per 100,000, which is estimated to be 25 percent of the world's prison population, while Americans make up only 5 percent of the world's total population.

A number of researchers and academics realized early on that it was ideologically wrong to incarcerate large numbers of nondangerous offenders in a violent world. Policymakers and prison population fore-casters consistently argued that a corrections system based solely on prison is a costly endeavor with few benefits or rewards. U.S. prison statistics indicate that nearly one-third of people admitted to prison violated their conditions of probation or parole (Sabol, Minton, and Harrison 2007). At the same time, the rates of parole and early release had declined so low in most states that more people were going in than were coming out of prison. Massive building efforts and the use of private companies attempted to ease the crowding, but often prisons would be full to capacity as soon as they opened their doors. The real problem was not that treatment and supervision did not work but that the criminal laws and practices had widened the net too much and had become too punitive.

Changes to the correctional system have come about slowly over time, with a decrease in prison populations reported in 2009. This was the first time that U.S. state prison populations experienced a marked decline in 40 years (West, Sabol, and Greenman 2010). The next section addresses the conditions that brought about these changes and what they hold for the future.

Focal Issue: Decreased Reliance on Prisons

Justice system changes such as the ones discussed earlier in the chapter take a long time before they influence the correctional system. Changes made more than a decade earlier reflected findings about why people fail on parole and probation. Most of the time, people on probation and parole supervision had violated a number of rules or conditions (such as failure to report, failure to pay fees, drug use) but had not committed new misdemeanor or felony crimes. A change in correctional practices was necessary to distinguish between people who committed new felony and violent crimes versus keeping people with technical violations and misdemeanor, nonviolent crimes on community supervision. Areas that had the largest prison population reductions actually *increased* the number of prisoners using community-based programs. For example, probation violators in Texas now go to treatment and diversion programs instead of prison for violating terms of their probation and parole (Pew Center on the States 2010).

Another change in correctional practices that occurred over the past decade is increasing emphasis on predicting recidivism with greater accuracy so that parole boards can make better decisions about the fates of those eligible for release. Predicting recidivism using risk assessments helps distinguish who can be safely paroled and who should remain behind bars longer. Using factors that statistically predict their likelihood of reoffending allows states to increase the number of people on parole and address the safety concern, thereby reducing prison populations. One study of the drop in crime and its effect on the state prison populations found that the number of people going to prison for new crimes decreased starting around 2007 (Pew Center on the States 2010).

However, these are not the only factors at work. The crime rate had been decreasing for several decades. Additionally, in 2008, a national economic recession forced states to reduce spending even further in all areas, including prisons. The fiscal crisis between 2008 and 2011 clearly prompted states to reconsider their sentencing and release policies. As a result, the number of released prisoners continued to grow as parole again became a more viable alternative. During the recent recession, prison construction stopped, and some states, such as Michigan, closed prisons.

Tied to the economic recession was the realization by some states that arrest and prosecution of drug offenders was costing too much and was not decreasing the rate of drug use, especially for marijuana. A different response toward felony drug offenders who were in possession of a controlled substance has signaled the beginning of a national movement away from reliance on imprisonment to respond to drug offenders. Starting with Proposition 36, California voters agreed in 2000 to allow judges more flexibility in sentencing first- and second-time felony offenders convicted of drug possession. Eligible offenders could receive drug treatment instead of imprisonment. More offenders participate in evidence-based substance abuse treatment programs in the community instead of going to prison.

Following California's lead, Michigan legislators repealed many of the state's mandatory minimum drug statutes in 2003. The legislators replaced the nondiscretionary determinate sentencing they had passed decades before with sentencing guidelines that returned discretion back to judges. At least 20 states have legalized marijuana for medical purposes. Other states, such as Colorado and Washington, have legalized the recreational use of marijuana for adults.

Even states traditionally perceived as notorious for tough sentencing laws quietly decriminalized possession of controlled substances charges. For example, the Texas legislature changed the designation of possession of less than two ounces of marijuana (a felony punishable by up to two years in prison) to a Class A misdemeanor (punishable by up to one year in jail). In 2014, the Texas legislature introduced a different bill to reduce the penalty even further down to a Class C misdemeanor, which would result in no jail time.

Decriminalization is an increasingly common legislative response. California reduced possession of less than one ounce of marijuana from a misdemeanor to a maximum fine of $100. Records tracking the effect of this law since 2010 reveal that decriminalizing offenses will lead to fewer arrests and convictions for both adults and juveniles. The numbers of prisoners confined nationwide have continued to decline (Carson and Golinelli 2013). We predict that eventually, if we continue in the direction of reducing reliance on prisons, the corrections system will indeed become more effective at differentiating violent offenders needing incarceration from nonviolent and drug offenders who deserve a more integrative, community-based correctional response, such as probation coupled with evidence-based treatment programs. However, there is another way to make our public prison system appear to shrink yet be responsive if there are increased short-term needs: private prisons. As Box 14.5 notes, this movement is gaining traction around the world.

MAKING SENSE OF JUVENILE JUSTICE

One of the interesting features of the juvenile justice system is that localities and states created it to remove youthful offenders from the harsh treatment of the adult justice system. Now we have started to rethink or reimagine what juvenile justice should be in the future. This endeavor is chock full of questions: Should authorities reintegrate juveniles into the adult justice system? Should we leave the juvenile justice system largely unchanged? Alternatively, should we divert more youngsters from the juvenile justice system into something even less punitive? We turn next to some possible answers.

Box 14.5   Globalized Justice: Private Prisons Around the World

Chapter 11 discusses the prison's origins and the parallel development of private prisons. In fact, England used private prisons as early as the 16th century. However, early in the 20th century, U.S. states moved away from this practice, while leasing prison labor to private enterprise continued for several decades. This situation changed in the 1980s and 1990s, as the ever-larger prison populations and declining revenues pushed states toward alternatives to publicly run prisons.

The United States is not alone in its use of private prisons. Across North America, South America, Europe, Africa, and Oceania, at least 11 nations with a variety of legal systems use private prisons on some level. The United States leads the world in the total number of individuals incarcerated in private prisons. However, Australia, Scotland, England, Wales, and New Zealand incarcerate a higher percentage of their total prison populations in private prisons. For example, Australia's private prisons hold 19 percent of that nation's prisoners, while in the United States that figure is roughly 8 percent. Germany, France, Brazil, Japan, Chile, and Canada also have private prisons. Enabling legislation for such prisons is being considered in Israel, Mexico, and Greece, although in Israel the use of for-profit prisons has already been declared as potentially causing "harsh and grave damage to the basic human rights of prisoners and to their personal freedom and human dignity" (Izenberg 2009).

Whether the international growth of private prisons will continue unabated or face court challenges, as in Israel, remains an open question. Indeed, human rights groups are marshaling their forces in opposition to private prisons. Clearly, such prisons will continue to house relatively low-risk inmates, allowing nations that employ them to expand or contract their prison populations as dictated by current policies and practices.

SOURCES: Human Rights Advocates 2010; Izenberg 2009; Mason 2013.

Focal Issue: Juvenile Justice—To Be or Not to Be?

It seems that juvenile justice in the United States currently reflects two conflicting trends or orientations. First, since the 1970s, there has been a discernible movement toward diverting more youngsters away from the juvenile justice system (see Mays and Winfree 2012: 120-130). Many of these youngsters are first-time offenders or have committed relatively minor offenses (shoplifting items worth small dollar amounts or spray-painting graffiti). For them, a treatment other than formal adjudication seems desirable and hopefully effective.

The **diversion movement** that began in the 1970s largely is a direct reflection of the notion of **labeling**, which means that if society tags, stigmatizes, or otherwise singles out a child as different and deserving of special treatment, then that child in fact becomes different (see especially Lemert 1951). There is some debate over whether labeling is a theory, but whatever its status, it clearly has had an impact on juvenile justice policy in the United States. Spurred on by passage of the Juvenile Justice and Delinquency Prevention Act of 1974, the subsequent creation of the Office of Juvenile Justice and Delinquency Prevention, and two National Advisory Committee reports (1976, 1980), diversion became an official federal policy. The Office of Juvenile Justice and Delinquency Prevention (OJJDP) made diversion one of its first primary goals, and grants-in-aid to state and local governments frequently stipulated that all juvenile justice reform programs explicitly incorporate diversion efforts.

Fundamental to the diversion movement was the idea that the juvenile justice system should remove most first-time offenders and virtually all nonserious offenders from the formal adjudication process. It was better to refer them to alternative community-based programs that could address the issues that brought the youngsters to the attention of the justice system. Thus, youngsters would avoid the labeling process and would not suffer the negative consequences that such labels carry. Because of this movement, communities nationwide developed and funded a wide array of diversion programs. Many of these programs began with the best of intentions, and some proved to be successful in keeping their clients from having further contacts with the juvenile justice system. Nevertheless, a number of these programs proved to be largely ineffective or, worse, widened the justice net and brought more youngsters under some form of social control than previously had been the case (see, for example, Henningsen 2003; Polk 1984; Sullivan 2001). The diversion movement is alive and well in juvenile justice, and each day its programs remove minor offenders from the jurisdiction of the formal justice system.

Diversion movement: federal efforts to encourage state and local governments to remove some juvenile offenders from the formal adjudication process

Labeling: the idea that youngsters formally processed by the justice system obtain the label of "delinquent" and as a result begin to act in accordance with the label that has been placed on them; something of a self-fulfilling prophecy

Aside from minor offenders, existing programs remove another group of youngsters—those who commit very serious personal crimes—from the juvenile justice system. These individuals may have long offense histories or have committed one very serious crime. The judicial response to such juveniles is their transfer to the criminal justice system, where they await trial (and punishment) as adults.

From the creation of the juvenile court, the juvenile justice system in the United States has had a variety of mechanisms for removing youngsters from the jurisdiction of the juvenile court to courts that try them as adults. The primary mechanism is the judicial waiver or transfer. In such cases, a juvenile court judge conducts a hearing to determine whether the youngster should remain under that court's jurisdiction. Moreover, states may legislatively exclude certain offenses, ranging from traffic offenses to homicide, from the juvenile court jurisdiction; some give authority to prosecutors to bypass the juvenile courts completely and to file cases directly with the adult criminal courts (Mays and Ruddell 2012).

Two groups move rather easily to the adult court jurisdiction. Persistent delinquent offenders are the first and, by far, the largest group. These youngsters typically are property offenders, and their chronic delinquency causes judges to deem them "not amenable to treatment" in the juvenile justice system. Ironically, when youthful property offenders appear in adult courts, they often receive probation rather than the incarceration that awaited them in the juvenile justice system. The second and smaller group transferred to the adult courts consists of those youngsters who have committed very serious personal crimes, especially homicide. Tried as adults, they face adult punishments, including the possibility of life without the possibility of parole.

Removing these two groups of youngsters leaves the juvenile justice system with what some have called "normal delinquents." The next question is do we maintain a separate system for these adolescents, or do we completely merge them into the criminal justice system? In 1999, when the juvenile court celebrated its 100th anniversary, it was questionable whether the entity would see another 100 years. Indeed, the 21st century may see the juvenile justice system expanded beyond its current boundaries, or it may see a separate system of juvenile justice disappear. As the international example summarized in Box 14.6 reveals, we share two issues with other nations, the question of immigrants' children and diversion from the system, questions that help to reshape the juvenile justice system (see Mays and Winfree 2012).

> ### Box 14.6 Globalized Justice: The Treatment of Juvenile Immigrant Offenders in Italy
>
> Illegal immigration is a hot-button issue in the United States. Juvenile offenders who happen to be undocumented aliens also present a problem for the U.S. juvenile justice system. Even the case of a legal resident alien youth accused of an act that could result in a trip to youth court or adult court presents a moral dilemma. If the court's decision is that the youth is a delinquent, the minor child could continue to stay in the United States. However, if the case occurs in adult court and the verdict is guilty, an immigration court could strip the youth of legal resident alien status and order deportation. Odds are that minor youths accused of delinquent acts or status offenses will be summarily deported to their nation of birth or incarcerated for an undetermined period of time if they are determined to be "stateless"—that is, if their national citizenship is in question and there is no nation willing to take them.
>
> Other nations wrestle with these concerns. Italy presents an interesting set of issues and responses. Italian penal law allows charging youths between 14 and 17 residing in Italy,
>
> irrespective of citizenship. Non-Italian youths (i.e., ethnic minority youth) have the same rights as citizens and, if detained, are eligible for the national healthcare system. Thirty-eight percent of all convicted youths processed through Italy's primary reception centers are non-Italians. These children are more likely than Italian youths to be incarcerated, primarily because such individuals do not have access to the resources necessary to keep them out of detention (e.g., a family, a stable home, employment).
>
> Italy employs "cultural mediators" who facilitate contacts between ethnic minority youths and Italian social services, the goal being to assist such youths in avoiding detention. The success of this system is variable; in some regions such mediators find themselves underutilized, marginalized, and relegated to mediator-as-interpreter status. Meeting the broad range of needs tied to these ethnic minority youths, aided in some instances by such mediators, remains a challenge for the Italian justice system.

SOURCE: Grattagliano et al. 2013.

SUMMARY

As Thomas Friedman (2007) observed in his influential book *The World Is Flat: A Brief History of the 21st Century*, because of increasing globalization, existing geopolitical divisions, including those associated with crime and justice, are becoming less meaningful in the 21st century. Thus, if we are to understand fully criminal justice in the 21st century, we must also know how the rest of the world responds to crimes, criminals, and the administration of justice, as what they do has the potential to impact what happens in the United States, for good or bad.

We trust that this look into the future of criminal justice, at least the adoption of an internationalist perspective, has proved instructive. Our goal was to provide both a globalizing framework and a series of comparison points by which to assess our own system. You should view this chapter, and the entire text, as a starting point and not an end to your search for a better understanding of criminal justice. As you continue studying the processes of justice in the United States, it is imperative that you look beyond the geopolitical boundaries of your hometown, your state, and even the nation when adopting a global perspective. If we as a nation have learned anything from September 11, 2001, it is that we have much to learn about the global aspects of crime.

REVIEW QUESTIONS

1. What is globalization? Why should criminal justice students develop a globalized view of crime and justice issues?
2. Compare and contrast transnational and international crime. We describe how only the former is the direct concern of the world's criminal justice systems. Can you think of an argument for making international crime part of the same equation? Explain your thinking on this important idea.
3. Which specific form of transnational crime do you think is the greatest threat to our nation and why?
4. Balanced and restorative justice (BARJ) has its roots in restorative justice practices of various contemporary indigenous peoples around the globe. Such practices may represent the most equitable and fair form of justice. What do you think? If not BARJ, what do you see as the next model of justice for the United States? Integrate the cross-national responses to such crime into your answer.
5. Attack or defend the following statement: "The militarization of police is the greatest threat to democracy currently facing the nation."
6. This chapter references six sources of wrongful convictions. Rank the sources from one to six, with one being the source about which our justice system is best able take corrective action and six being the source about which our justice system is least able to take corrective action. Explain the basis for your rankings.
7. Discussions about corrections, rightly or wrongly, tend to focus on prison first and on jails to a lesser extent. Does this emphasis accurately reflect the state of the nation's correctional system? Explain how you came to your conclusion.
8. As the chief juvenile justice policy analyst for your state's legislature, you have the task of providing an alternative plan for the treatment of juvenile offenders. What do you propose? Whatever you propose, explain your rationale.

KEY TERMS

bribery
corruption
crimes against cultural heritage
cybercrime/computer crime
disintegrative shaming
diversion movement
globalization
human organ trafficking
illicit drug trafficking/illegal drug trade
international crime
International Criminal Police Organization (INTERPOL)
jailhouse snitches
labeling
militarization of the police
money laundering
moral panic
reintegrative shaming
rule of law
sea piracy
special weapons and tactics (SWAT)
swatting

terrorism
trafficking in persons
transnational crime

United Nations Office on Drugs and Crime (UNODC)
wrongful convictions

NOTES

1. Such crimes are committed in the name of a government, such as in Nazi Germany during World War II, but individuals are indicted, tried, and, if guilty, punished for them.

2. Only in Iran is the sale of human organs legal, although other nations are attempting to legalize such trafficking.

3. At any given time, 2.5 million people are in forced labor—essentially a form of modern-day slavery—in 161 nations serving as source, transit, or destination nations.

GLOSSARY

actus reus the wrongful act associated with a crime

administrative law the type of law developed by regulatory agencies, especially those of the federal government

administrative office of courts state (or federal) agencies created to administer the ongoing business details of the judicial branch of government

administrative services services that provide for police recruitment and training, technical services, planning, analysis and research, and records and communications; generally but not exclusively nonsworn personnel

admiralty cases dealing with maritime law or those related to legal matters occurring around or on waterways

affirmative defenses justifications and excuses offered by criminal defendants explaining why their seemingly wrongful acts should not be considered criminal

aggravated assault an unlawful attack by one person on another for the purpose of inflicting severe or aggravated bodily injury

alibi Latin term meaning "elsewhere"; the affirmative defense alleging that the accused could not have committed the crime as a result of being somewhere else at the time

Anti-Federalists one of two original political parties in the United States; they opposed a strong national government, preferring instead to allow the states to have broad political powers

appellate jurisdiction, courts of courts that review the proceedings of trial courts in instances in which errors of law are alleged

arraignment a legal proceeding in which the accused is informed of the charges resulting from the grand jury indictment or similar process; the judge reviews the charges and addresses issues such as bail and legal representation at this point

arson any willful or malicious burning or attempting to burn, with or without intent to defraud, a dwelling house, public building, motor vehicle or aircraft, personal property of another, etc.

"assembly line" justice the method by which the crime control model enables crime suppression; ensures the swift and expeditious movement of a defendant through the justice system to punishment predicated on factual guilt

Asset Forfeiture Program Justice Department program for taking ill-gotten gains from criminals; run by the U.S. Marshals Service

attempts crimes that have been undertaken but, for some reason beyond the control of the offender, were not completed

automatic appeals cases such as those involving death penalty sentences that do not depend on filing an appeal by the convicted person but instead are sent for review to the appropriate appellate court

bail the process of securing a person's release prior to the next court appearance; see also *bond*

bail bond company a private, for-profit business that provides bonds to allow individuals to secure their release rather than having to wait in jail until the next court hearing

bench trial any trial before a judge without a jury

beyond a reasonable doubt the standard of proof in criminal cases necessary to establish guilt

Bill of Rights collective name for the first ten amendments to the U.S. Constitution passed largely in response to Anti-Federalists who were concerned about the expanding power of a strong central government

"blue curtain" refers to the veil of secrecy separating the police from the citizenry they protect and serve

"blue flu" work slowdowns by police, generally achieved by officers calling in sick and failing to report for duty

bona fide occupational qualifications (BFOQ) job requirements that the courts have recognized as necessary prerequisites for employment, either upon entry or because of in-service assessment

bond the surety (money or other property) posted to secure bail or pretrial release; see also *bail*

bounty hunters quasi-law enforcers, usually employed by a bail bond agency, who capture fugitives for a monetary reward, sometimes called a bounty; also known as skip tracers

Bow Street Constables a London-based 18th-century privately funded policing and investigative agency operating under the leadership of the Fielding brothers

bribery see *corruption and bribery*

building tender system the warden's use of handpicked inmates to control the larger inmate population in exchange for special privileges

burden of proof the requirement that a particular side must establish that a crime has been committed (the prosecutor) or that an affirmative defense is valid (the defense)

burglary the unlawful entry of a structure to commit a felony or theft; the use of force to gain entry need not have occurred

canon law religious or church law

cave dweller an inmate who is afraid to leave his or her cell because of perceived or actual victimization from other inmates

celebrated cases high-profile or particularly newsworthy cases

chancery courts specialized equity courts found in a limited number of states

charge to the jury instructions provided by the judge to the jury relating to the law and other considerations they must take into account in the process of their deliberations

circuit riding the practice of judges traveling to several locations to conduct trials or appellate proceedings

civilian employees nonsworn police personnel

civilian review boards panels of citizens and police experts that either reviewed the findings of internal police reviews or conducted their own investigations, depending on local police and practice

civil law in contrast to criminal law, legal disputes involving private parties; may involve civil wrongs or torts

civil rights actions legal actions (particularly in federal courts) alleging that certain protected rights of an individual or group have been violated, particularly under color of law

clearance by arrest classifying a crime as cleared by arrest

clearance by exceptional means classifying a crime as cleared other than by an arrest; may include the death of the offender (e.g., suicide or justifiably killed by police or citizen), the victim's refusal to cooperate with the prosecution after the offender has been identified, or denial of extradition because the offender committed a crime in another jurisdiction and is being prosecuted for that offense; in the UCR Program, the recovery of property alone does not clear an offense

COINTELPRO an "age of protest" FBI operation that implanted agents in alleged criminal groups and brought much discredit to the bureau

command element the highest-ranking part of an agency, responsible for developing policies and procedures; typically a highly politicized office

common law unwritten, judge-made law developed through the application of precedence in deciding similar cases in similar ways over a period of time

Community-Oriented Policing Services (COPS) an office with the Department of Justice that disseminates information and provides grants for community-oriented policing

community policing a philosophy that promotes organizational strategies that support the systematic use of partnerships and problem-solving techniques to proactively address the immediate conditions that give rise to public safety issues, such as crime, social disorder, and fear of crime

computer crime any criminal activity that requires or employs the use of a computing device; may also use various communications networks, including the Internet, in their commission; examples include illegal bank transfers and fraud by e-mail

concurrence in criminal law, the meeting of the guilty mind (*mens rea*) and the wrongful act (*actus reus*)

concurrent sentences multiple sentences imposed by the court that can be served at the same time; see also *consecutive sentences*

consecutive sentences multiple sentences imposed by the court that must be served one after the other; see also *concurrent sentences*

conspiracy the inchoate offense that results when two or more people plan to commit a crime and have a "meeting of the minds" relative to the commission of a crime

constable a type of law enforcer, dating from medieval England, assigned to a parish or local area in the community

constitutional courts federal courts created under Article III of the U.S. Constitution

constitutional law interpretations of state and federal constitutions by appellate courts; may be called case law

contingency fee attorney practice of accepting civil cases based on the likelihood of winning and receiving a certain percentage of the award

continuum of compromise the notion that the movement from good cop to bent cop to broken cop is one of stages; a slippery-slope hypothesis

contraband items that inmates are not allowed to have in their possession

contract attorneys lawyers who represent indigent defendants based on annual contracts awarded by the courts or the appropriate funding agencies

contributive justice a form of justice that essentially focuses on what the individual can bring to the group or society

corporate crime an offense committed either by a corporation or by individuals acting on behalf of a corporation or other business entity

corpus delicti Latin for "the body of the crime"; these are the elements the state must prove to establish that a crime has occurred

correctional officers institutional staff whose primary responsibilities are enforcing correctional law, prison policies, and ensuring a safe and secure facility for inmates, other staff, visitors, and the general public

corruption and bribery acts that rightly are viewed as a form of international crime when it involves public officials, party officials, or other elected representatives; the corrupting/bribing entity may be from the nation where the acts occur or from a second nation; these crimes can contribute to global crime and threaten basic democratic principles and the rule of law

counts (comites) a form of medieval political leader under the Frankish kings who was responsible for all elements of civil government

court-appointed attorneys lawyers assigned by judges to represent indigent defendants based on a list of eligible attorneys maintained by the courts

court security officers nonmarshal members of the U.S. Marshals Service who provide physical security for the nation's federal courts and buildings

courts of limited jurisdiction trial courts limited to small civil disputes and minor criminal cases (petty misdemeanors or misdemeanors)

courts of original jurisdiction courts where civil and criminal cases first originate; may be called trial courts

courts of record courts where a verbatim transcript is kept of the proceedings

crew an informal group of friends who provide support and backup when necessary but are not members of a prison gang

crime any behavior contrary to the group's moral code for which there are formalized group sanctions, whether or not they are law (sociological); an act or failure to act proven in a court of law to be in violation of a criminal code and punished by a lawful authority (legal)

crime control model (CCM) a way of viewing the administration of justice in which the goal is crime suppression; includes the ideas of presumed guilt, factual guilt, and "assembly line" justice

crimes against cultural heritage the theft of art and other cultural objects that are considered part of a nation's patrimony or property left to the nation by its forbearers

crimes against persons a category of crime whereby the victim of the crime is an actual person or persons; the UCR Program includes murder and nonnegligent manslaughter, rape, robbery, and aggravated assault

crimes against property a category of crime whereby the victim of the crime is property owned by an individual or individuals; the UCR Program includes burglary, larceny-theft, motor vehicle theft, and arson

crimes against public decency and morality public order offenses, generally considered classic examples of *mala prohibita* crimes or victimless crimes; the "victims" are often willing participants, and the offenses can include public indecency, prostitution, and public intoxication

crimes against society like many *mala prohibita* crimes, these represent society's prohibitions and include such specific crimes as gambling, weapons violations, prostitution, child pornography, and drug abuse offenses; see also *crimes against public morality*

crimes against the state crimes that threaten to disrupt the operation of the government; include treason and terrorism

criminal information an alternative to grand jury indictment; an official accusation of wrongdoing filed by the prosecutor with the court

criminal justice the entire sociolegal process whereby fairness is sought in matters involving laws that define what is and is not a crime as well as what happens to those found to be engaged in such activities

criminal justice system an apparatus society uses to enforce the standards of conduct necessary to protect individuals and the community

criminal law laws that define wrongful acts in which the prosecutor acts on behalf of the citizens of the state; often called penal law in that it provides for various punishments for those convicted of violations

criminology refers to the scientific study of crime, criminals, and society's response to both

crisis intervention teams a team composed of a specially trained social worker and police officer who work together to respond to dispatched police calls when the perpetrator may be showing signs of mental distress or has a history of mental illness

"CSI effect" the idea that juries and other decision makers in criminal justice case processing have come to expect either supporting or exculpatory scientific evidence, including DNA testing, in nearly every criminal case

custodial interrogations any situation in which the police focus on questioning a person suspected of a crime and the individual cannot leave of his or her free will

customary law unwritten laws that develop in tribal or primitive societies; based on group norms, mores, and folkways

cybercrime see *computer crime*

dark figure of crime term used by sociologists and criminologists to refer to unreported or unrecorded crimes

defendant in civil law, the person against whom a suit is brought; in criminal law, the person charged with committing a crime

Department of Homeland Security (DHS) a cabinet-level department created in the aftermath of the events of September 11, 2001; includes new law enforcement entities and existing ones taken from other federal law enforcement divisions with the goal of protecting the United States and its territories from and responding to terrorist attacks, human-originated accidents, and natural disasters

depersonalized policing the idea that physically removing police officers from their beats effectively cuts them off and isolates them from the citizenry

deprivation model theory that prisoners get around the formal rules to circumvent the pains of imprisonment and make their experience more pleasurable

determinate sentences sentences provided for by statute that are of a fixed length in terms of months or years (for example, 39 months); sentence reductions are often limited to the accumulation of good time credits; see also *indeterminate sentences*

direct examination the questioning of a witness in a trial by the attorney calling the witness

discretionary appeals appeals over which appellate courts have complete freedom of choice whether to accept

disintegrative shaming public and private practices that label and stigmatize offenders, making their reentry into society difficult if not impossible

disproportionate minority contact a movement which began in the 1990s to reduce the overrepresentation of juveniles of African American and Hispanic descent in the juvenile justice system

distributive justice refers to a form of economic justice whereby the benefits, services, rewards, and resources accrued by society are shared fairly with all members

disturbances short-term chaotic events involving a small group of inmates in which correctional staff maintain control

diversion removal of an accused person from the formal adjudicative process; often used with juveniles and minors or first-offense adult offenders

diversion investigators DEA investigators who specialize in finding the ways legal drugs are diverted to the illicit drug market

diversion movement federal efforts to encourage state and local governments to remove some juvenile offenders from the formal adjudication process

diversity of citizenship constitutional questions relating to opposing parties from different states or those involving citizens of foreign countries

due process clause a section of the Fourteenth Amendment of the U.S. Constitution that provides general guidelines as to when rights must be provided to individuals when issues relevant to life or liberty are at stake

due process model (DPM) a way of viewing the administration of justice in which the goal is fairness; includes the ideas of presumed innocence, legal guilt, and "obstacle course" justice

duress the affirmative defense alleging that the wrongful act was committed under some form of external compulsion (such as the threat of bodily harm or death to the person or the person's family)

Eighth Amendment law that prohibits levying excessive bail (whatever the word "excessive" might mean); also prohibits imposing cruel and unusual punishment

entrapment the affirmative action alleging that the idea for a crime was conceived by law enforcement officials and that the suspect would not normally have committed such an offense

equitable relief in civil law, the legal remedy that intends to put all parties back to their original status before some act or injury took place

excuses affirmative defenses that acknowledge the wrongfulness of the act but assert that there were acceptable reasons for the act

factual guilt the CCM idea that only all evidence, no matter how it was obtained, may be used to establish a defendant's guilt in or out of a court of law

Federalists the political party of George Washington; this party supported a strong national government with broad political powers

felonies the most serious crimes, calling for incarceration of one year or more in prison; they may be graded into different categories of seriousness

field services provide such activities as police patrol, traffic, community services, and investigations; generally sworn police personnel

Fifth Amendment law that requires a grand jury indictment for serious crimes in federal cases; protects against double jeopardy (being tried twice for the same crime) and against criminal defendants being compelled to testify against themselves (self-incrimination); and guarantees that no person shall be deprived of life, liberty, or property without due process of law

filed case case for which an indictment is held in abeyance with neither a dismissal nor a final judgment because the judge determined that a prison sentence was too harsh and no other options existed at that time

fine a monetary penalty imposed by the court that is statutorily defined by severity of the offense committed

first-line managers supervisory staff, usually serving at the rank of sergeant

fleeing felon rule the English common law rule that allowed police to use deadly force to apprehend any felon who was fleeing arrest

folkway an informal norm based on traditional ways of acting in social relationships

forcible rape by the traditional UCR definition, the carnal knowledge of a female forcibly and against her will, including attempts or assaults to commit rape by force or threat of force; however, statutory rape (without force) and other sex offenses are excluded

Fourth Amendment refers to the legal protections governing search warrants and arrest warrants: they must be based on the notion of probable cause (not merely the suspicion of one or more criminal justice actors) for a warrant to be issued and the search or arrest to be reasonable

Fraternal Order of Police (FOP) a social organization for police, begun in the late 19th century, that in 1915 morphed into a formal police union

Frye **test** a test applied by the courts to determine the validity of certain forms of scientific evidence

Fugitive Operations a U.S. Marshals Service program intended to bring to justice escaped prisoners and others wanted under federal arrest or detainment orders

gender-specific programs correctional treatment programs for women that address trauma linked to substance abuse

general services law enforcement agencies public agencies whose mission statement includes crime prevention, crime investigation and criminal apprehension, maintenance of order, and related law enforcement services

general trial jurisdiction, courts of courts authorized to hear a broad range of civil and criminal cases

globalization the interconnectivity of modern life around the world, including all aspects of culture from industry and economics to crime and justice

good time credits sentence reductions accumulated by prison inmates for good behavior and treatment program participation

grand jury a group of citizens convened by a court to review cases presented by the prosecuting attorney to determine if there is sufficient probable cause for the case to move forward to trial

"grass eaters" Knapp Commission designation for police officers who accepted bribes for overlooking crimes but who did not actively solicit such bribes

gratuities gifts, whether solicited or unsolicited, to police officers as a result of their official positions

hands-off period the era prior to 1964 when the courts refused to become involved in prisoner rights cases and left prison administrators to decide their own prison conditions

hate crimes a criminal act in which the perpetrator intentionally selects the victim because of the victim's actual or perceived race, gender, religion, sexual orientation, ethnicity, or disability

Hate Crimes Statistics Act of 1990 law passed by Congress requiring the U.S. Attorney General to record and report on hate crime or hate-motivated crimes; see 28 U.S.C. §534 (HCSA), passed in 1990 and modified in 2009

hierarchy rule technique used in the UCR Program whereby only the highest-ranked category crime in any criminal event is reported in the annual report

home detention when defendants or offenders are restricted to staying at home, with permission to leave only for work, court dates, or court-ordered treatment

hostage rescue team (HRT) a highly trained and specialized unit with the FBI dedicated full time to counterterrorism and hostage rescue

hue and cry a call for all able-bodied persons to apprehend an offender

human organ trafficking the for-profit, commercial trade in internal human body organs for transplantation; also trade in human body parts

hundreds a sociopolitical unit in Anglo-Saxon Britain that was based on the geographic area where 100 families resided

hung jury any jury that cannot come to a definite conclusion concerning the defendant's guilt or innocence

illicit drug trafficking a global black market or illegal economy that ranks among the largest in the world; this market cultivates, manufactures, distributes, and sells drugs that are subject to lawful governmental control; also called illegal drug trade

impeachment the formal process of removing an unfit public servant (including judges) from office as a result of official misconduct; used with federal and some state judicial systems

importation model prisoner behaviors are present on the streets in outside society and are brought into the prison

inchoate offenses incomplete criminal acts, including attempts, conspiracies, and solicitations

indeterminate sentences statutory sentences that provide for a range of punishment (for example, one to five years) in which the judge imposes the sentence, but the actual time served is determined by the paroling authority; see also *determinate sentences*

indictment the official accusation of a crime by a grand jury in which sufficient probable cause is found for a trial; also known as a true bill

indigent defendants criminal defendants who cannot afford their own attorneys

infancy the affirmative defense alleging that the accused was too young to form criminal intent

initial appearance appearance before a judge or magistrate shortly after arrest; charges are preliminary, and issues of bail and appointment of counsel are first addressed at this stage

inmate code the unwritten and suggested behavior that inmates live by to make doing time easier

insanity a legal (not medical) concept; an affirmative defense alleging that as a result of some mental incapacity occurring at the time of the wrongful act, the accused was incapable of forming criminal intent

intensive probation supervision a form of probation with the most restrictions and monitoring for offenders thought to be at the highest risk of recidivism

interim appointments the temporary appointment to the office of judge until the normal process of judicial selection (election or whatever) can be employed

intermediate courts of appeal courts that hear appeals from trials courts before they can progress to courts of last resort

international crime criminal activities that threaten world order and security; includes crimes against humanity, war crimes, and genocide

International Criminal Police Organization (INTERPOL) a treaty-based organization consisting of 190 member nations dedicated to the suppression and reduction of crime on a global scale; headquartered in Lyon, France

International Union of Police Associations (IUPA) an affiliate of the AFL-CIO that represents police across the nation

intoxication being under the influence of alcohol or drugs; voluntary intoxication is not a defense to crime, and involuntary intoxication may be so in very limited circumstances

Irish system mid-19th-century system credited to Sir Walter Crofton that emphasized reformation and increased freedom over time

jailhouse snitch prisoners who are willing to inform on other prisoners to receive leniency from the prosecuting attorney or court; one of the major sources of wrongful convictions

"jammed up" the idea that the police are being investigated, internally or externally, for possible malfeasance, misfeasance, or nonfeasance

judicial conduct commissions investigative bodies constituted to receive allegations of misconduct on the part of sitting judges; they may be empowered to impose disciplinary actions, or they may make disciplinary recommendations to the court of last resort

judicial independence the idea that the judiciary should be insulated from undue political influence from the executive and legislative branches of government

judicial marshals specialized police agencies that serve courts in their jurisdiction

judicial review courts' ability to review the acts of executive agencies and legislative bodies to determine the constitutionality of their actions; originally asserted in the case of *Marbury v. Madison* (1803)

Judiciary Act of 1789 one of the first congressional acts under the newly constituted United States; established the structure and jurisdiction of federal courts (below the Supreme Court) and created the offices of U.S. marshal, U.S. attorney, and attorney general

jurisdiction the right of a legal recognized entity to govern or otherwise exert control over a specific geographic area

justice fairness or reasonableness in the way people are treated or decisions are made

justice of the peace elected judicial officials who serve in a limited number of states; historically they were paid based on the fees they collected, and in most instances they were not required to be trained in the law

Justice Prisoner and Alien Transportation System (JPATS) the air wing of the U.S. Marshals Service that moves prisoners and undocumented aliens around the nation

justifications acts (such as self-defense) that would otherwise be wrong but given the circumstances are allowable and even expected

juvenile justice system part of the overall justice system that is responsible for processing legal minors who have violated the law

Kefauver Committee an investigative body in Congress that looked into the ties between organized crime and corrupt police in 1950s America

Knapp Commission a special investigation team in the 1970s that found widespread corruption in the NYPD, mostly related to protection and graft

labeling the idea that youngsters formally processed by the justice system obtain the label of "delinquent" and as a result begin to act in accordance with the label that has been placed on them; something of a self-fulfilling prophecy

larceny-theft the unlawful taking, carrying, leading, or riding away of property from the possession or constructive possession of another; examples include thefts of bicycles, motor vehicle parts and accessories, shoplifting, pickpocketing, or stealing any property or article that is not taken by force and violence or by fraud, including attempted larcenies

Law Enforcement Assistance Administration (LEAA) part of the federal government from 1969 to 1982 that administered funding to state and local law enforcement agencies; specifically, it funded educational programs, research, state planning agencies, and local anticrime initiatives

Law Enforcement Education Program (LEEP) a part of LEAA intended to provide free or nearly free college and university education for police and correctional officers; preservice could have debts excused; in-service could receive substantial educational subsidies; largely ended with demise of LEAA, although some states continue to provide in-service subsidies and rewards for higher education

legal aid societies groups of attorneys who donate time to represent individuals who cannot afford to pay for legal representation

legal clinics courses offered by law schools that allow second- and third-year students to gain practical legal experience under the supervision of clinical professors

legal guilt the due process model idea that only factual evidence obtained and presented in a procedurally correct fashion may be used in a court of law to substantiate a criminal charge

legality principle the concept that says that citizens have the right to know what conduct is illegal and that the law should establish such behavior specifically enough to minimize discretion by law enforcement authorities

legal justice the fairness being sought, which is specifically defined by law

legal precedent   an established legal standard that exists as a result of a series of cases being decided the same way over some period of time; see also *precedent*

legislative courts   federal courts created under Article I of the U.S. Constitution granting such authority to Congress

less-lethal force   types of physical, mechanical, or chemical force used by police officers that are not intended to produce great bodily harm or death

lethal force   types of force, usually as a result of discharging weapons, designed to incapacitate or kill

line staff   sworn officers who populate the operational divisions and units of the agency

local legal culture   the legal environment that exists in a particular jurisdiction based on the history and traditions of the location

London Metropolitan Police   a police agency, dating from 1829 and operating today, that is considered the first modern police force

magistrate judges   judges who preside over courts of limited jurisdictions in some states; most are popularly elected and may or may not be required to possess law degrees

mala in se   behaviors that are considered bad in and of themselves; those types of offenses that are inherently bad or evil

mala prohibita   offenses that are not inherently bad or evil but are prohibited as a result of laws prohibiting them

mandatory appeals   cases that must be heard (by constitutional mandate or statute) by an appellate court

mandatory sentences   sentences that must be imposed by a judge as a result of conviction of a certain offense

marital rape exception   the archaic and currently unlawful idea that a husband may rape his wife, even using force, as this is an act permissible under the bonds of marriage

marks system   a behavioral modification system credited to Captain Alexander Maconochie that rewards inmates who exhibit good behavior with credits toward early release

master list   the list containing the names of all persons eligible for jury service in a particular jurisdiction

"meat eaters"   Knapp Commission designation for police officers who actively sought opportunities for corruption, mostly related to drug trade and violence

mens rea   the guilty mind or criminal intent

merit selection   a method of judicial selection that combines elements of appointment with those of election; also known as the Missouri Plan for the state that pioneered this method; see also *retention ballot*

Metropolitan Police Improvement Bill of 1829   English Parliamentary legislation that created the London Metropolitan Police

middle management   personnel in an agency responsible for directly administering or overseeing the operations of the various divisions or units in the agency

militarization of the police   the movement to make civilian police departments more like military units in appearance and operations

misdemeanors   the least serious crimes; often call for fines or incarceration in a local detention facility for less than one year

Missouri plan   merit selection system of choosing judges, first established in Missouri in the 1940s, that combines some elements of appointment along with retention elections

Model Penal Code   a series of volumes prepared by the American Law Institute that provide examples of statutory provisions that can be copied and followed by states seeking to revise their criminal codes

Mollen Commission   a special investigation team in the 1990s that found widespread corruption in the NYPD

money laundering   when one party engages in activities intended to hide the origins or destination of funds or negotiable monetary instruments; "dirty" money enters at one end of the process, and "clean" money comes out the other end

moral panic   an emotive sense or feeling expressed in the general public about a specific issue or concern that threatens fundamental values within the community where it is expressed

mos (mores)   a moral code of significant importance to the group

motor vehicle theft   the theft or attempted theft of a motor vehicle, defined as a self-propelled vehicle that runs on land surfaces and not on rails, including sport utility vehicles, automobiles, trucks, buses, motorcycles, motor scooters, all-terrain vehicles, and snowmobiles; farm equipment, bulldozers, airplanes, construction equipment, or watercraft such as motorboats, sailboats, houseboats, or jet skis are generally excluded, as is taking a motor vehicle for temporary use by persons having lawful access

murder the unauthorized killing of another person; in law, often labeled criminal homicide

National Incident-Based Reporting System (NIBRS) crime statistics collection method that looks at every crime as an incident with several possible parts and possibly multiple participants with the information coming voluntarily from local law enforcement agencies; see also *Uniform Crime Report*

natural law the notion that law is unchangeable and its source is divine authority

necessity the affirmative defense alleging that a violation occurred as a result of forces of nature; considered a lesser-of-evils defense

nolo contendere a plea of "no contest" meaning that the defendant does not contest the charges, but the judge may impose a sentence as if there were a guilty plea

nonnegligent manslaughter the killing of another person with lesser intent than that required by murder (or homicide); a lesser degree of the unauthorized taking of the life of another than homicide

nonpartisan elections election of judges in a process where the candidate's political party affiliation does not appear on the ballot; see also *partisan elections*

nonsworn personnel see *civilian personnel*

norms rules or expectations shared by at least two people regarding behavior that is considered acceptable and unacceptable and, moreover, what happens when someone fails to conform to these standards

"obstacle course" justice the method by which the due process model ensures the protection of the rights of the accused; creating hurdles or barriers for the state to overcome as it demonstrates legal guilt

occupational crime criminal offenses associated with a person's job; these may be crimes committed on behalf of or against the company

Omnibus Crime Control and Safe Streets Act (1968) a sweeping anticrime act of Congress that was largely in response to the assassination of John F. Kennedy and what was perceived to be a general lawlessness and civil unrest associated with both the antiwar and civil rights movements of the 1960s; created a number of federal bureaucracies, including LEAA; suspended interstate trade in handguns; provided direct funds to deal with urban riot control and organized crime

organized crime any type of criminal activity associated with groups who plan and engage in the behavior as an economic enterprise

parole agreement/order terms and conditions set by the parole board to which the parolee agrees during the first meeting with his or her parole officer

parole board a politically appointed group that meets regularly to review files of prisoners who are eligible for early release

partisan elections election of judges in a process where the candidate's political party affiliation appears on the ballot; see also *nonpartisan elections*

penal transportation the removal of convicted criminals to a remote location where they were forced to work as indentured slaves and laborers as their sentence

peremptory challenges exclusion of potential jurors for no stated cause

petty misdemeanors the least serious misdemeanor offenses; often these violations result in only fines or very short periods of incarceration

plaintiff in civil law, the person who brings suit against another (the defendant)

plea bargain the agreement between the prosecutor and the defendant (defense attorney) that there will be a guilty plea in exchange for some type of leniency

police corruption all forms of misuse of authority by law enforcement, ranging from accepting gifts and gratuities to officer-involved criminal homicide

police division a group of police personnel who share a common police function

police misconduct any action by a police officer that violates a standard of professional conduct as defined by the employing department

Police Officer Standards and Training (POST) statewide entities that standardize and certify officers and their training

police personality the idea that there is a special type of person who is either attracted to police work or is produced by it; that person tends to be authoritarian and cynical

police unit a smaller and discrete part of a division that has a specialized activity to perform

police use of force amount of police effort required to compel compliance by an unwilling subject

policing the actions of a person or group in authority to ensure fairness and legality in an area of public life

positive law (legal positivism) the notion that law is not derived from divine authority but results from the interactions and processes that occur within a society

Posse Comitatus Act congressional legislation that limited the use of the U.S. military for essentially policing functions

Praetorian Guard Roman paramilitary group that protected the emperor and the city of Rome; politicized early in its existence; served as an early "secret service" or spy group

precedent a decision by a judge or other body that decides an issue in one case but may serve as the basis for resolving similar cases in the future; see also *legal precedent*

prefect of the watch the administrator in charge of the Roman *vigiles* who watched for fires and crimes in ancient Rome

preliminary hearing a probable cause hearing that typically occurs before a case is referred to the grand jury

preponderance of the evidence in civil law, the standard of proof that must tip the evidentiary scales in favor of one side or the other

presentence investigation report a summary report submitted to the court after a defendant's plea of guilty for a felony in which a sentence is recommended based on the totality of the defendant's situation and ability to handle probation

presumptive sentences the normal or typical sentence that should be imposed based on the stipulations provided for in statutes or in sentencing guidelines

prison argot the slang terms, symbols, and gestures that make up prison inmate communication

prisonized state in which prisoners identify with and have fully adopted the convict code of conduct over the conventional value system outside prison

Prison Rape Elimination Act (PREA) a federal act passed in 2003 to prosecute predatory inmates and staff who commit sexual assaults and to protect sexual assault victims in prisons

proactive policing anticipatory police actions intended to reduce or prevent crime

probable cause belief that a crime has been committed and that a particular person is suspected of having committed the crime

probate courts courts established to deal with issues such as wills, inheritance, and related matters

problem-oriented policing (POP) a strategy employed by police agencies to identify, analyze, respond to, and assess specific crime and disorder problems with the goal of creating effective responses to them

problem-solving courts judicial forums based on the notion of therapeutic jurisprudence; these courts are created to solve social problems such as drug use, driving while intoxicated, and domestic violence rather than merely adjudicating legal cases

procedural criminal law provides the legal road map for determining guilt or innocence in cases of criminal law violations; procedures that must be followed by the state

procedural law the "rules of the game"; the processes by which the substantive (statutory) law is to be applied

process a series of steps or actions taken in the furtherance of some clearly identified goal or outcome

professional model of policing an idea advanced by O.W. Wilson to make the police less prone to corruption

professional standards unit (PSU) an internal unit dedicated to investigating complaints and charges against the police force

prosecutor the attorney representing the state (government) who initiates criminal charges against the accused (defendant)

pro se proceedings court proceedings where parties represent themselves without the assistance of an attorney

pseudofamilies a make-believe family structure composed of women inmates who are not related to each other

public defenders publicly funded attorneys who represent indigent defendants

public information office (PIO) an internal unit that provides information to the media and the general public about programs, projects, and events affecting the community and the police department; community relations unit

public order offenses crimes affecting the peace, safety, and well-being of society

public welfare crime a criminal activity related to an act that normally would be lawful but owing to certain qualities becomes a crime by placing portions of the public at risk for loss, including health- and welfare-related problems; for example, producing a health- or life-threatening product such as a contaminated food

quaestores investigative agents in ancient Rome

Racketeer Influenced Corruption Organization (RICO) statutes laws passed first by the federal government and then by states to control organized crime; enacted by section 901(a) of the Organized Crime Control Act of 1970 (Pub. L. 91-452, 84 Stat. 922, enacted October 15, 1970); codified as Chapter 96 of Title 18 of the United States Code, 18 U.S.C. §1961-1968

rape by the new UCR definition, penetration, no matter how slight, of the vagina or anus with any body part or object, or oral penetration by a sex organ of another person without the consent of the victim

reactive policing police actions after a crime is committed or in response to it

regulator movement a group of pre-Revolutionary War vigilantes in North and South Carolina who took the law into their own hands

reintegrative shaming public and private practices that focus on offender rehabilitation within a supportive and engaging community that assists in various processes designed to receive the offender back into the community

release on recognizance a type of pretrial release in which the accused offers his or her word (through a signed document) to return to court at the next scheduled appearance

repealed removal or reversal of existing law

restitution a means of paying back a crime victim for losses or damages suffered

restorative justice an approach to justice that takes into account the needs of the victim, the offender, and the larger community; provides a means of individual and community healing for all three in the aftermath of a criminal event

retention ballot the method used to select judges in merit selection systems once the judge has been elected to office; retention ballots present voters with a yes-or-no choice about whether the judge should remain in office

retributive justice retribution, or punishment for the sake of punishment alone, with no other more lofty goals in mind

right to counsel based on the Sixth Amendment of the U.S. Constitution, the protection that accused criminal defendants may to be represented by an attorney at all critical stages of legal proceedings

robbery the taking or attempting to take anything of value from the care, custody, or control of a person or persons by force or threat of force or violence and/or by putting the victim in fear

rule of law an elusive international principle of law that is generally taken to mean that no one is above the law, that the law must clearly specify what is a crime and how guilt must be determined, and that all actions of government must be open and transparent; however, even on these notions, there is much disagreement

Runners see *Bow Street Constables*

Rural Constabulary Act of 1839 British Parliamentary act that mandated local police organizations throughout Britain along the lines of the London Metropolitan Police

Salic Code the basic civil law system found throughout much of modern Western Europe in medieval times; based on local tribal norms and rules, it owed much to Roman law

SARA model a method used in problem-oriented policing to provide workable solutions to community-based crime and public-disorder issues

sea piracy the apprehension, boarding, and robbery of vessels and/or persons at sea

security threat group a collective group of confirmed gang members that pose a threat to institutional safety and security

sentencing disparity a type of injustice when individuals are sentenced differently for the same crime

sentencing guidelines statutory provisions that consider the present offense and the offender's criminal history in determining the appropriate sentence to be imposed by the judge

sequestered jury a jury that is not allowed to return home at the end of court sessions each day; jury members are housed in hotels under the watch and care of court bailiffs to prevent them from being exposed to prejudicial publicity concerning the trial

serious mental illness disorders of the brain that affect thinking and behavior and are identified by the *Diagnostic and Statistical Manual* of the American Psychological Association

sharia law religious law in Islamic countries that covers all secular and moral aspects of human interaction

shire reeve an Anglo-Saxon official who represented the king or queen in the county; collected taxes and maintained order; precursor of the modern sheriff

Sixth Amendment a variety of provisions related to the administration of justice including the rights to a jury trial, speedy trial, and public trial; the right to be informed of the charges, the right to confront accusatory witnesses; and the right to be assisted by counsel

skell an informal police term to describe an unsavory character with whom the officers come into contact on the job

skip tracers see *bounty hunters*

snitches inmates who overidentify with correctional officers or who are perceived to be informing on other prisoners

solicitation the inchoate (incomplete) offense where one person encourages another person to commit a crime on behalf of the person doing the encouraging

special weapons and tactics (SWAT) military-style tactical units used by police agencies for situations such as barricaded armed suspects and hostage taking

Speedy Trial Act federal statute that provides for specific guidelines concerning the amount of time the government has to bring criminal cases to trial

spoils system system that allowed politicians to appoint individuals to jobs on the public purse based on patronage, political affiliation, and graft

spousal rape the crime committed when a husband engages in nonconsensual sex with his wife; in theory, could involve the reverse case as well or same-sex rape in marriage

Statute of Winchester a decree by Edward I concerning the existing office of constable, which would henceforth be assigned to a local hundred

statutory law statutes (laws) are passed by legislative bodies and codified (compiled in volumes) to spell out the various elements associated with different crimes

strict liability crimes the limited number of cases that do not require the state to prove criminal intent; common examples include speeding in a car and statutory rape

sub rosa economy the underground and black market economic system of inmate supply and demand

substance abuse treatment nonresidential or residential treatment of drugs and/or alcohol in different phases depending on the severity of the client's addiction

substantive criminal law the acts passed by the U.S. Congress and the various state legislatures

that define the elements associated with each criminal offense

substantive law the type of law that defines the nature of criminal offenses

supervised mandatory release legislatively defined release from prison once a prisoner has completed the mandatory minimum time on his or her sentence

supplementary homicide report a part of the *Uniform Crime Report* after 1962 that provided the age, sex, and race of murder victims; the weapon used; and the circumstances surrounding the offense

swatting a practice whereby an anonymous call falsely alerts the police to a barricaded suspect or shooting incident in progress that requires a SWAT team

sworn officers police personnel who are certified by a statewide agency and may exercise the full range of police duties, responsibilities, and powers

system a set of connected parts or elements that, taken together, create a complex whole

team policing a New York City Police Department program whereby officers were assigned to neighborhoods where they handled all aspects of local crime and disorder

terrorism a violent act or series of acts that is intended to instill high levels of fear, intimidation, and anxiety in the general population or to influence public policy or effect changes in government; can involve assassination, warlike activities, mass destruction, or kidnapping

Thames Police Office an early 19th-century group placed on the public purse that maintained order on the Thames River docks of London

therapeutic communities (TCs) peer-led confrontational-style drug treatment for severe drug addicts

"thin blue line" a term that has several different meanings but generally refers to the police, who are either socially and psychologically distant from the public or stand between the public and anarchy

tithingman an appointed or elected member of a tithing who represented that tithing and was responsible for issuing the hue and cry

tithings an Anglo-Saxon term referring to a group of ten families; ten tithings made up a hundred

trafficking in persons viewed as the transportation of human beings, usually for the purposes of involuntary servitude or slavery, across international boundaries; generally involves coercion or deception at some point; not to be confused with human smuggling, or the for-profit transportation of human beings across international boundaries

transnational crime "ordinary" crime (i.e., not international crime) that spans the boundaries and laws of two or more nations; includes such activities as computer/cybercrime, corruption and bribery of public persons, illegal drug trafficking, money laundering, sea piracy, crimes against cultural heritage, human organ trafficking, trafficking in persons, and terrorism, inter alia

trial amendment the Sixth Amendment, related to the administration of justice, including the rights to a jury trial, speedy trial, and public trial; the right to be informed of the charges; the right to confront accusatory witnesses; and the right to be assisted by counsel

trial de novo to try a case anew; cases appealed from limited jurisdiction courts (courts of non-record) go to general jurisdiction courts, where a whole new trial is conducted

triumviri nocturne Latin term for "the group of three responsible for the night"; in ancient Rome, the individuals responsible for organizing and overseeing the slaves who served as a night watch

true bill a finding of probable cause by a grand jury; see also *indictment*

truth-in-sentencing shorthand for the requirement that prison inmates must serve a substantial portion of their sentences (often 85 percent) before they are eligible for release

unconditional release when a prisoner leaves a correctional institution after completing his or her entire sentence behind bars and there is no period of post-release supervision

Uniform Crime Report a summary of crime in the United States, published annually since 1930, as gleaned from the nation's local-, county-, and state-level law enforcement agencies; coordinated by the FBI with the help of the International Association of Chiefs of Police and the National Sheriffs' Association

United Nations Office on Drugs and Crime (UNODC) a partnership between the UN Drug Control Program and the Centre for International Crime Control that supports field-based technical projects, provides crime-based research and analytical work, and helps provide member nations with a local normative basis for international crime-fighting treaties; headquartered in Vienna, Austria

urban cohorts a daytime patrol founded by Augustus as a counterbalance to the growing power of the Praetorian Guard

urban prefect the commander of the urban cohort in ancient Rome

use-of-force continuum a device designed to guide officer decision making in the process of the use of physical and other force in citizen encounters

U.S. Marshal an appointed member of a U.S. District Court; kept the peace in the court and enforced federal law in the area under the court's jurisdiction, including the apprehension of escape prisoners and warranted offenders

venires the pool of potential jurors from which a trial jury is chosen

vicarious liability a form of strict liability; when an employee commits a tort as a result of something that the employer had a responsibility to do or not to do, then the liability passes to the employer (*respondeat superior*), who becomes the tortfeasor

victim compensation fund a fund managed by the state attorney general's office and subsidized through offender fees that dispenses financial assistance to victims of violent crime

vigilantism a form of behavior whereby an individual or group of individuals claim to act on behalf of the community to catch and punish norm violators; in the modern era (i.e., since the creation of formalized structures of law and justice), this practice has continued and is generally viewed as problematic for an ordered society

vigiles public employees in ancient Rome who looked for fires and criminals at night

voir dire "to speak the truth"; the process of questioning and selecting a trial jury from the larger pool of jury candidates; see also *venires*

Volstead Act congressional act that essentially criminalized the manufacture, distribution, transportation, and possession of nonmedicinal alcohol under the provisions of the Eighteenth Amendment to the U.S. Constitution

voucher systems the method of indigent defense whereby criminal defendants are provided a form worth a certain amount of money (depending on the nature of the case), which then allows them to hire their own attorney

warrant clause　the part of the Fourth Amendment stating that no warrants "shall issue, but upon probable cause, supported by Oath or affirmation, and particularly describing the place to be searched, and the persons or things to be seized"

watch and ward system　medieval English police protection system whereby watchers looked for fires and criminals at night and warders kept the cities and towns safe in the daytime; also used in colonial America

wedding cake model　the four-layer model developed by Samuel Walker to explain the different ways the courts process celebrated cases, serious felonies, less serious felonies, and misdemeanors

weight of evidence　the amount of proof necessary to secure a conviction (in criminal law) or a judgment (in civil law)

Wickersham Commission　reported in 1931 that the Volstead Act was basically unenforceable and the source of much corruption within the law enforcement community; also known as the National Commission on Law Observance and Enforcement

witness security program　a U.S. Marshals Service program that gives at-risk federal witnesses new identities; also called the witness protection program, or WitSec

writs of certiorari　discretionary appeals in which courts (especially the U.S. Supreme Court) ask lower-level courts to send up the record of a particular case to make a decision about whether it will be accepted for review

writs of habeas corpus　to "have the body"; a legal document for appeal that requires the state to come forward and to establish why an offender's conviction is legitimate and why incarceration should be continued

wrongful convictions　situations in which an innocent person is convicted of a crime or in which a person is convicted despite insufficient evidence

Abadinsky, Howard, and L. Thomas Winfree Jr. 1992. *Crime and Justice: An Introduction.* Chicago: Nelson-Hall.

Abraham, Henry J. 1986. *The Judicial Process.* 5th ed. New York: Oxford University Press.

Administrative Office of the U.S. Courts. n.d. "District Courts." Available at http://www.uscourts.gov/FederalCourts/Understandingthe FederalCourts/DistrictCourts.aspx.

Administrative Office of the U.S. Courts. 2012a. *Federal Court Management Statistics Archive.* Available at http://www.uscourts.gov/Statistics/ FederalCourtManagementStatistics/FederalCourt ManagementStatistics_Archive.aspx.

Administrative Office of the U.S. Courts. 2012b. *Judicial Business of the United States Courts, 2011.* Washington, DC: Administrative Office of U.S. Courts.

Administrative Office of the U.S. Courts. 2013. "Defender Organizations." In *Guide to Judiciary Policy.* Vol. 7, *Defender Services.* Available at http://www.uscourts.gov/FederalCourts/Appointment OfCounsel/CJAGuidelinesForms/vol7PartA/ vol7PartAChapter4.aspx.

Administrative Office of the U.S. Courts. 2014. "Federal Public and Community Defender Directory." Available at http://www.fd.org/docs/ defender-contacts/federal-public-and-community-defender-directory.pdf.

Alarid, Leanne F. 1996. "Women Offenders' Perceptions of Confinement: Behavior Code Acceptance, Hustling and Group Relations in Jail and Prison." Ph.D. diss., Sam Houston State University.

_____. 2000. "Sexual Assault and Coercion Among Incarcerated Women Prisoners: Excerpts from Prison Letters." *Prison Journal* 80 (4): 391-406.

Alarid, Leanne F., Carlos D. Montemayor, and Summer Dannhaus. 2012. "The Effect of Parental Support on Juvenile Drug Court Completion and Postprogram Recidivism." *Youth Violence and Juvenile Justice* 10 (4): 354-369.

Alarid, Leanne F., and Maureen Rubin. 2013. "The Challenges of Having a Mental Illness and a Criminal Record: Can Outpatient Mental Health Services Reduce Recidivism?" Paper presented at the Academy of Criminal Justice Sciences, Dallas, TX, March 19-23.

Alarid, Leanne F., Barbara A. Sims, and James Ruiz. 2011a. "Juvenile Probation and Police Partnerships as Loosely Coupled Systems: A Qualitative Analysis." *Youth Violence and Juvenile Justice* 9 (1): 79-95.

_____. 2011b. "School-Based Juvenile Probation and Police Partnerships for Truancy Reduction." *Journal of Knowledge and Best Practices in Juvenile Justice and Psychology* 5 (1): 13-20.

Alarid, Leanne F., and Ofelia L. Vega. 2010. "Identity Construction, Self Perceptions, and Criminal Behavior of Incarcerated Women." *Deviant Behavior* 31 (3): 704-728.

Alarid, Leanne F., and Shonna Webster. 2013. "The Effect of Community-Based Drug Treatment Intensity and Participation on Probationer Recidivism." Unpublished manuscript.

Allen, Ronald J., and Richard Kuhns. 1985. *Constitutional Criminal Procedure.* Boston: Little, Brown.

Alpert, Geoffrey P. 1997. "Police Pursuits: Policies and Training." *Research in Brief,* May. Available at https://www.ncjrs.gov/pdffiles/164831.pdf.

Alpert, Geoffrey P., and Patrick R. Anderson. 1986. "The Most Deadly Force: Police Pursuits." *Justice Quarterly* 3:1-14.

Al-Rodhan, Nayef R.F., and Gerard Stoudmann. 2006. *Definitions of Globalization: A Comprehensive Overview and a Proposed Definition.* Geneva, Switzerland: Geneva Centre for Security Policy.

Altschuler, Bruce E., and Celia A. Sgroi. 1996. *Understanding Law in a Changing Society.* 2nd ed. Upper Saddle River, NJ: Prentice Hall.

Altstein, Howard, and Rita J. Simon. 2003. *Global Perspectives on Social Issues: Marriage and Divorce*. Lexington, MA: Lexington Books.

Ambagtsheer, F., and W. Weimar. 2012. "A Criminological Perspective: Why Prohibition of Organ Trade Is Not Effective and How the Declaration of Istanbul Can Move Forward." *American Journal of Transplantation* 12 (3): 571-575.

American Bar Association. 2013. *Supporting Justice III: A Report on the Pro Bono Work of Lawyers*. Chicago: ABA.

American Judicature Society. 2008. *Judicial Selection in the States: How It Works, Why It Matters*. Denver, CO: Institute for the Advancement of the American Legal System.

_____. 2012. "Welcome to the Center for Judicial Independence." Available at http://216.36.221.170/cji/default.asp.

_____. 2013. "Selection FAQs." Available at https://www.ajs.org/index.php/judicial_selection/selection-faqs.

American Law Institute. n.d. "ALI Overview." Available at http://www.ali.org/index.cfm?fuseaction=about.overview (accessed September 2, 2014).

_____. 1985. *Model Penal Code and Commentaries*. Philadelphia: American Law Institute.

Anderson, Robert U., Theodore Bartel, Frieda Gehlen, and L. Thomas Winfree Jr. 1976. "Support Your Local Police—On Strike?" *Journal of Police Science and Administration* 4:1-8.

Anson, Richard, J. Dale Mann, and Dale Sherman. 1986. "Niederhoffer's Cynicism Scale: Reliability and Beyond." *Journal of Criminal Justice* 14:295-305.

Armstrong, Michael F. 2012. *They Wished They Were Honest: The Knapp Commission and New York City Police Corruption*. New York: Columbia University Press.

Arnold, Guy. 2005. *The International Drug Trade*. New York: Taylor and Francis.

Austin, James, Kelly Dedel Johnson, and Maria Gregoriou. 2000. *Juveniles in Adult Prisons and Jails: A National Assessment*. Washington, DC: Bureau of Justice Assistance.

Auten, James H. 1981. "The Paramilitary Model of Police and Police Professionalism." *Police Studies* 4 (2): 67-78.

Ayres, Richard A. 1977. "Police Strikes: Are We Treating the Symptoms Rather than the Problem?" *Police Chief* 44:64-67.

Babwin, Don. 2013. "Chicago Police Misconduct Settlements Surge as the City Pays Out Millions in Taxpayer Dollars." *Huffington Post*, March 15. Available at http://www.huffingtonpost.com/2013/03/15/chicago-police-misconduct_0_n_2883433.html.

Bailey, W.G. 1989. *The Encyclopedia of Police Science*. New York: Garland.

Baillie Reynolds, Paul Kenneth. 1926. *The Vigiles of Imperial Rome*. London: University of Oxford Press.

Bales, William D., and Alex R. Piquero. 2012. "Racial/Ethnic Differentials in Sentencing to Incarceration." *Justice Quarterly* 29 (5): 742-773.

Balko, Radley. 2013. *Rise of the Warrior Cop: The Militarization of America's Police Forces*. New York: Perseus.

Banner, Stuart. 2002. *The Death Penalty: An American History*. Cambridge, MA: Harvard University Press.

Banton, Michael Parker. 2014. "The History of Policing in the West: Ancient Policing." *Encyclopedia Britannica*. Available at http://www.britannica.com/EBchecked/topic/467289/police/36611/The-history-of-policing-in-the-West.

Barclay, Scott. 1998. "Keeping Their Distance: Appellate Courts and Local Communities." *Judicature* 82 (1): 35-43, 45.

Bastian, Lisa D. 1994. *Criminal Victimization in the United States: 1973-92 Trends*. Washington, DC: U.S. Department of Justice.

Baumer, Eric P., Richard B. Felson, and Steven F. Messner. 2006. "Changes in Police Notification for Rape, 1973-2000." *Criminology* 41 (3): 841-870.

Bayley, David H., and Egon Bittner. 1984. "Learning the Skills of Policing." *Law and Contemporary Problems* 47:35-59.

Beck, Allen J., Paige M. Harrison, Marcus Berzofsky, Rachel Caspar, and Christopher Krebs. 2010. "Sexual Victimization in Prisons and Jails Reported by Inmates, 2008-09." Available at http://www.bjs.gov/content/pub/pdf/svpjri0809.pdf.

Beck, Allen J., and Timothy A. Hughes. 2005. "Sexual Violence Reported by Correctional Authorities, 2004." NCJ 210333. Available at http://www.ncdsv.org/images/BJS_SV-reported-by-correctional-authorities-2004_7-2005.pdf.

Beckett, Katherine, and Alexes Harris. 2011. "On Cash and Conviction: Monetary Sanctions as Misguided Policy." *Criminology and Public Policy* 10 (3): 509-537.

Becknell, Conan, G. Larry Mays, and Dennis M. Giever. 1999. "Policy Restrictiveness and Police Pursuits." *Policing: An International Journal of Police Strategies and Management* 22 (1): 93-110.

Beech, Anthony R., and Jaymini Chauhan. 2013. "Evaluating the Effectiveness of the Supporting Offenders Through Restoration Inside (SORI) Programme Delivered in Seven Prisons in England and Wales." *Legal and Criminological Psychology* 18:229-239.

Bergelson, Vera. 2011. "A Fair Punishment for Humbert Humbert: Strict Liability and Affirmative Defenses." *New Criminal Law Review* 14 (1): 55-77.

Berrick, Cathleen A., and Gregory C. Wilshusen. 2008. "Aviation Security: Transportation Security Administration Has Strengthened Planning to Guide Investments in Key Aviation Security Programs, but More Work Remains." Available at http://www.gao.gov/new.items/d08456t.pdf.

Bhati, Avinash Singh, John K. Roman, and Aaron Chalfin. 2008. *To Treat or Not to Treat: Evidence on the Prospects of Expanding Treatment to Drug-Involved Offenders*. Washington, DC: Urban Institute. Available at http://www.ncjrs.gov/pdffiles1/nij/grants/222908.pdf.

Bianchi, Robert Steven. 2004. *Daily Life of the Nubians*. Westport, CT: Greenwood Press.

Bingham, Sandra J. 1997. "The Praetorian Guard in Political and Social Life of Julio-Claudian Rome." Ph.D. diss., University of British Columbia. Available at https://circle.ubc.ca/bitstream/id/24987/ubc_1998-271064.pdf.

_____. 2013. *The Praetorian Guard: A History of Rome's Elite Special Forces*. London: I.B. Taurus.

Blackstone, William. (1771) 1979. *Commentaries on the Laws of England*. Chicago: University of Chicago Press.

Blumberg, Abraham S. 2004. "The Practice of Law as a Confidence Game." In *The Criminal Justice System: Politics and Policies*, 9th ed., edited by George F. Cole, Marc G. Gertz, and Amy Bunger, 211-226. Belmont, CA: Wadsworth.

Bonczar, Thomas P., and Tracy L. Snell. 2005. "Capital Punishment, 2004." NCJ 211349. Available at http://www.bjs.gov/content/pub/pdf/cp04.pdf.

Bonneau, Chris W., and Melinda Gann Hall. 2009. *In Defense of Judicial Elections*. New York: Routledge.

Bopp, William J., Paul Chignell, and Charles Maddox. 1977. "The San Francisco Police Strike of 1975: A Case Study." *Journal of Police Science and Administration* 5:32-42.

Bothwell, Robert K., John C. Brigham, and Roy S. Malpass. 1989. "Cross-racial Identification." *Personality and Social Psychology Bulletin* 15 (1): 19-25.

Boyle, Douglas J., Laura Ragusa, Jennifer Lanterman, and Andrea Marcus. 2011. "Outcomes of a Randomized Trial of an Intensive Community Corrections Program—Day Reporting Centers—for Parolees." Available at http://ubhc.rutgers.edu/vinjweb/publications/DRC236080.pdf.

Brennan, Pauline K., and Cassia Spohn. 2008. "Race/Ethnicity and Sentencing Outcomes Among Drug Offenders in North Carolina." *Journal of Contemporary Criminal Justice* 24 (4): 371-398.

Briar, Bob, and Hoyt Hobbs. 2008. *Daily Life of the Ancient Egyptians*. Revised ed. Westport, CT: Greenwood Press.

Brooks, Michael E. 2001. "Law Enforcement Physical Fitness Standards and Title VII." *FBI Law Enforcement Bulletin* 70:26-31.

Brown, Richard Maxwell. 1975. *Strain of Violence: Historical Studies of American Violence and Vigilantism*. New York: Oxford University Press.

Brown, Robert L. 1998. "From Whence Cometh Our State Appellate Judges: Popular Election Versus the Missouri Plan." *University of Arkansas at Little Rock Law Journal* 20 (Winter): 313-324.

Bruce, Alistair. 1999. *Keepers of the Kingdom: The Ancient Offices of Britain*. New York: Vendome Press.

Bureau of Justice Statistics. 2014. "NCVS Redesign." Available at http://www.bjs.gov/index.cfm?ty=tp&tid=91.

Burnett, Jennifer. 2010. "Justice in Jeopardy: Budget Cuts Put State Public Defense Systems Under Stress." *Capitol Ideas*, July-August. Available at http://www.csg.org/pubs/capitolideas/jul_aug_2010/hottopic_publicdefendervsprosecutors.aspx.

Burrough, Bryan. 2004. *Public Enemies*. New York: Penguin Books.

Butts, Jeffrey A., and John Roman, eds. 2004. *Juvenile Drug Courts and Teen Substance Abuse*. Washington, DC: Urban Institute Press.

Call, Jack E. 1995. "The Supreme Court and Prisoners' Rights." *Federal Probation* 59 (1): 36-46.

Calvi, James V., and Susan Coleman. 2008. *American Law and Legal Systems*. 6th ed. Upper Saddle River, NJ: Prentice Hall.

Caplan, Joel M. 2010. "National Surveys of State Paroling Authorities: Models of Service Delivery." *Federal Probation* 74 (1): 34-42.

Capps, L.E. 1998. "CPR: Career-Saving Advice for Police Officers." *FBI Law Enforcement Bulletin* 67 (7): 14-18.

Carceral, K.C. 2004. *Behind a Convict's Eyes: Doing Time in a Modern Prison*. Edited by Thomas J. Bernard, Leanne F. Alarid, Bruce Bikle, and Alene Bikle. Belmont, CA: Wadsworth.

Carp, Robert A., and Ronald Stidham. 1998. *Judicial Process in America*. Washington, DC: CQ Press.

Carpenter, Catherine L. 2003. "On Statutory Rape, Strict Liability, and the Public Welfare Offense Model." *American University Law Review* 53 (2): 313-404.

Carson, E. Ann, and Daniela Golinelli. 2013. "Prisoners in 2012—Advance Counts." NCJ 242467. Available at http://www.bjs.gov/content/pub/pdf/p12ac.pdf.

Case, Brian, Henry J. Steadman, Seth A. Dupuis, and Laura S. Morris. 2009. "Who Succeeds in Jail Diversion Programs for Persons with Mental Illness? A Multi-site Study." *Behavioral Sciences and the Law* 27 (5): 661-674.

Casper, Gerhard, and Hans Zeisel. 1972. "Lay Judges in German Criminal Courts." *Journal of Legal Studies* 1 (1): 135-191.

Cato Institute. 2010. "NPMSRP 2009 Preliminary Police Misconduct Statistical Report." Available at http://www.policemisconduct.net/npmsrp-2009-preliminary-police-misconduct-statistical-report/.

CBS Corporation. 2010. "CSI: Crime Scene Investigation Is the Most Watched Show in the World!" June 11. Available at http://www.cbscorporation.com/news-article.php?id=652.

Center for Problem-Oriented Policing. n.d. "About Us." Available at http://www.popcenter.org/about/ (accessed September 3, 2014).

Chicago Police Department. n.d. "Mission Statement and Core Values." Available at http://directives.chicagopolice.org/directives-mobile/data/a7a57bf0-12e6d379-71512-e6d5-9e3d1c3316a9aa46.html?ownapi=1 (accessed September 12, 2014).

Christian, J. 2005. "Riding the Bus: Barriers to Prison Visitation and Family Management Strategies." *Journal of Contemporary Criminal Justice* 21:31-48.

Civilian Complaint Review Board. 2014. "2013 Report: 20 Years of Independent Investigations." Available at http://www.nyc.gov/html/ccrb/downloads/pdf/CCRB%20Annual_2013.pdf.

Clemmer, Donald. 1966. *The Prison Community*. New York: Holt.

"Code of Hammurabi." n.d. Available at http://www.commonlaw.com/Hammurabi.html (accessed September 2, 2014).

Cohen, Thomas H. (court research associate, National Center for State Courts). 2000. Personal correspondence, August 25.

Cohen, Thomas H., and Tracey Kyckelhahn. 2010. "Felony Defendants in Large Urban Counties, 2006." NCJ 228944. Available at http://www.bjs.gov/content/pub/pdf/fdluc06.pdf.

Cole, George F. 2004. "The Decision to Prosecute." In *The Criminal Justice System: Politics and Policies*, 9th ed., edited by George F. Cole, Marc G. Gertz, and Amy Bunger, 178-188. Belmont, CA: Wadsworth.

Collins, William C. 1993. *Correctional Law for the Correctional Officer*. Laurel, MD: American Correctional Association.

Collins English Dictionary. 2014. "Policing." Available at http://www.collinsdictionary.com/dictionary/english/policing.

Colquitt, Joseph A. 2007-2008. "Using Jury Questionnaires: (Ab)Using Jurors." *Connecticut Law Review* 40 (1): 1-52.

Colvin, Mark. 1997. *Penitentiaries, Reformatories, and Chain Gangs: Social Theory and the History of Punishment in Nineteenth-Century America*. New York: St. Martin's Press.

Community Oriented Policing Services. n.d. "Use of Force." Available at http://www.cops.usdoj.gov/default.asp?Item=1374 (accessed September 3, 2014).

_____. 2013. "US Department of Justice Office of Community Oriented Policing Services Announces Awards for Innovative Policing Projects." Available at http://www.cops.usdoj.gov/Default.asp?Item=2696.

Connelly, Michael. 2005. *The Lincoln Lawyer*. New York: Little, Brown.

Cooley, Andrew G., and Brock Gavery. 2006. "Police Pursuits and High-Speed Driving Lawsuits." *Police Chief* 73 (10): 26, 28-30, 32-33, 35.

Cooley, Valerie A. 2011. "Community-Based Sanctions for Juvenile Offenders: Issues in Policy Implementation." *Criminal Justice Policy Review* 22 (1): 65-89.

Courtney, Ross. 2009. "After Change in Law, Few 'Lay Judges' Remain." *Yakima Herald-Republic*, November 27. Available at http://seattletimes .com/html/localnews/2010369833_apwasmalltown judges1stldwritethru.html.

Courts and Tribunals Judiciary. n.d. "Magistrates." Available at https://www.judiciary.gov.uk/about-the-judiciary/who-are-the-judiciary/judicial-roles/magistrates/.

Covington, Stephanie. 1999. *Helping Women Recover: A Program for Treating Substance Abuse Addiction*. San Francisco: Jossey-Bass.

Crank, John P. 1990. "Police: Professionals or Craftsmen? An Empirical Assessment of Professionalism and Craftsmanship Among Eight Municipal Police Agencies." *Journal of Criminal Justice* 18:333-349.

Crank, John P., Betsy Payn, and Stanley Jackson. 1993. "The Relationship Between Police Belief Systems and Attitudes Toward Police Practices." *Criminal Justice and Behavior* 20:199-221.

Critchley, T.A. 1978. *A History of Police in England and Wales*. London: Constable.

Currier, Katherine A., and Thomas E. Eimermann. 2009. *The Study of Law: A Critical Thinking Approach*. 2nd ed. Austin, TX: Wolters Kluwer Law and Business.

Cutler, Brian L., and Steven D. Penrod. 1995. *Mistaken Identity: The Eyewitness, Psychology, and the Law*. New York: Cambridge University Press.

Dale, W. Mark, Owen Greenspan, and Donald Orokos. 2006. *DNA Forensics: Expanding Uses and Information Sharing*. Sacramento, CA: SEARCH.

Dansky, Kara, and Sarah Solon. 2013. "Local Police, Armed with the Weapons of War, Too Often Mistakenly Shoot and Kill." *ACLU Blog of Rights*, March 6. Available at https://www.aclu.org/blog/criminal-law-reform/local-police-armed-weapons-war-too-often-mistakenly-shoot-and-kill.

Dardick, Hal. 2013. "Key Aldermen Back $33 Million in Police Misconduct Settlements." *Chicago Tribune*, January 16. Available at http://articles .chicagotribune.com/2013-01-16/news/ct-met-chicago-police-settlements-20130116_1_burge-cases-chicago-police-cmdr-attorney-flint-taylor.

DeFrances, Carol J. 2001. "State-Funded Indigent Defense Services, 1999." NCJ 188464. Available at http://www.bjs.gov/content/pub/pdf/sfids99.pdf.

DeFrances, Carol J., and Marika F.X. Litras. 2000. "Indigent Defense Services in Large Counties, 1999." NCJ 184932. Available at http://www .bjs.gov/content/pub/pdf/idslc99.pdf.

Deitch, Michele. 2009. "Keeping Our Kids at Home: Expanding Community-Based Facilities for Adjudicated Youth in Texas." *Texas Public Policy Foundation Policy Perspective*, May. Available at http://www.texaspolicy.com/center/effective-justice/reports/keeping-our-kids-home.

Dickman, Matthew. 2009. "Should Crime Pay? A Critical Assessment of the Mandatory Victim's Restitution Act of 1996." *California Law Review* 97:1687-1718.

Dodge, Mary, John C. Harris, and Alison Burke. 2009. "Calling a Strike a Ball: Jury Nullification and 'Three Strikes' Cases." In *Courts and Justice*, 4th ed., edited by G. Larry Mays and Peter R. Gregware, 393-401. Prospect Heights, IL: Waveland Press.

Domanick, Joe. 2014. "How 'Warrior Policing' Fails the Homeless Mentally Ill." *Crime Report*, April 15. Available at http://www.thecrimereport .org/viewpoints/2014-04-how-warrior-policing-fails-the-homeless-mentally-ill.

Dressler, Joshua. 2009. *Understanding Criminal Law*. 5th ed. Newark, NJ: Matthew Bender.

Dufton, Emily. 2012. "The War on Drugs: How President Nixon Tied Addiction to Crime." *The Atlantic*, March 26. Available at http://www.the atlantic.com/health/archive/2012/03/the-war-on-drugs-how-president-nixon-tied-addiction-to-crime/254319/.

Durham, Alexis. 1994. *Crisis and Reform: Current Issues in American Punishment*. Boston: Little, Brown.

Eck, John E., and William Spelman. 1987. "Who Ya Gonna Call? The Police as Problem-Busters." *Crime and Delinquency* 33:31-52.

Emsley, Clive. 1984. *Policing and Its Context, 1750-1870*. New York: Schocken.

Encinas, Gilbert L. 2001. *Prison Argot: A Sociolinguistic and Lexicographic Study*. Lanham, MD: University Press of America.

English, Kim, Peggy Heil, and Robert Dumond. 2010. *Sexual Assault in Jail and Juvenile Facilities: Promising Practices for Prevention and Response*. Denver: Colorado Division of Criminal Justice. Available at https://www.ncjrs .gov/pdffiles1/nij/grants/236738.pdf.

Etter, Gregg W., Michael L. Birzer, and Judy Fields. 2008. "The Jail as a Dumping Ground: The Incidental Incarceration of Mentally Ill Individuals." *Criminal Justice Studies* 21 (1): 79-89.

Farole, Donald J., Jr., and Lynn Langton. 2010. "County-Based and Local Public Defender Offices, 2007." NCJ 231175. Available at http://www.bjs.gov/content/pub/pdf/clpdo07.pdf.

Federal Bureau of Investigation. n.d.a. "COINTEL-PRO." Available at http://vault.fbi.gov/cointel-pro (accessed September 3, 2014).

———. n.d.b. "Estimated Crime in United States—Total." Uniform Crime Reporting Statistics. Available at http://www.ucrdatatool.gov/Search/Crime/State/RunCrimeStatebyState.cfm (accessed September 2, 2014).

———. n.d.c. "Quick Facts." Available at http://www.fbi.gov/about-us/quick-facts (accessed September 3, 2014).

———. 2004. *Uniform Crime Reporting Handbook.* Washington, DC: U.S. Department of Justice.

———. 2008. "Don't Make the Call: The New Phenomenon of 'Swatting.'" *Stories*, February 4. Available at http://www.fbi.gov/news/stories/2008/february/swatting020408.

———. 2009. "Offense Definitions." Available at https://www2.fbi.gov/ucr/cius2009/about/offense_definitions.html.

———. 2010a. "Burglary." Available at http://www.fbi.gov/about-us/cjis/ucr/crime-in-the-u.s/2010/crime-in-the-u.s.-2010/property-crime/burglarymain.

———. 2010b. "Murder." Available at http://www.fbi.gov/about-us/cjis/ucr/crime-in-the-u.s/2010/crime-in-the-u.s.-2010/violent-crime/murdermain.

———. 2010c. "Robbery." Available at http://www.fbi.gov/about-us/cjis/ucr/crime-in-the-u.s/2010/crime-in-the-u.s.-2010/violent-crime/robberymain.

———. 2011a. "Aggravated Assault." Available at http://www.fbi.gov/about-us/cjis/ucr/crime-in-the-u.s/2011/crime-in-the-u.s.-2011/violent-crime/aggravated-assault.

———. 2011b. "Arson." Available at http://www.fbi.gov/about-us/cjis/ucr/crime-in-the-u.s/2011/crime-in-the-u.s.-2011/property-crime/arson.

———. 2012. "Summary of the Uniform Crime Reporting (UCR) Program." Available at http://www.fbi.gov/about-us/cjis/ucr/crime-in-the-u.s/2011/crime-in-the-u.s.-2011/about-ucr.

Federal Bureau of Prisons. n.d. "RRC Contact Directory." Available at http://www.bop.gov/business/rrc_directory.jsp (accessed September 25, 2014).

Felson, Richard B., and Paul-Philippe Paré. 2005. "The Reporting of Domestic Violence and Sexual Assault by Nonstrangers to the Police." *Journal of Marriage and Family* 67:597-610.

Fields, Cassi. 2012. "Are Physical Tests Fair to Females? Physical Ability Tests Often Rule Out Qualified Female Applicants for Entry Level Police Jobs." *Women in Law Enforcement Blog*, July 13. Available at http://www.policemag.com/blog/women-in-law-enforcement/story/2012/07/are-physical-tests-fair-to-females.aspx.

Financial Action Task Force. 2013. *International Standards on Combating Money Laundering and the Financing of Terrorism and Proliferation: The FATF Recommendations.* Paris: FATF.

Finer, S.E. 2003. *The History of Government.* Vol. 1, *Ancient Monarchies and Empires.* New York: Oxford University Press.

Finkelhor, David, and Kersti Yllo. 1985. *License to Rape: Sexual Abuse of Wives.* New York: Free Press.

Fletcher, George P. 1998. *Basic Concepts of Criminal Law.* New York: Oxford University Press.

Fogel, David. 1975. ". . . We Are the Living Proof . . ." The Justice Model for Corrections.* Cincinnati, OH: Anderson.

Fogelson, Robert M. 1977. *Big City Police.* Cambridge MA: Harvard University Press.

Ford, Julian, and Robert L. Trestman. 2005. "Evidence-Based Enhancement of the Detection, Prevention, and Treatment of Mental Illness in the Corrections System." Available at https://www.ncjrs.gov/pdffiles1/nij/grants/210829.pdf.

Fradella, Henry F. 2007. "Why Judges Should Admit Expert Testimony on the Unreliability of Eyewitness Testimony." *Federal Courts Law Review* 2:1-29.

Francis, Russell. 1975. *A City in Terror: Calvin Coolidge and the 1919 Boston Police Strike.* Boston: Beacon Press.

Frankel, Jack E. 1991. "Looking Back and Looking Forward." *Judicature* 75 (2): 83-85, 113.

Freiburger, Tina L., and Brian M. Iannacchione. 2011. "An Examination of the Effect of Imprisonment on Recidivism." *Criminal Justice Studies* 24 (4): 369-379.

Friedman, John S., ed. 2005. *Secret Histories: Hidden Truths That Challenged the Past and Changed the World.* New York: Picador.

Friedman, Thomas E. 2007. *The World is Flat: A Brief History of the 21st Century.* New York: Picador/Farrar, Straus, and Giroux.

Frulli, Micaela. 2011. "The Criminalization of Offences Against Cultural Heritage in Times of Armed Conflict: The Quest for Consistency." *European Journal of International Law* 22:203-217.

Fyfe, James J. 2004. "Police Use of Deadly Force: Research and Reform." In *The Criminal Justice System: Politics and Policies*, 9th ed., edited by George F. Cole, Marc G. Gertz, and Amy Bunger, 152-167. Belmont, CA: Wadsworth.

Gaes, Gerald G., and Andrew L. Goldberg. 2004. *Prison Rape: A Critical Review of the Literature.* Washington, DC: National Institute of Justice.

Gaines, Larry, Victor Kappeler, and Joseph Vaughn. 1999. *Policing in America.* 3rd ed. Cincinnati, OH: Anderson.

Gardner, Martin R. 2003. *Understanding Juvenile Law.* 3rd ed. Newark, NJ: Matthew Bender.
_____. 2009. *Juvenile Law.* 3rd ed. Newark, NJ: LexisNexis.

Gartner, Rosemary, and Candace Kruttschnitt. 2004. "A Brief History of Doing Time: The California Institution for Women in the 1960s and in the 1990s." *Law and Society Review* 38 (2): 267-304.

Gau, Jacinta M., William Terrill, and Eugene A. Poaline III. 2013. "Looking Up: Explaining Police Promotional Aspirations." *Criminal Justice and Behavior* 40 (3): 247-260.

Gaughan, Judy. 2010. *Murder Was Not a Crime: Homicide and Power in the Roman Republic.* Austin: University of Texas Press.

Gershman, Bennett L. 2009. "Why Prosecutors Misbehave." In *Courts and Justice*, 4th ed., edited by G. Larry Mays and Peter R. Gregware, 321-331. Prospect Heights, IL: Waveland Press.

Gilmartin, Kevin M., and John (Jack) J. Harris. 1998. "The Continuum of Compromise." *Police Chief* 65:25-28.

Glaze, Lauren E., Thomas P. Bonczar, and Fan Zhang. 2010. "Probation and Parole in the United States, 2009." NCJ 231674. Available at http://www.bjs.gov/content/pub/pdf/ppus09.pdf.

Glaze, Lauren E., and Erika Parks. 2012. "Correctional Populations in the United States, 2011." NCJ 239972. Available at http://www.bjs.gov/content/pub/pdf/cpus11.pdf.

Glensor, Ronald W., Mark E. Correia, and Kenneth J. Peak. 2000. *Policing Communities: Understanding Crime and Solving Problems.* Los Angeles: Roxbury.

Global Commission on Drug Policy. 2011. "War on Drugs." Available at http://www.globalcommissionondrugs.org/wp-content/themes/gcdp_v1/pdf/Global_Commission_Report_English.pdf.

Goldsmith, Andrew John, and Colleen Lewis. 2000. *Civilian Oversight of Policing: Governance, Democracy and Human Rights.* Portland, OR: Hart.

Goldstein, Herman. 1979. "Improving Policing: A Problem-Oriented Approach." *Crime and Delinquency* 25:236-243.

Gonzales, G., and Davak, M. 2006. "Out of Jail and into Treatment." *Behavioral Health Care* 16 (8): 24-26.

Grant, Heath B., and Karen J. Terry. 2008. *Law Enforcement in the 21st Century.* 2nd ed. Boston: Allyn and Bacon.

Grant, Michael. 1978. *History of Rome.* New York: Charles Scribner's Sons.

Grattagliano, Ignazio, Andrea Lisi, Ylenia Massaro, Valentina Stallone, Filippo Compobasso, Anna Cannito, Christian Signorile, Nicola Petruzzelli, and Roberto Catanesi. 2013. "Incarcerated Foreign Minors in Italy: How to Treat Them?" *International Journal of Criminology and Sociology* 2:118-128.

Gray, M. Kevin, Monique Fields, and Sheila Royo Maxwell. 2001. "Examining Probation Violations: Who, What, and When." *Crime and Delinquency* 47 (4): 537-557.

Grisham, John. 2006. *The Innocent Man: Murder and Injustice in a Small Town.* New York: Doubleday.

Grossman, Rhea. 2008. "Law Enforcement Liability Risk: Claims for Failure to Supervise and Train and Liability for Off-Duty Police Officers." In *Loss Control Best Practices*, edited by Florida Partnership for Safety and Health. Tampa, FL: Partnership for Safety and Health. Available at http://www.riskinstitute.org/peri/images/file/Chapter9lawenforcementliabilitytext.pdf.

Hall, James Wesley. 2009. Written statement for *Indigent Representation: A Growing National Crisis; Hearing Before the Subcommittee on Crime, Terrorism, and Homeland Security of the Committee on the Judiciary, House of Representatives, 111th Congress.*

Hall, Katy. 2013. "CCA Letters Reveal Private Prison Industry's Tactics." *Huffington Post*, April 11. Available at http://www.huffingtonpost.com/2013/04/11/cca-prison-industry_n_3061115.html#slide=2322956.

Halsall, Paul. 1998. "Ancient History Sourcebook: Code of Hammurabi, c. 1780 BCE." Fordham University. Available at http://www.fordham.edu/halsall/ancient/hamcode.asp.

Handler, J.G. 1994. *Ballentine's Law Dictionary: Legal Assistant Edition.* Albany, NY: Delmar.

Harlow, Caroline Wolf. 2000. "Defense Counsel in Criminal Cases." NCJ 179023. Available at http://www.bjs.gov/content/pub/pdf/dccc.pdf.

Harris, Casey T., Darrell Steffensmeier, Jeffrey T. Ulmer, and Noah Painter-Davis. 2009. "Are Blacks and Hispanics Disproportionately Incarcerated Relative to Their Arrests? Racial and Ethnic Disproportionality Between Arrest and Incarceration." *Race and Social Problems* 1:187-199.

Hatley, Allen G. 1999. *Texas Constables: A Frontier Heritage*. Lubbock: Texas Tech University Press.

Hawken, Angela, and Mark Kleiman. 2009. *Managing Drug Involved Probationers with Swift and Certain Sanctions: Evaluating Hawaii's HOPE*. Washington, DC: National Institute of Justice. Available at https://www.ncjrs.gov/pdffiles1/nij/grants/229023.pdf.

Henningsen, Rodney J. 2003. "Deinstitutionalization Movement." In *Encyclopedia of Juvenile Justice*, edited by Marilyn D. McShane and Frank P. Williams III, 114-119. Thousand Oaks, CA: Sage.

Hensley, Christopher, Tammy Castle, and Richard Tewksbury. 2003. "Inmate-to-Inmate Sexual Coercion in a Prison for Women." *Journal of Offender Rehabilitation* 37 (2): 77-87.

Heumann, Milton. 2004. "Adapting to Plea Bargaining: Prosecutors." In *The Criminal Justice System: Politics and Policies*, 9th ed., edited by George F. Cole, Marc G. Gertz, and Amy Bunger, 189-210. Belmont, CA: Wadsworth.

Hickman, Matthew J., and Brian A. Reaves. 2003. "Local Police Departments, 2000." NCJ 196002. Available at http://static.prisonpolicy.org/scans/bjs/lpd00.pdf.

Hill, John. 2002. "High-Speed Police Pursuits: Dangers, Dynamics, and Risk Reduction." *FBI Law Enforcement Bulletin* 71 (7): 14-18.

Hippen, Benjamin E. 2008. "Organ Sales and Moral Travails: Lessons from the Living Kidney Vendor Program in Iran." *Policy Analysis* 614:1-20.

Hockenberry, Sarah, Melissa Sickmund, and Anthony Sladky. 2011. "Juvenile Residential Facility Census, 2008: Selected Findings." Available at https://www.ncjrs.gov/pdffiles1/ojjdp/231683.pdf.

Huber, Peter W. 1993. *Galileo's Revenge: Junk Science in the Courtroom*. New York: Basic Books.

Huff, C. Ronald, and Martin Killias. 2008. Introduction to *Wrongful Convictions: International Perspectives on Miscarriages of Justice*, edited by C. Ronald Huff and Martin Killias, 3-10. Philadelphia: Temple University Press.

Huff, C. Ronald, Arye Rattner, and Edward Sagarin. 1996. *Convicted but Innocent: Wrongful Conviction and Public Policy*. Thousand Oaks, CA: Sage.

Hughes, Timothy A., Doris James Wilson, and Allen J. Beck. 2001. "Trends in State Parole, 1990-2000." NCJ 184735. Available at http://www.bjs.gov/content/pub/pdf/tsp00.pdf.

Human Rights Advocates. 2010. "Privatized Prisons and Human Rights: Report to the 13th Session of the Human Rights Council." Available at http://www.humanrightsadvocates.org/wp-content/uploads/2010/05/HRC13_Privatized_Prisons_and_Human_Rights.pdf.

Hunter, Virginia. 1994. *Policing Athens: Social Control in the Attic Lawsuits, 420-320 B.C.* Princeton, NJ: Princeton University Press.

Hutson, H. Range, Phillip L. Rice, Jasroop K. Chana, Demetrios N. Kyriacou, Yuchiao Chang, and Robert M. Miller. 2007. "A Review of Police Pursuit Fatalities in the United States from 1982-2004." *Prehospital Emergency Care* 11 (3): 278-283.

Innocence Project. n.d.a. "About the Innocence Project." Available at http://www.innocenceproject.org/about (accessed September 18, 2014).

———. n.d.b. "About the Organization: FAQs." Available at http://www.innocenceproject.org/Content/What_is_the_Innocence_Project_How_did_it_get_started.php (accessed September 25, 2014).

———. n.d.c. "Other Projects Around the World." Available at http://www.innocenceproject.org/about/Other-Projects.php (accessed September 18, 2014).

International Association of Chiefs of Police. 1944. *Police Unions and Other Police Organizations*. Washington, DC: IACP.

———. 2001. *Police Use of Force in America, 2001*. Available at http://www.theiacp.org/Portals/0/pdfs/Publications/2001useofforce.pdf.

International Chamber of Commerce. 2013. "Piracy at Sea Falls to Lowest Levels in Seven Years, Reports IMB." Available at http://www.icc-ccs.org/news/873-piracy-at-sea-falls-to-lowest-level-in-seven-years-reports-imb.

International Criminal Court. n.d. "All Cases." Available at http://www.icc-cpi.int/en_menus/icc/situations%20and%20cases/cases/pages/cases%20index.aspx (accessed September 18, 2014).

Irwin, John. 1980. *Prisons in Turmoil*. Boston: Little, Brown.

Irwin, John, and Donald R. Cressey. 1962. "Thieves, Convicts, and the Inmate Culture." *Social Problems* 10:142-155.

Izenberg, Dan. 2009. "High Court Prohibits Privately Run Prisons." *Jerusalem Post*, November 20.

James, Doris J., Lauren E. Glaze. 2006. "Mental Health Problems of Prison and Jail Inmates." NCJ 213600. Available at http://www.bjs.gov/content/pub/pdf/mhppji.pdf.

James, Nathan. 2011. "Community Oriented Policing Services (COPS): Background, Legislation, and Funding." Congressional Research Service report. Available at https://www.fas.org/sgp/crs/misc/RL33308.pdf.

Jensen, Gary F., and Maryaltani Karpos. 1993. "Managing Rape: Exploratory Research on the Behavior of Rape Statistics." *Criminology* 31:363-385.

Johnson, David R. 1981. *American Law Enforcement: A History*. St. Louis, MO: Forum Press.

Jones, Mark. 2005. *Criminal Justice Pioneers in U.S. History*. Boston: Pearson.

Kadish, Sanford H. 1967. "The Crisis of Over-criminalization." *Annals of the American Academy of Political and Social Science* 374 (1): 157-170.

Kamisar, Yale, Wayne R. LaFave, Jerold H. Israel, Nancy J. King, and Orin S Kerr. 2008. *Basic Criminal Procedure*. 12th ed. Eagan, MN: West/Thomson Reuter.

Kane, Robert J., and Michael D. White. 2013. *Jammed Up: Bad Cops, Police Misconduct, and the New York City Police Department*. New York: New York University Press.

Karberg, Jennifer C., and Doris J. James. 2005. "Substance Dependence, Abuse, and Treatment of Jail Inmates, 2002." NCJ 209588. Available at http://www.bjs.gov/content/pub/pdf/sdatji02.pdf.

Kassin, Saul M. 2009. "The American Jury: Handicapped in the Pursuit of Justice." In *Courts and Justice*, 4th ed., edited by G. Larry Mays and Peter R. Gregware, 154-183. Prospect Heights, IL: Waveland Press.

Keegan, John. 1993. *A History of Warfare*. New York: Vintage Books.

Kelling, George L., and Mark H. Moore. 1988. "The Evolving Strategy of Policing." *Perspectives on Policing*, no. 4. Available at https://ncjrs.gov/pdffiles1/nij/114213.pdf.

Kelling, George L., and James Q. Wilson. 1982. "Broken Windows: The Police and Neighborhood Safety." *Atlantic Monthly*, March, pp. 29-38.

Kim, Dae-Young, Hee-Jong Joo, and William P. McCarty. 2008. "Risk Assessment and Classification of Day Reporting Center Clients." *Criminal Justice and Behavior* 35 (6): 792-812.

King, Nancy J., Fred L. Cheesman II, and Brian J. Ostrom. 2007. "Habeas Litigation in U.S. District Courts: An Empirical Study of Habeas Corpus Cases Filed by State Prisoners Under the Antiterrorism and Effective Death Penalty Act of 1996 (Executive Summary)." Available at https://www.ncjrs.gov/pdffiles1/nij/grants/219558.pdf.

King, William E. 2009. "Civilianization." In *Implementing Community Policing: Lessons from 12 Agencies*, edited by Edward Maguire and William Wells, 65-70. Washington, DC: U.S. Department of Justice.

King, William E., and Edward Maguire. 2000. "Police Civilianization, 1950-2000: Continuity or Change?" Paper presented at the annual meeting of the American Society of Criminology, San Francisco, November 15-18.

Klein, Andrew R. 1997. *Alternative Sentencing, Intermediate Sanctions and Probation*. 2nd ed. Cincinnati, OH: Anderson.

Klockars, Carl B. 1985. *The Idea of Police*. Newbury Park, CA: Sage.

Knapp, Kay A. 1984. *The Impact of the Minnesota Sentencing Guidelines*. St. Paul: Minnesota Sentencing Commission.

Knapp, Kay A., and Denis J. Hauptly. 1989. "U.S. Sentencing Guidelines in Perspective: A Theoretical Background and Overview." In *The U.S. Sentencing Guidelines: Implications for Criminal Justice*, edited by Dean J. Champion, 3-18. New York: Praeger.

Knapp Commission. 1972. *Knapp Commission Report on Police Corruption*. New York: George Braziller.

Knoll, C., and M. Sickmund. 2010. "Delinquency Cases in Juvenile Court, 2007." NCJ 230168. Available at https://ncjrs.gov/pdffiles1/ojjdp/230168.pdf.

Knox, George W. 2005. "The Problem of Gangs and Security Threat Groups (STGs) in American Prisons Today: Recent Research Findings from the 2004 Prison Gang Survey." Available at http://www.ngcrc.com/corr2006.html.

Kraska, Peter B. 2007. "Militarization and Policing: Its Relevance to 21st-Century Police." *Policing* 1 (4): 501-513.

LaMance, Ken. 2013. "Marital Rape Lawyers." Legal-Match, November 5. Available at http://www.legalmatch.com/law-library/article/marital-rape.html.

Lanciani, Rodolfo. 1898. *Ancient Rome in the Light of Recent Discoveries*. 12th ed. New York: Houghton, Mifflin.

Langeler, John. 2013. "State May Buy Portion of McNeil Island Prison Property." *KING5*, February 16. Available at http://www.king5.com/story/local/2014/09/18/13225910/.

Langton, Lynn. 2009. "Aviation Units in Large Enforcement Agencies, 2007." NCJ 226672. Available at http://www.bjs.gov/content/pub/pdf/aullea07.pdf.

———. 2010. "Women in Law Enforcement, 1987-2008." NCJ 230521. Available at http://www.bjs.gov/content/pub/pdf/wle8708.pdf.

Langton, Lynn, and Donald J. Farole. 2009. "Census of Public Defender Offices, 2007: Public Defender Offices, 2007—Statistical Tables." NCJ 228538. Available at http://www.bjs.gov/content/pub/pdf/pdo07st.pdf.

———. 2010. "Census of Public Defender Offices, 2007: State Public Defender Programs, 2007." NCJ 228229. Available at http://www.bjs.gov/content/pub/pdf/spdp07.pdf.

Lankenau, Stephen E. 2001. "Smoke 'Em If You Got 'Em: Cigarette Black Markets in U.S. Prisons and Jails." *Prison Journal* 81 (2): 142–161.

Larsson, Thomas. 2001. *The Race to the Top: The Real Story of Globalization*. Washington, DC: Cato Institute.

La Vigne, Nancy, and Julie Samuels. 2012. "The Growth and Increasing Costs of the Federal Prison System: Drivers and Potential Solutions." Available at http://www.urban.org/UploadedPDF/412693-The-Growth-and-Increasing-Cost-of-the-Federal-Prison-System.pdf.

Lawson, Tamara F. 2009. "Before the Verdict and Beyond the Verdict: The *CSI* Infection Within Modern Criminal Jury Trials." *Loyola University Chicago Law Journal* 41:119-173.

Le Bohec, Yann. 2000. *The Imperial Roman Army*. London: Routledge.

Legal Grind. 2011. "Law Versus Equity." In *A Little Law Book*. Available at http://www.legalgrind.com/index.php/law-library/113-law-library-category/the-little-law-book/236-law-versus-equity.

Lemert, Edwin. 1951. *Social Pathology*. New York: McGraw-Hill.

Leo, Richard A., and Richard J. Ofshe. 1998. "Consequences of False Confessions: Deprivations of Liberty and Miscarriages of Justice in the Age of Psychological Interrogation." *Journal of Criminal Law and Criminology* 88 (2): 429-496.

Levin, Mark, and Virginia Tice. 2013. "Japan's New Citizen Judges: How Secrecy Imperils Judicial Reform." *Asia-Pacific Journal*. Available at http://www.japanfocus.org/-Mark-Levin/3141.

Levine, James P. 2009. "The Impact of Sequestration on Juries." In *Courts and Justice*, 4th ed., edited by G. Larry Mays and Peter R. Gregware, 184-197. Prospect Heights, IL: Waveland Press.

Levine, Marvin J. 1988. "A Historical Overview of Police Unionization in the United States." *Police Journal* 61:334-343.

Lieberman, Joel D., and Bruce D. Sales. 2006. *Scientific Jury Selection*. Washington, DC: American Psychological Association.

Linke, Uli. 2010. "Fortress Europe: Globalization, Militarization, and the Policing of the Interior Borderland." *TOPIA: Canadian Journal of Cultural Studies* 23-24:100-120.

Liss, Carolin. 2003. "Maritime Piracy in Southeast Asia." *Southeast Asian Affairs* 29:52-68.

Livingstone, K. 2002. "Sea Piracy." In *Encyclopedia of Crime and Punishment*, edited by D. Levinson, 1145-1148. Thousand Oaks, CA: Sage.

Livsey, Sarah. 2012. "Juvenile Delinquency Probation Caseload, 2009." Available at http://www.ojjdp.gov/pubs/239082.pdf.

Loftus, Elizabeth F. 1996. *Eyewitness Testimony*. Cambridge, MA: Harvard University Press.

Lofty, Mel. 2002. "Restorative Policing." Paper presented at Third International Conference on Conferencing, Circles and Other Restorative Practices, Minneapolis, MN, August 8-10. Available at http://www.iirp.edu/pdf/mn02_lofty.pdf.

Loh, Elizabeth E. 2009. "Breaking the Law to Enforce It: Undercover Police Participation in Crime." *Stanford Law Review* 62:155-198.

Los Angeles County Public Defender's Office. 2012. "Our History: The Public Defender Concept—Why and When?" Available at http://pd.co.la.ca.us/About_history.html.

Loughman, Brian P., and Richard A. Sibery. 2012. *Bribery and Corruption: Navigating the Global Risks*. New York: John Wiley and Sons.

Lovgren, Stefan. 2004. "'CSI' Effect' Is Mixed Blessing for Real Crime Labs." *National Geographic News*, September 23. Available at http://news.nationalgeographic.com/news/2004/09/0923_040923_csi.html.

Lubitz, Robin L., and Thomas W. Ross. 2001. "Sentencing Guidelines: Reflections on the Future." *Executive Sessions on Sentencing and Cor-*

rections, no. 10. Available at https://www .ncjrs.gov/pdffiles1/nij/186480.pdf.

Lurigio, Arthur J. 2011. "Examining Prevailing Beliefs About People with Serious Mental Illness in the Criminal Justice System." *Federal Probation* 75 (1): 11-18.

Maguire, Edward, and William Wells, eds. 2009. *Implementing Community Policing: Lessons from 12 Agencies*. Washington, DC: U.S. Department of Justice. Available at http://www.cops.us doj.gov/files/RIC/Publications/ImpCP-Lessons-FINAL-080811-508.pdf.

Maguire, Kathleen, ed. 2013. *Sourcebook of Criminal Justice Statistics*. Washington, DC: Bureau of Justice Statistics. Available at http:// www.albany.edu/sourcebook.html.

Mahoney, Patricia, and Linda M. Williams. 1998. "Sexual Assault in Marriage: Prevalence, Consequences, and Treatment for Wife Rape." In *Partner Violence: A Comprehensive Review of 20 Years of Research*, edited by Jana L. Jasinski and Linda M. Williams, 116-162. Thousand Oaks, CA: Sage.

Mansfield, Cathy Lesser. 1999. "Disorder in the People's Court: Rethinking the Role of Non-Lawyer Judges in Limited Jurisdiction Court Civil Cases." *New Mexico Law Review* 29:119-200.

Martinson, Robert. 1974. "What Works? Questions and Answers About Prison Reform." *Public Interest* 35 (Spring): 22-35.

Marvell, Thomas. 1989. "State Appellate Court Responses to Caseload Growth." *Judicature* 72 (2): 282-291.

Marx, Gary T. 1982. "Who Really Gets Stung? Some Issues Raised by the New Police Undercover Work." *Crime and Delinquency* 28:165-192.

_____. 1988. *Undercover: Police Surveillance in America*. Berkeley: University of California Press.

Mason, Cody. 2013. *International Growth Trends in Prison Privatization*. Washington, DC: Sentencing Project.

Matejkowski, Jason. 2011. "Exploring the Moderating Effects of Mental Illness on Parole Release Decisions." *Federal Probation* 75 (1): 19-26.

Mays, G. Larry. 2012. *American Courts and the Judicial Process*. New York: Oxford University Press.

Mays, G. Larry, and Rick Ruddell. 2008. *Making Sense of Criminal Justice*. New York: Oxford University Press.

_____. 2012. *Do the Crime, Do the Time: Juvenile Criminals and Adult Justice in the American Court System*. Santa Barbara, CA: Praeger.

Mays, G. Larry, Stephen G. Ryan, and Cindy Bejarano. 1997. "New Mexico Creates a DWI Drug Court." *Judicature* 81 (3): 122-125.

Mays, G. Larry, and L. Thomas Winfree Jr. 2012. *Juvenile Justice*. 3rd ed. New York: Wolters Kluwer Law and Business.

_____. 2014. *Essentials of Corrections*. 5th ed. Malden, MA: Wiley Blackwell.

McGowen, Randall. 1995. "The Well-Ordered Prison: England, 1780-1865." In *The Oxford History of the Prison: The Practice of Punishment in Western Society*, edited by Norval Morris and David J. Rothman, 79-100. New York: Oxford University Press.

McNiven, Jennifer. 2014. "The Agency of Slaves in Ancient Mesopotamian State Formation." Available at http://www.academia.edu/4398718/ The_Agency_of_Slaves_in_Mesopotamian_State_ Formation.

McNulty, Thomas L., and Bellair, Paul E. 2003. "Explaining Racial and Ethnic Differences in Serious Adolescent Violent Behavior." *Criminology* 41:709-748.

Meador, Daniel J. 1991. *American Courts*. St. Paul, MN: West.

Michel, Caroline, Bruno Rossion, Jaehyun Han, Chan Sup Chung, and Roberto Caldara. 2006. "Holistic Processing Is Finely Tuned for Faces of One's Own Race." *Psychological Science* 17 (7): 608-615.

Minnesota Sentencing Guidelines Commission. 2014. *Minnesota Sentencing Guidelines and Commentary*. St. Paul: Minnesota Sentencing Guidelines Commission.

Minton, Todd D. 2013. "Jail Inmates at Midyear 2012: Statistical Tables." NCJ 241264. Available at http://www.bjs.gov/content/pub/pdf/jim12st.pdf.

Mollen Commission. 1994. *Commission Report: Anatomy of Failure; A Path to Success*. Available at http://www.parc.info/client_files/Special%20 Reports/4%20-%20Mollen%20Commission%20-%20NYPD.pdf.

Moore, Elizabeth. 2011a. "The Use of Police Cautions and Youth Justice Conferences in NSW in 2010." *Crime and Justice Statistics Bureau Brief*, no. 73. Available at http://www.bocsar .nsw.gov.au/agdbasev7wr/bocsar/documents/pdf/ bb73.pdf.

_____. 2011b. "Youth Justice Conferences Versus Children's Court: A Comparison of Time to Finalisation." *Crime and Justice Statistics Bureau*

Brief, no. 74. Available at http://www.bocsar .nsw.gov.au/agdbasev7wr/bocsar/documents/pdf/ bb74.pdf.

Morris, Norval. 2002. *Maconochie's Gentlemen: The Story of Norfolk Island and the Roots of Modern Prison Reform.* New York: Oxford University Press.

Mumola, Christopher J. 2000. "Incarcerated Parents and Their Children." NCJ 182335. Available at http://www.bjs.gov/content/pub/pdf/iptc.pdf.

Murphy, Jeffrie G. 1992. *Retribution Reconsidered: More Essays on the Philosophy of Law.* Norwell, MA: Kluwer Academic.

Natarjan, Mangai. 2005. "International Crime and Justice: An Introduction." In *Introduction to International Criminal Justice*, edited by M. Matarjan, xv-xxiii. Boston: McGraw-Hill.

National Advisory Committee on Criminal Justice Standards and Goals. 1976. *Juvenile Justice and Delinquency Prevention.* Washington, DC: U.S. Government Printing Office.

National Advisory Committee on Juvenile Justice and Delinquency Prevention. 1980. *Standards for the Administration of Juvenile Justice.* Washington, DC: U.S. Government Printing Office.

National Heritage Board of Poland. 2011. *Stop Heritage Crime: Good Practices and Recommendations.* Warsaw: National Heritage Board of Poland.

National Institute of Justice. 2012. "Police Use of Force." Available at http://www.nij.gov/topics/ law-enforcement/officer-safety/use-of-force/pages/ welcome.aspx.

Newell, Tim. 2002. "Restorative Practice in Prisons: Circles and Other Restorative Practices." Paper presented at the Third International Conference on Conferencing, Circles and Other Restorative Practices, Minneapolis, MN, August 8-10. Available at http://www.iirp.edu/ar ticle_detail.php?article_id=NDQ1.

New Jersey State Association of Chiefs of Police. 2007. "Police Department Regionalization, Consolidation, Merger and Shared Services: Important Considerations for Policy Makers." Available at https:// www.njslom.org/documents/whitepaper.pdf.

Niederhoffer, Arthur. 1969. *Behind the Shield: The Police in Urban Society.* Garden City, NY: Anchor Press.

North Carolina Domestic Violence Commission. 2013. "North Carolina Batterer Intervention Programs: A Guide to Achieving Recommended Practices." Available at http://www.councilforwomen.nc.gov/ documents/publications/BattererInterventionHand book.pdf.

Office for Victims of Crime. 2010. "OVC Fact Sheet: What Is the Office for Victims of Crime?" April. Available at http://www.ovc.gov/publica tions/factshts/what_is_OVC2010/fs_000321.html.

Office of Justice Programs. 1996. "LEAA/OJP Retrospective: 30 Years of Federal Support to State and Local Criminal Justice." Available at https://www.ncjrs.gov/pdffiles1/nij/164509.pdf.

Office of Juvenile Justice and Delinquency Prevention. n.d. "Balanced and Restorative Justice: Program Summary." Available at https:// www.ncjrs.gov/pdffiles/bal.pdf (accessed September 18, 2014).

O'Neal, Bill. 1979. *Encyclopedia of Western Gunfighters.* Norman: University of Oklahoma Press.

Online Dictionary. 2013. "Watch and ward." Available at http://onlinedictionary.dataseg ment.com/word/watch+and+ward.

Oxford Dictionary. 2014. "Justice." Available at http://www.oxforddictionaries.com/us/definition/ american_english/justice.

Packer, Herbert. 1968. *The Limits of the Criminal Sanction.* Stanford, CA: Stanford University Press.

Padgett, Kathy G., William D. Bales, and Thomas G. Blomberg. 2006. "Under Surveillance: An Empirical Test of the Effectiveness and Consequences of Electronic Monitoring." *Criminology and Public Policy* 5 (1): 201-232.

Palmer, Charles Steven. 2004. "Economics, Grievances, Protective-Employee Unionization, and the 1978 Memphis Fire and Police Strikes." *Essays in Economic and Business History* 22:183-197.

Parent, Dale G., and Ronald P. Corbett. 1996. "Day Reporting Centers: An Evolving Intermediate Sanction." *Federal Probation* 60:51-54.

Parent, Dale, Terence Dunworth, Douglas McDonald, and William Rhodes. 1997. "Key Legislative Issues in Criminal Justice: Mandatory Sentencing." *National Institute of Justice Research in Action*, January. Available at https:// www.ncjrs.gov/pdffiles/161839.pdf.

Paterson, Craig, and Kerry Clamp. 2012. "Exploring Recent Developments in Restorative Policing in England and Wales." *Criminology and Criminal Justice* 22:593-611.

Peak, Kenneth J. 2000. *Policing America: Methods, Issues, Challenges.* 3rd ed. Upper Saddle River, NJ: Prentice Hall.

_____. 2012. *Policing America: Challenges and Best Practices*. Upper Saddle River, NJ: Prentice Hall.

Pelissier, Bernadette, Mark Motivans, and Jennifer L. Rounds-Bryant. 2005. "Substance Abuse Treatment Outcomes: A Multi-site Study of Male and Female Prison Programs." *Journal of Offender Rehabilitation* 41 (2): 57-80.

Pennsylvania State Police. n.d. "History: Pennsylvania State Police." Available at http://www.psp-hemc.org/history/psp.html (accessed September 3, 2014).

Perry, Steven W. 2006. "Prosecutors in State Courts, 2005." NCJ 231799. Available at http://www.bjs.gov/content/pub/pdf/psc05.pdf.

Peters, Edward M. 1995. "Prison Before the Prison: The Ancient and Medieval Worlds." In *The Oxford History of the Prison: The Practice of Punishment in Western Society*, edited by Norval Morris and David J. Rothman, 3-48. New York: Oxford University Press.

Peters, Roger H., and Marc L. Steinberg. 2000. "Substance Abuse Treatment in U.S. Prisons." In *Drugs and Prisons*, edited by D. Shewan and J. Davies, 89-116. London: Gordon and Breach.

Pew Center on the States. 2010. "Prison Count 2010: State Population Declines for the First Time in 38 Years." Available at http://www.pewtrusts.org/~/media/legacy/uploadedfiles/wwwpewtrustsorg/reports/sentencing_and_corrections/PrisonCount2010pdf.pdf.

Poaline, Eugene A., III, and William Terrill. 2007. "Police Education, Experience, and the Use of Force." *Criminal Justice and Behavior* 34 (2): 179-196.

Police Foundation. 1981. *The Newark Foot Patrol Experiment*. Washington, DC: Police Foundation.

Polk, Kenneth. 1984. "Juvenile Diversion: A Look at the Record." *Crime and Delinquency* 30 (4): 648-659.

Pollock, Jocelyn M. 2002. *Women, Prison, and Crime*. 2nd ed. Belmont, CA: Thomson/Wadsworth.

Poole, Eric D., and Robert M. Regoli. 1980. "Police Professionalism and Role Conflict: A Comparison of Rural and Urban Departments." *Human Relations* 33:241-252.

Pound, Roscoe. 1930. *Criminal Justice in America*. New York: Henry Holt.

Poynton, Suzanne. 2013. "Rates of Recidivism Among Offenders Referred to Forum Sentencing." *Contemporary Issues in Crime and Justice*, no. 172. Available at http://www.bocsar.nsw.gov.au/agdbasev7wr/_assets/bocsar/m71685412/cjb172.pdf.

President's Commission on Law Enforcement and Administration of Justice. 1967a. *The Challenge of Crime in a Free Society*. Washington, DC: U.S. Government Printing Office. Available at https://www.ncjrs.gov/pdffiles1/nij/42.pdf.

_____.1967b. *Task Force Report: The Police*. Washington, DC: U.S. Government Printing Office.

"Prison Violence." 2002. *Corrections Compendium* 27 (5): 6-14.

Puzzanchera, Charles. 2009. "Juvenile Arrests, 2008." NCJ 228479. Available at https://www.ncjrs.gov/pdffiles1/ojjdp/228479.pdf.

Radelet, Louis A., and David L. Carter. 1994. *The Police and the Community*. New York: Macmillan.

Radosh, Polly F. 2008. "War on Drugs: Gender and Race Inequities in Crime Control Strategies." *Criminal Justice Studies* 21 (2): 167-178.

Ramakers, Anke, Robert Apel, Paul Nieuwbeerta, Anja Dirkzwager, and Johan van Wilsem. 2014. "Imprisonment Length and Post-prison Employment Prospects." *Criminology* 52 (3): 399-427.

"Ramsey Renews Call for National Crime and Justice Study Commission." 2013. *Crime Report*, October 21. Available at http://www.thecrimereport.org/news/crime-and-justice-news/2013 10-ramsey-renews-call-for-national-crime-study-commissi.

Ratcliffe, Jerry H., Travis Taniguchi, Elizabeth R. Groff, and Jennifer Wood. 2011. "The Philadelphia Foot Patrol Experiment: A Randomized Controlled Trial of Police Patrol Effectiveness in Violent Crime Hotspots." *Criminology* 49 (3): 795-831.

Reaves, Brian A. 2011. "Census of State and Local Law Enforcement Agencies, 2008." NCJ 233982. Available at http://www.bjs.gov/content/pub/pdf/csllea08.pdf.

_____. 2012a. "Federal Law Enforcement Officers, 2008." Available at http://www.bjs.gov/content/pub/pdf/fleo08.pdf.

_____. 2012b. "Hiring and Retention of State and Local Law Enforcement Officers, 2008: Statistical Tables." Available at http://www.bjs.gov/content/pub/pdf/hrslleo08st.pdf.

Rehnquist, William H. 2001. *The Supreme Court*. New York: Alfred A. Knopf.

Reichel, Philip L. 2008. *Comparative Criminal Justice Systems: A Topical Approach*. Upper Saddle River, NJ: Pearson/Prentice Hall.

_____. 2013. *Comparative Criminal Justice Systems: A Topical Approach.* 6th ed. Boston: Pearson.

Reid, Traciel V. 1999. "The Politicization of Retention Elections." *Judicature* 83 (2): 68-77.

Reiss, Albert J. 1971. *The Police and the Public.* New Haven, CT: Yale University Press.

Rennison, Callie Marie. 2002. "Rape and Sexual Assault: Reporting to Police and Medical Attention, 1992-2000." NCJ 194530. Available at http://www.bjs.gov/content/pub/pdf/rsarp00.pdf.

Renzema, Marc, and Evan Mayo-Wilson. 2005. "Can Electronic Monitoring Reduce Crime for Moderate to High-Risk Offenders?" *Journal of Experimental Criminology* 1:215-237.

Richardson, James F. 1974. *Urban Police in the United States.* Port Washington, NY: Kennikat Press.

Robertson, John A. 1974. *Rough Justice: Perspectives on Lower Criminal Courts.* Boston: Little, Brown.

Rogers, Brian. 2012. "Hundreds of Cases to Be Reviewed Because of Errors by Crime Lab Worker." *Houston Chronicle*, May 1. Available at http://www.chron.com/news/houston-texas/article/Hundreds-of-cases-to-be-reviewed-because-of-3525028.php.

Rosenmerkel, Sean, Matthew Durose, and Donald Farole Jr. 2009. "Felony Sentences in State Courts, 2006: Statistical Tables." NCJ 226846. Available at http://www.bjs.gov/content/pub/pdf/fssc06st.pdf.

Rothman, David J. 1995. "Perfecting the Prison: United States." In *The Oxford History of the Prison: The Practice of Punishment in Western Society*, edited by Norval Morris and David J. Rothman, 111-130. New York: Oxford University Press.

Rothman, Emily F., Alexander Butchart, and Magdalena Cerda. 2003. *Intervening with Perpetrators of Intimate Partner Violence: A Global Perspective.* Geneva: World Health Organization. Available at http://apps.who.int/iris/bitstream/10665/42647/1/9241590491.pdf.

Rotman, Edgardo. 1995. "The Failure of Reform: United States, 1865-1965." In *The Oxford History of the Prison: The Practice of Punishment in Western Society*, edited by Norval Morris and David J. Rothman, 169-198. New York: Oxford University Press.

Rottman, David B., and Shauna M. Strickland. 2006. *State Court Organization, 2004.* Washington, DC: Bureau of Justice Statistics, U.S. Department of Justice.

Rubenstein, Jonathan. 1973. *City Police.* New York: Farrar, Straus, and Giroux.

Rutledge, John P. 2001. "They All Look Alike: The Inaccuracy of Cross-racial Identifications." *American Journal of Criminal Law* 28:207-228.

Rydberg, Jason, and William Terrill. 2010. "The Effect of Higher Education on Police Behavior." *Police Quarterly* 13:82-120.

Sabol, William J., and John McGready. 1999. "Time Served in Prison by Federal Offenders, 1986-97." NCJ 171682. Available at http://bjs.gov/content/pub/pdf/tspfo97.pdf.

Sabol, William J., Todd D. Minton, and Paige M. Harrison. 2007. "Prison and Jail Inmates at Midyear, 2006." NCJ 217675. Available at http://www.bjs.gov/content/pub/pdf/pjim06.pdf.

Sabol, William J., Heather C. West, and Matthew Cooper. 2009. "Prisoners in 2008." NCJ 228417. Available at http://www.bjs.gov/content/pub/pdf/p08.pdf.

Sampson, Robert J., and Stephen W. Raudenbush. 1999. "Systematic Social Observation of Public Spaces: A New Look at Disorder in Urban Neighborhoods." *American Journal of Sociology* 105 (3): 603-651.

Sanborn, Joseph B., Jr. 2009. "Pleading Guilty and Plea Bargaining: The Dynamics of Avoiding Trial in American Criminal Courts." In *Courts and Justice*, 4th ed., edited by G. Larry Mays and Peter R. Gregware, 109-128. Prospect Heights, IL: Waveland Press.

Santayana, George. 1905. *The Life of Reason.* Vol. 1, *Reason in Common Sense.* New York: Charles Scribner and Sons. Available at http://www.gutenberg.org/files/15000/15000-h/vol1.html.

Santos, Michael G. 2004. *About Prison.* Belmont, CA: Wadsworth/Thomson.

Sayer, Andrew. 2009. "Contributive Justice and Meaningful Work." *Res Publica* 15:1-16.

Schauffler, Richard Y., Neal B. Kauder, Robert C. LaFountain, William E. Raftery, Shauna M. Strickland, and Brenda G. Otto. 2006. *State Court Caseload Statistics, 2005.* Williamsburg, VA: National Center for State Courts.

Scheck, Barry, Peter Neufeld, and Jim Dwyer. 2000. *Actual Innocence: Five Days to Execution and Other Dispatches From the Wrongfully Convicted.* New York: Doubleday.

Scheider, Matthew. 2008. "Community Policing Nugget." *Community Policing Dispatch*, January. Available at http://cops.usdoj.gov/html/dispatch/january_2008/nugget.html.

Schmitt, Glenn R. 2006. "Drug Courts: The Second Decade." NCJ 211081. Available at https://www.ncjrs.gov/pdffiles1/nij/211081.pdf.

Schmitz, Leonhard. 1875. "Quaestor." In *A Dictionary of Greek and Roman Antiquities*, edited by William Smith, 980-982. London: John Murray. Available at http://penelope.uchicago.edu/Thayer/E/Roman/Texts/secondary/SMIGRA*/Quaestor.html.

Schubert, Frank August. 2010. *Criminal Law*. Austin, TX: Wolters Kluwer Law and Business.

Schultz, David P., Ed Hudak, and Geoffrey P. Alpert. 2010. "Evidence-Based Decisions on Police Pursuits: The Officer's Perspective." *FBI Law Enforcement Bulletin* 79 (3): 1-10.

Schweitzer, N.J., and Michael J. Saks (2007). "The *CSI* Effect: Popular Fiction About Forensic Science Affects the Public's Expectations About Real Forensic Science." *Jurimetrics* 47:357-364.

Sedlak, Andrea J., and Carol Bruce. 2010. "Youth's Characteristics and Backgrounds: Findings from the Survey of Youth in Residential Placement." NCJ 227730. Available at https://www.ncjrs.gov/pdffiles1/ojjdp/227730.pdf.

Selman, Donna, and Paul Leighton. 2010. *Punishment for Sale: Private Prisons, Big Business, and the Incarceration Binge*. Lanham, MD: Rowman and Littlefield.

Senna, Joseph J. 1974. "Criminal Justice Higher Education: Its Growth and Directions." *Crime and Delinquency* 20:389-397.

Shalakany, Amr. 2006. "Comparative Law as Archaeology: On Sodomy, Islamic Law and the Human Rights Activist." Paper presented at New York University Kevorkian Center for Middle East Studies, October 9. Available at http://www.utexas.edu/law/centers/humanrights/events/speaker-series-papers/Shalakany.pdf.

Shank, Michael, and Elizabeth Beavers. 2013. "The Militarization of U.S. Police Forces." *Reuters*, October 22. Available at http://www.reuters.com/article/2013/10/22/us-opinion-shank-idUSBRE99L12420131022.

Shelton, Donald E. 2008. "The 'CSI Effect': Does It Really Exist?" *NIJ Journal* 259:1-7.

Sheppard, Stephen Michael, ed. 2012. *Bouvier Law Dictionary*. New York: Wolters Kluwer Law and Business.

Sifakis, Carl. 2005. *The Mafia Encyclopedia*. 3rd ed. New York: Facts on File.

Simon, A. Josias. 2013. "Paramilitary Policing in the Implementation of Police Department Tasks: The National Police of the Republic of Indonesia (POLRI)." *International Journal of Criminology and Sociology* 2:519-524.

Slate, Risdon N. 2004. "Mental Health Courts: Striving for Accountability While Looking to the Future and Holding Civil Liberties and Public Safety in the Balance." In *Courts and Justice*, 3rd ed., edited by G. Larry Mays and Peter R. Gregware, 423-429. Prospect Heights, IL: Waveland Press.

Slate, Risdon N., Jacqueline K. Buffington-Vollum, and W. Wesley Johnson. 2013. *The Criminalization of Mental Illness: Crisis and Opportunity for the Justice System*. 2nd ed. Durham, NC: Carolina Academic Press.

Smith, Christopher E. 1991. *Courts and the Poor*. Chicago: Nelson-Hall.

Smith, Christopher E., and Anne M. Corbin. 2008. "The Rehnquist Court and Corrections Law: An Empirical Assessment." *Criminal Justice Studies* 21 (2): 179-191.

Smith, Nadine, and Don Weatherburn. 2012. "Youth Justice Conferences Versus Children's Court: A Comparison of Re-offending." *Contemporary Issues in Crime and Justice*, no. 160. Available at http://www.bocsar.nsw.gov.au/agdbasev7wr/bocsar/documents/pdf/cjb160.pdf.

Snell, Tracy L. 2011. "Capital Punishment, 2010: Statistical Tables." NCJ 236510. Available at http://www.bjs.gov/content/pub/pdf/cp10st.pdf.

_____. 2013. "Capital Punishment, 2011: Statistical Tables." NCJ 242185. Available at http://www.bjs.gov/content/pub/pdf/cp11st.pdf.

_____. 2014. "Capital Punishment, 2012: Statistical Tables." NCJ 245789. Available at http://www.bjs.gov/content/pub/pdf/cp12st.pdf.

Snyder, Howard N., and Melissa Sickmund. 2006. *Juvenile Offenders and Victims: 2006 National Report*. Washington, DC: U.S. Department of Justice.

Soler, Mark, and Lisa M. Garry. 2009. "Reducing Disproportionate Minority Contact: Preparation at the Local Level." *Disproportionate Minority Contact*, September. Available at https://www.ncjrs.gov/pdffiles1/ojjdp/218861.pdf.

Sorg, Evan T., Cory P. Haberman, Jerry H. Ratcliffe, and Elizabeth R. Groff. 2013. "Foot Patrol in Violent Crime Hot Spots: Longitudinal Impacts of Deterrence and Post-treatment Effects of Displacement." *Criminology* 51 (1): 65-102.

Soulé, Dave, Denise Gottfredson, and Erin Bauer. 2008. "It's 3 p.m. Do You Know Where Your Child Is? A Study on the Timing of Juvenile

Victimization and Delinquency." *Justice Quarterly* 25 (4): 623-646.

Southerland, Mittie D. 2002. "Criminal Justice Curricula in the United States: A Decade of Change." *Justice Quarterly* 19 (4): 589-601.

Spangenberg, Robert L., and Marea L. Beeman. 1995. "Indigent Defense Systems in the United States." *Law and Contemporary Problems* 58 (1): 31-49.

Spelman, William. 2000. "Prisons and Crime." In *Crime and Justice: A Review of Research*, edited by M. Tonry, 419-494. Chicago: University of Chicago Press.

Spierenburg, Pieter. 1995. "The Body and the State: Early Modern Europe." In *The Oxford History of the Prison: The Practice of Punishment in Western Society*, edited by Norval Morris and David J. Rothman, 49-78. New York: Oxford University Press.

Spohn, Cassia. 2007. "The Deterrent Effect of Imprisonment and Offenders' Stakes in Conformity." *Criminal Justice Policy Review* 18 (1): 31-50.

Spohn, Cassia, and David Holleran. 2000. "The Imprisonment Penalty Paid by Young, Unemployed Black and Hispanic Male Offenders." *Criminology* 38 (1): 281-306.

Stark, Rodney. 1972. *Police Riots: Collective Violence and Law Enforcement*. Belmont, CA: Wadsworth.

"Statute of Winchester 1285." 2013. *Documents in English History*, February 3. Available at http://historyofengland.typepad.com/documents_in_english_hist/2013/02/statute-of-winchester-1285.html.

Steele, Walter W., and Elizabeth G. Thornburg. 2009. "Jury Instructions: A Persistent Failure to Communicate." In *Courts and Justice*, 4th ed., edited by G. Larry Mays and Peter R. Gregware, 141-153. Prospect Heights, IL: Waveland Press.

Steffens, Lincoln. 1957. *The Shame of the Cities*. New York: Hill and Wang.

Steffensmeier, Darrell, and Stephen Demuth. 2000. "Ethnicity and Sentencing Outcomes in U.S. Federal Courts: Who Is Punished More Harshly?" *American Sociological Review* 65 (5): 705-729.

_____. 2001. "Ethnicity and Judges' Sentencing Decisions: Hispanic-Black-White Comparisons." *Criminology* 39 (1): 145-178.

Stefko, Joseph, and Scott Settig. 2012. "Modeling Options for a Consolidated Law Enforcement Agency: City of Jamestown and Chautauqua County, NY." Available at http://www.cgr.org/jamestown/docs/Baseline-and-Prelim-Options-11-9-2012.pdf.

Stephan, James J. 2008. "Census of State and Federal Correctional Facilities, 2005." NCJ 222182. Available at http://www.bjs.gov/content/pub/pdf/csfcf05.pdf.

Stephens, Otis H., and Gregory J. Rathjen. 1980. *The Supreme Court and the Allocation of Constitutional Power*. San Francisco: W.H. Freeman.

Stephens, Sheila. 2006-2007. "The 'CSI' Effect on Real Crime Labs." *New England Law Review* 41:590-607.

Stewart, Gary. 1998. "Black Codes and Broken Windows: The Legacy of Racial Hegemony in Anti-Gang Civil Injunctions." *Yale Law Journal* 107 (7): 2249-2279.

Stolz, Barbara A. 1997. "Privatizing Corrections: Changing the Corrections Policy-Making Subgovernment." *Prison Journal* 77 (1): 92-111.

Strodtbeck, Fred L., Rita M. James, and Charles Hawkins. 1957. "Social Status in Jury Deliberations." *American Sociological Review* 22 (6): 713-719.

Strodtbeck, Fred L., and Richard D. Mann. 1956. "Sex Role Differentiation in Jury Deliberations." *Sociometry* 19 (1): 3-11.

Sullivan, Jacqueline. 2001. "Widening the Net in Juvenile Justice and the Dangers of Prevention and Early Intervention." Available at http://www.cjcj.org/uploads/cjcj/documents/widening.pdf.

Sumner, William Graham. 1906. *Folkways: A Study of the Sociological Importance of Usages, Manners, Customs, Mores, and Morals*. Boston: Ginn.

Sykes, Gresham M. 1958. *The Society of Captives*. Princeton, NJ: Princeton University Press.

Sykes, Gresham M., and Sheldon Messinger. 1960. "The Inmate Social System." In *Theoretical Studies in Social Organization of the Prison*, by Gresham M. Sykes, Sheldon L. Messinger, Richard A. Cloward, Richard McCleery, Donald R. Cressey, Lloyd E. Ohlin, and George H. Grosser, 5-19. New York: Social Science Research Council.

Tanner, Samuel, and Massimiliano Mulone. 2012. "Private Security and Armed Conflict: A Case Study of the Scorpions During the Mass Killings in the Former Yugoslavia." *British Journal of Criminology* 53:41-58.

Terry, Charles M. 2003. *The Fellas: Overcoming Prison and Addiction*. Belmont, CA: Wadsworth.

Thatcher, David. 2004. "Order Maintenance Reconsidered: Moving Beyond Strong Causal Reasoning." *Journal of Criminal Law and Criminology* 94 (2): 381-414.

Theodorson, George A., and Achilles G. Theodorson. 1969. *Modern Dictionary of Sociology: The Concepts and Terminology of Sociology and Related Disciplines*. New York: Thomas Y. Crowell.

Thompson, R. Alan, Lisa S. Nored, and Kelly Cheeseman Dial. 2008. "The Prison Rape Elimination Act (PREA): An Evaluation of Policy Compliance with Illustrative Excerpts." *Criminal Justice Policy Review* 19 (4): 414-437.

Tillyer, Rob. 2012. "Opening the Black Box of Officer Decision-Making: An Examination of Race, Criminal History, and Discretionary Searches." *Justice Quarterly* 31 (6): 961-985.

Tjaden, Patricia, and Nancy Thoennes. 2006. "Extent, Nature, and Consequences of Rape Victimization: Findings from the National Violence Against Women Survey." NCJ 210346. Available at https://www.ncjrs.gov/pdffiles1/nij/210346.pdf.

Tonry, Michael. 2004. *Thinking About Crime: Sense and Sensibility in American Penal Culture*. New York: Oxford University Press.

Torres, Donald A. 1987. *Handbook of State Police, Highway Patrol, and Investigative Agencies*. Westport, CT: Greenwood Press.

Turley, Alan, Tim Thornton, Craig Johnson, and Sue Azzolino. 2004. "Jail Drug and Alcohol Treatment Program Reduces Recidivism in Nonviolent Offenders: A Longitudinal Study of Monroe County, New York's, Jail Treatment Drug and Alcohol Program." *International Journal of Offender Therapy and Comparative Criminology* 48 (6): 721-728.

Twerksy-Glasner, Aviva. 2005. "Police Personality: What Is It and Why Are They Like That?" *Journal of Police and Criminal Psychology* 20 (1): 56-67.

Tyler, Tom R. 2006. "Viewing *CSI* and the Threshold of Guilt: Managing Truth and Justice in Reality and Fiction." *Yale Law Review* 115:105-155.

United Nations Global Initiative to Fight Human Trafficking. n.d. "Human Trafficking: The Facts." Available at http://www.unglobalcompact.org/docs/issues_doc/labour/Forced_labour/HUMAN_TRAFFICKING_-_THE_FACTS_-_final.pdf (accessed September 18, 2014).

United Nations Office on Drugs and Crime. n.d. "About UNODC." Available at http://www.unodc.org/unodc/en/about-unodc/index.html?ref=menutop (accessed September 18, 2014).

_____. 2013. *World Drug Report 2013*. New York: United Nations. Available at http://www.unodc.org/unodc/secured/wdr/wdr2013/World_Drug_Report_2013.pdf.

Uphoff, Rodney J. 2009. "The Criminal Defense Lawyer: Zealous Advocate, Double Agent, or Beleaguered Dealer?" In *Courts and Justice*, 4th ed., edited by G. Larry Mays and Peter R. Gregware, 332-365. Prospect Heights, IL: Waveland Press.

U.S. Census Bureau. 2012. "Table 344: Employment by State and Local Law Enforcement Agencies by Type of Agency and Employee: 2008." Available at http://www.census.gov/compendia/statab/2012/tables/12s0344.pdf.

U.S. Courts. 2012. "Federal District Court Workload Increases in Fiscal Year 2011." *Third Branch News*, March 13. Available at http://news.uscourts.gov/federal-district-court-workload-increases-fiscal-year-2011.

U.S. Department of Justice. 1986. "Report of the Tort Policy Working Group on the Causes, Extent, and Policy Implications of the Current Crisis in Insurance Availability and Affordability." Available at http://files.eric.ed.gov/fulltext/ED274437.pdf.

_____. 2012. "Attorney General Eric Holder Announces Revisions to Uniform Crime Report's Definition of Rape." January 6. Available at http://www.justice.gov/opa/pr/2012/January/12-ag-018.html.

U.S. Equal Employment Opportunity Commission. n.d. "EEO-1 Job Classification Guide 2010." Available at http://www.eeoc.gov/employers/eeo1survey/jobclassguide.cfm (accessed September 16, 2014).

U.S. General Accounting Office. 1980. *The Law Enforcement Education Program Is in Serious Financial Disarray*. Washington, DC: General Accounting Office.

U.S. Government Accountability Office. 1998. *Law Enforcement: Information on Drug-Related Police Corruption*. Washington, DC: Government Accountability Office. Available at http://www.gao.gov/products/GGD-98-111.

_____. 2006. *Federal Law Enforcement: Survey of Federal Civilian Law Enforcement Functions and*

Authorities. Washington, DC: Government Accountability Office. Available at http://www.gao.gov/products/GAO-07-121.

U.S. Marshals Service. n.d. "History—How Much Did It Cost to Find Billy the Kid?" Available at http://www.usmarshals.gov/history/billythekid.htm (accessed September 3, 2014).

———. 2014. "Fact Sheet: U.S. Marshals Service 2014." Available at http://www.usmarshals.gov/duties/factsheets/overview-2014.pdf.

U.S. Senate. n.d. "Impeachment." Available at http://www.senate.gov/artandhistory/history/common/briefing/Senate_Impeachment_Role.htm#4.

Vago, Steven. 2009. *Law and Society*. 9th ed. Upper Saddle River, NJ: Prentice Hall.

Vera Institute of Justice. 2010. *The Continuing Fiscal Crisis in Corrections: Setting a New Course*. New York: Vera Institute of Justice.

Visher, Christy A., Laura Winterfield, and Mark B. Coggeshall. 2005. "Ex-Offender Employment Programs and Recidivism: A Meta-analysis." *Journal of Experimental Criminology*, 1 (3): 295-316.

Wachtel, Julius. 1992. "From Morals to Practice: Dilemma of Control in Undercover Policing." *Crime, Law, and Social Change* 18:137-158.

Walker, Daniel. 1968. *Rights in Conflict: Convention Week in Chicago, August 25-29, 1968*. New York: E.P. Dutton.

Walker, Donald R. 1988. *Penology for Profit: A History of the Texas Penal System, 1867-1912*. College Station: Texas A&M University Press.

Walker, Samuel. 1980. *Popular Justice: History of American Criminal Justice*. New York: Oxford University Press.

———. 1993. "Does Anyone Remember Team Policing?" *American Journal of Police* 22 (1): 33-55.

———. 2011. *Sense and Nonsense About Crime, Drugs, and Communities: A Policy Guide*. 7th ed. Belmont, CA: Wadsworth.

Walker, Samuel, and Charles M. Katz. 2007. *The Police in America: An Introduction*. 6th ed. Boston: McGraw-Hill.

Wall, David S. 2007. *Cybercrime*. Cambridge, UK: Polity Press.

Walmsley, Roy. 2013. "World Prison Population List." 10th ed. Available at http://www.prisonstudies.org/sites/prisonstudies.org/files/resources/downloads/wppl_10.pdf.

Walsh, Anthony, and Craig Hemmens. 2008. *Law, Justice, and Society*. New York: Oxford University Press.

Wasby, Stephen L. 1988. *The Supreme Court in the Federal Judicial System*, 3rd ed. Chicago: Nelson-Hall.

Watson, Richard, and Randal G. Downing. 1969. *The Politics of the Bench and Bar*. New York: John Wiley.

Webber, Andrew. 2012. "Youth Justice Conferences Versus Children's Court: A Comparison of Cost-Effectiveness." *Contemporary Issues in Crime and Justice*, no. 164: 1-8.

Weber, Max. 1954. *Law in Economy and Society*. Cambridge, MA: Harvard University Press.

Webster, Peter D. 1995. "Selection and Retention of Judges: Is There One 'Best' Method?" *Florida State University Law Review* 23:1-42.

Weiss, Robert P. 2001. "Repatriating Low-Wage Work: The Political Economy of Prison Labor Reprivatization in the Postindustrial United States." *Criminology* 39 (2): 253-291.

Weitekamp, Elmar G.M. 1993. "Reparative Justice: Towards a Victim-Oriented System." *European Journal of Criminal Policy and Research* 1 (1): 70-93.

Wells, Gary L. 2006. "Eyewitness Identification: Systemic Reforms." *Wisconsin Law Review* 2006 (2): 615-643.

Wells, Gary L., Mark Small, Steven Penrod, Roy S. Malpass, Solomon M. Fulero, and C.A.E. Brimacombe. 1998. "Eyewitness Identification Procedures: Recommendations for Lineups and Photospreads." *Law and Human Behavior* 22 (6): 1-39.

Wertham, Frederic. 1954. *Seduction of the Innocent*. New York: Rinehart.

West, Heather C., William J. Sabol, and Sarah J. Greenman. 2010. "Prisoners in 2009." NCJ 231675. Available at http://www.bjs.gov/content/pub/pdf/p09.pdf.

Wheeler, Russell R. 1992. "Origins of the Elements of Federal Court Governance." Available at https://bulk.resource.org/courts.gov/fjc/governce.pdf.

Wheeler, Russell R., and Cynthia Harrison. 1994. *Creating the Federal Judicial System*. 2nd ed. Washington, DC: Federal Judicial Center.

White, Michael D. 2007. *Current Issues and Controversies in Policing*. Boston: Allyn and Bacon.

White, Michael D., Justin T. Ready, Robert J. Kane, and Lisa M. Dario. 2014. "Examining the Effects of the TASER on Cognitive Functioning: Findings from a Pilot Study with Police Recruits." *Journal of Experimental Criminology* 10 (3): 267-290.

Whittenburg, James. 1977. "Planters, Merchants, and Lawyers: Social Change and the Origins of the North Carolina Regulation." *William and Mary Quarterly* 34:215-238.

Wicker, Tom. 1994. *A Time to Die: The Attica Prison Revolt.* Lincoln: University of Nebraska Press.

Wilson, James Q. 1968. *Varieties of Police Behavior.* Cambridge, MA: Harvard University Press.

Wilson, Jeremy M., and Clifford Grammich. 2012. "Police Consolidation, Regionalization, and Shared Services: Options, Considerations, and Lessons from Research and Practice." *BOLO,* February. Available at http://ric-zai-inc.com/Publications/cops-w0641-pub.pdf.

Wilson, Jeremy M., Alexander Weiss, and Steven Chermak. 2014. "Contracting for Law-Enforcement Services: Perspectives from Past Research and Current Practices." Available at http://policeconsolidation.msu.edu/sites/default/files/ContractingReport_021714FINAL.pdf.

Wilt, G. Marie, and James D. Brannon. 1976. "Cynicism or Realism: A Criticism of Niederhoffer's Research into Police Attitudes." *Journal of Police Science and Administration* 4:38-45.

Winfree, L. Thomas, Jr. 2009. "Restorative Policing and Law Enforcement in the United States of America: Problems and Prospects." In *Victimology, Victim Assistance and Criminal Justice: Perspectives Shared by International Experts at the Inter-University Centre of Dubrovnik,* edited by Otmar Hagemann, Peter Schäfer, and Stephanie Schmidt, 245-254. Mönchengladbach, Germany: Niederrhein University of Applied Sciences.

Winfree, L. Thomas, Jr., Greg Newbold, and S. Houston Tubb III. 2002. "Prisoner Perspectives on Inmate Culture in New Mexico and New Zealand: A Descriptive Case Study." *Prison Journal* 82 (2): 213-233.

Winterdyk, John, and Richard Ruddell. 2010. "Managing Prison Gangs: Results from a Survey of U.S. Prison Systems." *Journal of Criminal Justice,* 38 (4): 730-736.

Wodahl, Eric J., and Brett Garland. 2009. "The Evolution of Community Corrections: The Enduring Influence of the Prison." *Prison Journal* 89 (1): 81S-104S.

Wodahl, Eric J., Brett Garland, Scott E. Culhane, and William P. McCarty. 2011. "Utilizing Behavioral Interventions to Improve Supervision Outcomes in Community-Based Corrections." *Criminal Justice and Behavior* 38 (4): 386-405.

Wodahl, Eric J., Robbin Ogle, and Cary Heck. 2011. "Revocation Trends: A Threat to the Legitimacy of Community-Based Corrections." *Prison Journal* 91 (2): 207-226.

Women in Federal Law Enforcement. 2011. "Pregnancy and the Federal Law Enforcement Officer." FedAgent.com, April 21. Available at http://www.fedagent.com/columns/hear-it-from-wifle/278-pregnancy-and-the-federal-law-enforcement-officer.

Worden, Alissa Pollitz. 2009. "Privatizing Due Process: Issues in the Comparison of Assigned Counsel, Public Defender, and Contracted Indigent Defense Systems." In *Courts and Justice,* 4th ed., edited by G. Larry Mays and Peter R. Gregware, 366-392. Prospect Heights, IL: Waveland Press.

Worley, Robert, James W. Marquart, and Janet L. Mullings. 2003. "Prison Guard Predators: An Analysis of Inmates Who Established Inappropriate Relationships with Prison Staff, 1995-1998." *Deviant Behavior* 24:175-194.

Worley, Robert M., and Vidisha Barua Worley. 2013. "Games Guards Play: A Self-Report Study of Institutional Deviance Within the Texas Department of Criminal Justice." *Criminal Justice Studies* 26 (1): 115-132.

Wrobleski, Henry H., and Kären M. Hess. 2000. *An Introduction to Law Enforcement and Criminal Justice.* Belmont, CA: Wadsworth.

Yao, Allan Y. 2001. "Police and Culture: A Comparison Between China and the United States." *Police Quarterly* 4:156-185.

Zedner, Lucia. 1995. "Wayward Sisters: The Prison for Women." In *The Oxford History of the Prison: The Practice of Punishment in Western Society,* edited by Norval Morris and David J. Rothman, 329-361. New York: Oxford University Press.

TABLE OF CASES AND STATUTES

399

INDEX

Italic page numbers indicate material in boxes, tables, or figures.